D1490966

THOUGHT AND EXPRESSION
IN THE SIXTEENTH CENTURY

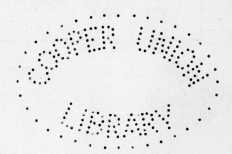

THOUGHT
AND EXPRESSION
IN THE
SIXTEENTH CENTURY

BY

HENRY OSBORN TAYLOR

Vol. II

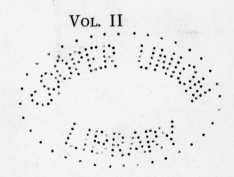

New York
THE MACMILLAN COMPANY
1920

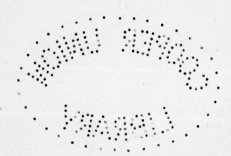

TO

J. I. T.

CONTENTS

BOOK IV

ENGLAND

CONTENTS

CHAPTER XXVII

CHAPTER XXVIII

CHAPTER XXIX

BOOK V

PHILOSOPHY AND SCIENCE

CHAPTER XXX

CHAPTER XXXI

CHAPTER XXXII

CHAPTER XXXIII

CHAPTER XXXIV

CHAPTER XXXV

BOOK IV
ENGLAND

CHAPTER XVIII

ENGLISH EDUCATION IN LETTERS

THE English were the progeny of Britons, Saxons, Danes, and Gallicised Normans. After the Conquest, newcomers from the Continent constantly freshened this racial mixture, uniting with those who by a few, or many, generations had preceded them. Social fashions and enlightenment from abroad also affected these islanders, and such elements of Latin education as the more favored ones received.

An English speech developed, as well as political institutions and a common law; also an insular point of view, an English patriotism, and in fine an English genius which should set its stamp upon the achievements of an English race and find expression in its intellectual creations. Yet the language betrayed its heterogeneous constituents, and foreign currents were to remain evident in English thought and literature. Continental conditions and intrigues constantly affected the English political situation; and foreign elements will be seen to enter, and sometimes neutralize each other, in the insular religious revolution of the sixteenth century.

Of all centuries the sixteenth most strikingly exhibits the plastic power of the English genius, which was then masterfully appropriating the foreign matter and compelling it to contribute to the expression of the mental and emotional experiences of the race. The products or expressions of this English genius will be seen in English legislation, in English conduct, in fortified modes of English thinking, in Anglican forms of Christianity, and most gloriously in English songs and dramas.

With different emphasis or elusiveness these phenomena testify to the continuity of the English past and present, and evince the medial qualities of a people whose racehood

3

was composite, and whose language was not wholly Teutonic or Romance either in its genius or vocabulary.   One
will constantly encounter the effect of recent foreign
fashions, or foreign thought, foreign learning, including
the invigorated humanism which entered from abroad and
which Englishmen went abroad to seek; or, again, all
foreign elements are sunk in the creative power, and lost
in the magnificence, of the English imagination.

To trace the evolution of English political institutions
out of an insular experience, instructed by foreign suggestions or impelled by external exigencies; to follow English
education; note the use of antique or foreign material in
secular English thinking or philosophy; observe the construction of an Anglican Christianity from the edicts of a
King chiming with popular approvals, which were affected
by the ideas of Luther, Zwingli, or Calvin; and witness the
English literary genius leaping forth from conventions
and conceits, insular or continental, and even from Latin
and Greek translations — all this were to attempt the
intellectual history of England.   A few of the illustrative
features of these vast assimilative and creative processes
may be noted in this and the following chapters.

During no mediaeval century did the influence of the
antique civilization fail to act upon England; nor did
English students whether at home in Oxford or Cambridge, or at Paris, Chartres or Orleans, fail to prosecute
some form of classical or antique study, impelled by love
of letters or philosophy, or by a more conventionally pious
motive.   The English were not leaders here; yet John of
Salisbury who passed much of his life in France, and died
as bishop of Chartres in the year 1180, was one of the
best scholars and most genial teachers of his time.
Robert Grosseteste, an emphatic English personality, carried learning from Paris to Oxford, and there did
much to foster a closer knowledge of the tongues; a work
which his great pupil Roger Bacon strove vigorously to
further.[1]

In the early fourteenth century, England sent forth

---

[1] Cf. *The Mediaeval Mind*, Vol. II, p 146 sqq.

revolutionary scholastics, like Duns Scotus and Occam; but she was scarcely conscious of the renewal of classic studies issuing from the personalities and writings of Petrarch and Boccaccio. Intellectually as well as geographically, England was one stage further than France from the rising Italian ardor for a classical humanism. The times were violent, and were to prove disastrous for her as well as for her chief continental neighbor, involved with her in an interminable war, which for France turned the first coming of letters from Italy into a false dawn, and for England issued finally in defeat upon the Continent and in dynastic war at home. Not even then were letters altogether quenched in Englishmen. Humphrey, duke of Gloucester, (b. 1391 d. 1447) brother of Henry V., tempered a rather malign career by an interest in books. He was a reader of Dante, Petrarch and Boccaccio as well as of the Latin classics. He collected books, which he gave or left to Oxford; he patronized Italian humanists, and, among his own countrymen, the poet Lydgate and the rather too clairvoyant ecclesiastic Pecock.[2] Lydgate knew no Greek, and his favorite ancient author was Seneca. He was still more occupied with Boccaccio and mediaeval Latin writers, from whom, rather than from the classic sources, he drew his knowledge of antiquity.

Some Englishmen of Duke Humphrey's generation, or close to it, were drawn to Italy. There was the highborn and scholarly William Grey, who died as bishop of Ely, leaving to Balliol College his manuscripts of the writings of Poggio, Guarino and other Italians. His protégé was John Free (d. 1465) or Phreas, who lived in Italy, and translated a Greek work of Synesius. At the same time John Tiptoff, earl of Worcester, travelled there, lived with humanists and bought their manuscripts. The shrewd reign of Henry VII (1485-1509) established commercial relations with Italian cities and drew Italian craftsmen, artists, and even diplomats to the service of a King who knew their worth. Intellectually Italian influence counts from the latter part of his reign; Dante and Petrarch became great names, while Boccaccio was trans-

[2] Cf. post, p. 40, sqq.

lated and read and imitated: other Italian poets and humanists also in their turn.[3]

Henry VIII was a highly educated youth, whose succession to the throne was hailed by Erasmus as ushering in a millennium of letters for England. In fact, it followed closely upon the coming of a better scholarship to Oxford. An early leader was Grocyn, apparently the first Englishman since Roger Bacon to teach Greek. Born about 1444, he taught Greek at Oxford before 1488, when he went to Italy, where he learned more Greek, to teach on his return. He was the eldest of the band of Scholars — Linacre, Colet, More — whom Erasmus met upon his first visit to England in 1499. Grocyn left an influence and a library, but apparently no writings of his own, when he died in 1519.

Thomas Linacre, a somewhat younger man of ampler genius, handed on the torch of classic study and of medicine. Elected fellow of All Souls in 1484, he spent the following years in Italy, where fortune proved kind. Lorenzo dei Medici permitted him to attend the lessons which Politian was giving Lorenzo's sons; he stayed in Rome and Venice under favorable auspices, and at Padua was made Doctor of Medicine. He became a good Latinist and Grecian, and was devoted to such medical study as the times afforded. Returning to England, he incidentally taught Greek to Thomas More, and was tutor to Prince Arthur, Henry VII's eldest son. Afterwards he became physician to Henry VIII, and had Wolsey and other great ones for patients. Receiving, according to the custom, a number of ecclesiastical preferments, he devoted his income and his energies to founding the College of Physicians. This medical humanist translated works of Galen into Latin, and, dying in 1524, left his considerable property to support the College of Physicians and provide for medical studies in Oxford.

The coming of Erasmus to England in 1499, and his subsequent return and lengthy sojourns at London, Oxford and Cambridge were an inspiration and a financial

[3] See generally the valuable study of Mary A. Scott. *Elizabethan Translations from the Italian*, (1916).

burden to these English humanists, like More and Colet, whose friendship for this rising star of humanists lasted till death. Erasmus had scarcely entered on his career of Latin authorship when he first arrived, nor did he know much Greek. In fact he left England to study Greek in Paris. Some years later he lectured for a while at Cambridge. In England, as elsewhere, his works won vogue and influence, and were a power making for humane and religious enlightenment,— an enlightenment from a foreign source, which might be dimmed crossing the Channel.

No man in England worked more earnestly to spread learning and piety than John Colet, who was of the same age as Erasmus. Born in affluence, he was educated at Oxford, and then travelled and studied in France and Italy. Whether or not he ever listened to Ficino and Pico della Mirandula, he was influenced by their writings, and by the *Hierarchies* of pseudo-Dionysius the Areopagite. He was a man of humane piety; and was strongly drawn to the Epistles of St. Paul, which he studied only in the Vulgate. Returning to his native land, he lectured at Oxford during portions of the years from 1497 to 1499, chiefly upon *Romans* and *Corinthians;* and presented in these lectures a sound appreciation of the actual circumstances under which Paul wrote. He made an understanding of the historical situation a basis of his pious exposition of the text. This was indeed to introduce the new learning in biblical studies to his hearers.

In 1504 Henry VII made Colet Dean of St. Paul's Cathedral. He had always spoken out about church abuses, and as Dean found much that needed change. He began to preach in the Cathedral on Sundays and other festivals, in itself an innovation which was no more agreeable to his Chapter than his insistence upon temperance in food and drink. In fact, he did and said much to draw the dislike of his clerical brethren. His most memorable sermon was preached before a Convocation of the church called in 1511 to consider heresies and other matters. Colet showed them another kind of heresy, very unpleasant to their ears, the heresy of their own evil lives. His sermon, animated with instincts reappearing in the English Reformation, shows this English man utilizing whatever enlightenment he had obtained and remaking it into the expression of convictions of his own.

The text was from the twelfth chapter of Romans: " Be not conformed to this world, but be ye reformed in the newness of your understanding, that ye may prove what is the good will of God, well pleasing and perfect." Unwillingly, yet in obedience to the Archbishop's command, he had come to preach before them, and to warn them to set their minds upon the reformation of the Church. The apostle forbids them to be conformed to the world, to wit, " in devilish pride, in carnal concupiscence, in worldly covetousness, in secular business." The preacher amplifies his theme from the worldly lives and customs of the clergy, through which the dignity of the priesthood is brought down to contempt, the order of the Church confused, and the laity given occasion to stumble by the example set them of the love of the world that casts men headlong into hell. " We are also nowadays grieved of heretics, men mad with marvellous foolishness. But the heresies of them are not so pestilent and pernicious unto us and the people, as the evil and wicked life of priests; the which, if we believe St. Bernard, is a certain kind of heresy, and the chief of all and most perilous."

The reform and restoration of the Church's estate, continues the preacher, must begin with " you our fathers (the bishops), and so follow in us your priests and in all the clergy." The Church needs no new laws, but the enforcement of what she has. Let them be recalled and rehearsed: those which warn you bishops to admit only worthy men to holy orders, and which command that benefices shall be given only to such; those which condemn simony and enjoin personal residence; those which forbid the clergy to be merchants, usurers, or to haunt taverns and carry arms, and consort with women; those which command them to walk the straight and narrow way, and not to concern themselves with secular business or sue in princes' courts for earthly things; those which govern the election of you bishops and enjoin your duties and " the good bestowing of the patrimony of Christ"; and those which prevent the uncleanness of courts and provide for provincial and general councils. Let it not be said of them that they lay grievous burdens on other men's backs, and will not so much as touch them with their little finger. If ye keep the laws, ye will give us the light of your example; and we shall set an example to the laity: and " you will be honored of the people." [4]

This sermon was a broad undoctrinal program of the need for a practical self-abnegating reformation. No wonder that reputed " Lollards " liked to hear Colet preach, and that certain of the clergy whose withers were not unwrung made a futile attempt to have him tried for heresy. Young King Henry said Colet was a good enough doctor for him. He has another title to fame, as founder of St. Paul's School, which was to continue a beneficial factor in the education of English boys. Although a Cathedral school existed, Colet founded his separately about the year 1510, " desiring nothing more than education and bringing up children in good manners and literature "; and he set as " patrons and defenders, governors and rulers of that same school the most honest and faithful fellowship of the Mercers of London." [5]

The statutes of the founder prescribed the duties of master, undermaster, and chaplain, and rules for the pupils: " Children of all nations and countries indifferently to the number of 153 according to the number of seats in the school." The school hours were set and rules of behavior. As to what should be taught, says the founder, " it passeth my wit to devise and determine in particular, but in general to speak and somewhat to say my mind, I would they [the pupils] were taught always in good literature, both Latin and Greek, and good authors such as have the very Roman eloquence joined with wisdom, especially Christian authors that wrote their wisdom with

---

[4] This sermon was preached in Latin. The old English version is given in an appendix to J. H. Lupton's *Life of Dean Colet,* (London, 1887), who has also edited with an English translation, Colet's lectures on *Romans* and *Corinthians.*

[5] From the prologue to the Statutes, which are printed in an appendix to Lupton's *Life.*

clean and chaste Latin either in verse or prose, for my intent is by this school specially to increase knowledge and worshipping of God and our Lord Christ Jesu and good Christian life and manners in the children." So he wishes them first to learn the Catechism which he wrote in English, and sundry school books by Erasmus; then certain of the best among the early Christian authors who still used the speech of Tully, Salust and Virgil, before the coming of " that filthiness and all such abuse which the later blind world brought in, which more rather may be called *blotterature* than literature; [this] I utterly banish and exclude. . . ." Foreseeing the shifts of time, and considering the wisdom and goodness of the fellowship of Mercers, he leaves it to their discretion to alter and amend his statutes; thus further evincing the broad wisdom of the man who entrusted his school to a Merchants' Guild rather than to any ecclesiastical corporation.

Colet, dying in 1519, had the good fortune to pass away before Englishmen had to take sides between Henry and the pope. His illustrious and somewhat younger friend, Sir Thomas More, suffered death for his conviction that the pope and not Henry VIII was the supreme head of the Church in England. And long before he died, the soul of More must have been riven by some sense of the inconsistency between the ideal radicalism of his *Utopia,* with its suave tolerance in religion, and the violent language of the later controversial writings of its author and his stern suppression of heresy when Lord Chancellor. To explain this problem of More's possible duality, there may be no need to assume changes in the man himself between early manhood and middle age. The same nature may always have existed in this admirable person; but life's exigencies may have permitted some of his qualities to slumber while they enlisted others in active service, turning potency perhaps to strident fact.

Nature had endowed him with many talents, and circumstance favored their development. Having passed a part of his boyhood in the household of Cardinal Morton, one of Henry VII's ablest and best advisers, he went to Oxford. There he devoted himself to the humanities, and seems also to have felt the counter yearning for an ascetic religious life. His father, a prominent lawyer, shortly took him from the university, and placed him in the Inns of Court. Not long after, he is found lecturing upon Augustine's *City of God,* and then acting as a law reader. The religious ascetic instinct still struggled with the duties and opportunities of a temporal career, and for several years he dwelt "religiously without vows" in the Carthusian house of London ("the Charterhouse of London"). On the other hand, his desire to marry was strengthened by the advice of his "ghostly father" Dean Colet, and by pleasing intercourse with the marriageable daughters of an Essex gentleman. The virtuous propriety of More's character was shown in his selection of the elder and less attractive daughter for his wife; fearing to put a slight upon her if he chose her preferable younger sister.

Once married, he applied himself to the duties of his profession and budding public career, still appeasing his ascetic yearning by wearing a hair shirt, which he did not relinquish till he gave it to his daughter Margaret a few days before his death. Elected a member of the Commons at the age of twenty-six, he successfully opposed the King's demand for the ancient feudal aids to knight his eldest son and dower his eldest daughter. In this early action he evinced the moral and physical courage which never was to fail him. Clear-minded, diligent and eloquent, More rapidly rose in his profession, acting as counsel in the notable cases of the time. He was appointed to sundry public offices, attracted the notice of Wolsey and won the favor of the young King Henry VIII. Through him, he was made Privy Councillor, elected speaker of the House, made chancellor of the Duchy of Lancashire, and finally succeeded Wolsey as Lord Chancellor, in the first office of the realm. His administration of the Chancellorship was marked by an extraordinary efficiency and an exceptional probity. For his energy in the suppression of heresy, as well as for his defense of the Catholic Faith in these times which had become parlous, the bishops in Convocation raised a princely sum to reward him, which More refused. Having been Chancellor for three years, he returned the Great Seal to the King's hands in 1532 hoping thus to escape from embroilment, against his conscience, in the royal supremacy and divorce, and devote the remainder of his life to piety and quiet work. It turned out otherwise. The King was set upon forcing this most admired of his subjects to take the oath supporting his headship of the Church of England. He no longer bore him any love — if indeed that King's love ever went beyond a quickened satisfaction at a subject's ministration to his will. When others were swearing to this oath, and men's eyes were naturally turned on More, how could that King tolerate such an example of recalcitrancy? The exigencies of Henry's policy impelled him to an execution which was not repugnant to his mood or nature. There is no need to re-tell that marvellous story of the imprisonment and execution of this noble and saintly man.[6] We turn to earlier and lighter phases of his personality.

More was a man of wit and imagination, with the tastes and aptitudes of a scholar. He learned his Greek from Grocyn and Linacre, and doubtless later through collaboration with Erasmus.[7] From the latter's first visit to England a strong friendship and mutual admiration arose between the two, which continued unshaken till the day when Erasmus with a good part of the learned world was horrified at the news of More's execution. More was always interested in theology, and liked to argue its points with this good friend. Together, they translated into Latin a number of the Dialogues of Lucian.[8] In selecting this brilliant and scandalous Ancient, More appears simply as a lover of the classics, with his Christian theology tucked well away. About the same period he translated into English an Italian Life, and letters, of Pico della Mirandula, in which congenial task the nobility

---

[6] It is best told in the *Life of More* by his son-in-law Roper, (Margaret's husband), and in the letters of More written in his captivity.

[7] Seebohm's *Oxford Reformers* (Third ed., 1887) is the standard, but not always accurate, account of the relations between Colet, More, and Erasmus.

[8] First published in 1506.

of his nature and the beauty of his English were manifested at their brightest.

Erasmus wrote the *Praise of Folly* in More's house in 1509, and dedicated it to him. We may think of the *Utopia* as the answering note of More's Erasmian humanism, just as the ocean setting of the piece answered to the stir in men's minds made by the recent voyage and narrative of Americus Vespucius. Erasmus despised all vernaculars, and the *Utopia* was written in Latin, and not in that mother tongue of which More was a master. It was pacifist and socialistic, keenly denunciatory of the follies of avarice and the accumulation of wealth. It gently ridiculed the Friars and deprecated the needless number of priests. It argued against cruel and ineffective punishments, like hanging men for theft, and reflected upon the economic and social ills of England. There were no idlers in Utopia; all men and women labored. Hence six hours daily work sufficed to supply the common needs, and the remainder of the day was spent according to the tastes of a people who deemed human felicity to lie in the free cultivation and garnishing of the mind,—" animi libertatem cultumque." None cared for gold; they used it for chamber-pots, but drank from glass and earthen vessels. They prefer a dim light in their churches (here speaks the author's esthetic taste). They still obeyed the decree of their founder King that every man should be free to follow what religion he would, and to argue peaceably in its support.

The last principle, the much spoken of religious tolerance of the *Utopia,* was of a piece with the rest of this Platonic composition. It was a congruous part of its humanistic idealism, having no connection with actual life, enforcement of law, and maintenance of the Catholic faith, in sixteenth century England. There was no time in the life of this most reverent and legal minded Catholic when he would actually have tolerated any denial of the religion of the Roman Catholic Church. And as for innocent dallyings with the idea of toleration in some unreal Atlantis, it must be remembered that the *Utopia* was published in 1516, a good year before Luther posted those fateful theses on the Wittenberg church door. The Lutheran revolt from the doctrine and authority of the Church awakened the self-consciousness of Catholics, and dispelled their tolerant security. No strict Catholic thereafter might indulge in wayward gambols. Had More foreseen the Lutheran revolt and the Anabaptist social upheavals apparently springing from it, he would not have written the *Utopia*. That indeed would have been playing with hell-fire, quite consciously. His later anxious mind is shown by his words to his son-in-law: " Son Roper, I pray God that some of us, as high as we seem to sit upon the mountains treading heretics under our feet like ants, live not the day that we gladly would wish to be at a league and composition with them to let them have their churches quietly to themselves, so that they would be contented to let us have ours quietly to ourselves." So More spoke, before the King's divorce was broached, as Roper was congratulating him on " the happy state of the realm that had so Catholic a prince, that no heretic durst show his face." More already had forebodings.

There is no need to give the details of More's polemic against Tyndale and other, mainly Lutheran, heretics. Earnestly, and perhaps eagerly, he used the powers of his Chancellorship to suppress heresy, persecute it, if one will use the term. It is superfluous to say that he thought himself fulfilling his highest duty. Likewise during his Chancellorship and the years following his retirement, he wrote indefatigably and voluminously; for there was then a huge crop of persons and books to write against. As he says in 1532: " Our Lord send us now some years as plenteous of good corn as we have had some years of late, plenteous of evil books. For they have grown so fast and sprongen up so thick, full of pestilent errors and pernicious heresies, that they have infected and killed, I fear me, more silly simple souls than the famine of the dear years destroyed bodies."

This passage which opens *The Confutation of Tyndale's Answer,* is followed by a descriptive list of these chief pestilent books. If Tyndale seemed his chief an-

tagonist, there were many other heresy mongers.   More
took upon himself the defense of all the teachings of the
Church.   He supports purgatory, auricular confession,
celibacy, image-worship, pilgrimages.   He shows himself
far more close-minded and conservative than Erasmus.
But his was a hard position, writing controversial compositions in a crisis, when indeed men were suspecting that
Henry secretly favored the heretics.   Even a man as
honest and sincere as More might find himself forced to
support what it might have amused him to ridicule after
the manner of Erasmus.

The circumstance that early in his life More lectured
as well as studied in the Inns of Court, suggests the rôle
of that veritable Law-school in enabling the Common Law
of England to surmount the impact of the Civil Law in
the sixteenth century, and in the end make most beneficial
use of the principles of Roman jurisprudence.   A vigorous and vital renewing of the study of Justinian's *Digest*
was taking place in France and Italy, a renewal which,
under such great leaders as Alciatus, Budé, and finally
Cujas, was sloughing off the mummifying wrappings of
the Commentators, and restoring to their virility the
living and eternal texts.

If the Roman law was then about to be " received " in
a Teutonic Germany, why should it not subdue the Common Law of a less purely Teutonic England?   Persuasion
lay within its excellence everywhere, and in both England
and Germany mighty influences were impelling its acceptance.   But the Common Law of England proved
tougher; and nothing had done more to toughen it than
the yearly publication of law reports and the constant
discussion and inculcation of its tenets in the Inns of
Court.   It was destined to triumph in the masterful
career and influence of Sir Edward Coke, and thereafter
still triumphantly intact, it proved capable of mollifying
its harshness and amplifying its meagre experience from
the equity and commercial law of Rome.[9]

From the law and from Sir Thomas More who suffered

[9] F. W. Maitland, *English Law and the Renaissance.* (Cambridge,
1901.)

death in 1535, we turn to two younger men, scholars as well as educators, who will serve to illustrate the lack of epoch-making qualities in English scholarship. One was Sir Thomas Elyot, an official in the time of Wolsey and Crumwell. He died in 1546. Various published works show him a well read Latinist, not uninfluenced by Italian humanism. In 1531 he published his *Boke named the Gouvernour,* which treated of the education proper to those who were likely to be called upon to exercise authority in the Commonwealth as prince or magistrate.[10] As he says in the Proheme addressed to the King, he would " describe in our vulgar tongue the form of a just public weal: which matter I have gathered as well of the sayings of our most noble authors (Greek and Latin) as by my own experience." The book " treateth of the education of them that hereafter may be deemed worthy to be governors of the public weale under your highness." " A public weale " to Elyot's well read and experienced mind " is a body living compact or made of sundry estates and degrees of men, which is disposed by the order of equity and governed by the rule and moderation of reason." He regarded the welfare of the whole Commonwealth as the right end to be held in view, yet inasmuch as " the base and vulgar inhabitants not advanced to any honor or dignity " are not likely to hold authority, his book has to do with the education of men of gentle birth. As was natural, and prudent in addressing Henry VIII, he says that " the best and most sure governance is that of one king or prince."

The book proceeds, with no tangibly original ideas, to set forth a suitable scheme of studies and education. It is filled with classic examples drawn from Plutarch and many other writers. The author evinces the broadening effect of the classics upon himself by the range of instructive incident and story, which he culls from them for the benefit of his readers. He inculcates the need of a good and beneficent character in rulers, and describes the moral

---

[10] *The Boke named the Gouvernour,* devised by Sir Thomas Elyot, Knight, edited with a Life and full notes by H. H. S. Croft, 2 Vols. (London, 1880).

education calculated to evoke it.   In spite of the fact that the *Gouvernour* was so largely drawn from Plutarch, Plato and Aristotle, it has an English quality and vitality of its own, gained from the personal experience, and indeed springing from the personality, of its worthy author.

This practical and personal English element is less noticeable in the works of Roger Ascham, (1515–1568), a professional scholar, equipped with an ample store of Greek and Latin learning.   His was largely an academic career passed as a fellow of St. John's College, Cambridge, and crowned by the attainment of the Public Oratorship of the University.   But he hankered for the light of courts and their emoluments; and became to his delight, and moderate profit, the tutor of the Princess Elizabeth.   He has left famous descriptions of her early studies and proficiency,[11] and has also told of that ill fated paragon of young womanhood, Lady Jane Grey, whom he found " in her chamber, reading *Phaedo Platonis* in Greek, and that with as much delight as some gentlemen would read a merry tale of Boccace."[12]   He was afterwards given the post of secretary to Edward VI, and discharged the duties of a like office under Mary and the young queen Elizabeth.   A man of anti-papal convictions and occasional bold expression, he could also realize the golden quality of silence.

Ascham was a diligent man with a retentive memory, and an excellent letter writer in both Latin and English. He associated with the scholarly and the great, and besides his interesting correspondence, and his enthusiastic, but pedantic, *Toxophilus,* on archery, he wrote his *Scholemaster,* toward the end of his life, and dedicated it to Elizabeth as he had dedicated the *Toxophilus* to her father.   It betrays the thoroughly English satisfaction of its author at the privilege of associating with those of better birth than himself.   It was " specially purposed for the private bringing up of youth in Jentlemen and noble mens houses, and commodious also for all such as had

---

[11] E.g. in Ep. XCIX, (Giles' ed., 1550).
[12] *Scholemaster,* Bk. I, cf. Ep. CXIV, in Giles' edition.

forgot the Latin tonge, and would, by themselves, without a Scholemaster, in short tyme, and with small paines,
recover a sufficient habilitie, to understand, speake and
write Latin." Just how the book would assist forgetful
maturity to recover its youthful Latinity may not be clear.
Yet it has an abundance of Latin and Greek quotations,
with some seasonable advice on the education of children
and a considerable amount of formal pedantic definitions.
It is not so strongly and personally put together as Elyot's
Gouvernour.

These earlier examples of study and scholarship in
England are suggestive of several points. First, that
the progress of English scholarship in the fifteenth and
sixteenth centuries came through the studies of Englishmen upon the continent, or through the coming of learned
foreigners to England. Secondly, profane studies with
Englishmen might quickly turn to serve the ends of a
rational Christian piety, and proceed hand in hand with
study of the Sacred Text and the Church Fathers,— as
was indeed the case with Erasmus, who after all was
England's chief enlightener. Thirdly, through the sixteenth century, Englishmen will contribute little to pure
scholarship, profane or sacred; but in secular life and
church reform will make practical English application of
their studies. Fourthly, when, as in the case of the
Scotchman George Buchanan,[13] these islanders confine

---

[13] George Buchanan, 1506–1582, was Scotland's chief humanist, nor did
any contemporary Englishman equal him in reputation. The ties were
close between Scotland and France, and at the age of fourteen Buchanan
was sent to study in Paris. He spent the better part of twelve years
studying and teaching at that University. After a brief visit to Scotland, he next is found spending three years at Bordeaux and five in Portu-
gal, where he suffered at the hands of the Inquisition. But he had gained
fame from his metrical Latin version of the Psalms, which rendered them
with pseudo-classic taste and feeling. This complete humanist returned
to stay in Scotland at the age of fifty-five. He became a sort of court
poet to the Queen of Scots, and although a follower of the Reform, preserved her favor. Upon Darnley's murder and Mary's marriage with
Bothwell, and subsequent flight to England, Buchanan turned against her
in his *Detectio*. He was afterwards tutor to the young King James, and
wrote a Latin history of Scotland. His repute was great while he lived
and for another century. But when one thinks of his metrical rendering of
the Psalms and his great poem "De Sphaera," which was also written
in classic metre and consecrated to a presentation of a rapidly exploding
theory of the universe, one is impressed with the futility of his accomplishment.

themselves to pure scholarship, and the production of polite pseudo-classic literature, the result is empty. For their energy passed out from scholarship into politics, church reform, voyages of discovery and the creation of an English literature which was not classical. English scholarship had also its ups and downs. The suppression of the monasteries by Henry VIII cut off a considerable supply of funds used in the support of scholars at the Universities. Because of this and the distraction and confusion of ecclesiastical changes, the cult of letters was unfavorably affected by the English Reformation during the reigns of Henry VIII, Edward VI and Mary.[14] In Elizabeth's reign, especially the latter half, the genius of the time passed beyond the cult of classic letters, however much it had directly or indirectly drawn from them.

[14] Ascham's letters — e.g. Ep. LXXIX (Giles' Ed.) of 1547 speak of the decline of learning at Cambridge. See more at large Strype, *Ecclesiastical Memorials,* II, I, Chapter XXXI, and II, II, Chapter XXIV.

CHAPTER XIX

THE ENGLISH REFORMATION: WYCLIF

HISTORICAL events are not always to be accepted under the tags which have been attached to them, nor for what their movers assumed or supposed them to be. The so-called English Reformation was not predominantly a religious movement having to do with the saving of souls and their lot in the world to come. Its chief dramatic incidents sprang from the political constitution of England. In its entire course it was a catholic expression of the taste and temper and the formative genius of the English people. It cannot be treated by itself, separate from the consideration of all the rest that made England. For it was a part and parcel of the whole, and scarcely more other-worldly than the rest.

The Lutheran revolution was German, and the French Reform was French. But, among other obvious traits, one vital circumstance distinguishes them essentially from the English Reformation. The inspiration of the German Reformation, the explosion which it was, flared from the personality of perhaps the greatest of Germans, Martin Luther. The French Reform finds its form and culmination, its intensive actualization, in the work and genius of Calvin. In either case Luther or Calvin centres the human interest of the modern student upon himself. But the course of the English Reformation, unless at the very beginning in Wyclif, offers no man whose personal genius dominates and impels the story. It is a social, political, and if one will, religious, movement among a people; moulded by the political and social conditions of the country, and dominated by no single personality, except when temporarily driven by the passions and policy of Henry VIII. It has very little that is intellectually original; it borrows ideas from abroad, from any quarter.

Its makers, the English people, were neither blessed nor burdened with abstract conceptions. In the end we find ourselves interested in the ecclesiastical-political-social form which is worked out.

The English Reformation, so convincingly and amusingly English, was composite, even heterogeneous, in its antecedents and moving elements. Underlying, enveloping, and through attraction or repulsion, affecting the whole movement was the Roman Catholic Church. Although this was to be cast loose from as an organization, it supplied the bulk of the doctrines which any reformed national Christian church must retain. Assuming this Catholic matrix, a vital element of the reform was the " new learning " from abroad, both sides of it, secular and sacred: that is to say, the " new learning " in the sense of the humanistic revival and extension of classical studies, Greek as well as Latin; and the " new learning " lying in the study of Old Testament Hebrew and New Testament Greek, and in the Pauline teachings of Luther, Zwingli, Calvin, and the legion of their followers. English factors were the indigenous Protestant tendencies, obscurely traceable to the tenets of Wyclif and the Lollards. An immediate efficient cause was the lust of Henry VIII and his desire for a son and heir. The vicissitudes of politics and the consolidation of the royal prerogatives under Henry VII had placed autocratic power in the hands of his successor, and contributed to the realization of his will to supersede the Pope as Supreme Head of the English Church.

There were two long strains of preparatory and at last efficient forces entering the English reform of religion and separation from the Church of Rome — two strains which might collaborate, but more constantly exhibited intolerance on the one side, and on the other dissent and occasional revolt. The one was the self-assertion of the English realm against papal encroachments; [1] the other

---

[1] The course of the royal and parliamentary self-assertion of the realm, expressed in statutes, will be noticed as introductory to the statutes of Henry VIII. Post, Chapter XXII.

the protest of an evangelical and independent conscience against an ecclesiastical authority which seemed both irrational and unjustified by the faith of Christ.

Both of these strains joined in Wyclif, at whose preaching, says Milton, " all the succeeding reformers more effectually lighted their tapers." That preaching, continues Milton, " was to his countrymen but a short blaze, soon damped and stifled by the pope and prelates for six or seven kings' reigns." [2]

There were gusts of righteous anger in the air which Wyclif breathed. Some one had experienced and given utterance to those powerful allegorical visions of human life, called after *Piers Plowman*.[3] They voiced the indignation of a man who saw, as the people should have seen, the clergy and laity in their evil shortcomings and haphazard repentances. One will find no obvious plan in these visions, but ample denunciations of all forms of greed and sham, and declarations of the worth of Truth, which lies in honest virtues and the soul practising them. The author recoiled as sharply from the spiritual falsity of absolution purveyed to the wicked through the Church, as from the sins which need the pardon that only repentance and right conduct can merit or receive. Christian verities are taught by precept and by the illustrative drama of the vices, virtues, and sorrows of a society composed of all sorts and conditions of men. The writer is very close to the Bible, and always gives the pregnant Scripture text which sums up his alliterative speech. He is English in the savor of his scenes and personages, as in his language and verse. The vision of the ills of laity and clergy does not bring him to rebel against king and state, or refuse obedience to the Church. Yet his words

[2] *Of Reformation in England.*
[3] The authors, one or several, are unknown, or disputed. The massive edition is by Skeat in four volumes (*Early Eng. Text Society*). For a vivid presentation of its contents, see Jusserand's *Piers Plowman* (Putnam's, 1894). For discussion of authorship, see J. M. Manly in the *Cambridge Hist. of Eng. Lit.*, and *The Piers Plowman Controversy* (Manly, Jusserand, Chambers, *Early Eng. Text Soc.* 1910). The sincerity and power of these poems will impress any reader who can overcome his repugnance to alliterative verse, which is as disagreeable to us as it was to Chaucer, and less familiar.

were taken as their own by rioters against the social orders and by rebels against the Church. It was no easier for these people than for the twentieth century historian, to distinguish between denunciations of the abuse and rebellion against the system on which it poisonously blossoms. This difficulty will recur in considering the career of Wyclif.

He appears as a half-sculptured giant held in the rough marble. Yet, through a life of contest with surrounding acceptances and corruptions, he freed himself from the matrix of his earlier years, and emerged at last an egregious and prophetic heretic. The difficulties of the struggle, even the obstacles in the way of entering upon it at all, cannot be realized by us who live in a world divided between Catholics and Protestants of every hue. How should a man discover for himself that the atmosphere which he and all men breathe is poisonous? How should Wyclif, a child of mediaeval thought, begin to break away from universal acceptances? What spiritual fulcrum could he use, and on what outer certainty should he set it beyond the beliefs enveloping him? Whither should he revolt from a religious State controlling much of this world and salvation in the next? Following Wyclif's career, we see that even this man of new insight would not have broken with the universal Church, had not conditions prepared the way and events jostled him along. As for supposing him to have foreseen the outcome of his gradually shaped convictions, that is not to be thought of.

Wyclif belongs to England. Elsewhere his career could not have been what it was, nor could it have progressed by the stages one observes in it. Yet only its earlier part seems manifestly a result of Wyclif's situation as an Englishman of academic station, and somewhat involved in politics. The later part is more disengaged, and more personal to the man who had finally become a religious reformer.

He was born at an undetermined place in England about the year 1320; he died at his parish of Lutterworth in Leicestershire on the thirty-first day of December 1384.

His closing years of astonishing intellectual activity, of
vehement advocacy of church and doctrinal reform, of
bitter denunciation of Popes and Friars, were passed in
this little town where he never suffered personal moles-
tation, although a generation after his death his bones
were cast out from his tomb by order of the Council of
Constance.   His earlier life, his education, his development prior to those last years of militant emancipation,
are identified with Oxford,— he was master of Balliol in
1360.   There he studied, taught, and wrote; and thence
from time to time he was drawn to London by public
business, or to stand trial.[4]

Wyclif's education made him a scholastic logician and
theologian.   Scholasticism is inseparable from its own
scholastic Latin, in which it was expressed; its thoughts
were unsuited to vernacular expression, especially where
the vernacular was English or German, and not a
Romance tongue.   When reasoning and writing in Latin,
Wyclif's style and method never cast off the scholastic
bands.   But in English he is another man: " Two virtues
be in mannes soule by which a man should be ruled:
holynesse in mannes wille, and good cunning in his witt.
Holynesse should put out sin, and good cunning should
put out folly."   Reading this, after Wyclif's scholastic
Latin, is like entering a sunny field.[5]

So in his Latin treatises Wyclif, to the end of his days,
never cast off the scholastic goitre afflicting the formal

[4] For the scanty and uncertain facts of Wyclif's life see G. Lechler,
Johann von Wiclif und die Vorgeschichte der Reformation, (2 Vols.
Leipsic, 1873, also in Eng. translation); F. D. Matthew, *The English
Works of Wyclif hitherto unprinted,* Introduction (Early Eng. Text Soc.,
1880 and 1902); W. W. Shirley, *Fasciculi Zizaniorum,* Introduction
(Master of the Rolls Series, 1858); G. M. Trevelyan, *England in the
Age of Wycliffe,* (1899).

[5] Matthew, *Eng. works of Wyclif,* On Confession, pp. 327–345. While
commonly the Latin of the theologians and controversialists of the fourteenth century is bad, the bad qualities vary somewhat with the education
and nationality of the writer.   Dr. R. L. Poole says that Wyclif's "Latin
is base even as compared with that of such of his predecessors as Ock-
ham; there is a gulf between it and that of Thomas Aquinas.   Wycliffe
in fact belongs to a time when scholars were ceasing to *think* in Latin.
It is significant of his position that he is one of the founders of English
prose-writing.   To understand his Latin it is often necessary to translate it into English."   Preface to Dr. Poole's edition of Wyclif's *De
Civili Dominio,* (Wyclif Society, 1885).

Latin compositions of his time.   His last elaborate Latin
work, the *Trialogus*,[6] completed the year of his death,
is a final compend of doctrine as to God and things divine,
in fact a concise *Summa Theologiae*.   The arrangement
of its four books follows the four books of the *Sentences*
of Peter Lombard.   It is not easy reading, yet in its
entirety bears interesting evidence of the whole Wyclif.
It shows that the major part of him and of what he taught
came directly from his scholastic forbears, yet it contains
the novel matters which made Wyclif's importance both in
his own time and after.   These consisted of his incisive,
heretical, clear-seeing arguments against transubstantiation, the riches of the clergy, and against the Friars altogether, their principles, their teachings, and the foundations of their Orders; also against privy confession, priestly absolution, papal indulgences and many superstitions.
He had reached them in the course of controversies which
may be briefly followed.

In the year 1371 the Commons petitioned the Crown
that the bishops should not hold great offices of state.
There was also talk of seizing their endowments.   The
next year the coming of a papal collector turned popular
distrust in the direction of Avignon.   The Commons
prayed the king to deprive any priest holding a benefice,
when persistently guilty of immoral life.   In 1374 a mission, of which Wyclif was a member, was sent to Bruges
to treat with papal envoys.   There he seems to have
won the confidence of John of Gaunt, the chief man in
the realm since his brother, the Black Prince, had died and
Edward III was old and imbecile.   Gaunt was bent on
confiscating the superfluous property of the Church, a
measure which Wyclif advocated, having held for many
years that the wickedness of the clergy annulled the
Church's right to its possessions.[7]   He had urged his

---

[6] Ed. by Lechler (Macmillan, 1867).

[7] Wyclif's arguments, partly borrowed from the recent *De pauperie
Salvatoris* of Fitzralph, Archbishop of Armagh, are curiously mediaeval
and feudal.   He defined *dominium,* or lordship, as a habit belonging to
the rational nature in virtue of which it is said to be set over that which
serves it.   "God has lordship by reason of creation, possession by reason
of conservation, and use by reason of governance. . . . God is lord *not
mediately,* as other kings are, through the rule of subject vassals, since

opinions publicly at Oxford, and after his return from Bruges came up to London to preach clerical disendowment, apparently at the Duke's invitation. If he found ready listeners among all social grades, he also roused the wrath of the more masterful clergy, and was summoned for trial at St. Paul's, in February 1377. He appeared supported by the Duke and Lord Percy, who were both intent upon depriving the mayor of London of his power over the city. Hot words passed between these lords and the imperious Bishop Courtenay, till the excited crowd broke in, and the abortive trial ended in confusion. The next day the Londoners drove the Duke and Lord Percy from the town. Yet the defeat was not for long. Edward III died in June; the Londoners and John of Gaunt came to terms, and the son of the Black Prince was crowned king as Richard II.

In the meanwhile Rome took up the conflict,— Gregory XI had migrated back to the Eternal City. The pope was at war with Florence, and there had been recent friction between the papacy and the English government over the excommunication of the Florentines in England, whom the king took under his protection. Papal Bulls arrived. One of them, addressed to the University of Oxford, prohibited it from permitting Wyclif to defend his teachings there, and commanded that he be arrested and delivered into the custody of the Bishop of London or the Archbishop of Canterbury: they in turn were enjoined to warn the King against Wyclif's errors, to examine him and report to Rome, and keep him in prison till the papal decision was returned. The matters of which he was

immediately and of himself he makes, maintains, and governs all that which he possesses, and helps it to perform its works according to other uses which he requires." Every man holds from God by the tenure of obedience. In giving, God does not surrender His lordship, but gives possession and use. His grants are made "to men in their several stations and offices, on condition of obedience to His commandments. Mortal sin, therefore, breaks the link, and deprives man of his authority. Thus no one in a state of mortal sin has, in strict right, either priesthood or lordship. . . . This is the meaning of Wyclif's favorite expression, that all dominion is founded in grace." The last is from Shirley, *Fasiculi Zizaniorum*, Introduction, p. lxiii. The above translations are from R. L. Poole's edition of Wyclif's *De Dominio divino* (Wyclif Soc., 1890), who prints in an appendix the first four books of Fitzralph's *De pauperie Salvatoris*.

accused related mainly to the order and governance of the Church: he had questioned the powers of the pope to bind and loose, had maintained that excommunication if unjust had no effect; had urged the right of kings and lords to deprive the Church of its possessions when misused, and had questioned the exclusive privilege of the bishops to administer certain sacraments. He was also charged with communism. Marsiglio of Padua and John of Jandun were named as the sources of his false teachings.

Men were just then occupied with the succession to the throne. The government, with or without John of Gaunt, remained rather anti-papal. The bishops feared to move; while Wyclif, already master of men's minds at Oxford, was becoming the popular champion of the realm against papal encroachments. He defended himself before Parliament.[8] Probably his defense was well received since he was soon called on to advise the government " whether the realm of England may legitimately, under the need of providing for defense, keep its treasure from being drawn abroad, even though the pope commands it under pain of censures and in virtue of obedience." [9]

In his Response he says: " Every natural body has power from God to resist its contrary, and preserve itself in its rightful being. . . . Since therefore the realm of England, in the language of Scripture, ought to be one body, and the clergy, lords and Commonalty its members, it seems that the same realm has such power given from God " — and therefore may keep its treasure for its own defense when necessary. Then he argued that the Pope could not demand this treasure as alms under the gospel injunction of *caritas:* because the title to the alms falls with the same necessity: " for since all *caritas* begins from itself, it would be no work of *caritas* but of folly to send the kingdom's alms to foreigners (ad exteros), the realm itself needing them."

[8] Shirley, *Fasic. Zizaniorum*, pp. 245–257.
[9] Wyclif's *Responsio*, from which this and the following extracts are taken, is printed in Shirley, *Fas. Zis.*, pp. 258–271.

With these and other arguments Wyclif combated the pope's right to drain the country of its treasure. He said the pope would be unlikely to lay an interdict on the realm, considering his love and our well-known piety, " but supposing that Antichrist's disciple should break out in such insanity, one solace is that God does not desert those who hope in Him." An unjust and therefore in-valid excommunication may work fear and damage; but such temporal trouble may be met. Christians are not bound to maintain the pope in pomp; and if it be said to be bad for the realm to keep so much loose money, let that be remedied by a prudent administration and distri-bution of church property, and a return of the endow-ments to the founders. He was setting forth sundry others matters of like tenor when silence was imposed on him.

Wyclif's trial came to nothing. At Oxford the heads of the University would not proceed against its dis-tinguished son, with whose opinions they were in sympa-thy. And when the abortive proceedings were re-opened before the bishops in London, the Princess of Wales, who was the mother of young Richard II and virtually regent, forbade Wyclif's condemnation, and a tumultuous inroad of London folk broke up the session. Wyclif was now an important person with the authorities and popular with the people.

In 1378 the Great Schism broke out, induced by the harsh ways of the newly elected Urban VI, and the lust of power on the part of the French cardinals. These made an Antipope, Clement VII, and set up a rival pa-pacy in their congenial Avignon. Europe fell into two ecclesiastical camps, France and Spain supporting Clem-ent, England and the Teutonic lands supporting Urban. Each pope proclaimed a crusade against the other, and rival venders of indulgences and pardons overspread Europe. This scandalous condition changed Wyclif's attitude toward the papacy. Having hitherto in all spiritual matters acknowledged the papal authority, he began to hold it an encumbrance and detriment to the Church of God. His religious energies seemed now to break forth in power, turning him altogether from politics to the reform of religious practices and doctrine.

One great reforming measure was his translation of the Gospels from the Vulgate into English. His efforts to render the Bible accessible to the people sprang from his zeal to spread the true religion disencumbered of its corruptions, and also accorded with the tendency of the time to turn from Latin to English in the conduct of both secular and spiritual affairs. Another effective and constructive measure lay in the training and sending out of "poor priests" to preach the English Bible to the English people. They were not necessarily poor in understanding or education; but it was theirs to realize Wyclif's conception of true Christian ministry through voluntary poverty and earnest preaching of the living faith. He worked untiringly to send them forth equipped for their labors and devoted to their mission. The result must have cheered his last years of physical debility; for the poor priests brought the Gospel to the homes of thousands.

With Wyclif's evangelical activities his doctrinal dissent became more incisive and its promulgation more eager. He insisted upon the acceptance of Scripture as the sole authority in religion; he attacked the priestly power of issuing indulgences and granting absolution, and denied the priestly claim of transubstantiating bread and wine into the divine body and blood of Christ.

The last denial was a clear heresy, biting at the root of the divine or miraculous power given to the Church; if the miracle of the Mass was imposture, around what function might the Church assemble its authority? Good churchmen, moreover, might here take up the gauntlet without fear, the matter being purely doctrinal and disconnected with abuses which laid the Church open to attack. Wyclif's teaching was condemned at Oxford, probably in 1381, and on his appeal to the king (not to pope or bishop) John of Gaunt sent to forbid him to say more upon this subject. But Wyclif only stated his position the more clearly,[10] and the University still sup-

---

[10] In his *Confessio,* printed in *Fasic. Ziz.,* pp. 115-132.

ported him. The Friars were ranged against him, and from this time he became unbounded in his denunciation of them and their corruptions.

In the year 1381 the rebellion of the peasants of the Eastern counties broke out under Wat Tyler, " John Ball " and other leaders. The preaching of Wyclif's followers against the wealth of the clergy may have fallen as a spark into the explosive mass of discontent and destitution. Much destruction of church property, some murders of church dignitaries, followed, before the rebellion was bloodily put down. It probably affected Wyclif as the revolt of the German peasants affected Luther, making him more conservative in his political views and more careful of his utterances.

After all this turmoil, Archbishop Courtenay (Archbishop Sudbury's head had been cut off by the rioters) summoned a synod in May 1382 at Blackfriars. There Wyclif's teachings on the Eucharist and other matters were condemned, but with no mention of Wyclif by name. The storm fell upon his supporters at Oxford and elsewhere. Wyclif himself, apparently unmolested, retired to Lutterworth, where he died two years later in 1384. These two closing years of physical weakness, for he was partly paralyzed, were the period in which he most completely expressed his convictions.

Wyclif's doctrine of divine and civil lordship was pointed with ever increasing acerbity against the excessive possessions of the Church and the secular power of the pope.[11] Thereupon he developed the principle that

[11] Cf. *ante,* page 25, note. The *Dialogus sive Speculum Ecclesie militantis,* ed. by Alfred W. Pollard (W. Socy., 1886), was written between 1379 and 1382, and is mainly directed against clerical ownership of property. In the last year of his life, Wyclif wrote a letter to Pope Urban (printed in *Fas. Ziz.,* p. 241). The following is a contemporary translation of a passage: " This I take as hoolsome counseil, that the pope leeve his worldly lordship to worldly lordis, as Crist gaf hom, and move spedely all his clerkis to do so." *Select English Works of John Wyclif,* ed. by T. Arnold (Oxford, 1871), Vol. 3, p. 505. Wyclif had already said in his *De Civili Dominio,* i, 17, " For to rule temporal possessions after a civil manner, to conquer kingdoms and exact tributes, appertain to earthly lordship not to the Pope; so that if he pass by and set aside the office of spiritual rule, and entangle himself in those other 'concerns, his work is not only superfluous but also contrary to holy Scripture." (R. L. Poole's translation.)

the Bible alone is the authoritative vehicle of God's truth; everything in the Church going beyond it is useless and erroneous, while whatever contravenes it is damnably false. In studying it, he would follow the light of reason and also the authority of the Church Fathers, who are fallible however. Scripture should be understood as a whole so that one part may explain another. And the Holy Spirit must guide our efforts.[12] It was his habit, especially in his sermons, to give the literal sense of the English Scriptural text which he had quoted, and then to follow with its allegorical application in simple and temperate fashion.

Some time after the papal and episcopal attack on him, he gave out a defense in his condemned *Conclusions* in a Latin and an English version.[13] In the latter, having shown that priests should content themselves with alms and not " curse " for their tithes, and that all holding cures should perform the duties of their posts, and that God's unadulterated law should be preached in the tongue understanded of the people, he continues:

" For we should take as belief that goddes lawe passeth alle other, both in autorite and in truthe and in wit. First in autorite; for as god passeth men, so goddes lawe must passe in autorite mannus lawe and therefore god bade his apostlis not to preche mannus lawe but for to preche the gospel to all maner of men. Much more ben they to blame that prechen japes and lies; for goddes word is more wholesome to men since it is belief, and it techeth to follow crist, and that must each man do that shal be saved, and therefore thinke we thereon night and day, both wakinge and slepinge, for when other lawes may have ende then it shall dwell in bliss: and the heart of this lawe is the gospel of iesu crist. Preche prestes this heart to men and teche them to love crist; for he is cursed that loveth him not and sueth [followeth] him not, as Paul saith. And certes that prest is to blame that should so freely have the gospel and leeveth the preching thereof and turneth hym to mannus fables."

He denounces the Friars: " Why should not men flee from these false prophets as Christ biddeth in the gos-

---

[12] See Lechler's *Wyclif* (Eng. Trans.) I, pp. 473-483.
[13] The Latin form was published by Lechler (Leipsic, 1863) *Johannis de Wiclif Tractatus de Officio Pastorali*, and the English is in Matthew, *Eng. Works of W. hitherto unpublished*, pp. 405-457.

pel? But Bulls of the court of Rome blinden many men here, for it seemeth the head of error and proper nest of antichrist." Antichrist cannot show that Christ ordained these orders of clergy, these " new rotten sects " of monks and canons. " No man should sue (follow) either pope or bishop or any angel, but in as much as he sueth Christ." [14]

Wyclif was opposed to gorgeous ceremonial, which he dubs *judaizing* after the ways of carnal sense, and placing the symbol above the meaning. He set his face against the worship of images, which entangle the imagination. Herein lay the peril, the poison of idolatry (venenum idolatriae), beneath the honey, drawing men to adore the image (signum) in the place of what it signifies.[15] He thought ill of the many saints' festivals and the worship of relics, and deemed that men would to do better to observe the precepts of God at home than go pilgrimaging to the threshold of the Saints. He also drew away from worship of the Virgin, which in earlier years he had approved; and from much of the Church's teaching as to Purgatory: it might be that the suffrages of the Church helped the dead, but the least good deed of the dead man would help him more.[16] It was also his opinion that while the virgin state might be the very highest, it were better for most people, including priests, to marry.[17]

There is no doubt that Wyclif became more hostile to

[14] " Ordo vel religio catholica quam Christus instituit, excellit omnes istos ordines quodammodo infinite." *Trialogus* Lib. IV, cap. 33, cf. ib. cap. 24 *et seq*. Wyclif also argues that the king, and not the pope, should appoint prelates.

[15] Liber Mandatorum as given by Lechler, o. c. I, p. 556.

[16] See Lechler, o. c., pp. 563, 564.

Christ's Church " hath three parts. The first part is in bliss, with Christ head of the Church, and containeth angels and blessed men that now ben in heaven. The second part of this church be saints in purgatorie; and these sin not of the new, but purge their old sins. And many erours fallen in praying for these saints; and sith they alle been dead in bodi, Christ's words may be taken of them,— sue (follow) we Christ in oure lif, and let the dead bury the deade. The third part of the Church be true men that here live, that shall be after saved in heaven, and live here Christen men's lives." Arnold, o. c. Vol. 3, p. 339,— In the same tract Wyclif opines (p. 344) that many a canonized man is deep damned; the pope is very fallible.

[17] Cf. a tract " Of wedded men and wives," Arnold, Select Eng. Works, etc., Vol. 3, pp. 188–201 — which may have been the work of a Wiclifite. Also Lechler, o. c, I, pp. 571, 572.

the papacy from the time of the Schism, the popes' " un-
couthe dissension " as he called it.[18] About 1380, he
wrote a tract against the pope in which the term Antichrist is freely used.[19]

" It were to wit besides how God shewed love to his Church by
division of these popes that is now lately fallen. Our belief teacheth by Paul that all things fall to good to God's children that
dread him, and thus should Christian men take them. . . . And so
some men take it that the holy prayer of the church made to Christ
and his mother moveth him to send this grace down to divide the
head of Antichrist, so that his falsehood be more known. And it
seemeth to them that the pope is antichrist here on earth. For he
is against Christ both in life and in lore. Christ was most poor
man from his birth to his death, and left worldly riches and begging, after the state of innocence; but antichrist against this from
the time that he be made pope till the time that he be dead here,
coveteth to be worldly rich and casteth by many shrewd ways how
that he may thus be rich. Christ was most meke man, and bade
learn this of him; but men say that the pope is most proud man of
earth and maketh lords to kiss his feet where Christ washed his
Apostles' feet. Christ was most homely [familiar] man in life,
in deed and in word; men say that this pope is not next Christ in
this, for where Christ went on his feet both to cities and little
towns, they say this pope will be closed in a castle with great array."

Wyclif continues through a series of telling contrasts
between the ways of Christ and the ways of popes as he
knew of them. As for the Schism, " this division of these
popes may turn to good of many realms, that men trow
to neither of them, but, for love of Jesus Christ, in as
much as they suen [follow] Christ in their life and in their
lore." If the realms would obey the pope only in so far
as he followed God's law they would be free from the
" blasphemies of indulgences and of other false feignings;
for it may fall that the pope grant to rich men that they
should go straight to heaven without pain of purgatory,
and deny this to poor men, keep they never so god's law."

In another tract,[20] probably written in the last year
of his life, Wyclif, having argued against the pope's infallibility and shown that monks, canons and friars act

18 Arnold, o. c. 3, p. 242. It is a pity that Marsiglio and Occam and
Wyclif did not perceive that Constantine's Donation was a forgery.
19 Printed in Matthew, o. c. pp. 458–482.
20 Arnold, o. c. Vol. 3, pp. 338–365.

more like servants to Antichrist than of the Apostles, points out that Peter had no more power than the other apostles:

" Christian men believe that Peter and Paul and other apostles took power from Christ, but only to edify the Church. And thus all priests that be Christ's knights have power of him to this end. Which of them hath most power is fully vain of us to treat; but we suppose of priests' deeds that he that profiteth more to the Church hath more power of Christ, and else they be idle with their power. And thus by power that Christ gave Peter may no man prove that this priest, the which is bishop of Rome, hath more power than other priests."

After a while Wyclif shows how little Christian men should fear interdicts or excommunications or crusades, which can " do no harm to a Christian man but if he do harm first to himself. . . . And thus dread we them not for censures that they feign, but dread we ever our God lest we sin against him. . . ."

Of Confession Wyclif speaks temperately. The practice has varied, says he:

" For first men confessed to God and to the common people, and this confession was used in the times of the apostles. Afterwards men were confessed more especially to priests, and made them judges and counsellors of their sinful lives. But in the third time since the fiend was loosed, pope Innocent [21] ordained a law of confession that each man once a year should privily be confessed of his proper priest, and added much to this law that he could not ground. And if this pope's ordinance do much good to many men, natheless many men think that it harmeth the Church." [22]

Auricular confession pointed to absolution by the priest, the falsehood and demoralizing effects of which Wyclif never tired of denouncing. Privy confession is an innovation of the fiend, and a device to subject men to the pope. To grant absolution belongs to God: " a priest should not say ' I assoil,' when he know not whether God assoil." [23] The confessors of great men are highly paid, those with whom the rich treat privily as to their sins, from whom, also privily, they are wont to receive evil

[21] Innocent IV at the Lateran council of 1213.
[22] Arnold o. c. Vol. 3, p. 255, in a long tract on the Schism.
[23] Matthew, o. c. pp. 327–345.

counsel, as they make confession without contrition, to the damnation of both parties :

" thus sin might be bought for money as one buys an ox or a cow; and so rich men had occasion to dread not for to sin, when they might for a little money be thus assoiled of all their sins; and poor men might despair, for they had not to buy thus sin. . . . And he that trusteth to popes' bulls or assoilings from pain and sin, or other words of confessors that they feign besides God's law, is foolishly deceived in his belief and hope, but we should believe that the grace of God is so great and plenteous that if a man sin never so much nor so long in his life, if he will ask God's mercy and be contrite for his sin, God will forgive him his sins without such japes feigned of priests. But be men ware of this peril, that continuance of man's sin without sorrow and displesaunce will make his sin hard and bereeve him of power to sorrow therefore and to get mercy; and thus men should ever dread sin, and flee to knit [make fast] on to another: for when a man sinks in the mire, at the last he may not help himself." Yet Wyclif returns to the thought that secret repentance may atone for sins of conscience; " men should understand that the courtesy of God asketh not of each man to shrive him thus by voice of mouth." [24]

Denunciation of the feigned miraculous power of priests and pope was one path by which Wyclif advanced to his denial that the natural elements in the Eucharist were changed. No false teaching " was ever more cunningly brought in by hypocrites, or cheats the people in more ways." [25] Moreover, transubstatiation disturbed his scholastic reasoning upon substance and accidents. He says in a Latin sermon: " It seems enough for the Christian to believe that the body of Christ is in some spiritual and sacramental manner at every point of the consecrated host, and that next after God honor is to be chiefly rendered to that body, and in the third place to that sensible sacrament, as to an image or tomb of Christ." [26]

[24] Touching the supererogatory merits of the saints, on which the pope might draw, Wyclif's words are full of scorn: "And so this fond fantasy of spiritual treasure in heaven, that each pope is made dispenser of this treasure at his own will, this is a light word, dreamed without ground. For then each pope should be lord of this heavenly treasure, and so he should be lord of Christ and other saints in heaven, yea, if he were a fiend, as was Judas Iscariot." Arnold, o. c. Vol. 3, p. 262.

[25] *Trialodus*, IV, 2. Matthew's translation.

[26] Matthew, o. c. p. xxii, where the Latin is given and from where I have taken the above translation. Wyclif's *Confessio, Fas. Ziz.* 115-132 states his position elaborately. The following extract will be under-

The *Wyckett,* a popular controversial tract question-ably ascribed to Wyclif, stript the mystery from all the sacraments, including the Eucharist:

" Therefore all the sacramentes that be lefte here in earth be but myndes of the body of Christ, for a sacrament is no more to saye, but a sygne or mynde of a thynge passed or a thynge to come, for when Jesu spake of the breade and sayde to his disciples, *As ye do this thyng, do it in mynde of me* (Luke xxii) . . . Also Christ say-eth (John xv) *I am a very vyne.* Wherefore worshyppe ye not the vyne for God as ye do the bread? Wherein was Christ a very vyne, or wherein was the bread Christ's bodye? In figurative speech, which is hid to the understanding of synners. Then if Christ became not a material either [or] an earthly vyne, neither material vyne became the bodye of Christ. So neither the material bread was changed from his substance to the flesh and body of Christ."

stood by anyone interested in these attempted formulations of a magic-mystery: Non tamen audeo dicere quod Corpus Christi sit essentialiter, substantialiter, corporialiter, vel identice ille panis. . . . Credimus enim quod triplex est modus essendi corporis Christi in hostia consecrata, scilicet virtualis, spiritualis, et sacramentalis. Virtualis est quo bene facit per totum suum dominium, secundum bona naturae vel gratiae. Modus autem essendi spiritualis est, quo corpus Christi est in eucharistia et sanctis per gratiam. Et tertius modus essendi sacramentalis, quo corpus Christi est singulariter in hostia consecrata.

CHAPTER XX

LOLLARDY AND PECOCK AND GASCOIGNE

It may have been, as Milton says, that Wyclif's preaching "was to his countrymen but a short blaze, soon damped and stifled." Yet we shall find his true succession not merely in such lights of the subsequent reformation as Latimer and Hooper, but in the English people themselves, as in the stirrings of the Puritan movement, with its hatred of prelacy and "Judaizing" ceremonial and its insistence upon Scripture as the sum and limit of religious truth. Of a surety these tendencies had lived on after Wyclif's death, "damped" to be sure, but hardly "stifled."

His followers were soon called Lollards, a name of unknown origin. It is hard to see in them more than faintly glowing embers,— or their time was not yet come. Far and wide the realm was dominantly, but not violently, orthodox. Innovations in belief were not favored. Men and women were accustomed to being "assoiled" by priests and Friars, and needed just such solemn tinsel of assurance, especially when they came to die. Indulgences, relics, pilgrimages were popular. People are not readily disturbed in beliefs and practices which are well suited to their unenlightenment. As for the Mass, it was the central authoritative saving miracle; attack upon it or any paring down of its efficiency roused anger. Here and there men perceived the dupery by which Friars and Pardoners filled their pouches. But there was little indignation. Few are so keen-minded as to be angered by what is monstrous only to the mind. For wide-spread wrath, men's passions must be roused; their money must be taken in ways and for persons they dislike. Some general hatred of the popes or the priests and the prelates of the land was roused by tithes and other exactions, or hungry eyes were cast on the fat abbey lands. Thus it had been with the tumultuous mob ranging with John Ball and Wat Tyler.

Again, the English people did not like to persecute or be persecuted. They were not cruel or intolerant in that way, nor as yet stiffnecked. In 1382, relying on an ordinance passed by the king and lords, Richard sent writs to the Bishops commanding them to arrest all Lollards. The Commons objected vigorously, till they compelled the recall of the ordinance in which they had not concurred. " Let it now be annulled, for it was not the intention of the Commons to be tried for heresy, nor to bind over themselves or their descendants to the prelates more than their ancestors had been in time past." [1] Only after some years could the Commons be brought to take steps against the Lollard heresy, by passing the statute *De Haeretico Comburendo* in 1401.

Nor on their side, did the Lollards wish to be burnt for their convictions. They evaded persecution as they might, or usually recanted when caught in its grip. Conflicts were neither stubborn nor embittered, in comparison with religious wars or persecutions elsewhere. It may be that their dissenting opinions were not clear enough to die for. In fine there was little zeal either to inflict or endure martyrdom. Lollardy never spread so far in England as to invite foreign Catholic intervention. The trouble mercifully remained a family affair, and the horrible embroiling factors of national or racial hate did not burst in and make the hell of England which the invasion of northern Catholics had made of Provence in the Albigensian Crusade, or which rancor between Czechs and Germans was to make of Bohemia in the generation following Wyclif's death.

As for the substance of Lollardy, that consisted of Wyclif's teachings.[2] But it was a Wyclifism always tend-

---

[1] Rolls of Parliament, iii, 141, cited by Trevelyan, *England in the Age of Wycliff*, p. 311.

[2] See The Lollard Conclusions of about the year 1394 printed in *Fasciculi Zizaniorum* (Master of Rolls Series) ed. by Shirley, and in Gee and Hardy, *Documents illustrative of English Church History* (1914), pp. 126–132.

ing to disintegrate, become desultory and unreasonable. It clung to Scripture rather crudely understood; it protested against images and ceremonies; it detested popery and prelacy, and in a general way conformity. This "lay party" lacked organization; its adherents lacked education and intelligence, and that enormous experience and knowledge of human nature which rounded out the Roman Catholic Church, and gave it stability even in its abuses. If Lollardy was some sort of evangelical purification of Catholic Christianity, it also afforded proof, if such was needed, that society cannot be conducted on principles which lack the wisdom of the world.

Undoubtedly as the fourteenth century passed into the fifteenth, a large number of men were known as Lollards, among whom the more intelligent held themselves Wyclif's followers. They were chiefly laity of the common sort, with here and there a priest strayed from his pasturage, or a layman of position. Such was Sir John Oldcastle, who doughtily refused to admit his errors, and with his armed friends and followers made some sort of blind assault upon authority in the reign of Henry V. He was at last executed in 1417,[3] and a number of his adherents. This did much to finish Lollardy as a tangible movement, religious, social or political. Its doctrines were loosely maintained in the so-called "lay party," a term, which aptly designated a tendency among plain Englishmen to distrust priests and prelates, and think them not entitled to their emoluments when they failed egregiously in their duties; or a tendency to rely on the direct reading of Scripture and to regard excessive worship of images as idolatry.

The reading of Scripture by the laity in their own tongue, and the circulation of translations made by Wyclif, are uncertain and thorny topics. The English reading public was extremely limited, and French quite as much as English was the language of the Court and high nobility, though doubtless not of country squires. Gower wrote as lengthily in French and Latin as in English, and his English works, as well as those of Geoffrey Chaucer,

---

[3] On Oldcastle see Gairdner, *Lollardy*, etc., I, pp. 72 sqq.

were not made public before Wyclif's death. Nevertheless there is some evidence of English versions of parts of
Scripture possibly preceding those which probably Wyclif
made and had his " poor priests " use when preaching.
But it is improbable that his translations extended beyond
the Gospels. As for the ecclesiastical attitude, the proof
is somewhat lame that the Catholic Church opposed the
reading of Scripture by the laity, under proper super-
vision; but the Church authorities forbade as they were
able the putting of unlicensed versions into the hands of
ignorant persons who might be misled and mislead others.
And of necessity the Church set its face against the right
of the individual to interpret Scripture after his own
mind, and stand by it against authority.[4]

There was more learning, and occasionally a broader-
mindedness, among the opponents of Lollardy. One of
these was Thomas Netter or Walden as he is usually
called after his native town in Essex, a Carmelite and
confessor to Henry V. A zealous opponent of the
Wycliffites or Lollards, he has given a convenient synopsis
of their teachings in his chief work against them.[5] An
opponent of the " lay party," far more interesting intellectually, was Bishop Pecock, whose character was as
supple as his mind. He opposed Lollardy and defended
the Church in its practices, even in its abuses, possibly
with ill-judged officiousness, and certainly with dangerous
arguments, which in the end brought this curious person
within scorching distance of the stake. His career has
its ludicrous elements.

The year and place of birth of Reginald Pecock, sometime Lord Bishop of Chichester, are unknown. He was
undoubtedly a Welshman. His boyhood is alleged to
have been studious. Election to a fellowship at Oriel
College, Oxford, in 1417 is the first definitely known point
of his career. In due time he passed from acolyte and
deacon to priest. At the same time pursuing his studies

[4] The matter is briefly discussed by Gairdner, *Lollardy,* &c. I, p. 100
sqq. Gasquet, *Pre-Reformation English Bible* (1895) argues that the ex-
tant versions known as Wycliffite are authorized Catholic translations.
The subject is obscure and lends itself to temperamental argument.

[5] See Gairdner, *Lollardy,* &c. I, p. 86 sqq.

sacred and profane with ardor and success, he was made
Bachelor of Divinity.   Afterwards summoned to court,
he became useful to princes and received the first of
various sleek preferments from the " good," but none
too good, Duke Humphrey Plantagenet, Protector of the
kingdom.   Pecock now wrote many books, which refuted
the errors of the Lollards, and were pleasing to those
whom it was well to please.   His fortunes blossomed
cheerily, and he was made bishop of St. Asaph in 1444,
through the Protector's influence.   Two or three years
later he defended somewhat over zealously or over spe-
ciously the order of bishops, to which he was pleased to
belong.   Not only Wyclif and the Lollards, but earnest
priests of unblemished standing held that the decline of
preaching was owing to the example and indeed to the
precepts of the bishops led by his Grace of Canterbury.
Save with themselves, the bishops were not popular.
Pecock pleaded for them in a famous sermon, maintaining
that their loftier duties freed them from the burden of
preaching, and likewise from the obligation of residence,
since Court or Parliament might need their talents.   He
vindicated also the papal right of provisional preferment
to benefices not yet vacant.   In fine he upheld what serious men regarded as the manifest abuses of the hierarchy.
So pleased was he with his own discourse that he wrote it
out in the form of conclusions, and sent them to his
friends, deeming that they would be held true by all men
learned in divinity and the Canon Law.   The result
proved otherwise, when denunciation rather than acclaim
broke forth from both the learned and the ignorant.   Attempts were made to censure him, but the episcopal
authorities showed themselves lenient to his errors, even
though soon afterwards it came to him to speak slightingly
of the authority of the great Church Fathers.

Pecock himself was not a lazy bishop, but a preacher
as well as writer.   He seems to have believed in the positions taken in his argument, which in fact accorded with
the practices of his order.   So he continued writing, pro-
ducing many tracts.   His prejudices and circumstances
led on to the composition of his most interesting work,

the *Repressor of overmuch blaming* (*wijting* was the old word he used) *the clergy*. In that he vindicated his opinions with arguments verily leading back through Abaelard to the *De divisione naturae* of Erigena, and with the occasional employment of such critical historic insight as had not been shown by Occam or Marsiglio or Wyclif, or any man indeed except Lorentius Valla, who about the same time likewise was exposing the spuriousness of " Constantine's Donation." Before relating Pecock's further rise and luckless downfall it were well to make some mention of the contents of his book.[6]

The *Repressor* primarily directs itself against those tenets of the " lay party " (i. e. the Lollards) which make Scripture to be the sole and sufficient rule of life, and hold that meek and godly and ignorant man can understand Scripture as well as the educated clergy. By overthrowing this position, Pecock prepares the way for a full justification of many clerical practices and ordinances which are not, explicitly at least, commanded by Scripture. His attack upon the scriptural fetishism of the lay party and his exalting of reason's *doom of kinde* (the judgment of the law of reason), and the education and skill pertaining to its due exercise, is of interest as well as portent. For these tenets of the " lay party " were to exercise enormous influence, and even reach dominance in Puritan England, while in Pecock's book we hear two voices opposing them, the one voice that of tradition and church usage, and the other that of reason implanted in man but duly trained by the accepted discipline and accumulated wisdom of the ages.

The first error of this lay party is that Christians should

[6] Pecock's *Repressor* is edited, with an introduction, by C. Babington in the Rolls Series (1860). A full account of the book is given in Gairdner's *Lollardy and the Reformation*, etc., Vol. I, p. 202 sqq (Macmillan, 1908). Pecock in *Repressor*, pp. 350–366, argues at some length against the truth of the story of the reproving angel's voice at the time when Constantine made his Donation, and then against the historical fact of any such great donation having been made by Constantine. He is seeking to show that the temporalities of the Church came, unreproved by any angel's voice, from other times and sources. Very different was the intent of Valla's *De falso credita Constantini donatione*, which by closer criticism showed that document to have been a forgery. Pecock wrote a few years later than Valla, but without knowledge of the latter's argument.

hold no " governaunce " (ordinance) to be " the service or the law of God, save it which is grounded in Holy Scripture." They are set so fast in this

" trowing or holding . . . that whenever any clerk affermeth to them any governaunce contrary to their wit or plesaunce, though it lie full open and full surely in doom of reason, and therefore surely in moral law of kinde, which is law of God for to be done, yet they anon asken, ' Where groundest thou it in the New Testament? ' or in the Old ' in such place which is not by the New Testament revoked? ' "

The second error in which they are set is

" that whatever Christian man or woman be meek in spirit and will for to understand truly Holy Scripture, shall without fail find the true understanding of Holy Scripture in whatever place he or she shall read and study, though it be in the Apocalypse or anywhere else; and the more meek he or she be, the sooner he or she shall come into the very true and due understanding of it."

And the third error is that these meek understanders will listen to no argument from any clerk.

Pecock proceeds to set out as counter considerations the value of logic and the irrefragable conclusion of the syllogism, " though all the angels in heaven would say and hold that thilk conclusion were not true." He deemed it would be a great advantage if the common people might study logic in their mother tongue. All this, however, is but preliminary to the deeper rationalism of his argument. Herein in the first place he argues that it is not the office of Scripture to " ground any governaunce or deed or service of God, or any law of God or any truth, which man's reason by nature may find, learn, and know." Pecock's positions are more interesting than his arguments in their support; for these are often cumbered with redundant logic, and the form is not as good as that of thirteenth century scholasticism. His polemic sometimes gets the better of his humor, as when in showing that Scripture does not contain all that is needed for man's guidance, he points out the meagreness of its teaching upon matrimony, amounting not to " the hundredth part of the teaching upon matrimony which I teach in my book on matrimony;

and yet who will read will find the teaching of that book little enough or over little for to teach all that is necessary to be learned and known upon matrimony."

While Scripture does not *ground* the things of reason, it requires and assumes the use of reason. If Scripture bids a man be just to his neighbor, reason teacheth him the same; and what justice is must be found in reason and not in Scripture. Christ changed the ceremonial law of the Old Testament, but not the moral law, but added some new sacraments. And the said *law of kinde* was before both Testaments, and was " not grounded in Holy Scripture, but in the book of the law of kinde written in men's souls with the finger of God."

Having established his first main conclusion, Pecock puts the following portentous corollary,

"that whenever in Holy Scripture or out of Holy Scripture be written any point of any governaunce of the said law of kinde it is more verily written in the book of man's soul than in the outward book of parchment or velum; and if any seeming discord be betwixt the words written in the outward book of Holy Scripture and the doom of reason written in man's soul and heart, the words so written ought to be expounded and interpreted and brought for to accord with the doom of reason in thilk matter; and the doom of reason ought not for to be expounded, glossed, interpreted and brought for to accord with the said outward writing in Holy Scripture."

Evidently the uninterpreted letter of Scripture is not the supreme law with Pecock.

Although Scripture is not the ground of " natural or moral governaunce or truth into whose finding, learning, and knowing man's reason may by himself come," nevertheless it witnesseth these ordinances and truths not grounded in it, reminding and exorting men to perform and fulfil the same. Pecock further concludes that " the whole office and work into which God ordained Holy Scripture is for to ground articles of faith and for to rehearse and witness moral truths of law of kinde grounded in moral philosophy, that is to say in the doom of reason." [7] And the greater part of God's law for man on

―――――――――

[7] Pecock seems to go back to Duns Scotus for his position "that the

earth is grounded " in the inward book of the law of kinde and of moral philosophy," the truths for example, that there is one God, creator of all, that man is made for an end which is union with God.   On the other hand, without moral philosophy no man can know the whole law of God.   So all unlearned persons of the lay party ought to make much of the clerks who are learned in moral philosophy, that the clerks may help them rightly to understand Scripture.

Then as it were to comfort and assure himself of the validity of his positions, Pecock boldly puts forth these words:

" If any man make of Holy Scripture and apprise it, even as truth is and no more than truth is, God is therein pleased; and if any man will make of Holy Scripture or any creature in heaven or in earth more than truth is, God is therein displeased.   And further thus: If any man be feared lest he trespass to God if he will make over little of Holy Scripture, which is the outward writing of the Old Testament and the New, I ask why is he not a-feared lest he make over little and apprise over little the inward Scripture of the before spoken law of kinde written by God himself in man's soul, when he made man's soul to his image and likeness?   Of which inward Scripture Paul speaketh, Romans ii.   For certes this inward book or Scripture of law of kinde is more necessary to Christian men, and is more worthy than is the outward Bible and the cunning thereof, as far as they both treat of the more part of God's law to man."

Long before Pecock's time scholastic theologians, including the great Aquinas, had exalted the *lex naturalis* above the decrees of secular and even ecclesiastical authority.   Its source was the *summa ratio in Deo existens*, as Aquinas puts it, which man may perceive by the light or judgment of his natural reason,— an idea which is not far removed in significance from Pecock's *doom of kinde*. Unconditional supremacy was ascribed to this *lex naturalis*, even as the same was ascribed to the *jus divinum* revealed in Holy Scripture.   These two supremacies had been kept in close accord.   But Pecock's argumentation with its emphasis on the inward Scripture of the law of

faculty of the said moral philosophy and the faculty of pure divinity or the Holy Scripture be two diverse faculties, each of them having his proper bounds and marks, and each of them having his proper truths and conclusions."

kind, in contrast or possible opposition with " the outward Bible," opened yawning gulfs of rationalism;— and such were not closed by our author's handling of the objection that experience often shows that judgments of reason are fallible, whereas " Holy Scripture is a reverend thing and worthy, since by and from it the Christian Church of God taketh her faith." It is possible moreover that our bishop was not free from inconsistency in despising the narrow trust in Scripture of unaided and unteachable ignorance, and yet relying on the sometimes fatal " doom of reason " guided by policy and interest and passion. One cannot refrain from quoting a passage of great interest and even charm, in which he points to the danger of rash Bible reading. A " great cause," says he, of the errors of the " lay party " is this,

" that the reading in the Bible, namely in the historical [narrative] parts of the Old Testament and of the New, is much delectable and sweet, and draweth the readers into a devotion and a love of God, and from love and deinte [delight] of the world. . . . And then because the said reading was to them so graceful and so delectable, and the said end so profitable, it fell into their conceit for to trow full soon . . . that God had made or purveyed the Bible to men's behoof after or by the utterest degree of his power and cunning for to so ordain, and therefore all the whole Bible (or as some trowed, the New Testament) should contain all that is to be done in the law and service to God by Christian men, without need to have therewith any doctrine. And . . . soothly it has been said to me thus, ' that never man erred by reading or studying in the Bible ' . . . notwithstanding that there is no book written in the world by which a man shall rather [sooner] take occasion for to err."

Pecock thought there was a dearth of clergy learned in logic, moral philosophy and divinity, to expound Scripture; hence heresy had become rife among the laity,— and the king would have been better occupied in rooting it out than in conquering France. The subsequent three parts of his book (we have been drawing only from part I) are devoted to the defense (as against the lay party) of images and pilgrimages, of the revenues of the clergy, of the ranks and degrees among the clergy, of the lawfulness of papal and episcopal decrees, and of the religious

orders. Evidently the matter of this book contained very much that should have been pleasing to the church authorities; yet for its dangerous
arguments and for its author's views unguardedly
expressed elsewhere, this zealous prelate was brought
to grief. But not immediately, for he was translated to
the richer see of Chichester in 1450, through the interest
of the Duke of Suffolk and the Bishop of Norwich who
were suspected of complicity in the supposed murder of
Duke Humphrey, Pecock's former patron! The downfall of these hated lords left him defenceless and detested.
He was then writing his *Treatise on Faith*, in which he
was again busy sustaining the clergy by arguments that
rather tended to undermine their infallible authority and
possibly shadowed forth religious toleration! He was
a man not altogether fortunate in his arguments and his
zeal. The hate of the lords temporal and spiritual broke
out against him in a council at Westminster in 1457. It
was said that he had pooh-poohed the Doctors of the
Church, had made a new creed of his own. Pecock and
his books were brought up for examination before the
Archbishop at Lambeth. We are not very credibly informed as to the actual dispute, and the method and substance of his examination. The accounts are from his
enemies. He was condemned for many of his conclusions, the archbishop in a curious closing speech (as reported not very reliably), offering him the choice of public
abjuration or being made " as the food of fire and fuel for
the burning."

Naturally, perhaps one may say pitifully, he elected
to abjure his errors; and before a vast crowd at Paul's
Cross, made a full recantation and abject confession of
error and presumption, and with his own hand delivered
his books to be burned. His works were also burnt at
Oxford, and doggerel verses expressed the contempt in
which men chose to hold him. After various appeals and
measures, the shorn heretic was consigned to permanent
detention in a chamber of the abbey of Thorney in
Cambridgeshire.[8]

[8] For these uncertain facts see Babington's Introduction, and R. L.

Much of our information regarding Pecock comes from the *Liber Veritatum* (otherwise called *Dictionarium Theologicum*) of an orthodox contemporary who hated him well, Doctor Thomas Gascoigne.[9] Pecock may have been in this Doctor's mind when the latter was defining " Haereticus " in his Dictionary, and stating as the first characteristic of the tribe that they do not follow the authority of the Scriptures but the pointings (sensum) of human reason. They are men of lust, yet endowed with ardent and acute minds, for only men so gifted can construct a heresy; and they change from one contrary error to another.

Gascoigne was a man of birth and property, greatly respected at his university of Oxford, where he was chosen chancellor more than once; his integrity and his loyalty to church and crown were above all cavil. This exemplary doctor's *Dictionarium* gives a motley picture of the ecclesiastical debasement of his times. Its illustrations are vivid and direct, and filled with varied interest and entertainment as he tells of the preferment of boys and drunken fools to bishoprics, and of a bishop drawing revenue from the concubinage of his clergy.[10] The author opposed the Lollards and also detested their opponent Pecock; he was a fearless and constant denouncer of those evils which later moved Luther to revolt, to wit, papal pardons, indulgences, and dispensations from onerous duties.[11] Also he set an example of abstention from the fruits of ecclesiastical abuses, plural preferments and the like. For the reform of all these evils he could find no place but Rome to look to; and at the same time he was convinced that the condition of the papal court was such that nothing good could come from it. He had no thought of revolt; and an extract from his book will show how utter and how

Poole's article in the *Dictionary of National Biography*. Apparently Pecock's examination dwelt mainly on matters other than those arousing our interest in him.

[9] Edited with a full introduction by Thorold Rogers, (Oxford, 1881). Dr. Gairdner gives much of interest from it in his *Lollardy,* etc., I, p. 243 sqq.

[10] Gower in *Mirour de l'Omme,* lines 20149–20160, speaks of deans drawing revenue from harlots. Macaulay's ed. of Gower; French Works (Clarendon Press).

[11] See pp. 76 sqq., 86 sqq., 92 sqq., and 118 sqq. of Roger's edition.

sweeping, and yet how devoid either of revolutionary intent, or of hope of reform within the Church, might be the rebukes and upbraidings of a churchman:

" For Rome as a singular and chief wild beast has laid waste the vineyard of the Church, by reserving to themselves [i. e. to the Roman Curia] the elections of the bishops, that none may confer an episcopal church on anyone unless he first pay the annates or firstfruits and revenue of the vacant church.   Likewise she has destroyed the vineyard of the Church of God by annulling the elections of all bishops in England.   Likewise she destroys the Church by promoting evil men as the king and himself [i. e. the Pope] agree.   Likewise Rome as a wild beast has ravaged the churches by annulling all the elections of bishops made in cathedral churches, ordaining that all elections of bishops pertain to the Apostolic Chamber, to wit, to the decision of the pope and his cardinals. Likewise because Rome does not name anyone bishop save whom the pope and cardinals choose as bishop or archbishop, having rendered and prepaid at Rome thousands of marks in fruits and having made gifts to the Roman or papal courtiers."

Time and again Gascoigne declares and instances his proofs, that the pope, even if he would, dared not take measures for reform, from fear of poison or death by open violence.

This much has been said of Pecock and Gascoigne because they are interesting people, and also in order to cover the barrenness of the record of the " lay party " through the fifteenth century.   Yet one feels or may infer its inarticulate existence, representing in those disturbed and bloody English decades a certain laicizing of life and opinion in England, as opposed to sacerdotalism or ecclesiasticism, and perhaps monkery.   There was scant feeling that church lands were sacrosanct.   In 1410 the Commons petitioned for their confiscation in part or altogether; and through this century far fewer monasteries were founded, while foundations of hospitals and schools and colleges increased.   Undoubtedly by the time of Henry VIII's accession, there was a wide lay intelligence in England, instructed or largely ignorant, yet prepared for the acceptance of Protestant ideas from the Continent, and ready at the royal behest to separate from papal Rome.

CHAPTER XXI

SOCIAL DISCONTENT AND LUTHERAN INFLUENCE: TYNDALE

I

TURNING the pages of Gascoigne, one hears the resonant echoes of ancient denunciations — of mankind, of knights and bourgeoisie, and so often of the Church. These satires or denunciations might be general or specifically pointed at the particular abuse or crime. Much also has been recorded, or more lately has been written, upon the state of the Church in England, and especially upon the state of its monasteries, at the time when Henry VIII bestrode the throne. Yet just how good or bad the Church and its monasteries were, one queries still.

The Church had been and still was part of English society, in which the gentry were the favorite sons, and estates were inherited from one generation to the next. The landed classes furnished the Church's maintenance, and the nobility and gentry put their younger sons and needy relations into the bishoprics and other goodly benefices. This regular operation of family interest was but one remove from the law of inheritance of secular landed estates. It was much the same in Germany and elsewhere. The condition of the Church paralleled that of society at large; it was not abnormally bad, but merely permeated with normal human slackness, selfishness, materialism and ignorance, with occasional instances of a better energy and enlightenment in its upper or lower orders. The monasteries possessed large revenues or small; the denizens managed their fat lands, or subsisted leanly; generally they lived slackly enough and, like normal human beings, were disinclined to exert themselves beyond the goading of their needs. The monasteries also exercised charity and hospitality, and the richer ones provided funds for the support of scholars at the universities.

Probably the poorer monasteries were spiritually the more squalid and inert.

Sadly general statements these, sounding like truisms! the clergy are part of society, and made what they are by education, convention and environment; they are good or bad, but on the whole tending, by virtue of their education, to be a little better than the corresponding upper or middle classes from which they are drawn.   And as one part of society is jealous of another, and not apt to sympathize with its difficulties and temptations, so the laity tended to be captious as to the clergy, and to envy them the wealth which they did not seem to earn.   It was thus in England, as we might assume, if we were not so informed.

The matter may, however, be regarded in another light. There come times when some order in society fails to function in correspondence with the demands of society at large.   Or the ideas conventionally represented by a certain order may no longer meet the best thoughts of contemporaries.   This touches the clergy and their functions.   The needs of society, and its somewhat clearer or advancing ideas, may pass beyond the current observances and practices of the Church.   And therefore, from this point of view, the question of church abuses and clerical corruption resolves itself into the question whether the habits of the clergy and the methods and institutions of the established religion fittingly correspond with the ideas, and meet the needs, of the time.   An answer in the negative means that Church and clergy are no longer suited to the time, and reform is needed.   Contemporary verdicts will declare that Church and clergy are corrupt.   The clergy may be as good, as moral, as the laity, or even better; but methods and institutions, and perhaps principles of belief, need refashioning.   What is called for, is the application of intelligence and the best available knowledge in matters of religion.

In fact, to make one more general statement before turning to specific illustration of the English situation, it may be said that the German, French, and English reformations represent intellectual advance, rather than moral or religious improvement, except as the latter is involved in the former. For example, to give up image worship, relics, pilgrimages, and indeed to renounce the authority of the Roman bishop, was to become more intelligent, rather than better.

In the reign of Henry VIII two currents, or perhaps three, of popular criticism assailed the established Church. Distinguishable in origin, in their working they tended to unite. The one was the surviving loosely heterodox dissent of the so-called " lay party "; which was no longer (if it ever was) a " party," or anything so concrete and articulate. The other current, confusedly Lutheran or Zwinglian, came from the Continent, where it also may have had its ancient sources. But in England it represented the " new learning." Thirdly, if one will, social and economic discontent, the stress of poverty, the sense of disadvantage. This was aggravated by the enclosure of parks and pastures by great proprietors, which dispossessed many tenants, and by the middle of the sixteenth century, may have thrown out of employment ten per cent. of the Kingdom's population.[1] Such sense of poverty and oppression had always made part of the indigenous condemnation of the clergy's wealth, and readily combined with the " new learning " when it came from the Continent. Indeed one may say that most reforms which have issued out of Christianity against its own corruptions, as they have been called for by the avarice and lusts of priests and prelates and rich seculars, so have they carried the motive of relieving the distress of the poor. In some way they all seem popular movements, and to represent some assertion of popular rights as against the oppression of the rich. So had it been with Wyclif and the Lollards, so was it with the Lutheran reform, in spite of Luther's violent protests, and so was it to be in England. Thus, although distinguishable, these

---

[1] A tract on "the decay of England by the great multitude of sheep" (Early. Eng. Text. Soc. Extra series XIII), written about 1550 in the reign of Edward VI, shows with statistics and calculations the vast number of plows rendered idle by the enclosing of arable land for pasture. See also on "the economic evils of Edward's time Crowley's *Petition against the Oppressors of the Poor Commons,* in Strype, *Ecclesiastical Memorials* II, II, p. 217 (Chapter XVII), also ib. II, II, Chapter XXIII.

three factors in English sixteenth century disaffection toward the Church often joined together, and became as indigenous soil, with native harrowings and foreign informing seed.

It was none too easy for clever contemporaries to distinguish them; and dispute arose as to which cause to ascribe the dissatisfaction (the degree was in dispute) with the Church.   A notable debate took place between a clever lawyer, Saint-German, and Sir Thomas More, in the years 1532 and 1533, when the King already had proceeded far in his conflict with the pope.   Saint-German contended that " the division between spiritualitie and temporalitie," in other words, the laity's dissatisfaction with the wealth and laxity of the clergy, was both general and of long standing; while More insisted that it was special or local, and of recent origin: " The division is nothing such as this man makes it, and is grown as great as it is only since Tyndale's books and Frith's and Friar Barnes' began to be spread abroad." [2]

Probably Saint-German was right in contending that the disaffection was old, in its roots at least, and that it was then general; and More was doubtless right in ascribing its current prevalence largely to the recently disseminated literature.   That contained social protest as well as religious novelty; yet the proportions varied with the writers.   Instances may be given first of those in which the social protest outbulks all else, and then of those in which principles of religious reform are clear and trenchant.

To the former belongs the famous *Supplicacion of Beggars* written by one Simon Fish about the year 1528 or 1529, who had already fled the kingdom, through fear of Cardinal Wolsey.   For the Cardinal was enraged against him for acting in a play a part which travestied his Grace.   Then he wrote the *Supplicacion of Beggars*,

---

[2] The tracts in question are Christopher Saint-German's *Dyalogue in English between a Student of Law and a Doctor of Divinity; A Treatise concerning the division between the spiritualitie and temporalitie; A Dyalogue between two Englishmen, whereof one is called Salem and the other Bizance;* and More's *Apology* and *Debellacyon of Salem and Bizance.* The controversy is given in Gasquet, *Eve of the Reformation.*

which Henry VIII came by and secretly read. Henry liked the book so well that he sent word to Fish that he could safely return to the realm; which is a proof that it was a diatribe against the clergy, and had no theological heresy; for Henry was as jealous of his orthodoxy as he was open to complaints against the Church which he was battering.

The burden of the piece is the oppression of the poor through the wealth, avarice, and extortion of the clergy. They are no shepherds, but ravenous wolves, all of them:

"Bishops, Abbots, Priors, Deacons, Archdeacons, Suffragans, Priests, Monks, Canons, Friars, Pardoners, and Somners. And who is able to number this idle ravinous sort, which (setting all labor aside) have begged so importunately that they have gotten into their hands more than a third part of your Realm. The goodliest lordships, manors, lands and territories are theirs. Besides this, they have the tenth part of all the corn, meadow, pasture, grass, wool, colts, calves, lambs, pigs, geese, and chickens . . . of every servant's wages . . . milk, honey, wax, cheese and butter. Yea, and they look so narrowly upon their profits, that the poor wives must be countable to them of every tenth egg, or else she getteth not her rights at Easter, shall be taken as an heretic. . . . What money pull they in by probates of testaments, privy tithes . . . and at their first masses? Every man and child that is buried must pay somewhat for masses and diriges to be sung for him, or else they will accuse the dead's friends and executors of heresy."

The invective, which is addressed to the King, passes on to other exactions, and the enormous mulcting of the Realm by the begging Friars. The clergy get half the revenues of the entire Realm. And they are bad. No man's wife or daughter is safe from them; none may for certain know his own child. They draw women from their husbands, and spread disease. Why should not you, the King, punish them as you do other men? Through them, your people are beggars and thieves. They are stronger in Parliament than yourself. Who dares lay any charge against them, when "so captive are your laws unto them, that no man that they list to excommunicate, may be admitted to sue any action in any of your courts."

The only color for these exactions is "that they say that they pray for us to God, to deliver our souls out of the pains of purgatory." But many learned men deem purgatory " a thing invented by the covetousness of the spirituality." The only remedy is to be rid of them. "Tie these holy idle thieves to the carts, to be whipped naked about every market town till they fall to labor, that they, by their importunate begging, take not away the alms that the good Christian people would give unto us sore, impotent, miserable people, your bedesmen." Then shall crime and poverty diminish, your people shall obey you, the marriage vows shall be kept, the commons increase in numbers and in wealth, and the gospel shall be preached.[3]

This exaggerated diatribe is only here and there heretical, as when it hints that priests were better married, and that purgatory is their invention; also in its implication that they do not preach the gospel. Yet Sir Thomas More, in the lengthy answer which he immediately wrote, seized upon this denial of purgatory as his starting point. He termed his tract *The Supplicacion of Souls,* and opened it with the heart-rending cry of souls in Purgatory, " poor prisoners of God," imploring their late spouses, kindred and companions not to forget them, but " rather by your good and charitable means vouchsafe to deliver us hence." Purgatory was indeed a cardinal Catholic doctrine, and quite as essential for the lengthening of the Church's purse as for the shortening of the pains of the departed. More devotedly upheld purgatory, as he did every Catholic doctrine.

Any attack upon clerical abuses or extortions was likely to disparage some doctrine of the Church. Whether the disparagement was incidental or a direct assault, would usually depend on the writer's interest, since he was not likely to be an unconditional accepter of Church teachings. In the sixteenth century any active opponent of Church abuses was apt to be a heretic, or liable to become one. This holds true of the authors of tracts against the clergy, and even of those which were occupied with economic abuses and the misery of the people. Belonging to the latter was the *Complaynt of Roderic Mors,* " some-

[3] Edited by J. M. Cowper, Early English Text Society, Extra Series XIII (1871).

time a gray friar " by Henry Brinklow, written in 1542.[4]
Its premise is that all men should obey the laws of Prince
and Parliament when not contrary to God's law: even
then none should resist violently, but suffer death rather
than obey.   The theme of the tract is the economic distress caused by oppressive or improper laws and practices.
Between the year 1529, when the *Supplicacion of Beggars*
appeared, and 1542, the date of the " Complaynt," Henry
had wrenched England from the papacy, and had permitted changes in the services of the Church, as the mood
was on him, or foreign relations served.   But usually with
vigorous hand he upheld Catholic doctrine and smote rash
innovators, as will be seen hereafter.   The monasteries
had been suppressed, and their lands seized by the King,
or delivered to his followers, who would hold them fast
and become a power in the realm opposed to papal
restoration.

The *Complaynt of Roderic Mors* first directs itself
against those wicked recipients of abbey lands who have
raised the rents, or evicted the tenants who could show no
leases.   " What a shame is this to the whole realm, that
we say we have received the Gospel of Christ, and yet it
is worse now in this matter than it was over fifty or three
score years, when we had but the Pope's law, as wicked
as it was, for then leases were not known."   This means
that in the former times landlords, lay and spiritual, commonly accepted such rents as the tenants, from father to
son, had paid.   The new landlords were squeezing the
last penny from the land.

" Look well upon this, ye Christian burgesses; for this
inhansing of rents is not only against the common wealth,
but also, at length, shall be the chiefest decay of the principal commodity of this realm.   For why?   This in-
ordinate inhansing of rents . . . must needs make all
things dear, as well pertaining to the back as to the belly,
to the most great damage of all the King's subjects, landed
men only except."   Brinklow argues that the raising of
the rents is the root of all economic evils.   If they were
reduced, English cloth could be produced more cheaply,

[4] Early Eng. Text Soc., Extra Series XXII.

and would find a better market. With high prices "everyone eateth out another."

Another trouble is the forfeiting of the lands or goods of those who are executed for treason or other crime; by which their wives and children are reduced to poverty. Another is the enclosing of parks, forests and chases; and the deer destroy the neighboring crops, while a man may be hanged for killing the beast devouring his corn or grass. "The thing is too manifest. God grant the King grace to pull up a great part of his own parks, and to compel his lords, knights, and gentlemen to pull up all theirs by the roots, and to let out the ground to the people at such reasonable price as they may live at [by] their hands. . . . Ye lords, see that ye abuse not the blessing of the riches and power which God has lent you, and remember, that the earth is the Lord's, and not yours."

The tract passes to the abuse of the selling of wards for ill assorted marriages, by which adultery increases; then to the old story of the law's delay and cost, and the pitiful state of prisoners lodged like hogs, lying in prison for years without trial. Moreover, when men are accused by the bishops for their preaching, they should not be suffered to lie in the Bishops' prisons, which are the prisons of their accusers. " Why should not both parties be put in prison till the matter be tried, as well as one?" Then the bishops would not be so hasty in accusing.

He turns again to the Church lands: " When an Antichrist of Rome durst openly . . . walk up and down through England," he and his children had the wit to get the best lands there, and goodly parsonages and vicarages. Yet alms were given, through the monks, and the distress of the poor relieved, who now utterly lack support. By the confiscation of the abbey lands, the matter is mended as the devil mended the old woman's leg, by breaking it altogether! " My lord parsons " are thieves and robbers, who entered not by the door of the sheepfold, but by act of Parliament; and the temporal landlords now even exceed the spirituality in covetousness.

The tract wanders on through the varied abuses

troubling the realm, and turns to the need of reform in religion, which was unreformed enough in these last years of Henry VIII, in spite of severance from Rome. Let men leave off calling upon creatures in heaven and earth, and worship one God only and rely on one mediator, Jesus Christ. Away with holy days and idols and images, and auricular confession. Let the priests marry, if they will. " But now through God's help, to bring these godly acts . . . to a good and godly purpose, ye must first down with all your vain chantries,[5] all your proud colleges of canons, and specially your forked wolves the bishops; leave them no temporal possessions, but only a competent living. . . . Now for the good of these chantries, colleges, and bishops, for the Lord's sake take no example at the distribution of the abbey goods and lands; but look rather for your erudition to the godly politic of the Christian Germans in this case "— a last recommendation disclosing the influence of the German reform upon the writer. He points out how the bishops' wealth should be distributed among the poor of city and country, with part of it given to the King.

But the "pope's shavelings" still blaspheme Holy Writ, and men are imprisoned for reading it. "The pope remaineth wholly still in England, save only that his name is banished. For why? his body (which be the bishops and other shavelings) doth not only remain, but also his tail, which be his filthy traditions, wicked laws, and beggarly ceremonies . . . yea and the whole body of his pestiferous canon law." Every bishop now is pope and antichrist! And never were they so eager to defend the pope as since the King took from him the tribute. The body of the realm is still oppressed. We remain " in a perpetual bondage and spiritual captivity." The tract closes with a cry to England to wake from sleep, lest her blood be upon her head.

This long tract was written in those years of Henry's cruel reactionary orthodoxy; as was the same writer's later " Lamentation of a Christian against the City of

[5] Where masses were sung for souls in purgatory.

London," which was printed in Nuremberg in 1545.[6]   Its
cry has become even shriller, its cry against idolatry, and
lament for the rejection of Christ's Testament.   The
bishops are abominations, and the greatest idol is the
Mass.   " Do ye not see how the whore of Babylon hath
altered the supper of the Lord, which was instituted to
have the blessed Passion in continual remembrance ? "

Two " Supplications " also belong to these last repres-
sive years of Henry, when the poor may have felt the oppression of the bishops and many-beneficed clergy as bitterly as ever in the days when the pope was still the
ghostly lord of England.   Both tracts are anonymous.
The one, belonging to the year 1544 is entitled " A Supplicacion to our most Soveraigne Lorde Kynge Henry the
Eyght "; and the other, of the year before Henry died
(1546) is entitled " A Supplication of the Poore Commons." [7]   Both denounce the ignorance, slothfulness,
avarice and oppressive wealth of the clergy, and the laws
which load them with unearned benefices, and forbid the
poor to read the Word of God.   It is " the crafty policy
of the clergy to keep the knowledge of God's Word from
all men, that they might indulge their avarice and iniqui-
ties ";— and thus nourish the ungodly trust in masses for
the dead by which men are impoverished.   Even the
studies of the clergy may work ill: " It is a dangerous
thing to admit one to be a spiritual pastor, whose profession and study all his youth hath been in decrees and
popish laws.   For such a study, for the most part, ingen-
dereth a popish heart."   The King should abolish the
great lordships of the bishops, who live like heathen
princes, having too much worldly business and authority.
If this were reformed, faith would abound.

The second tract denounces those same " sturdy beggars " as it calls the clergy, and inveighs against the
statutes which permitted only the wealthy laity to have a
Bible in their houses, and forbade men to read the Scriptures in the Churches during service.   Curious laws, we
think them, to prevent the misunderstanding of Scrip-

[6] Early Eng. Text Soc., Extra Series XXII.
[7] Both printed in Early Eng. Text Soc., Extra Series XIII.

ture! Words of reproachful warning are addressed to
the King:

"Oh gracious Prince, here are we, your natural and most obedient liege people, constrained to forget (with all humble subjection
we speak it) that we are of nature and by the ordinance of God
your most bounden subjects, and to call to remembrance that by
our second birth we are your brothers and fellow servants (although in a much inferior ministry) in the household of the Lord
our God. . . We beseech you (most dear Sovereign) even in the
hope you have in the redemption by Christ, that you call to remembrance that dreadful day, when your Highness shall stand before the judgment seat of God in no more reputation than one of
those miserable creatures which do now daily die in the streets for
lack of their due portion, wherewith you and your nobles do reward
those gnatonical elbowhangers, your chaplains."

The author tells a story of one of these parasitical
chaplains riding abroad for his pastime, having with him,
as his custom was, a scroll in which were written the names
of the parishes of which he was the parson.

"He espied a church standing upon a fair hill, pleasantly beset
with groves and plain fields, the goodly green meadows lying beneath by the banks of a crystalline river garnished with willows,
poplars, palm trees [sallows] and alders, most beautiful to behold.
This vigilant pastor, taken with the sight of this territorial para-
dise, said unto a servant of his: 'Robin,' said he, 'yonder benefice
standeth very pleasantly; I would it were mine.' The servant answered, 'Why sir,' quoth he, 'it is your own benefice,' and named
the parish."

The tract turns grimly to the greed of those who have
the abbey lands; it bids the King remember his hoary hair,
— surely he would desire to leave a Common Weale to
his son, and not an island of brute beasts; it bids him also
beware of God's judgment: "For the blood of all them
that, through your negligence shall perish, shall be required at your hand."

These protesters and dissenters may be taken to represent currents of English social and religious disaffection
coming down from Wyclif. As there had been continuous or sporadic strains of protest against the doctrines and
practices of the Roman Catholic Church, so after Henry's
breach with Rome, there continued or arose like strains

of protest against the established Church of England, which acted with as high a hand, and, at the close of Henry's reign, still carried well nigh the whole volume of Catholic doctrine, not to say superstition — as will be noted more particularly. From the time, however, that the Lutheran revolt broke out in Germany, and a corresponding movement began in Switzerland and France, English dissent was stimulated and informed by ideas from the Continent, and indeed blown up into a flame by them, as Sir Thomas More said. From that moment it becomes difficult to distinguish indigenous English thoughts, though one can readily identify as continental certain conceptions, like that of justification by faith.

A general idea of what these recalcitrants were supposed to hold and teach may be gathered from articles of accusation brought by ecclesiastical authorities, who represented, in the first instance selected, the Roman Catholic Church, and in the second, the Church of England. Humphrey Monmouth was a wealthy London draper, who had entertained John Tyndale and furnished funds for printing (on the Continent) his English translation of Scripture, and other books in English. This was shortly after the year 1521 when Luther was proclaimed a heretic in England, and his writings and opinions prohibited. In May 1528 Sir Thomas More and another of the Privy Counsel made search in Monmouth's house for forbidden books, committed Monmouth to the Tower, and laid charges against him in twenty-four articles.[8] These accused him of adhering to the heresies of Luther, and possessing his books, and causing them to be translated; of assisting Tyndale and others to translate the Bible; of being concerned with the printing of detestable books beyond the seas against the Sacrament of the Altar and the observance of the Mass; of eating flesh in Lent; of affirming that faith, without works, is sufficient to save; of alleging that the Constitutions of the Church did not bind men; of maintaining that we should pray only to God and not to the saints, that pilgrimages were unprofitable,

[8] Given in Strype, *Ecclesiastical Memorials,* I, I, p. 488 of Oxford ed. of 1822, p. 317 in older edition.

that men should " not offer to images in the church, nor
set any light before them," that confession was unnecessary, that fasts need not be kept, that papal pardons are
nugatory.   Monmouth made his defense, and may have
been saved by the turn of the tide.   At all events he
lived to die nine years later, leaving a pious will which
would not have been to the taste of those who had committed him to the Tower.[9]

Probably some eight years after Monmouth's com-
mittal, the Clergy of the Lower House in the Canterbury
convocation, acknowledging the King's Highness to be the
" Supreme Head of the Church of England, according to
the commandment of God," and speaking doughtily of the
" Bishop of Rome " and his " usurped authority," nevertheless proceeded to protest certain errors and abuses:
that the sacrament of the altar is not esteemed, and people
speak lightly of it; that extreme unction is denied to be a
sacrament, and that priests are held to have no more
authority to administer sacraments than laymen.   Likewise it is held that all church ceremonies, not expressly
directed by Scripture, should be abolished; that those are
antichrists who refuse the cup to the laity; " that a man
hath no free will "; that God gives no knowledge of
Scripture to the rich; that vows are contrary to Christ's
religion; that priests should have wives; that the saints'
images are not to be reverenced, and that it is plain idolatry to set lights before them; that one may christen a
child in a tub of water at home; " that the priests' crowns
are the whore's marks of Babylon; that the stole about
the priest's neck is nothing else but the Bishop of Rome's
rope "; that it is no sin to eat meat in Lent and on Good
Friday; that auricular confession, absolution and penance
are unprofitable; " that bishops, ordinaries, and ecclesiastical judges have no authority to give any sentence of excommunication . . . nor yet to absolve from the same ";
that churches are but conveniences to assemble in, and
burials in church-yards are vain; that the mass is only a
deluding of the people; that saints are not to be invoked,

[9] His petition of defense and his will are given in Strype, o. c. I, II
(appendix No. LXXXIX and XC).

for they know nothing of our prayers and cannot mediate between us and God; that there is no purgatory, but departed souls go straight to heaven or hell; that hallowed water, holy days, pilgrimages, fasts, and alms are vain; that it is sufficient to believe, without good works; " that no human constitutions or laws do bind any Christian man, but such as be in the Gospel, Paul's Epistle, or in the New Testament."

II

The absorption of Lutheran and even Zwinglian elements by an ardent reforming Englishman is exemplified in William Tyndale. He appears to have been born not later than 1490, and is said by Foxe to have been " brought up from a child in the university of Oxford, where he, by long continuance, grew up, and increased as well in the knowledge of tongues and other liberal arts, as especially in the knowledge of the Scriptures, whereunto his mind was singularly addicted." He also became a reader of Erasmus, and translated his *Enchiridion*. But the desire to render the Bible into English burned within him, till translation of Scripture became the labor of his life. In London he was entertained, as has been said, by Humphrey Monmouth, who, with other merchants, furnished him with funds for the journey to the Continent, which he undertook in order to obtain counsel in his work and have the fruit of his labor printed in safety. He was at Wittenberg with Luther in 1524, and stayed at Marburg, Cologne, and Worms, but spent most of his last years in Antwerp, where in the end he was decoyed into the hands of imperial officers, and was burnt for a heretic for 1536.

Tyndale made his translations from the Greek and Hebrew, and his vigorous renderings, pruned and corrected, form the basis of the " authorized version." His New Testament, printed at Worms, was brought into England in 1526, where the bishops, led by the Archbishop of Canterbury, took measures to suppress it. The bishop of London notified his clergy that " many children of iniquity, maintainers of Luther's sect, blinded through extreme wickedness and wandering from the way of truth and the Catholic faith, craftily have translated the New Testament into our English tongue, intermeddling therewith many heretical articles and erroneous opinions, pernicious and offensive, seducing the simple people, attempting by their wicked and perverse interpretations to profanate the majesty of the Scripture which hitherto hath remained undefiled, and craftily to abuse the most holy Word of God and the true sense of the same." [10]

England was still part of the papal church; and its prelates were of one mind as to the suppression of unsanctioned translations of the Bible which might impugn some part of the established doctrine. Tyndale's work, besides its alleged heretical renderings, stung them with its marginal comments. He took his stand on the authority of Scripture, and labored to set it before his countrymen according to his best understanding and interpretation of the text. That was his mission. He had no intention of expressing novelties of his own. Yet as he grasped the Scriptural meanings afresh and for himself, and doubtless was affected by Lutheran influence, his rendering was not likely to accord fully with the Catholic interpretation. He had a sound perception of the historical sense of Scripture, and sound ideas as to the limits of allegorical interpretation. The former appears, for example, in the Prologue to his translation of the Pentateuch:

"Behold how soberly, and how circumspectly, both Abraham and also Isaac behave themselves among infidels. Abraham buyeth that which might have been given him for nought, to cut off occasions. Isaac, when his wells, which he had digged, were taken from him, maketh room and resisteth not. Moreover they ear and sow, and feed their cattle, and make confederations, and take perpetual truce, and do all the outward things; even as they do who have no faith, for God hath not made us to be idle in this world."

In plain straight English he continues setting forth the acts and character of Jacob.

[10] As cited by Gairdner, *Lollardy*, &c. II, p. 228, citing " Foxe IV, 666–7."

In his Prologue to Leviticus he warns against the beguilement of allegories, whether in the Old Testament or the New. This matter should be handled sensibly. "Allegories prove nothing — and by allegories understand examples or similitudes borrowed of strange matters, and of another thing than thou entreatest of . . . But the very use of allegories is to declare and open a text, that it may be the better perceived and understood." [11]

He can state admirably the plain lessons of the palpable sense of Scripture; and he is Pauline and Lutheran with respect to faith and works. "But thou reader," says he in his prologue to the Prophet Jonas, "think of the law of God, how that it is altogether spiritual, and so spiritual that it is never fulfilled with deeds or works, until they flow out of thine heart, with as great love toward thine neighbour, for no deserving of his, yea though he be thine enemy, as Christ loved thee, and died for thee, for no deserving of thine, but even when thou wast his enemy."

Although more English, which is to say, less extreme and less logical than Luther, Tyndale holds to faith rather than to works. As he says in his tract, *The Wicked Mammon:* "That faith only before all works and without all merits, by Christ's only, justifieth and setteth us at peace with God, is proved by Paul in the first chapter to the Romans." But faith brings forth works naturally, and as of course; or it is a vain false faith, and the man "an unprofitable babbler." Both faith and works with Tyndale, as with Luther, are gifts of God. In the same tract he says: "All good works must be done freely with a single eye, without respect of any thing, and that no profit be sought thereby." But as good works naturally follow upon faith, so eternal life naturally follows upon faith and goodly living, without the seeking, just as hell naturally follows sin without the seeking. A Christian "feeleth that good works are nothing but the

---

[11] In his *Obedience of the Christian man,* p. 339 sqq., Tyndale speaks aptly concerning allegories, which men devise for illustration and instruction's sake, yet knowing that they prove nothing.

fruits of love, compassion, mercifulness, and of a tenderness of heart which a Christian has to his neighbour;
and that love springeth of that love which he has to
God."

Tyndale was no utter follower of Luther. His views
upon that momentous question of the nature of Eucharist,
which rent the religious bowels of the sixteenth century,
were rather those of Zwingli. Or we may say that his
English protestantism harked back to Wyclif, and that
he thus inherited his conception of the sacrament of the
altar, which resembled that of the Swiss reformer. As
a good Wycliffite, Lollard, or what one will, Tyndale
stood on the authority of Scripture as the law of God for
man. In his way, as a good Englishman of the Tudor
period (or a good Lutheran of Luther's age!) he next
stood firmly on the principle of obedience to the King.
This he inculcated as part of the natural law and constitution of human society in his *Obedience of a Christian
Man,* a discursive repetitious treatise, in which he writes
with power, but shows the inferiority of his composition
to the compactness and serried ordering of Luther's
writings.

Obedience is due from children to parents, from wives
to husbands, from subjects to princes. " The King is in
this world without law, and may at his lust do right or
wrong, and shall give account but to God only." Again:
" Princes are in God's stead, and may not be resisted, do
they never so evil, they must be reserved unto the wrath
of God. Nevertheless, if they command to do evil, we
must then disobey and say, we are otherwise commanded
of God: but not to rise against them." God giveth the
father power over his children, the husband over his wife:
" And even in like manner as God maketh the King head
over his realm, even so giveth he him commandment to
execute the laws upon all men indifferently. The King
is but a servant to execute the law of God, and not to rule
after his own imagination."

The pope's authority is vain against the King's: it cannot exempt monks and friars from their obedience to the
King. " God did not put Peter only under the temporal

sword, but also Christ himself " (citing Gal. iv, Mat. iii).
The pope has no authority from Christ except to preach
God's word, and Tyndale finds no power in pope or pre-
late to constitute a holiness of observance and ceremonial.

" Ye blind guides, said Christ, ye strain out a gnat and swallow
a camel. Do not our blind guides stumble at a straw, and leap
over a block, making narrow consciences at trifles, and at matters
of weight none at all? If any of them happen to swallow his
spittle, or any of the water wherewith he washed his mouth ere
he go to Mass; or touch the Sacrament with his nose . . . or happen to handle it with any of his fingers which are not anointed;
or say *Alleluia* instead of *Laus tibi Domine;* or *Ite missa est* instead of *Benedicamus Domino;* or pour too much wine in the
chalice; or read the gospel without light; or make not his crosses
aright, how trembleth he! How feareth he! What an horrible
sin is committed! 'I cry God mercy,' saith he, 'and you my
ghostly father.' But to hold an whore, or another man's wife, to
buy a benefice, to set one realm at variance with another, and to
cause twenty thousand men to die in a day, is but a trifle and a
pastime with them."

The true doctrine is otherwise:

" When a man feeleth that his heart consenteth unto the law
of God, and feeleth himself meek, patient, courteous, and merciful
to his neighbour, altered and fashioned like unto Christ, why should
he doubt but that God hath forgiven him, and put his Spirit in
him, though he never cram his sin into the priest's ear? . . . To
whom a man trespasseth, unto him he ought to confess. But to
confess myself unto thee, O Antichrist, whom I have not offended,
am I not bound."

The Obedience of a Christian Man appeared in 1528,
and however displeasing to pope and prelate, it was quite
acceptable to Henry, then about to assert his authority
against the pope. But Tyndale was no safe royal prop.
Two or three years later, his *Practice of Prelates* vehemently roused the King's displeasure; for it argued against
his divorce, and declared as its first head that " Prelates,
appointed to preach Christ, may not leave God's word,
and minister temporal offices; but ought to teach the lay
people the right way, and let them alone with all temporal
business."

There are few novel thoughts in Tyndale. He knew

the thinking of his day, and knew and felt his English antecedents. He was imbued with the common fund of Christian dogma and teaching, as held in the creeds and in the Gospel. All this made up his mental equipment. But he also felt the situation in which he moved, and his feelings, like those of all would-be reformers, reset and re-expressed the fund of thought at his disposal. He may be regarded as an English expression of Reform. He was practical, he could not be captured by any one principle, by any single syllogism, such as justification by faith. He would make room for all pressing considerations, especially those harmonizing with his prejudices. If he was influenced by Luther, he also comes straight down from Wyclif.

A caustic light is thrown upon the personality and situation of Tyndale and of those who wrote and argued on that side, from the impression made by these men and their writings upon their most illustrious antagonist.

" Howbeit, there be swine that receive no learning, but to defile it; and there be dogs that rend all good learning with their teeth. . . . To such dogs men may not only preach, but must with whips and bats beat them well and keep them from tearing of good learning with their teeth . . . till they lie still and hearken what is said unto them. And by such means be both swine kept from doing harm, and dogs fall sometimes so well to learning, that they can stand upon their hinder feet, and hold their hands afore them pretetely [prettily] like a maid, yea, and learn to dance after their master's pipe, such an effectual thing is punishment, whereas bare teaching will not suffice. And who be now more properly such dogs, than be those heretics that bark against the blessed sacraments, and tear with their dogs' teach [sic — is it ' teaching ' or ' teeth '?] the catholic Christian faith, and godly expositions of the old holy doctors and saints? And who be more properly such hogs, than these heretics of our days, of such a filthy kind as never came before, which in such wise defile all holy vowed chastity, that the very pure scripture of God they tread upon with their foul dirty feet, to draw it from all honest chastity, into an unclean shameful liberty of friars to wed nuns." [12]

Intelligent men to-day do not speak thus of those who differ from them in religion; though in our hearts we still

[12] *The maner and order of our election* — More's English Works, p. 586. Cf. as to More, ante, Chapter XVIII.

speak as violently of malignant anarchists who would destroy order, government and property. Vague in our
creeds, we hold fast to law and property. But the old
theological habit of exhausting the vials of vituperation
upon heretics was still strong in the sixteenth century,
when they swarmed as never before, and when their
arguments, as here in England, looked to social and
economic, as well as religious, change.

CHAPTER XXII

CHURCH REVOLUTION BY ROYAL PREROGATIVE AND ACTS OF PARLIAMENT

I

THE course of the self-assertion of the English realm and of its eventual separation from the papacy may be traced through a series of royal and statutory decrees. It opens, if one will, with the Conqueror's emphatic refusal to do fealty to Gregory VII, since " neither have I promised it, nor do I find that my predecessors did it to your predecessors." The chronicler Eadmer amplifies William's rejection of Gregory's enormous claims: " He would not then allow any one settled in all his dominion to acknowledge as apostolic the pontiff of the City of Rome, save at his own bidding, or by any means to receive any letter from him if it had not first been shown to himself." His masterful assertion of his will over his own bishops is shown in the same writing.[1]

The high hand of the Conqueror could not be maintained. Henry I compromised the matter of investitures with the saintly but unyielding Anselm, Archbishop of Canterbury; and a century later the royal self-respect sank to its nadir when John, overwhelmed by his offenses, in expiation surrendered his realm to the legate of Pope Innocent III, and received it back as a feudal fee, doing homage and promising an annual payment of one thousand marks.[2] Again the tide turned, and markedly under Edward I. The Mortmain Act of 1279 forbade the transfer of lands to the dead hand of the Church, and some years later the Barons of the realm in parliament denied the suzerainty of Rome over Scotland, which Ed-

---

[1] These extracts are from Gee and Hardy, *Documents illustrative of English Church History* (Macmillan, 1914), pp. 57, 59.

[2] Documents in Gee and Hardy, o. c. p. 75.

ward contemplated reducing to his obedience. A still later statute of the same reign prohibited English monasteries from sending gold to their superiors abroad.[3]

The important statutes of Provisors and Praemunire take form in the reigns of Edward III and Richard II. Those against Provisors raised an effective wall against the papal bestowal of English benefices in anticipation of their vacancy. The Praemunire legislation highly penalized the transferring to foreign courts of suits cognizable in the courts of the realm. The matter of these statutes might be, and subsequently was, much extended to meet other cases, especially during the reigns of Henry VIII and Elizabeth, and barred the exercise of papal authority in England.[4]

The feudal and dynastic Wars of the Roses ended in 1485 with the accession of Henry VII. For a year or more after Bosworth Field, Henry showed by word and conduct that he deemed his victory had straightened all obliquities in his title to the throne. Having thus carefully made his own right clear, he married the undoubted heiress of the opposing claims. All that was left of York and Lancaster was thus united. Then the shrewd and tireless King set himself to foster the surest interests of England. He abandoned the hapless policy of continental conquest, which had drained the country's blood and wealth, and had impeded the development of an insular nation. Instead, by intrigues and filibustering threatenings, and treaties patiently worked out, he advanced the foreign commerce of his people, and, aided by parliament, virtually created the cloth industry at home, so that England became an exporter of cloth as well as of her staple wools. His policy, moreover, favored the general distribution of wealth among all who were engaged in industry or trade, and did not permit its accumulation in the hands of the London merchants. Assisted by the institution of the court of the Star Chamber, he conciliated or subjected to himself the decimated

[3] Gee and Hardy, o. c. pp. 81, 91, 93.

[4] See post p. 77 sqq. Those of the reigns of Edward III and Richard II are given in Gee and Hardy, o. c. pp. 103–104, 112–125.

aristocracy, and made royal servitors of once feudal lords. But he created few new peerages, and appointed capable Commoners and Churchmen to the high offices of state. In his hands or those of his experienced councillors, the rents from the enormous confiscated crown lands of York and Lancaster increased; while the customs which had been granted him for life, added to his constant sources of revenue. He so manipulated those imposts paid by foreigners as to bring a greater revenue to himself and at the same time further his measures to enlarge the trade of England. This was an instance of his general policy, which was to enhance his royal power and revenue, while keeping these aims identified with the prosperity of his realm. His acts disclose no personal despotic purpose running counter to his people's interests. Abstention from costly foreign wars was certainly an advantage to England, even though it enabled the King to amass treasure, and rule without recourse to parliament for grants.

The benefits accruing from this autocratic reign, and the transmission of an unquestionable hereditary title, caused the accession of the eighth Henry to be greeted with universal acclaim. The dreadful lessons of a disputed succession and civil war had been branded into the English consciousness. Henceforth, for wellnigh a century, England was daily to rise up and lie down to rest in the security of the Tudor title to the throne and the authority of the occupant. Whatever might be the preferences of the people in religion or aught else, this ingrained conviction assured the succession of the child Edward VI, and upon his death, made vain the opposition to Mary, and when she died fastened men's hopes upon Elizabeth.

The preceding paragraphs may suggest some of the reasons why the power of Henry VIII proved resistless in his mortal conflict with the papacy. Sheer suddenness is rare in history. Although various tendencies, long gathering, were brought to a head and the explosion fired by royal passion, one will remember the organic preparation for the catastrophe. The old feeling and forms of expression are still carried on in royal or parliamentary utterances. A statute of Praemunire passed in 1393 in the sixteenth year of Richard II, a foolish futile King, apostrophizes " the crown of England, which has been so free at all times, that it has been in no earthly subjection, but immediately subject to God in all things touching the royalty of the same crown, and to none other," and decries the illegal practices through which it would " be submitted to the pope, and the laws and statutes of the realm defeated and avoided at his will, to the perpetual destruction of the sovereignty of our lord the King, his crown, and his royalty, and of all his realm, which God defend." So speaks the older statute; and Henry VIII when not yet twenty-five years old, about the year 1514, refusing to allow an appeal to the pope declared: " By the permission and ordinance of God, we are King of England; and the Kings of England in times past had never any superior, but God alone. Therefore, know ye well that we will maintain the right of our crown and of our temporal. jurisdiction . . . in as ample a manner as any of our progenitors have done before our time."

These words were uttered before any thought had come of the final rupture, and even before Henry had aired his theological and royal vanity in his book against Luther, for which he received from the pope the title of Defender of the Faith. And when the final rupture was approaching, in 1533, what one might dub a super-statute of Praemunire (enacted doubtless at the King's behest) prohibited all appeals to Rome, and proclaimed the sufficiency of the King's courts temporal and spiritual for the adjudication of all controversies. Its recital emphasized and expanded the old principles of sovereign independence declared in " divers sundry old authentic histories and chronicles . . . that this realm of England is an empire . . . governed by one supreme head and King, having the dignity and royal estate of the imperial crown of the same,"— unto whom the body politic composed of all sorts and degrees of people, divided into spirituality and temporality, owe, next to God, a natural and humble obedience.[5]

II

The antagonism between the King of England and the pope of Rome which became a mortal conflict, had nothing to do with the Christian faith or with doctrines necessary to salvation. It was personal and political. Henry, impelled by the desire for a male heir to his throne and driven by a specific passion for the person of Anne Boleyn, asked of Pope Clement VII an annulment of his marriage with Catharine of Aragon. The pope would not comply, because the counter-pressure of the Emperor Charles V was heavier than any influence Henry could bring to bear. There had been qualms as to the legitimacy of Henry's marriage with the probably virgin widow of his elder brother, and some transient doubt cast on the papal competency to grant the requisite dispensation. There is no evidence, however, that this question had worried Henry before the desire came for another and legitimate marriage, not an illicit connection with a mistress. As the prospects dwindled for favorable action from the pope, the facile-minded Cranmer suggested to the King that he obtain responses on the validity of his marriage with Catharine from the leading Universities. Persuasion, or pressure, brought the desired responses from Oxford and Cambridge, from Paris, Orleans, Angers, Bourges and Toulouse, Bologna and Padua — no mean array of authority. The universities within the Emperor's dominions were not asked! The intricate affair proceded. Henry was cited to appear in Rome, while the pope under pressure from the Emperor, threatened him with excommunication unless he put Anne away and took back Catharine. In response the Convocation of the English clergy declared that the King's marriage to Catharine was unlawful, and in April 1533 the court of the new archbishop, Cranmer, pronounced it null and void: — the King already had been married secretly to

---

[5] Gee and Hardy, o. c. p. 187 sqq. This statute will be given more fully, post p. 77 sqq.

Anne: whereupon in Rome the marriage to Catharine was confirmed and Henry excommunicated.

Such is the bare outline of the divorce itself. We turn to the measures by which the King in furtherance of his personal and royal ends, and in defiant opposition to the pope, made himself the supreme head of the Church of England. They are to be followed in the acts of parliament and the determinations of the English Church in Convocation. Although the prime movers were the King and his secretary, Thomas Crumwell, parliament was not unwilling to enact laws, prohibiting the despatch of revenue to Rome, abrogating the papal authority in England, and subjecting the clergy to the power of the King in parliament. On the other hand there was wide sympathy with Catharine and dislike of Anne. The King's divorce and remarriage were far more unpopular than the measures through which he became Head of the Church.

The parliament which met in November 1529, and was not dissolved for seven years, was the instrument which effected the breach with the papacy, established the King's supremacy over the English Church, and decreed the suppression of the monasteries. Wolsey had fallen; and the chancellorship was held by Sir Thomas More, the first of that distinguished line of laymen who ever since have conducted that office. It was in the air that parliament would cut the skirts of the unpopular clerical order, while the substitution of the King as head of the Church in place of the pope, was likely to depend upon the pope's rejection of the King's demand for a divorce.

Wolsey had woefully confessed himself guilty of a *praemunire* in having accepted the office of papal legate. Under the King's encouragement, parliament now fell upon clerical abuses, and after warm discussion, passed laws regulating the probate and mortuary fees of the ecclesiastic court, clerical non-residence and pluralities, and the farming of Church lands. It was becoming clear that the pope would not comply with Henry's will. So in December 1530 a *praemunire* was brought in the King's bench against the entire clerical body for having recognized Wolsey's legatine authority! The Convocations of the terror stricken clergy were informed that their guilt might be compounded by the payment of a large sum of money for the King's necessities, provided they would also recognize him as " the sole protector and supreme head of the Church and Clergy in England." After grievous debate, this condition also was accepted, with slight change of form and the addition of the somewhat unsatisfactory words " as far as the law of Christ allows."

The next marked step in the subjection of the clergy to the royal will was the doctrinally careful and orthodox Petition of the Commons, laid before the King in March 1532. This spoke of seditious books and " fantastical " opinions contrary to the true Catholic faith, and besought remedies against various clerical abuses and exactions, the delays and excessive fees of the ecclesiastical courts, their imprisonment of innocent people, the improper conferment of benefices and excessive number of holy days, but above all (the real point and gravamen of the matter) against the power of the bishops and other clergy in Convocation to make laws, constitutions, and ordinances without the consent of King and parliament.[6]

This was submitted to Convocation, which soon answered with an explicit defense of their acts and conduct and their law-making authority " grounded upon the Scripture of God and the determination of Holy Church." They protested their inability to " submit the execution of our charges and duty, certainly prescribed by God, to your highness' assent," ready as they were to listen to his opinion. The King handed this reply to a deputation from the Commons, saying " We think their answer will smally please you, for it seemeth to us very slender." The Commons should consider it, while he, the King, would be impartial.

Convocation now became alarmed, and attempted a compromise which proved unacceptable. The King sent for the Speaker and twelve members of the Commons, and said to them: " Well-beloved subjects, we thought that the clergy of our realm had been our subjects wholly;

[6] Given in Gee and Hardy, o. c. pp. 145 sqq.

but now we have well perceived that they be but half our
subjects — yea, and scarce our subjects. For all the prelates at their consecration make an oath to the pope clean
contrary to the oath they make to us, so that they seem
his subjects and not ours." He gave them a copy of
the two oaths, the incompatibility of which now struck
him so forcibly, and suggested further measures of constraint. Realizing the hopeless situation, Convocation
made submission in a formal document [7] (May 15, 1532),
in which they recognized the King's goodness and pious
zeal, his learning far exceeding that of other kings; they
promised to make no new canons, constitutions or ordinances, without the King's assent, and to submit existing
canons for abrogation or approval to a committee to be
composed of sixteen members of the upper and lower
house of Parliament and sixteen members of the clergy,
all appointed by the King.

Having brought the English clergy to subjection, the
King, with Parliament, proceeded against the pope. Already an act had been passed conditionally restraining
the payment of annates to the pope, and providing for
the consecration of bishops in case of hindrance from
Rome.[8] There followed now, after some debate as to
its untoward effect upon England's commercial relations
with Flanders, the passage of the great statute in Restraint of Appeals to Rome.[9] This declared England to
be an Empire "governed by one supreme head and
king . . . unto whom a body politic compact of all sorts
and degrees of people divided in terms and by names of
spirituality and temporalty, be bounden and ought to
bear, next to God, a natural and humble obedience."
The "English Church " within this realm possesses the
wisdom to resolve all questions "without the intermeddling of any exterior person or persons; " and the " laws
temporal, for trial of property of lands and goods, and
for the conservation of the people of this realm in unity
and peace," are sufficiently administered by temporal

[7] Called "The Submission of the Clergy," Gee and Hardy, o. c. p. 176.
[8] Gee and Hardy, o. c. pp. 178 sqq.
[9] Ib. pp. 187 sqq. Feby., 1533.

judges. The act refers to statutes of previous reigns passed to preserve the realm's prerogatives, notwithstanding which " sundry inconveniences and dangers, not provided for plainly by the said former acts . . . have arisen . . . by reason of appeals sued out of this realm to the see of Rome, in causes testamentary, causes of matrimony and divorces, right of tithes " and so forth; and enacts that all such causes pertaining " to the spiritual jurisdiction of this realm," shall be determined exclusively in the spiritual and temporal courts of the Kingdom; and that their sentences alone shall take effect, while appeals shall be determined within the realm. The clergy shall continue to administer the sacraments notwithstanding any interdicts from Rome; and any person endeavoring to procure such interdict, or make any appeal to Rome, shall be guilty under the statutes of Praemunire and Provisors.

This act made futile as well as fatal any appeal to Rome from the prospective annulment, in an English ecclesiastical court, of the King's marriage to Catharine. At the close of 1533, (when the King had been excommunicated) his Council went on preparing for complete severance with the pope, who henceforth should be called by no other title than " Bishop of Rome." In the following year three acts of Parliament carried out the program. The first provided for the complete submission of the clergy in pursuant of their declaration (already noted), and for the appointment of the committee therein contemplated, and forbade all appeals to Rome.[10] The second prohibited unconditionally the payment of annates and the presentation of persons to the pope for the office of bishop or archbishop. It provided for their election by dean and chapter on nomination by the King, and for their consecration and oath of fealty to the Crown.[11] Thirdly, a long and most elaborate act forbade the payment of Peter's pence, and much more besides. It recited the impoverishment of the realm through the intolerable exactions of the Bishop of Rome, and his usurpation of

[10] Gee and Hardy, o. c. pp. 195 sqq.
[11] Gee and Hardy, o. c. pp. 201 sqq.

power to dispense with human laws, all " in great derogation of your imperial crown and authority royal, contrary to right and conscience." The King's realm is
subject only to laws made within it, and the same may
be dispensed by the " High Court of Parliament " and
persons authorized by them. And, " forasmuch as your
majesty is supreme head of the Church of England, as the
prelates and clergy of your realm . . . have recognized,"
the act prohibited the payment of Peter's pence or any
other impositions, to the see of Rome, and declared that
neither the King or his subjects should henceforth sue
for any dispensation or license from the Bishop of Rome;
but the same should be had from the Archbishop of Canterbury, and, in all exceptional or novel cases, under the
approval of the King and his council. The solemn declaration was inserted that it was not the intention of the
act " to decline or vary from the congregation of Christ's
Church in any things concerning the very articles of the
Catholic faith in Christendom, or in any other things declared, by Holy Scripture and the word of God, necessary
for your and their salvations, [i.e. the salvation of the
King and his subjects] but only to make an ordinance by.
policies necessary and convenient to repress vice, and for
the good conservation of this realm in peace, unity, and
tranquillity. . . ."

The last proviso indicates the politico-ecclesiastical, but
undoctrinal, nature of the revolution which had been
brought about. In November of the same year (1534)
the first " Act of Succession " decreed the absolute nullity
of Henry's marriage to Catharine, and the unquestionable
validity of his marriage to Anne, and established the
succession to the crown in the heirs male of the latter
marriage, and in default of the same, in the Lady Elizabeth, and the heirs of her body. It was declared to be
high treason to impugn this marriage and succession, by
act or speech or writing; and an oath to maintain it was
prescribed for all the King's subjects, which it was to be
high treason to refuse. Renunciations of papal authority
were then obtained from the Convocations of Canterbury
and York, from the two universities, and from the monas-

teries generally, all declaring that the Bishop of Rome had no more jurisdiction in England than any other foreign bishop.

III

The revolution which had been brought about through the royal will and its effective embodiment in acts of parliament, consisted in the repudiation of the pope and his authority and in the recognition of the King as the supreme head of what had now become the Church of England. This revolution, which was for a time to be the main feature if not the chief propelling force in the larger movement called the English Reformation, did not affect directly the Christian faith and doctrine and the saving of souls. It would be an error to suppose that the King had become the Supreme Head of the Church of England *in the place of the pope*. The Roman Catholic Church, with its supreme head the Pope of Rome, was constituted primarily as a cure of souls, with the power of " the Keys " to admit to heaven or consign to hell. Its vast ecclesiastical and temporal power and its enormous wealth ministered to this, its true function. The King as supreme head of the Church of England had no power over the destinies of souls, nor had the Church of which he was the head. In this sense neither he nor it had ghostly or spiritual authority; but only temporal and ecclesiastical authority. The King was no shepherd of souls like the pope, with power to remit sin; nor was the English Church any such single and exclusive vehicle of salvation as the Church of Rome, but at most a minister of salvation. Both English King and English Church denied that the pope and his Church had any such power over souls as they had asserted; but neither English Church or King arrogated a like authority. While denying the validity of papal excommunications, neither English King or Church, any more than the Lutheran or the Calvinist Church, possessed the power to excommunicate and damn — a power which any Roman Catholic bishop might exercise within the sphere of his authority and duty.

A grasp of the essentially political and ecclesiastical character of this royal and parliamentary revolution and of the difference between King and pope, is essential to an understanding of all that followed, including all changes or modifications of church doctrine and church service. Listen to the enlightening words of perhaps the most universal and lucid exponent of the purport of these changes, Archbishop Cranmer. He is writing to his master Henry, apparently in August 1535. The letter refers to the King's command to the prelates of his realm fully to set forth to the people of their dioceses that the " Bishop of Rome's authority . . . was but a false and unjust usurpation, and that your Grace of very right, and by God's law, is the Supreme Head of this Church of England, next immediately unto God." The Archbishop accordingly had preached certain sermons, elucidating the position of the Bishop of Rome, showing

" that many of his laws were contrary to God's laws ; and some of them which were good and laudable, yet they were not of such holiness as would make them, that is, to be taken as God's or to have remission of sins by observing of them. And here I said that so many of his laws as were good and laudable, men ought not to contemn and despise them, and wilfully to break them ; for those that be good your Grace has received as laws of your realm, until such time as others should be made. And, therefore, as laws of your realm, they must be observed and not contemned. And here I spake as well of the ceremonies of the Church, as of the foresaid laws ; and that they ought neither to be rejected or despised, nor yet to be observed, with this opinion, that they of themselves make men holy, or that they remit sin. For seeing that our sins be re- mitted by the death of our Saviour Christ Jesus, I said it was too much injury to Christ to impute the remission of our sins to any laws or ceremonies of man's making. . . . But as the common laws of your Grace's realm be not made to remit sin, nor no man doth observe them for that intent, but for a common commodity, and for a good order and quietness to be observed among your subjects ; even so were the laws and ceremonies first instituted in the Church for a good order and remembrance of many good things, but not for the remission of our sins. And though it be good to observe them well for that intent they were first ordained, yet it is not good, but a contumely unto Christ to observe them with this opin- ion, that they remit sin, or that the very bare observation of them in itself is an holiness before God ; although they be remembrances of many holy things, or a disposition unto goodness. And even so do the laws of your Grace's realm dispose men unto justice, to peace, and other true and perfect holiness; wherefore I did conclude for a general rule, that the people ought to observe them as they do the laws of your Grace's realm, and with no more opinion of holiness or remission of sin, than the other common laws of your Grace's realm." [12]

If such was the view touching the laws and ceremonies of the hitherto established Roman Catholic Church, the royal Church of England could take no other view of its own laws and ceremonies, especially since in the last resort they emanated from the same law-giving power, to wit, the King in parliament, from which sprang the common laws of the realm. Obviously that law-making power, however supreme and royal, was human, and none of its enactments could make or mar, or affect directly, the salvation of a single soul. It could not remit sins or condemn a soul to hell. Temporal penalties must be relied upon to compel the payment of tithes, for example; for which the parish priests, of the former Roman Catholic Church, had been wont to "curse," with all the supposed consequences. [13]

Nevertheless, save for authority over the destinies of souls beyond the grave — or beyond the *stake* — with respect to this world of speech and writing and visible conduct, the Church of England under the authority of parliament and the headship of the King, continued to exercise the functions of the Church of Rome. Moreover, from the novelty or anomaly of its position as in fact a newly established national and independent, if not separate, church, it would be obliged to declare the principles of its adoption of the contents of Christian truth, and even to constitute *de novo* some body of Anglican doctrine. This state-church (there might be difficulty in distinguishing its two constituents) necessarily partook of the character of its political source and sanction; if it emanated from the King in parliament, and had the King for its head, did it not in some sense include its head and that which it emanated from? The King was soon to

[12] Ellis's *Letters,* &c, Third series, Vol. III, pp. 23 sqq.
[13] With reluctance, we may suppose, on the part of the good priests, at least. As Chaucer says: "Full loth he was to cursen for his tithes."

preside in Convocation, through his vicar Thomas Crumwell, and masterfully direct its action.   This English
Church, inclusive of its parliamentary source and kingly
headship, was not merely lawful and established; it was
enunciatory and law-giving.   It was law; and law means
obedience, either voluntary, or when withheld, enforced.
The principle of law, with its complement of obedience,
meant necessarily conformity, conformity to norm; and so
meant uniformity.   That also accorded with the spirit of
the laws common to all the realm, through which England
had become a nation.

Further, out of the necessities of the nature of this
Church proceeded the character and process of its development and self-formulation.   Its origin was in law and
institution; it emanated from the command and power of
the King in parliament.   It did not arise from any moving
conception of abuses and the need of definite reform; far
less, did it spring from an idea, such as that of justification
by faith.   Therefore its evolution and further progress
could not be as a leap from thought to another thought
new born, as light signals flash from peak to peak.   That
had been the way of Luther's development.   The official
English remaking or reformation of the Church must
proceed through official command and adaptation or
modification or abolishment of institutions; and through
enunciated formulae, of doctrine to be sure, but more
generally of *observance*.   It would thus attain to a body
of outer conformity; which might have sincere and
rational grounds for such men as were sincere and rational, and yet would proceed or function through state
oath and formal utterance and the fulfilment of a ceremonial painfully defined.

So it was also a very practical affair,— the English
Church and the course of its formation.   It moved from
the decision of one point of practice or doctrine to another, often impelled not merely by the exigencies of the
domestic situation, but by foreign diplomatic opportunities or dangers.   Likewise its supporters and opponents
within the Kingdom would be moved by points of practice and by ceremonial preference: a question of lay or

ecclesiastical jurisdiction might attract a man, or repel him through his attachment to old practices: and so his taste in vestments or no-vestments; and whether he preferred an altar or a communion-table, and where it should be placed. Each point of practice, every element of ceremonial, or its abolition, represented some conviction or idea, and therefore was a symbol. But more really and directly the moving or repelling influence was habit and association with the actual fact itself, rather than a consideration of the spiritual validity of what it stood for; and whether taken as a symbol or a fact, it was English. If its representation of spiritual truth was rather veiled than naked, it should at all events be seemly, entirely decent and respectable. This might represent much to Englishmen, who have always done a good deal of thinking in terms of the decencies of life.

IV

We turn for further illustration to the courses of events. In November 1534 a short act was passed making the King unqualifiedly " the only supreme head in earth of the Church of England." [14] It provided that he should " have and enjoy, annexed and united to the imperial crown of this realm . . . all honours, dignities, pre-eminences, jurisdictions, privileges, authorities, immunities, profits and commodities to the said dignity of supreme head of the same Church belonging and appertaining." It granted to the King, his heirs and successors full power and authority from time to time to repress, reform, restrain and amend all errors, heresies and abuses which might lawfully be reformed and restrained by " any manner spiritual authority or jurisdiction . . . to the pleasure of Almighty God, the increase of virtue in Christ's religion, and for the conservation of the peace, unity, and tranquillity of this realm; any usage, custom, foreign law, etc., . . . to the contrary notwithstanding." There was passed at the same time a confirmatory act of succession, giving the form of oath, and declaring that it

[14] It omitted the words "so far as the law of Christ allows."

should be sworn to by all the subjects of the King; also an act specifically making it treason to utter speech or writing derogatory to the king or queen, their title and dignities and orthodoxy.[15]

The executions of More and Fisher followed, and of certain heroic Carthusians, for refusing to take the oath. They would have sworn to the succession itself decreed by the act; but the oath involved repudiation of papal authority and approval of Henry's divorce, to which their consciences would not permit them to assent. On the other hand, King and Church vindicated their orthodoxy, and the decency and order of the realm, by burning a goodly number of Anabaptists. Henry was still as particular touching his doctrinal orthodoxy as he had been in those previous years when his demands upon the pope were progressing from insistency, through minatory pressure, to mortal conflict in the end. He had then sanctioned the burning of heretics more respectable than these rowdy Anabaptists.

The King, as head of the Church made Thomas Crumwell his vicar-general; and a commission was issued to him to hold a general visitation of churches, monasteries and collegiate bodies. There followed, through a lengthy process of investigation, report, and parliamentary action, the famous suppression of the monasteries, and the transfer of their lands and plate to the royal exchequer. About half of these huge domains were granted by the King to a number of nobles and influential commoners, who had aided in these measures, and whose support was thereby won permanently for the throne. These holdings became a vested interest calculated to rivet the royal Church upon the realm. There might be and were remonstrances and murmurs and revolts [16] against these changes in the Church; but they broke down before the power of the King and the strength of vested interests. Even the Papal restoration under Mary did not dare dis-

[15] Gee and Hardy, o. c. p. 243–247.
[16] For instance the famous "Pilgrimage of Grace" which embroiled the northern counties in the years 1537 and 1538. It is elaborately treated in *The Pilgrimage of Grace,* M. H. & Ruth Dodds. 2 Vols. (Cambridge, 1915).

turb the last, but confirmed the grants of abbey and such like lands in the hands of the possessors.[17]   The suppression of the monasteries, cruel as it was and unseemly in its details, liberated England from a spiritual incubus. Good, bad, or indifferent as these foundations were, the homes of lethargy and immorality, or well conducted establishments, which incidentally paid the expenses of many a scholar at the universities, they were no longer suited to the life, the progress, and the secularization of England, and the laicizing of her government and judiciary.

Another measure of less material, but great spiritual, effect, was the establishment of Biblical studies at the universities, and the removal of Duns Scotus and his like, together with the Canon Law from the curriculum.[18] For the Canon law was the very *rationale* of the papacy.

To return to the formulation of doctrine by the Church. The early Christian Church lived and breathed amid pagan acceptances and a conglomerate of pagan-Christian notions. Its formulation of dogma proceeded largely through disclaimer and counter-statement. Now the Church of England, based upon this ancient dogmatic formulation and surrounded by an abundance of contemporary Christian truth and error — Catholic, Lutheran, Zwinglian, not to mention indigenous Lollardy — was to proceed through selection and adoption, mainly. The influence of the tyrant theologian on the throne was strong, over-mastering usually. He had still plenty of thoughts upon theology. Beneath his altered views the conceit of his *Assertio septem sacramentorum* against Luther still puffed him up. He was no unfit representative of his people; his thoughts, his opinions, his self-assertion might be theirs, for he could listen closely for his people's voices; and as for their attitude toward religion and its royal exponent, the remark of the Venetian ambassador is to the point: " With the English, the example and authority of the Sovereign is everything, and

---

[17] See the second act of Repeal of Philip and Mary, 1554. Gee and Hardy, o. c. pp. 385, 394.
[18] See the sprightly letter of Layton to Crumwell, 1535. Ellis *Letters,* 2nd Series, Vol. II, p. 60.

religion is only so far valued as it inculcates the duty due from the subject to the prince." Although this has more absurdity than truth, one can understand how an ambassador, moving much in court circles, might have thought it. The people were to have, and eventually express and realize plenty of religious opinions having little to do with upholding the King's authority. And, of course, even as his divorce and all the ecclesiastical breaches which it involved were abhorrent to many and bitterly spoken against, many likewise detested the religious innovations promulgated under his authority. If but little appeared changed beyond the government and secular allegiance of the Church, men knew it was not so. It was just as clear to many a good Roman Catholic as it became to protesting sectaries and future Puritans, that Church government and constitution could not be severed from faith and doctrine, but all were part of the inseverable discipline and truth which saved, or of the idolatry and false doctrine which so surely damned.

Yet the Ten Articles of 1536, the first completed Formulary of the Church of England, asserted that the two were distinct and severable, and treated them separately under respective heads of matters " expressly commanded by God and necessary to our salvation," and such other things as belong to a decent and established Church usage. This true English attempt to select and formulate the seemly and convenient rightly bore the printed title: [19] " Articles devised by the Kinges Highnes Majestie, to stablyshe Christen Quietnes and Unitie Amonge us, and avoyde contentious opinions, which Articles be also approved by the consent and determination of the hole clergie of this realme." [20]

The King was not present at the Convocation in St. Paul's Church which approved them; but his place was taken by Crumwell as his vice-gerent, and the latter's

[19] I am following the text given in Appendix I to Hardwick's *History of the Articles* (1851).

[20] A year or more before, the King composed, or superintended the composition of a book called *King Henry's Primer,* which assembled the Christian teachings proper for his people. See Strype, *Ecclesiastical Memorials,* Vol. I, Pt. I, Chapter XXXI.

proctor. Crumwell set forth in vigorous language the King's solicitude over the situation, which called for concord instead of brawling, and the establishment of every article upon the Word of God. The house of bishops was divided in its tendencies. The lower house sent up a protestation, under sixty-seven heads, against errors and abuses, most of which were plainly Lutheran or Lollard; yet with a humble disclaimer of any intention of displeasing " the King's Highnes . . . supreme Head of the Church of England . . . to whom accordingly we submit ourselves." They vehemently abjured the usurped authority of the Bishop of Rome.[21] The Articles were passed,— a selection and compromise. They were not destined to much popularity, and were especially disapproved by the northern clergy in their convocation, who still opposed the headship of the king.[22]

A preface from the King bespoke the need of charitable concord and unity, and pointed out that the necessary articles of faith would first be stated, and then the honest ceremonies and good politic orders to be used in the churches, although not necessary to salvation.[23] The first Article ordains " that all bishops and preachers shall instruct and teach our people, *by us committed to their spiritual charge,*" to believe and defend as true " all those things . . . which be comprehended in the whole body and canon of the Bible and also in the three creeds or symbols . . ." the Apostles', the Nicene, and the Athanasian. All these things must be held and taken for " the most holy, most sure, and most certain, and infallible words of God," not to be altered, by any authority. They are necessary to be believed for man's salvation, and whosoever, after instruction, will not believe, will be damned. The decision of the ancient councils of Nice, Constantinople, Ephesus and Chalcedon, condemning contrary opinions, are to be accepted.

[21] Printed in Strype, *Ecc. Mem.* I, II. Appendix of Originals. No. LXXIII.

[22] Their opinion is given in Strype, ib. No. LXXIV.

[23] The Ten Articles are printed in Hardwick *On The Articles,* also in Lloyd's *Formularies of Faith* (Oxford, 1825), which also contains the *Institution of a Christian Man,* and *A Necessary Doctrine and Erudition,* etc.

The second article sustains the Catholic doctrine of baptism, and denounces Anabaptists and Pelagians. The third, upon penance, follows generally the Catholic view, making " the sacrament of perfect penance " to consist of " contrition, confession, and amendment of the former life, and a new obedient reconciliation unto the laws and will of God " by works of charity. Confession to a priest is declared necessary, the authoritative efficacy of his absolution is recognized, and the necessity of good works. No reference is made to indulgences and the supererogatory merits of the saints, which are spoken of in the tenth article. The fourth article asserts the real and corporeal presence of the selfsame body and blood of Christ under the form and figure of bread and wine. Nothing is said of the giving or withholding of the cup from the laity.

So far there was scarcely perceptible deviation from Catholic doctrine; which, however, was emphatically, though silently, departed from by the omission of the remaining four sacraments recognized by the Roman Catholic Church. The next (fifth) article is upon Justification, which is remission of our sins and acceptation into the grace of God. Sinners attain it " by contrition and faith joined with charity . . . not as though our contrition, or faith, or any works proceeding thereof, can worthily merit or deserve the said justification," but only the grace of the Father and the merits of the Son. Nevertheless besides inward contrition, faith, and charity, God requireth of us " that after we be justified we must also have good works of charity and obedience towards God . . . for although acceptation to everlasting life be conjoined with justification, yet our good works be necessarily required to the attaining of everlasting life."

This limping argument may have been one of the reasons why Melancthon spoke of the Articles as *confusissime compositum,* most confusedly put together. The remaining five articles, " concerning the laudable ceremonies used in the Church," also might have drawn his sarcasm. Yet even Luther's convictions only gradually reached their ultimate conclusions through the experiences of life and the goads of controversy; and one should not expect logical consistency in this the first selective and adoptive draft of Anglicanism, which was to be throughout a compromise and *via media,* with very little originality, and a consistency of expression, temperament, and fitness, rather than of logic.

The first of these latter articles touching meet, though unsaving, ceremonies, treats of images, which are an ancient and useful means of kindling men's minds, and should remain in Churches, but must not be worshipped. The next approves the honoring of saints, but not with that confidence in them which is due to God alone. It is laudable to supplicate the saints in heaven for their interceding prayers, yet not thinking of any of them as quicker to hear than Christ, or that any one of the saints " doth serve for one thing more than another, or is patron of the same." The ninth articles approves the rites and ceremonies of the Church, as putting " us in remembrance of those spiritual things that they do signify. . . . But none of these ceremonies have power to remit sin, but only to stir and lift our minds unto God, by whom only our sins are forgiven." The last article, of Purgatory, affirms " that it is a very good and charitable deed to pray for souls departed " and " it standeth with the very due order of charity [for] a Christian man to pray for souls departed and commit them to God's mercy, and also to cause others to pray for them in masses and exeqies, and to give alms to other to pray for them, whereby they may be relieved and holpen of some part of their pain; " but as their condition is not certified to us by Scripture, we remit the matter to God's mercy, " to whom is known their estate and condition. Wherefore it is much necessary that such abuses be put away, which under the name of purgatory have been advanced as to make men believe that through the Bishop of Rome's pardons souls might clearly be delivered out of purgatory " or that masses said at Scala Coeli could " send them straight to heaven."

There was nothing of greater import in the Articles than the fact that they were issued by the King, and appeared as the production of a convocation presided over by his vice-gerent. As is usual with compromises, they roused little enthusiasm and much dissatisfaction. In the north, in Lincolnshire and Yorkshire for example, a large protest very like a rebellion directed itself against all heresy and innovation, and against the destruction of the monasteries. This was " The Pilgrimage of Grace." The King suppressed it through his vigor, cruelty and astuteness, aided by the reluctance of the leaders of the Pilgrimage to oppose the King in arms. Apart from the Pilgrimage, however, it was clear that a goodly part of both laity and clergy throughout the country had no wish to see the hitherto accepted doctrines and practices of the Church disturbed even to the degree provided in the Articles. On the other hand such reform or innovation as they contained — and more besides! — was acceptable in London and the commercial cities of the south. Many within Convocation and thousands without desired still more of the " new learning." Their minds were surging with indigenous protestantism and thoughts from Germany.

The result was that within a year, Convocation again was summoned to agree upon a further statement, in view of wide dissensions by no means yet allayed. It issued another Formulary, called *The Institution of a Christian Man.* This expounded the Apostles' Creed, the Ten Commandments, the Lord's Prayer and the *Ave Maria;* but the most important addition, which must be taken as a concession to the conservative or reactionary revolt, was the restoration of the omitted four sacraments to a place among the authorized doctrines of the English Church. It contained a preface from the Convocation to the King. In fact it seemed more distinctly than the Ten Articles to issue from Convocation, and was also dubbed the " Bishops' Book." Yet it submitted itself wholly to the King for his approbation. He lacking, as he said, the time to study it carefully, nevertheless had tasted it and found nothing that was not laudable. So he directed that it should be read and taught in parish churches for the space of three years.

No Pilgrimage of Grace or other protest had succeeded in unseating Thomas Crumwell, who was hated by Catholics as the chief promoter of the royal heresies — if only they dared call them so. It was Crumwell who, as the King's vice-gerent, issued the first royal injunctions to the clergy [24] enjoining them to publish and inculcate the Articles and the acts of Parliament abolishing the Bishop of Rome's pretended jurisdiction. The clergy were admonished to forbear from superstitious ceremonies, to exhort their parishioners to keep God's commandments and fulfill works of charity, rather than go on pilgrimages; since it will more profit their soul's health to " bestow that on the poor and needy, which they would have bestowed on . . . images and relics." Let the clergy instruct their parishioners and promote the education of the young, avoid taverns, drinking, riot, and card-playing, devoting themselves instead to the study of Scripture.

After the appearance of the *Institution,* another vigorous set of Injunctions was issued, in 1538.[25] Titularly they were full-fledged.

" In the name of God, Amen. By the authority and commission of the most excellent Prince Henry, by the Grace of God King, etc., . . . in earth supreme head under Christ of the Church of England, I, Thomas, lord Crumwell, lord privy seal, vice-gerent to the King's said highness for all his jurisdictions ecclesiastical within this realm . . . give and exhibit unto you [blank] these injunctions following to be kept, observed, and fulfilled upon the pains hereafter declared."

The previous injunctions are confirmed, with added threats. Then comes the straight command to place one copy " of the whole Bible of the largest volume, in English " in every parish church for the parishioners to read. Moreover every person is to be exhorted to read the Scriptures privily or openly, avoiding contention, and referring his difficulties " to men of higher judgment in Scripture." The Lord's Prayer and the Creed are to be taught in English, sentence by sentence, and likewise the Ten Commandments. The very gospel of Christ shall be " purely and sincerely " declared, in four quarterly

[24] 1536, Gee and Hardy, o. c. pp. 269 sqq
[25] Gee and Hardy, o. c. pp. 275 sqq.

sermons, and all are to be exhorted " to the works of charity, mercy, and faith, specially prescribed and commanded in Scripture, and not to repose their trust . . . in any other works devised by men's phantasies besides Scripture; as in wandering to pilgrimages, offering of money, candles or tapers to images or relics, or kissing or licking the same, saying over a number of beads, not understood or minded on,"— all of which tend to idolatry and superstition, the offense most abhorrent to God. The " Feigned images " which are " abused with pilgrimages or offerings " are to be taken down; nor shall candles or tapers be set before any image or picture. You shall admonish your parishioners that images serve but as " books of unlearned men," to recall the lives of those they represent; " which images, if they abuse for any other intent . . . they commit idolatry." The clergy are forbidden to change the days of fasting; but the commemoration of Thomas à Becket " shall be clean omitted." For indeed Becket was a stench in Henry's nostrils, through the Injunctions do not say so!

If these second Injunctions seemed to point to a reformation of worship, they left small scope for personal deviation or discretion. That all things in the Church should be done under authority and as allowed, and no fantastic aberration permitted, was made still more emphatic in the King's proclamation, published late in the same year. It prohibited the importation, sale, or publication of unlicensed English books; no one was to print or sell unsupervised " books of Scripture," or dispute as to the Sacrament. The marriage of priests was sternly forbidden, while a number of very Catholic ceremonies were enjoined till the King should change them — thus making clear the point that their retention or discarding depended on his will. Yet one definite result of these decrees, was that an authorized English version of the Bible was recognized and commanded to be read. This efficaciously furthered the Reform, and proved a barrier against the assertions of the papal church. Besides the resonant beauty of the version, which in fact was largely Tyndale's, the foundation of the faith and simple structure of the early church was clearly shown, and the character of the precepts which had been metamorphosed, through sacerdotal formulation, into a sacramentary system. It was much to say " elder " instead of " priest," " congregation " instead of " church," and " repent " instead of " do penance," as the Vulgate had it.[26]

Nevertheless, in spite of such significant innovations, Henry's Catholic dogmatic orthodoxy continued adamantine, or at any rate, royal. With learning, patience and severity, he presided at the trial of one Lambert, a quondam priest, whose main heresy was the denial of the bodily presence of Christ in the eucharist. Henry directed his condemnation. This was in November 1538, and within six months drastic measures were taken to carry out the royal intent, and hew all men to a Procrustean conformity with the orthodoxy alike of King and Church and realm. In June 1539 Parliament passed the act of the Six Articles, or " six bloody whips." [27] It recited the King's Supremacy, and the great utility of " concord, agreement, and unity in opinions, as also the manifold perils which have heretofore . . . arisen, of the diversities of minds and opinions " in matters of religion; also, the summoning of both Parliament and Convocation to settle six certain Articles. It stated that the King had taken part in the debates having " most graciously vouchsafed, in his own princely person, to descend and come into his said High Court of Parliament and council, and there like a prince of most high prudence and no less learning, opened and declared many things of high learning and great knowledge, touching the said Articles . . . for a unity to be had in the same," and that upon the consent of the King's highness, and the assent of both houses as well as the clergy, it was resolved and agreed upon as follows:

[26] Sir Thomas More in his *Dialogue* published in 1529, Book III, Chapter VIII, objected to the myriad instances of mistranslations, as he deemed them, in Tyndale's New Testament; instancing the substitution of " seniors," " congregation " and " love " for " priests," " church," and " charity "; and the change of " grace " into " favour," of " confession " into " Knowledgeing," and " penance " into " repentance."

[27] Gee and Hardy, o. c. pp. 303 sqq.

First, the full truth of transubstantion.

Secondly, that a communion in both kinds is unnecessary.

Thirdly, that priests may not marry.

Fourthly, that vows of chastity are to be observed.

Fifthly, that private masses be continued.

Sixthly, that auricular confession is necessary.

The act decreed that dissent from the first Article should be heresy, to be punished by burning and forfeiture of goods as in cases of high treason; and that to teach and maintain on trial any matter opposed to the remaining articles, should likewise involve a felon's death with forfeiture; while forfeiture was prescribed for publishing or writing anything against the said Articles, with death for the second offense.   Effective means were provided for the detection of these felonious offenses and the carrying out of the set penalties.

This ineluctible act swung its scourges over the heads of recalcitrants at home, and flaunted them in the faces of the Lutheran princes of Germany.   Various negotiations looking towards some sort of religious union had taken place between Henry and the German Protestants, who sought to win the King to their Augsburg Confession, a document which exerted great influence upon the English formulations of belief.   In 1538 the Lutheran representatives in England insisted that the Lord's Supper should be ministered to the laity in both kinds, that private propitiatory masses should be abolished, and auricular confession also; and that the clergy be permitted to marry.[28]   They had left England with the correction of these abuses as they called them, unassented to.   And the next year the Act of the Six Articles was, as it were, hurled after them, denouncing Lutheran tenets under extreme penalties.   Henry was a great politician, as well as royal theologian.   He was apt to time his acts to the pulse of the international situation, constantly feeling for the varying dangers to which his heresy exposed him from the Emperor and the pope, and even the French

[28] See the document in Strype, *Eccl. Memorials,* I, II, No. XCVI, also ib. I, I, Chapter XLV.

King. He knew when to court and when to repulse the Lutherans who in fact had no confidence in him and small respect for his reforms.

At all events this Act of the Six Articles was the high watermark of the intolerance and asserted Catholic orthodoxy of the established English Church. And here may be remarked that in the conception, and in the process of attainment, of uniformity, or compulsory conformity, through the reigns of Henry and Edward and Elizabeth, three grades, or stages may be distinguished. The first was the formulation or adoption of cardinal matters in the saving articles of faith. Next comes the authorization and ordering of the chief ceremonies adopted or altered, or omitted from the Roman Catholic Church. Lastly in order if not in time, the process of regulation passes to the details of vestment, the placing of the communion table, and the like. The whole process is not inspiring, but seemly in the result. It was big with respect for form, for " good form " indeed, for the matter of correct social and religious convention. Its dogmatic eclecticism, its selective, moulding, plastic quality was as clearly English as Lutheranism, body and soul, was German. And the Church of England, if palpably body, had also a soul of service and conviction, a soul of beauty indeed, as well as a sightly body. The body was incorporate in a visible setting and ceremonial a little less impressive and magnificent than that of the Roman Catholic Church. Its soul found voice in the English liturgy, which may be taken as inclusive of the noble and convincing version of the Scriptures, of the rites of baptism, matrimony, burial, the Holy Communion; inclusive of daily church prayers and collects, chants, and absolutions, through which the worshipper carries from the church a stately peace.

" A necessary Doctrine and Erudition for any Christian man, set forth by the King's Majesty " in 1543, was the last comprehensive Formulary from the King. It was not improperly called " The King's Book "; for Henry had carefully corrected it. Yet the chief shaping hand is

reputed to have been Cranmer's [29]; and other divines took
part in its composition.   It opened with a striking Epistle
from the King to all his faithful and loving subjects,"
setting forth his " travail " to purge his realm of ignorance and superstition by publishing the Scriptures.   Yet
there is found in some of our people's hearts, " an inclination to sinister understanding of Scripture," with presumption, arrogance, carnal liberty and contention.   To
remedy this, " and for avoiding such diversity in opinion,"
he is constrained

" to set forth, with the advice of our clergy, such a doctrine and
true declaration of the true knowledge of God and his word, with
the principal articles of our religion, as whereby all men may uniformly be led and taught the true understanding of that which is
necessary for every Christian man to know, for the ordering himself in this life agreeable to the will and pleasure of Almighty God.
Which doctrine also the Lords both spiritual and temporal, with
the nether House of our Parliament, have both seen and like very
well."

With telling clarity the Epistle continues:

" And for Knowledge of the order of the matter in this book
contained, forasmuch as we know not perfectly God, but by faith,
the declaration of faith occupieth, in this treatise, the first place.
Whereunto is next adjoining, the Declaration of the articles of our
Creed, concerning what we should believe.   And incontinently
after them followeth the Explication of the seven Sacraments: [note
well, all the *seven Sacraments*] wherein God ordinarily worketh;
and whereby he participateth unto us his spiritual gifts and graces
in this life. . . .   Then followeth conveniently the Declaration of
the Ten Commandments, being by God ordained the highway
wherein each man should walk in this life: to finish fruitly his
journey here, and after to rest eternally in joy with him. . . ."

Then is

" expounded the seven petitions of our *Pater Noster,* wherein be
contained requests and suits for all things necessary to a Christian
man in this present life; with Declaration of the *Ave Maria,* as a

29 " To judge from Cranmer's writings and later statements, he must
have disapproved of much in the " Necessary Doctrine " as well as of the
Act of the Six Articles.   But there was politic adaptation in Cranmer, and
an apparent protestant evolution in his real opinions.   *A Necessary Doctrine,* etc., is printed in Lloyd's *Formularies of Faith* (Oxford, 1825),
pp. 215-377.

prayer containing a joyful rehearsal and magnifying of God in the work of the incarnation of Christ; which is the ground of our salvation, wherein the blessed Virgin our Lady, for the abundance of grace wherewith God endued her, is also with this remembrance honoured and worshipped.

"And forasmuch as the heads and senses of our people have been embusied, and in these days travailed with the understanding of *free will, justification, good works,* and *praying for the souls departed,* we have, by the advice of our clergy, for the purgation of erroneous doctrine, declared . . . plainly . . . the mere and certain truth in them: so as we verily trust, that to know God, and how to live after his pleasure, to the attaining of everlasting life in the end, this book containeth a perfect and sufficient doctrine, grounded and established in holy Scripture."

All people are exhorted to read and print its doctrine in their hearts: first those whose office is to teach others, and must to that end study the Old and New Testament. "But for the other part of the Church, ordained to be taught . . . the reading of the Old and New Testament is not so necessary . . . but as the Prince and the policy of the realm shall think convenient. . . ." And "the politic law of our realm hath now restrained it from a great many, esteeming it sufficient for those so restrained, to hear and truly bear away the doctrine of Scripture taught by the Preachers. . . ."

After such a preface there need be no surprise that the doctrines set forth should be substantially those of the Roman Catholic Church, save for the necessary denial of the authority of the pope and whatever flowed from that. The opening explanation of "Faith" was sufficiently Catholic, and likewise the exposition of the Creed, until the article concerning belief in "the holy Catholic Church." Here it was pointed out that the holy church

"is also catholic that is to say, not limited to any one place or region of the world, but is in every place universally through the world, where it pleaseth God to call people to him in the profession of Christ's name and faith. . . . And this church is relieved, nourished, and fortified by his holy and invincible word and his sacraments, which in all places have each of them their own proper force and strength, with gifts of graces also, distributed by the goodness of Almighty God in all places, as to his wisdom is seen convenient."
"Whereby it appeareth," continues the exposition, "that the unity of these holy churches, in sundry places assembled, standeth

not by knowledging of one governor in earth over all churches. For neither the whole church Catholic together, nor any particular church apart, is bound to acknowledge any one universal governor over the whole church other than Christ. . . . The unity therefore of the church is not conserved by the bishop of Rome's authority or doctrine; but the unity of the Catholic Church, which all Christian men in this article do profess, is conserved and kept by the help and assistance of the Holy Spirit of God, in retaining and maintaining of such doctrine and profession of Christian faith, and true observance of the same, as is taught by the Scripture and the doctrine apostolic."

The text goes on to speak emphatically of the usurpations of the bishop of Rome.

Very Catholic is the exposition of the Seven Sacraments — all of them, with none omitted.   For example:

" The sacrament of penance is properly the absolution pronounced by the priest upon such as be penitent for their sins, and do Knowledge and shew themselves to be.   To the obtaining of the which absolution or sacrament of penance be required contribution, confession, and satisfaction."

Likewise in the Sacrament of the Altar, the Catholic doctrine of transubstantiation is stated explicitly.   So matrimony is declared a sacrament, and ordination, though with much to say against the usurping claims of the bishop of Rome; and lastly extreme unction.   The article on Justification denounces " predestination," and declares it to be " plain that not only faith, as it is a distinct virtue or gift by itself, is required to our justification, but also the other gifts of the grace of God, with a desire to do good works, proceeding of the same grace."   And again: " no faith is sufficient to justification or salvation, but such a faith as worketh by charity. . . . Our good works which we do, being once justified, by faith and charity, avail both to the conservation and perfection of the said virtues in us, and also to the increase and end of our justification and everlasting salvation."

The next Article on Good Works, explains that by good works " we mean not the superstitious works of man's own invention," as those on which monks, friars and nuns rely; nor on the other hand such as are " done by the power of reason and natural will of man, without faith in Christ "; but such as men justified do work in charity and faith, or in remorse for sin. And the last article declares it to be

" a very good and charitable deed to pray for souls departed," and " to cause others to pray for them, as well in masses and exequies, as at other times, and to give alms for them, according to the usage of the Church and ancient opinion of the old fathers; trusting that these things do not only profit and avail them, but also declare us to be charitable folk, because we have mind and desire to profit them, which, notwithstanding they be departed this present life, yet remain they still members of the same mystical body of Christ whereunto we pertain."

The unctuousness of the last is admirable! And as in the *Ten Articles* and the *Institution*, the text proceeds to disclaim particular knowledge of the place and state of the departed and declares that in order to put away the abuses in this matter brought in by the maintainers of the papacy of Rome, it is better to " abstain from the name of purgatory," under color of which the papal abuses have been advanced, and the fond idea that masses said at *Scala Coeli* might profit the souls more than those said at some other place.

The *Necessary Doctrine* was no longer than the *Institution*, of which it was a revision and a clear improvement in form and language. And one notes, that however far these two formularies are from accepting the Augsburg Confession, in plan and form they appear as a combination of the *Ten Articles* with the *Shorter* and *Longer Catechisms* of Luther.

CHAPTER XXIII

PRAYER-BOOK AND ARTICLES AND THE ELIZABETHAN SETTLEMENT

I

THE death of Henry VIII on the twenty-eighth of January 1547 removed the chief obstacle from the path of protestant reform in the Church of England. There had been, perhaps, some late waverings from the severity of the act of the Six Whips; but in the main, Catholic doctrine and observance still made the ecclesiastical law and custom of the realm when Edward VI, a priggish child of eleven, succeeded to the throne. The royal finances were embarrassed, poverty was prevalent, and the government seemed uncertain. The English experience of Protectors had not been cheering. Vexed questions arose as to the late King's will. Yet out of the initial crisis, the earl of Hertford, Edward's uncle, emerged as Protector, and became Duke of Somerset. By this title he is known to history as a ruler of considerable capacity, and graciously inclined, in spite of personal avarice. But in political intrigue he was no match for the more sinister Warwick, who overthrew him within three years and assumed the leadership of the State as Duke of Northumberland. Both these men, while differing in honesty and motive, favored the Reform. The privy council could not be unanimous when so much was unsettled as to doctrine and ceremonial; but it leaned preponderantly toward the New Learning, with Archbishop Cranmer, a facile and constructive talent, promoting the same. The formal result, for the reign of Edward, consisted in the Prayer Books of 1549 and 1552, and the Forty-two Articles of Religion, called also of the latter date. The last, however, were agreed upon so near the close of Edward's reign that they did not become part of the ecclesiastical law of the land before Mary's reactionary changes overwhelmed both Articles and Prayer Book for the time. The Prayer Book of 1552 was to re-emerge nearly intact upon Elizabeth's accession. But the Articles were not confirmed and were formally superseded by the revision of 1562, which finally was reaffirmed with slight alterations in the thirty-nine Articles of 1571. These still present the doctrines of the English Church.

In 1547 Parliament and Convocation seemed to share the liberal mind of the Protector. The law of treason was relaxed and the old statute *de haeretico comburendo* was repealed along with the Act of the Six Articles and restrictions upon printing and reading the Scriptures. Convocation voted for the ministration of the communion in both kinds; and Parliament quickly turned their decision into law. The statute [1] making this decree, like so much English ecclesiastical legislation, emphasized the royal desire for " perfect unity and concord," and spoke of the abuse and reviling of the blessed Sacrament by wicked or ignorant men; who not only disputed irreverently " of that most high mystery, but also, in their sermons, preachings, readings . . . arguments, talks, rhymes, songs, plays, or jests, name or call it by such vile and unseemly words, as Christian ears do abhor to hear rehearsed."   So penalties were set on such revilings, and it was decreed that the people, with the priest, should receive the Sacrament in both kinds.

There was call enough for such an act, inasmuch as the repeal of the Six Whips and other highly penal statutes had loosed men's tongues. No seemly uniformity of usage prevailed; the streets resounded with disputes and ribaldry, while the press began to teem with satires. There was much image-breaking. Catholic reactionaries looked on malignantly or obstructed when they might, while the lack of a clearly defined and dominant strain of Protestant belief and practice deepened the confusion. The English people, with their leaping national English consciousness and Wycliffite backgrounds, would not take

[1] Gee and Hardy, o. c. pp. 322 sqq.

just what the German Luther taught, or Bucer advocated, nor what Bullinger, Zwingli's successor, inculcated even more congenially. Scandalous fighting over the Mass moved the Council to impose silence on this matter, and commit the disobedient Bishop Gardiner to the Tower. The conflicting ineffectiveness of partially repealed legislation called loudly for further authoritative action to restore some show of harmony and regain that seemly uniformity of usage so dear to the hearts alike of English kings and loyal subjects.

For a while the Protector and Council proceeded by royal proclamations and orders as to preaching. These were rather confusing, whether taken individually or when compared with each other. But they showed a genial intent to restrain divers and unauthorized changes in church services and ceremonial, while preparing men for a new order of service, when it should be declared. A number of books against the Mass appeared; and an English translation of Erasmus's *Paraphrase of the New Testament* stirred many readers. Translations were made of works of Melancthon, Luther, Zwingli, Bullinger, Calvin and others. The nature of the Sacrament was vehemently disputed over — that controversy which well may be called the central tragedy of Protestant reform in the sixteenth century. A disputation over it in the House of Lords lasted through a good part of December 1548, and was participated in by lay lords as well as bishops. In the end the views of Cranmer and Somerset prevailed by a good majority.

The Archbishop had gradually reached his convictions upon the nature of the Eucharist. Early in his career, transubstantiation had repelled him. The doctrine of the real presence expressed in the Ten Articles (1536) and the *Institution of a Christian Man* (1538) might be interpreted as consubstantiation, the Lutheran conception. Cranmer readily had subscribed to this. But he opposed in Parliament the Act of the Six Whips, and did not like the doctrine in *The Necessary Erudition* of 1543. As against the clear transubstantiation there asserted, he sheltered himself within his principle of submission to the royal supremacy. He had been strongly drawn toward Lutheranism from the time of his mission in Germany, whither the King sent him in 1531. There he became intimate with Osiander, then pastor in Nuremberg, and married his niece.[2] So he naturally inclined toward the Lutheran view of the Sacrament, and permanently adopted the doctrine of justification by faith alone.

In the first years of Edward, Cranmer, loosed from his anxious subservience to Henry, invited a number of foreign divines to England. Peter Martyr, an Italian, who was made professor of divinity at Oxford, à Lasco, a noble Pole, and Bucer from Strasbourg, who was made a professor of divinity at Cambridge, were among them. The foreign influence was thus strengthened in the official English national Church; and foreign pastors were installed for the congregations of German or Dutch, French, and Italian Protestants resident in England. This was urged by Cranmer and favored by other members of Somerset's Council as a measure combining Christian charity with Christian policy.[3] Cranmer issued a Catechism in 1548, which was a translation from a Lutheran original.

Before this, however, and clearly before the debate above referred to in the House of Lords, Cranmer's views of the Sacrament were loosened from the Lutheran insistence upon the real presence, which he acknowledged he had held to in error of the truth.[4] So he passed on to an opinion substantially in accord with that of Zwingli, Bullinger and Bucer, or one may say, of Wyclif. This is the view represented by the Prayer Book and the forty-two or, subsequently, the thirty-nine Articles.

In 1549 Edward's first Act of Uniformity [5] was en-

[2] He did not see fit to bring her home with him; but sent for her in 1534, after he was Archbishop. In the time of the Six Whips, 1539, he returned her to Germany. Malicious tongues alleged that he used to carry her about with him on his Archiepiscopal journeys, in a chest with breathing holes in it.

[3] See Strype, *Memorials of Cranmer,* pp. 335 (234) sqq. (Chapter XXII).

[4] See Strype, *Memorials of Cranmer,* Chapter XXV, pp. 364 (254) sqq. for Cranmer's writings upon the Sacrament and his Controversy with Gardiner and others (1550–1552).

[5] Gee and Hardy, o. c. pp. 358 sqq.

acted, with its great schedule, *The Book of Common Prayer*. It recited the existence of " divers forms of common prayer, commonly called the service of the Church; that is to say, the Use of Sarum [Salisbury], of York, of Bangor, and of Lincoln," and recently of various forms besides. Pointing out the inconvenience of such diversity as well as innovation, it stated that to obtain " a uniform quiet and godly order," the King had appointed Archbishop Cranmer and certain discreet bishops, with other learned men, to " draw and make one convenient and meet order, rite, and fashion of common and open prayer and administration of the sacraments." This is now accomplished by them with the aid of the Holy Ghost, and is set forth in the book delivered to his Majesty entitled, *The Book of the Common Prayer and Administration of the Sacrament*. The act enjoined the use of this, and laid penalties upon such of the clergy as might refuse, and upon persons who should satirize it in songs or plays. Psalms or prayers taken from the Bible might also be used on occasion. The same year an act was passed legalizing the marriage of priests.[6]

The church services in use when Edward came to the throne,— the " divers forms " referred to in the Statute of Uniformity — were much the same as they had been before his father's breach with Rome. The Prayer Book abolished this diversity and set a uniform " use " or service for the whole realm, and one which differed from any " use " previously followed.[7] Cranmer was the leading advocate of this change, and the chief author of the Book of Common Prayer, while Bishop Gardiner was the chief obstructionist. Between the two were other ecclesiastics and learned laymen, who would not go as far as Cranmer wished. So the book was the result of many arguments and compromises. Its Communion Service departed from the Catholic liturgies by discarding the conception of the Mass as a sacrifice and an oblation; which became instead a celebration, " with these thy

[6] Gee and Hardy, o. c. p. 366.
[7] See the statements of Gasquet and Bishop on page 2 of their *Edward VI and the Book of Common Prayer*, (1890) which I have used for the next few pages.

holy gifts " of bread and wine, " the memorial which thy Son hath willed us to make." A " sacrifice of praise and thanksgiving " was offered, not (as Cranmer explained) to reconcile us to God, but to testify the duty of those who have been reconciled by Christ. Thus, consciously or unconsciously, Cranmer and the Prayer Book fell in with Luther's denial of the sacrificial character of the Mass. And one may say that the rest of the Prayer Book had as much Lutheranism as it had of Roman Catholicism, allowing for the general fact that it was Christian and presented the fund of Christian prayer and teaching long domiciled in the Roman Catholic Church.

The substitution of a new English service for the old and mainly Latin rituals was received with some approval, but also with a dissent and hostility that in the Southwest of England broke out into a dangerous revolt.[8] Economic troubles contributed to this rebellious reaction, which may perhaps be regarded as a prelude to the more national return to Catholicism under Philip and Mary. It was suppressed with considerable difficulty and the shedding of blood. Indeed upon the fall of Somerset some expected that the Church of England might be turned back toward its earlier conservatism. This expectation was quickly dispelled by the bill to deface images and destroy old service books (Jan. 1550) and by Warwick's confirmatory letter in the King's name to Cranmer. It was plain that reforms were to be drastically pressed. The proceedings to deprive Gardiner, the ablest of all the reactionaries, of his bishopric of Winchester, which had been commenced under Somerset, were carried to a conclusion. He was imprisoned, with Bonner also, Bishop of London, who likewise was deprived, and Ridley made bishop in his stead.[9] A New Ordinal was prepared,

[8] See the very interesting Catholic reactionary articles of the Rebels, demanding the Mass in Latin, the Act of the Six Whips, the restoration of Images and the old services, prayer by name for the souls in Purgatory, a recall of the English Bibles, and so forth, with Cranmer's elaborate refutations, in Strype, *Memorials of Cranmer,* Appendix, No. XL (pp. 799–840).

[9] Not less than six reactionary bishops were deprived. See Strype, o. c., Chapter XX, for the manner and reasons of depriving the bishops of Worcester and Chichester.

and the Calvinistic Hooper,[10] was with great difficulty persuaded to submit even to its short rites, and be consecrated Bishop of Gloucester, He and Ridley were expected to destroy the Altars of Baal. The substitution of communion tables, properly placed, proceeded apace. Some of the old altars were made into hogsties — arae factae sunt harae — writes a correspondent of Bullinger.[11] The government's pruning of church revenue and confiscation of church valuables no longer needed in the reformed ritual, presented further obstacles to cumbrous rites and the support of supernumerary ministrants.

Thus ecclesiastic reform was driven along, while its more prudent friends, like Bucer, feared lest the land was insufficiently weaned from its old superstitions: a condition from which reactions might arise. At all events, the Prayer Book of 1549, detested by Catholics or reactionaries, and unsatisfactory to progressive Protestants, was hardly deemed final. It did not represent the last stage of religious thought even of its chief author Cranmer. From its first publication, a revision was looked for, and in fact shortly was begun. Possibly the design of Cranmer was to disavow and change those parts and phrases of the book of 1549, which Gardiner and other would-be Catholics had seized upon as evidence of the recognition of Catholic doctrine. The next Prayer Book should belong unquestionably and emphatically to the Reform. And so it did, with its alterations of the communion service, its discarding of the word " altar," its omission of the intercession for the dead, and other changes.[12] Judging from its recitals " a great number of people in divers parts of this realm " had refused to attend services in the churches, and doubts had arisen as to the manner of conducting them. All persons were now enjoined to attend under " pain of punishment by the censures of the Church," and were forbidden to frequent other forms of service.[13] There could be no doubt as to the progressively coercive intentions of its

[10] A very interesting person, see post p. 135 sqq.
[11] Gairdner, *Lollardy*, etc. III, p. 308.
[12] See more specifically, Gasquet and Bishop, o. c. Chapter XVI.
[13] Gee and Hardy, o. c. pp. 369 sqq.

authors. But the days of the boy Edward were numbered; and within a few months of the establishment of
the Prayer Book of 1552, Mary came to the throne and
abolished it. It was restored by Elizabeth in 1559, and
has endured with few changes to the present day.

The Book of Common Prayer was a product of the
mixed English race. Written in a language which was
Teutonic and Romance, it was itself an Anglican harmony
framed of Roman and Teutonic elements. As it has
helped ennoble the English language and evoke the harmonies of English prose, so has it enriched and
harmonized and beautified the religious mood and feeling
of generations of English worshippers. It was the finished form of expression of the Christian genius of England. One need not ask that it should have added to
religious thought.

Cranmer's share in the composition of the Forty-two
Articles of 1552 was as his share in the composition of
the Prayer Books. His was the chief constructive mind
and hand; but others took part in the work of drafting,
and of revision upon consultation.[14] Having apparently
been agreed upon by Convocation, the Articles were published by the King's command shortly before Edward died.
(May or June 1553). They were declared to have been
drawn up " for the avoiding of controversy in opinions,
and the establishment of a godly concord in certain matters of religion." It is clear that their composition was
influenced by the need to combat definite errors, as of the
Anabaptists and Millenarians for example; and also that
they could not be regarded as a complete formulation of
the tenets of the English Church. In part, both
language and substance were borrowed from the Augsburg Confession, as a comparison between the two documents makes evident.[15]

Apparently the Articles were not explicitly annulled in
the reign of Philip and Mary. Upon the accession of
Elizabeth they remained unnoticed for a time, while cer-

---

[14] Charles Hardwick's lucid *History of the Articles of Religion* (1851)
is still unsuperseded.

[15] See in detail Hardwick, o. c. pp. 100 sqq.

tain provisional articles were set forth by the bishops.
The excellent Parker had been made Archbishop of Canterbury, and a royal commission in 1559 was deputed to
visit the dioceses, and take note of the disturbance of
religion caused by Mary's reign, the use or rejection of the
Prayer Book, and like matters. The Convocations of
Canterbury and York were called to assemble in 1562.
In the meanwhile the archbishop, assisted by certain
bishops, had been revising the Forty-two Articles, using
the Latin version of 1552. The Lutheran strain was
still strong in the minds of these revisors. But since
in the course of years new errors had appeared, the revision was obliged to take notice of them in the framing
of its propositions, while certain specifically directed
articles of the former date were omitted as no longer
needed. It was thought expedient to state explicitly that
Confirmation, Ordination, Marriage, Penance and Extreme Unction were not " Sacraments of the Gospel "; the
authority of a national church to alter ceremonies was
declared and the meaning of the royal supremacy. The
laity were to receive both cup and bread.

After discussion and some revision of the archbishop's
draft, Convocation adopted the *Thirty-nine* Articles, to
which number they had been reduced. There is some uncertainty as to their ratification by the Privy Council
and the Queen; yet they would appear to have been
ratified in their Latin version. It was this Latin version
that was again slightly revised by Convocation in 1571,
and put into English. The same year Parliament passed
a statute compelling the clergy to subscribe to them in
the English version, which was spoken of in the act as
having been adopted in 1562.[16] The Queen reluctantly
gave her assent, bitterly as she was opposed to Parliament's initiative in Church affairs.

So the Articles of Religion of the Church of England
were formed through a combined process of selection and
repudiation, carried out by men possessing a talent for
harmonious construction. No originality was asserted;
no novelty was sought. Yet they sufficiently declared the

[16] Gee and Hardy, o. c. pp. 477 sqq.

position, and represented the temperament, of the Church of England.   Again, an English result is attained through materials not distinctively English, and in part even distinctly foreign.

Since the mind of Cranmer, with its gift of cadenced utterance, had a chief share in fashioning Prayer Books and Articles, these devotional and declaratory compositions accorded with his ecclesiastical persuasions, and represented a partial accomplishment of his main design. More than one group of motives swayed the purposes of this archbishop, in whom personal simplicity veiled his political faculties. If his great talents seemed adaptable and time-serving, they served as well what was or became his dominant ideal: a national church under the headship of the national ruler, but independent of the usurped authority of the pope.   He may have held this to be the best for all nations, with the fine hope of a doctrinal harmony uniting them in spiritual concord.   He assuredly held to it for England with all his mind and heart: the Church should obey the King, both of them freed from bondage to the Roman bishop.   Seeking pardon from Queen Mary for his brief support of Lady Jane Grey, in deference to Edward's Testament, he said truthfully:

"Now as concerning the state of religion, as it is used in this realm of England at this present, if it please your Highness to license me, I would gladly write my mind unto your Majesty.   I will never, God willing, be author of sedition, to move subjects from the obedience of their Heads and Rulers: which is an offense most detestable.   If I have uttered my mind to your Majesty, being a Christian Queen and Governor of this Realm . . . then I shall think myself discharged.   For it lies not in me, but in your Grace only, to see the reformation of things that be amiss.   To private subjects it apperteineth not to reform things, but quietly to suffer that they cannot amend." [17]

In his last hours he said before the Queen's Commissioners

"that the loss of his promotions grieved him not. . . . But what stuck closest to him and created him the greatest sorrow, was, to

[17] Strype's *Cranmer*, Appendix, No. LXXIV.

think that all the pains and trouble, that had been taken by King Henry and himself, for so many years, to retrieve the ancient authority of the Kings of England, and to vindicate the nation from a foreign power, and from the baseness and infinite inconveniences of crouching to the Bishops of Rome, should now thus easily be quite undone again." [18]

This ideal of the archbishop long dominated the English Church.

II

The return of the realm to Roman Catholicism and its reconcilement to the pope, under the half Spanish Mary and her altogether Spanish spouse, represented no lasting popular reaction. A part of the population had been Catholics at heart in Edward's time; their return to the papal fold might be a glad home-coming. But the national feeling was strong among them, and while they favored Catholic doctrines, rather than those of the Reform, a goodly proportion detested subservience to Rome. Besides these sincere Catholics, whether royal or papal-minded, many men were quick to take their cue from the royal impulsion. Altogether there was a reactionary majority in the Church. Accordingly in October 1553, a scant three months after Mary's accession, Convocation piously or servilly declared for the sacrament in one form for the laity, for transubstantiation, and for the adoration of the Eucharist. And through the reign of Philip and Mary the mass of the people dumbly turned back to Roman Catholicism.

Yet a good part of the realm had sincerely accepted the Protestant Anglicanism of Edward and Cranmer, and through this Catholic reign did but grudgingly or outwardly conform to the royal and parliamentary decrees, while a minority held back in stiff dissent. From the last, the roll of Marian martyrs — some three hundred in all — was recruited. Soon after Mary's accession, Cranmer, Ridley, Latimer, and Bradford found themselves in one chamber in the Tower, because the place was full.[19]

[18] Strype's *Cranmer*, p. 534 (372).
[19] So says Latimer in his protestation to Queen Mary's Commissioners. Strype, *Ecc. Memorials*, III, II, p. 292.

So either from ready conviction, or deference to the royal authority and fear of the consequences of refusal, the greater part of the bishops and other clergy, with their parishes, flocked back to popery. Yet Mary's reign was but an interlude, which had no lasting effect upon the subsequent gradual and permanent turning of the realm to Anglicanism — and beyond. The Marian legislation did not fail to acknowledge the vested right of the grantees of lands and property formerly belonging to the Roman Catholic Church.[20]   And one notes that the royal and national desire for uniformity still finds expression in proclamations and statutes, and that from the fair start of their preambles, the enactments might have proceeded to establish Edwardine prayer-books just as readily as Roman forms. And indeed one may think that this approbation of uniformity, and of conformity to law, as well as obedience to the royal will, and fear of consequences, was embodied in the conduct of such men as Cecil, and of that marvellous heir presumptive, the princess Elizabeth. Naturally exhortations to law-abiding obedience and tranquillity had prominent place in her first royal utterances and those of her first parliament when she had succeeded to the throne after that morning of November 17, 1558, when Mary died, and " all the Churches in London did ring, and at night [men] did make bonfires and set tables in the streets, and did eat and drink, and made merry for the new queen."

Cecil was in Elizabeth's confidence before she left Hatfield on the day of Mary's death, to begin her progress to London. He was to be her chief councillor for forty years. Two enigmatic words in the document which the next day proclaimed her Queen gave evidence of the consultation of this great political pair, and foreshadowed Elizabeth the woman as well as Elizabeth the Queen, and the policy of her reign. They were the words *et caetera*. She was proclaimed Queen of England, France, and Ireland, Defender of the Faith, *et caetera!* Those two words stood in the place of Mary's blank omission

[20] See e.g. in Mary's second act of repeal, 1554, Gee and Hardy, o. c. p. 394.

of the title " Supreme head of the Church," an omission which some people thought invalidated her Acts of Parliament.   For her successor to have continued this omission might have been taken to announce a Roman Catholic policy, while to have restored the " Supreme head " to its place, would have imprudently declared more perhaps than the Queen and her secretary had yet decided on.   It was not to be the custom of Elizabeth to announce her decisions before she had made them!   Certainly these were two prophetic words.

The same proclamation forbade " the breach, alteration, or change of any order or useage presently established,"— another note of prudent stepping, or rather of not stepping at all till the firm stepping-stones should be distinguishable in the troubled waters.   For they were troubled enough.   The Romanists were talking seditiously against the new Queen, the " gospellers " were rioting and pulling down images.   A goodly sprinkling of these disorderly people were quickly jailed; and before many weeks another proclamation forbade irregular preaching and dispute, tending to the breach of " common quiet . . . according to the authority committed to her highness for the quiet governance of all manner her subjects."   By this authority so unprovocatively stated, clergy and laity were directed neither to preach or listen to " any manner of doctrine or preaching " other than the Gospels and Epistles of the day, the Ten Commandments, the Common Litany used in her majesty's own chapel, the Lord's Prayer and the Creed — all in English.[21]   This use of the vernacular could not be objected to, since an unrepealed statute of Henry VIII permitted it.   The Spanish Ambassador might sneer that such use of English was the custom of heretics.   Elizabeth was content that others should notice this as well as he.   In her ride through London, to her coronation, when a lady clad in white silk as " Truth " had presented her a great English Bible, Elizabeth received it with thanks, and kissed it, laid it to her bosom in the sight of all, protesting that she would often read over that book.

[21] Gee and Hardy, o. c. p. 416.

But the Queen's position was netted with difficulties, while dangers beset England. Mary had just lost Calais. A treaty of peace hung in the balance, with England as unprepared to fight as Philip was reluctant to continue the war against the French King. Philip made Elizabeth a perfunctory offer of marriage, which she most courteously declined. So he sought the hand of the French king's daughter. Philip was Elizabeth's friend to this extent that he would not permit her to be crushed, and Mary Stuart, a niece of all the French Guises set up in her stead. Peace was made; Calais was judiciously abandoned. But still the coming Franco-Spanish marriage, the papal threat to proclaim Elizabeth a usurping heretic and bastard, the possibility of all manner of invasion from Scotland, France, the Netherlands, the realm unprepared and possibly divided, constituted perils enough.

The general situation and the stubborn convictions of many of the clergy, especially of the bishops, all of whom had been appointed in the former reign, retarded and confused the religious settlement. There was also some division of opinion among those who desired the reestablishment of the national and royal church. One suggestion was to proceed against the Marian bishops by *praemunire*, and defer legislation, while tacitly permitting such return to Anglicanism as might be had under existing statutes.[22] On the other hand a projected " Device for the Alteration of Religion," [23] composed within the circle of the Queen's Council, presented a searching consideration of foreign and domestic dangers, looked the situation in the face, and advised that the coming parliament should proceed at once. A book of services should be established, and the disloyal or reluctant Romanists on the one hand, and the over zealous innovators on the other, should both be constrained to conform for the quiet and safety of the whole realm.

An incident destined to become famous marked the

[22] Goodrich, " Divers Points of Religion."
[23] See Strype, *Annals of the Reformation,* I, I, p. 74. The document is given, ib. I, II, pp. 392–398.

opening of Parliament on January twenty-fifth. The abbot and monks of Westminster, advancing to meet the Queen with burning tapers, were met by her exclamation: "Away with those torches! we can see well enough." This, with the singing of the Litany in English and no elevation of the Host, showed the Queen's inclination.

Not long after the opening of the session, a Supremacy bill was introduced, which was destined to be " tossed about in both houses," as an old historian says.   Its fate seemed to hang not in one but in several balances.   Convocation, then in session and controlled by Roman minded priests and bishops, presented a protestation of their faith, affirming transubstantiation, the sacrificial nature of the Mass (points which had brought Cranmer, Ridley and Latimer to the stake) the supremacy of the pope, and the full authority of the clergy to regulate religion without the laymen.[24]

After this veritable challenge to the crown and parliament the settlement advanced but laggingly until March, when it was known that peace with France had been concluded.   Even then success seemed far from certain. Easter came, and with it a proclamation authorizing the laity to receive the communion in both kinds — on such questions hung England's quiet!   Riots and seditious preaching still made the flotsam on a tide that was turning rapidly from Rome.   There was a formal disputation at Westminster, which the Lord Keeper, Sir Nicholas Bacon, so arranged that it resulted in the confusion of the Catholic party, instead of the usual Protestant quarrel over the nature of the Sacrament.   Yet Elizabeth, affected by the foreign situation and her threatened excommunication, would not be called " Supreme Head," a title befitting Christ alone.   With changed phrases and substantial amendments, and after much adverse argument,[25] Parliament in April 1559 enacted that which was well entitled " An Act *restoring* to the crown the ancient jurisdiction over the State ecclesiastical and spiritual, and

[24] See the articles in Strype, *Annals,* &c. I, I, p. 80.
[25] See the speeches of Catholic bishops, &c. in Strype, *Annals,* &c., I, II, pp. 399–456.

abolishing all foreign powers repugnant to the same." [26]

It recited the " divers good laws " of King Henry VIII, " for the utter extinguishment and putting away of all usurped and foreign powers . . . as also for the restoring and uniting to the imperial crown of this realm the ancient jurisdictions, authorities . . .," and the repealing act of Philip and Mary, by which " your said humble subjects were eftsoons brought under an usurped foreign power and authority and do yet remain in that bondage."

Having with this reiterated emphasis harked back to the ancient jurisdiction of the Crown declared by Henry but renounced by Mary, the act proceeded to repeal certain statutes of the latter reign and revive those of the former, declaring that the statutes thus revived should extend and apply to Elizabeth. It revived as well the statute of Edward's reign suppressing revilers of the Sacrament and providing for its reception in both kinds; and next repealed Mary's revival of old statutes against heresy. It formally abolished all foreign authority within the Queen's dominions, and annexed to the crown all spiritual and ecclesiastical jurisdictions lawfully exercised heretofore by any spiritual or ecclesiastical authority. The Queen was authorized to appoint ecclesiastical commissioners, and an oath was prescribed declaring " that the Queen's highness is the only *supreme governor* of this realm . . . as well in all spiritual or ecclesiastical things or causes, as temporal," and renouncing the jurisdiction of any foreign prince or state or prelate. This oath was to be taken by every ecclesiastic and by every temporal official through the realm, under penalty of forfeiture of office and perpetual disability. Forfeiture of estate was set for the offense of asserting any foreign authority, a second offense to bring the offended within the statute of *praemunire,* while a third should render him guilty of treason. Certain provisions were made for a fair and speedy trial.

The energy and volubility of the reactionary opposition

[26] Printed in Gee and Hardy, o. c. 442–458, and in G. W. Prothero, *Select Statutes and other Constitutional documents* of the reigns of Elizabeth and James I, pp. 1–13 (Fourth edition, 1913), a very useful book.

spent itself on the Supremacy Act, with the result that the accompanying Act of Uniformity [27] passed with less storm. This reëstablished Edward's second *Book of Common Prayer*, with a few alterations; and enjoined its use in Church Services under severe penalties, penalizing with equal severity its defamation or interruption. In this respect constraining both those who were too slow and those who were too swift (in Elizabeth's phrase), it carried out the recommendations of the *Device for Alterations* referred to above.

The Marian bishops refused to take the oath, and held up the shining light of Mary's course, which if Elizabeth would follow, the " holy see would be pleased once more to take her and the realm into her bosom." The Queen's reply stirs the blood: " That as Joshua declared, saying, *I and my house will serve the Lord,* so she and her realm were resolved to serve him," and by no means the bishop of Rome, to whom Mary could not bind her or her realm. And she would hold those of her subjects to be her enemies and God's, who should own his usurped power.[28] One after another these episcopal recalcitrants were deprived of their sees, and the more rebellious and seditious among them constrained of their liberties. None of them, not even Bonner, was executed, a contrast to the ways of Mary's and Henry's reigns.

Not long after the dissolution of parliament, the Queen issued her Injunctions for the use of Church visitors upon their rounds,[29] which in the main revived those of Edward. They annulled most carefully all foreign or papal authority and proclaimed the queen's supreme power; they forbade the extolling of images, relics, and miracles, and directed monthly services against superstitions; commanded that the Bible and the Paraphrase of Erasmus be set up in the churches, to be read quietly and uncontentiously; provided for the licensing of preachers, who should lead godly lives; also for tithes and for

[27] Gee and Hardy, o. c. pp. 458–467; Prothero, o. c. pp. 13–20.
[28] Documents in Strype, *Annals of the Reformation,* I, I, pp. 207–208, and 217–219.
[29] Gee and Hardy, o. c. pp. 417–441. Cf. also Strype, *Annals,* etc., I, I, pp. 235 and pp. 312–330.

the Litany, and the observance of Sunday; regulated the marriage of priests, the licensing of all books, (save the works of profane authors used in universities and schools), prescribed reverential kneeling in time of common prayer, and bowing at the name of Jesus; provided for the orderly substitution of communion tables for altars,[30] and other matters. The Oath of Supremacy was explained as involving nothing new, but solely as according to the Queen the authority of Edward and Henry, " that is, under God to have the sovereignity and rule over all manner persons [ecclesiastical or temporal] born within these realms . . . so as no other foreign power shall or ought to have any superiority over them."

Plainly — but it is safer to reiterate it — the Elizabethan settlement of religion had as much to do with politics as with doctrine; and was above all an expression of England's sense of nationality,— that growing power which was irreconcilable with the recognition of a foreign ecclesiastical authority or any domestic ecclesiastical authority half independent of the royal parliamentary government. Likewise the spoliation of the Church, the diminution of its revenues through grants and leases and appropriation — this was a national policy, and no sheer robbery, no mere confiscation on the part of a needy government or its rapacious supporters. It safeguarded the national religious settlement, sealed the victory of the crown and parliament. For, as Cecil said, to have left the Church its wealth would have left it potentially the victory — the sinews of war for a later defense against the State, which must include the *ecclesia*.

The settlement made by the Acts of Supremacy and Uniformity evoked less general and less violent opposition than the Council had feared. If such a middle course aroused small enthusiasm, it probably prevented the rebellion either of reactionaries or innovators. The principle of coercion was acceptable in itself, for there was no spirit of tolerance in the realm. With all parties, the

[30] On this important change, which involved the renunciation of the sacrificial character of the Mass, see the contemporary arguments given in Strype, *Annals,* etc., I, I, pp. 237 sqq.

question as to submission or recusancy, would be solely as to the contents of the coercive measures.

Opposition was expected from the Catholics, whose bishops had voted against the settlement and afterwards had continued to protest. In fact, the visitors under the Injunctions met opposition in the Cathedral Chapters especially in the north; while the parochial clergy were generally submissive. In London the people were disposed to outrun the Injunctions, and destroy and burn images and like paraphernalia, rather than await their orderly removal. The rudiments of the Puritan spirit were stirring.

This Elizabethan settlement, like that of Henry or of Edward, included the declaration and enforcement of the major principles of Anglican Church doctrine as well as the ceremonies and usages which made for a uniform order, but could neither save nor damn. The Henrican revolution started with the greater principles: first renunciation of papal authority and then the statement of the major doctrines, and passed on apologetically to some regulation of ceremonial, as in the Ten Articles of 1536. The tone and color of the ceremonial, vestments, cult of images, had always been uppermost in the popular mind. And when the governing powers, royal, parliamentary, and ecclesiastical, had settled the main lines of national church and doctrine, they too would be obliged to turn to the demands for ceremonial regulation, which were insistent and might be riotous. As the reform progressed more rapidly under Edward, and under Elizabeth showed no signs of reversion to the conservatism of Henry, there came a larger need to modify or abolish the ceremonial in harmony with the more incisive doctrinal changes. Since every form was an expression or symbol of some doctrinal acceptance, the need for a close accord was pressing.

Moreover just as the main lines of the Anglican establishment had been from the first political and national, as well as ecclesiastical or religious, so every feature of the closely allied ceremonial (or abolishment thereof) had similar bearing and significance. To substitute communion tables for altars was to declare that the communion was not a sacrifice; the change was a Protestant demonstration, a renunciation of the Mass and with it a renunciation of the sacerdotal primacy of Rome. Likewise vestments belonged to the old Catholic priesthood, and implied the support of prelacy within the English Church. And what was not suggested by that most sacred symbol, the Crucifix?

Let us note some features of this ritualistic game, to us so comic, but deeply typical of the English Reformation. Ever and anon it threatened to become " the whole story." Strype, most diligent of annalists, says that apparently in 1539, Convocation " hammered out " a " book of ceremonies, which was mainly (he thinks) the work of Bishop Gardiner, and was intended to make a fair show of the old corruptions of the Church." [31] It recognized the distinction between works commanded by God in Scripture and ceremonies devised by man. Yet the latter make " for a decent order, quietness and tranquillity," and are worthy of reverent observance by the people. The book sets out the ceremonies to be used for the various church services, especially the Mass, explaining the symbolism of the celebrant's vestments, his words and acts. Regulations as to the observance of Sunday are given, the rules as to bells and vestments generally, candles, ashes, palms, the hallowing of oil and chrism, the washing of altars, all in the main following the Catholic rite.

The matter of ceremonial regulation is of chief interest in connection with Puritan dissent. But, before passing to that large topic, two not unhumorous instances may be noted of the English treatment of religious convention and form.

In the first year of King Edward, it was deemed advisable to recognize the time honored Lenten fast, and a proclamation was issued in the name of the King, as supreme head of the Church of England, by the advice of his beloved uncle, Somerset. His highness is informed

[31] *Ecclesiastical Memorials,* I, I, p. 546. Strype gives the text of it, ib. I, II, pp. 411–433.

that divers of his subjects despise such godly works as fasting, prayer and almsgiving, and especially the abstinence of Lent. He would not have his subjects think there was a difference in days and meats, so that one was more holy than another; but he approves the accustomed times of fasting, to the intent that men subdue their bodies unto the soul and spirit:

" And also for worldly and civil policy, certain days of the year to spare flesh and use fish, for the benefit of the Commonwealth and profit of this his Majesty's realm, whereof many be fishers and men using that trade of living. . . . So that hereby both the nourishment of the land might be increased by saving flesh . . . and also divers of his loving subjects have good living and get great riches," by providing and selling fish.[32]

The other instance is that of Elizabeth's private Crucifix and candles. As an Englishwoman and a Queen, Elizabeth liked tangible religious symbols; she delighted also in having her way, in small things as in great; and quite as much she loved the game of politics. She hated to burn bridges behind her, and there was one little decorated bridge by which she preserved a way of dalliance with Catholic powers and suitors, with her own Catholics at home, and even, for a while, possibly with the Bishop of Rome. This pretty little bridge, which was not really meant to be walked on, much less crossed, was the Queen's Crucifix and candles in her private chapel. These were Elizabeth's pious bijoux, and symbols of her own sweet will. She would set them on her Communion table, and make it look like an Altar, and be a sign to over zealous Protestants, Calvinists, or Puritans, that the Queen was not all theirs. They became a little more in evidence, a tantalizing beacon, whenever a Catholic suitor, like the French Duke of Anjou, hove in sight. The Queen's reign could not please everyone. And it was no part of Elizabeth's policy never to horrify those on whom she most relied,[33] or to leave off coquetting with

[32] Strype, *Ecc. Memorials,* II, II, p. 343.
[33] In a shocked letter of protest, Bishop Cox of Ely tells of the " trembling fear of God " which compelled him to refuse the queen's request to officiate in her chapel, while the crucifix was there.

those whom she never meant to engage herself with or trust. The fortunes of Crucifix and candles in that private chapel of the Queen, make a funny story, indicative of Elizabeth's temperament and fancies, and of her position and her policy both at home and abroad.[34]

[34] See Strype, *Annals of the Reformation*, I, I, p. 259 sqq.; W. H. Frere, *English Church in the reigns of Elizabeth and James I*, pp. 53–54; F. W. Maitland in the *Cambridge Modern History*, Vol. II, pp. 575 sqq.

CHAPTER XXIV

HUGH LATIMER

An institution, once it is established, becomes somewhat of a husk to the historian, whose interest should lie in following advancing endeavor and achievement. The means by which the established institution maintains and defends itself may enlighten us as to human resourcefulness and policy; yet our inquisitiveness turns rather to the growing and developing antagonist attacking it. For the time of Henry VIII, it is the story of the establishment of the Church of England that holds us. The Roman Catholic defense has nothing new to offer to our minds, nor has its fortuitous reestablishment in Mary's reign. And, under Elizabeth, Catholic recusancy and treasonable plotting present but the barren reactionary side of the religious conflict.

As for the Church of England, its progressive protestantism under Edward is still new and interesting; and we watch to see what form its re-establishment and final settlement will take through the first years of Elizabeth. Then it too becomes dry for the historian; and his regard is turned to Puritanism, to the content of its convictions, and to the Puritan attack upon the vestments and ceremonies, upon the prelacy and autocracy, of the Church of England. This deflection of our interest does not reflect upon the balanced and Catholic excellences of the English Church or applaud the deterrent qualities of Puritanism. And, for a time at least, our sympathy and interest are likely to turn back to Anglicanism as we see its positions turn to principles in the hands of that young Anglican genius, Richard Hooker.

In via media tutissime ibis — especially when thou art thyself the *via media*. A *via media* was the English people, composite in race and language; a twisting *via media* was their great Queen; a seemly *via media* was the Anglican Church. On the one side of it the Catholic road deflected Romeward, somewhat evacuated of on-ward-pressing English *viatores*. On the other side, may we find the path of Lollardy, blazed by Wyclif, worked upon by Luther, by Zwingli and others, and next to be straightened (in both senses!) by Calvinistic Puritans? Was it the old promiscuous Lollard path which was still offering itself, with some discernible continuity, to be trodden by Elizabethan dissent and Puritanism? Can we make out any line of march from Lollardy to Puritanism?

It is to the purpose to see where marched the feet of brave old Hugh Latimer, who feared not the face of man, nor the stake at last. His father was a yeoman, and he was born in Leicestershire not later than 1490. While a boy he was sent to Cambridge University, where he spent many years in study and godly living. A zealous Catholic and student of Duns Scotus, Aquinas, and Hugo of St. Victor, he is reported to have advocated scholastic theology as a more profitable study than Scripture. As strong an opponent of the Lutherans as Henry himself, his bachelor's oration was an attack upon Melancthon. But by the time he was licensed to preach by the University in 1522, his thoughts must have been turning against the superstitions and practices, if not the doctrines, of the Church, which was still Catholic and Papal. He was roused by the indolence and worldliness of priests and bishops, the " dumb mouths " who cared so slackly for their flocks.

In 1525 the Bishop of Ely came in unexpectedly where the already noted preacher was preaching in Latin to the University. Latimer paused respectfully till bishop and retinue were suitably placed, and then began quite a different sermon upon " the honorable estate of a bishop," whereof Christ was himself " the true and perfect pattern." He handled this theme " fruitfully," impressing the bishop, who was of another breed. Yet his lordship chose to thank him for having so excellently set forth the bishop's office; only he would have him preach yet another sermon " against Martin Luther and his doctrine."   Latimer, perceiving how the wind sat, answered that he was unacquainted with Luther's doctrine, seeing they were all forbidden to read his works: " I have preached before you this day no man's doctrine, but only the doctrine of God out of the Scriptures.   And if Luther do none otherwise than I have done, there needeth no confutation of his doctrine.   Otherwise, when I do understand he doth teach against the Scripture, I will be ready with all my heart to confound his doctrine, as much as lyeth in me."

" Well, well, Mr. Latimer," replied the bishop, " I perceive that you somewhat smell of the pan: you will repent this gear some day."   So the bishop joined with Latimer's foes, and forbade his preaching in the University, which lay within his diocese of Ely.   And it was complained of Latimer to Cardinal Wolsey that he was preaching Lutheran heresy.   Wolsey sent for him, and after examining the man, his learning and his preaching, bade him go back and preach; and restored his license.[1]

The bishop and the others who complained of Latimer were mistaken in the turn of their accusation.   For he was no follower of Luther, though, like thousands of Englishmen, he was moved by the great German's inspiration.   He was not, like Luther and Calvin, predominantly Pauline, though he might have gained a vivid sense of Paul through some indirect influence from Colet's lectures on *Romans* and *Corinthians,* which had been delivered at Oxford.   Broadly evangelical, he accepted Paul's teachings, and found no difference between them and the Sermon on the Mount.   One may call him Biblical, for he drew upon the Old Testament as well as on the New, though it was the latter that he most constantly studied, reading it through seven times, as he says, in his last imprisonment, to see if he could find therein the doctrine of transubstantiation!

One of the texts he liked to preach on was Romans xv, 4: " All things that are written are for our instruction "; a text which was exemplified throughout his preaching; for he made the whole Bible teach.   As Montaigne used

[1] See Strype, *Eccl. Memorials,* III, 1, pp. 368 sqq.

Plutarch for a universal source of illustration of life and
conduct, so with another spirit Latimer used the whole
Bible, not only its precepts and exhortations, but its statements and narratives, which could point a moral, and
aptly illuminate precept with example.

A touching but nondescript disturber of ecclesiastical
quiet was Thomas Bilney, " little Bilney," as his friends
lovingly called him, who was burned as a heretic in 1531,
a year when Henry VIII was eager to evince his orthodoxy. His was a sensitive protesting soul, which could
not adjust itself with clerical practices. A constant Bible
reader, he found satisfaction in Paul's epistles, with their
justification by faith, and disliked images and pilgrimages.
But he was not a Lutheran; and the heresy in him was
exceptionally intangible, for he accepted transubstantiation, the sacrifice of the Mass, and papal authority.
Twenty years after his death, Latimer speaks movingly
of what passed between them:

" Here I have occasion to tell you a story which happened at
Cambridge. Master Bilney, or rather Saint Bilney, that suffered
death for God's word sake; the same Bilney was the instrument
whereby God called me to knowledge; for I may thank him, next
to God, for that knowledge that I have in the word of God. For
I was as obstinate a papist as any was in England, in so much
that when I should be made a bachelor of divinity, my whole oration went against Philip Melancthon and against his opinions.
Bilney heard me at that time, and perceived that I was zealous
without knowledge; and he came to me afterward in my study,
and desired me for God's sake, to hear his confession. I did so;
and, to say the truth, by his confession I learned more than before
in many years. So from that time forward I began to smell the
word of God, and forsook the school-doctors and such fooleries.
Now, after I had been acquainted with him, I went with him to
visit the prisoners in the tower at Cambridge; for he was ever
visiting prisoners and sick folk. So we went together and exhorted them as well as we were able to do; moving them to patience and to acknowledge their faults." [2]

Latimer was himself to be something of a greater Bilney; for his heresies were at first rather intangible, though
later they became sufficiently pronounced. In 1529 he

[2] Sermon on the Lord's Prayer, 1552. *Sermons by Hugh Latimer,* p. 334
(Parker Society).

preached some sermons " on the Card," the Card which Christ played in the game of his salvation. The injunctions of that card are enough for men to play, who would be saved, injunctions of love and mercy, rather than sacrifice. He is a good Christian who keepeth well Christ's rule, as he is a good Augustinian friar that keepeth well St. Augustine's rule. The preacher was levelling at " will-works," or " voluntary works " which go outside the rule of Christ's commandments. Such are pilgrimages, the setting up of candles, gilding saints and building churches, when Christ commands that men themselves shall be a holy temple to God. Such works may not be evil, but let men do them only when they have fulfilled the commands of Christ.[3]

These sermons gave offense in quarters where gilding images and painting churches were esteemed, and where monastic rules were thought to excell the Gospel, or to be its best interpretation. Although Latimer approved of Henry's divorce, and stood in favor with Crumwell, such a preacher was not likely to keep out of trouble. Still he was popular, and in 1535 Henry made him bishop of Worcester. The Catholics held him to be a promoter of heresy with the King; at all events this Bishop of Worcester was an ardent burner of images. In 1539, when it suited Henry to draw tight the cords of orthodoxy, and the Act of the Six Articles was passed, Latimer resigned his bishopric. He was given into the custody of a more obedient prelate, and ordered to cease from preaching. Little or nothing is heard of him, till Henry died. On Edward's accession he came by his own again as a great preacher, even before the King. It was clear, too that he had turned from transubstantiation. He was among those first accused in Mary's reign. Perhaps the authorities would have connived at his flight; but he would not. In the course of time he was tried and condemned in a trial famous or infamous. His offense was heresy as to the Eucharist and refusal to obey a government which knew no way of handling such high offenders save by execution. His offense was both heresy and treason, the

[3] *Sermons*, o. c. pp. 3–26.

combined capital enormity *par excellence*. Yet we still wonder to see sundry bishops and the Primate of England, somewhat rudely unfrocked and burnt for such a matter. The last words of " old Hugh Latimer " carried telling truth: " Be of good comfort, Master Ridley, we shall this day light a candle, by God's grace, in England as I trust never shall be put out."

Latimer could not have been one of the greatest of all English preachers, had he been more of a systematic or logical or scientific theologian. The Bible is free, unsystematic and spontaneous. Its living current of religious inspiration cannot be made to flow through one who has immured his soul in logical definition and metaphysical formulation. At all events, not in the sixteenth century, which was not a century of constructive theological metaphysics, like the fourth, but one when the advancing energies of life, with their renewed evangelical and Biblical inspiration, were beating on the potent conjoined scheme of dogma and ecclesiastical authority. Latimer was impassioned with his own acceptance and understanding of the Bible. Affected, of course, by the thoughts and controversies of his era, he nevertheless drew his convictions from the Scriptures as spontaneously as he drew their illustration from the world about him. His sermons reflected and absorbed the habits, the demands, the hardships, the very implements and incidents of English life, all presented in the homely imagery and vigorous Anglo-Saxon that carried straight from the preacher to his audience. Here was indeed an English Gospeller, whose thoughts and phrases seemed to echo Wyclif: " right prelating is busy labouring, and not lording." [4] might have been Wyclif's or Latimer's. The latter was not from Wittenberg or Zurich or Geneva, but something of a Lollard preacher and bishop of the English Church.[5]

Latimer stands before us in his most famous sermon, " on the plough," [6] preached at St. Paul's in London in

[4] *Sermons*, o. c. p. 65.
[5] Strype, *Ecc. Mem.*, III, I, p. 378 gives a good estimate of Latimer's preaching.
[6] *Sermons*, o. c. p. 59 sqq. There was a series of sermons " on the plough "; but only one is known.

1548. In previous sermons he had told his auditors
" what seed should be sown in . . . God's plough land
. . . that is to say, what doctrine is to be taught in
Christ's church and congregation. . . . And now I shall
tell you who be the ploughers." They are the preachers:
" For preaching of the gospel is one of God's plough
works, and the preacher is one of God's ploughmen."
" Be not offended," he continues, " with my homely similitudes, or because I liken a prelate to a ploughman. But
now you will ask me, whom I call a prelate. A prelate is
that man, whatsoever he be, that hath a flock to be taught
of him. . . . And well may the preacher and the ploughman be likened together; first for their labour of all
seasons of the year "; for there is no season when the
ploughman has not some work to do, ploughing, sowing,
tilling, ridging his land, weeding it and dunging it. So
the prelate, the preacher, " hath first a busy work to bring
his parishioners to a right faith, as Paul calleth it, and not
a swerving faith; but to a faith that embraceth Christ, and
trusteth to his merits; a lively faith, a justifying faith; a
faith that maketh a man righteous, without respect to
works." Next he has " to confirm them in the same
faith; now casting them down with the law, and with the
threatenings of God for sin; now ridging them up again
with the gospel, and with the promises of God's favour:
now weeding them by telling them their faults, and making
them forsake sin," and so forth. The preaching of the
word is the people's meat — " meat, and not *strawberries*
that come but once a year! " Alack! many are these
strawberry preachers that minister but once a year, and
that slackly! Woe to them!

Latimer utters a cry over London, with its rich citizens,
" Proud men of London, malicious men of London, merciless men of London,"— shall he call them? Yes, for
London is worse than Nebo — charity is waxen cold, none
helpeth the scholar or the poor. " Oh London, London!
repent, repent; for I think God is more displeased with
London than ever he was with the city of Nebo. Repent
therefore, repent, London, and remember that the same
God liveth now that punished Nebo! "

But how much fault is there with the lazy ploughmen, the unpreaching prelates!

"Methink I could guess what might be said for excusing of them. They are so troubled with lordly living, they be so placed in palaces, couched in courts, ruffling in their rents, dancing in their dominions, burdened with ambassages, pampering of their paunches, like a monk that maketh his jubilee; munching in their mangers, and moiling in their gay manors, and mansions. . . . They are otherwise occupied, some in the King's matters, some are ambassadors, some of the privy council, some to furnish the court, some are lords of the parliament, some are presidents, and comptrollers of mints."

"Well, well, is this their duty? Is this their office? Is this their calling? Should we have ministers of the church to be comptrollers of the mints? Is this a meet office for a priest that hath cure of souls? . . . I would fain know who controlleth the devil at home in his parish, while he controlleth the mint?"

And the preacher continues decrying the evil of secular occupations for the clergy. Let the bishop not try to divide himself, but be a whole man in his office, which is to teach his flock.

"And now I would ask a strange question: who is the most diligentest bishop and prelate in all England, that passeth all the rest in doing his office? I can tell, for I know him who it is; I know him well. And now I think I see you listening and hearkening that I should name him. . . . I will tell you: it is the devil. He is the most diligent preacher of all others; he is never from his diocese; he is never from his cure; ye shall never find him unoccupied; he is ever in his parish; he keepeth residence at all time . . . he is ever at his plough. . . . And his office is to hinder religion, to maintain superstition, to set up idolatry, to teach all kinds of popery. . . . Where the devil is resident, and hath his plough going, there away with books, and up with candles; away with Bibles, and up with beads. . . . Down with Christ's cross, and up with purgatory pickpurse, up with him, the popish purgatory I mean. . . ."

Oh that our prelates were as diligent! But the devil as a lion, goeth seeking, and not sleeping as our bishops do! He soweth his papal doctrines, "to evacuate the cross of Christ" and make Christ's death of small virtue. He who once was lifted up! — and now instead the devil would lift up a daily propitiatory sacrifice and oblation! And the sermon continues flaying the papistical doctrines which make vain the cross of Christ.   It was a sermon unforgettable, to us perhaps a little repetitious in the reading, but suited to drive home each point in preaching. The preacher's attitude is English, and his sermon deals with English abuses and English lethargy.

There is no need to belittle the influence of Wittenberg or Zurich on the English Reformation.   Christians had never denied that faith in Christ was the corner stone of the Christian salvation; without it no man can be saved. And after Luther and Zwingli had spoken, no voice that was lifted against the placing of man's righteousness and justification in acts which were not prescribed by the Gospel but by the clergy, no such protesting voice could fail to emphasize the counter, and even sole, efficacy of faith.[7]   But the English Church would not entrust itself to the utter logic of Paul or Luther, or of Calvin; it could not cast loose from the coordinate saving require- ment of fulfilling other Commands of Christ, especially the love enjoined upon his disciples, which inspires the Epistle of John, and which Paul himself proclaimed as greatest, in his thirteenth chapter of Second Corinthians. So having an English temperament, a Lollard tempera- ment, if one will, rather than a Lutheran or Calvinistic, Latimer emphasizes faith, and even speaks, in the pro- testant language of his age, of the faith which justifies " without respect to works."   But it is evident that he is not, like Luther, preaching mainly Paul, but the whole Gospel of Christ and all his saving works.   This attitude appears throughout his sermons, and is peculiarly illus- trated by the following extract from one preached before King Edward in 1549:

" Whatsoever the pain is, it is a great pain that he suffered for us.   I see no inconvenience to say, that Christ suffered in soul in hell.   I singularly commend the exceeding great charity of Christ, that for our sakes would suffer in hell in his soul   It sets out the unspeakable hatred that God hath to sin.   I perceive not that it doth derogate anything from the dignity of Christ's death; as in the garden, when he suffered, it derogates nothing from that he suffered on the cross.   Scripture speaketh on this fashion: ' He that

[7] See in Latimer's Sermon on the Epistle for the twenty-third Sunday after Trinity — *Sermons,* pp. 520–522.

believeth in me, hath life everlasting.' Here he sets forth faith as the cause of our justification; in other places, as high commendation is given to works: and yet, are the works any derogation from that dignity of faith? No. And again, Scripture saith, *Traditus est propter peccata nostra, et exsusitatus propter justificationem etc.* It attributeth here our justification to his resurrection, and doth this derogate anything from his death? Not a whit. It is whole Christ. What with his nativity; what with his circumcision; what with his incarnation and the whole process of his life; with his preaching; what with his ascending, descending; what with his death; it is all Christ that worketh our salvation." [8]

For this lack of insistent logic, Melancthon might have felt toward this passage as he felt toward certain parts of the Ten Articles of 1536.[9] But have the Gospels any insistent logical construction? No more had the English Church or Latimer's preaching: neither English Church or English preacher would put all salvation in one basket, though Luther and Calvin might demonstrate that there was none other. No logician, no great theologian, Latimer preaches the Bible,— the New Testament with illustrations from the Old — just as he finds it. He holds to his text from the fifteenth chapter of Romans: "All things that be written are written for our instruction"; a text even for a Good Friday sermon, in which he says: "This day we have in memory of his [the Saviour's] bitter death and passion, which is the remedy of our sin." [10] So he would put all the Gospel, not some formulation of it, into his Sermons on the Lord's Prayer [11] likewise into his Sermon on the words of John's Gospel: 'This is my commandment that ye love one another,' [12]—'By this shall all men know that ye are my disciples if ye shall have love one to another,— and Latimer continues:

"So that he maketh love his cognizance, his badge, his livery. Like as every lord, most commonly, giveth a certain livery to his servants, whereby they may be known that they pertain unto him; and so we say, 'Yonder is this lord's servant,' because he weareth his livery: so our Saviour, which is the Lord above all lords, would his servants to be known by their liveries and badge, which badge

[8] Seventh Sermon preached before King Edward — *Sermons*, o. c. p. 235.
[9] Ante page 89.
[10] *Sermons*, o. c. p. 217.
[11] Preached in 1552, *Sermons*, o. c. pp. 326 sqq.
[12] *Sermons*, o. c. pp. 447 sqq.

is love . . . for love is the token whereby you shall know such a servant that pertaineth to Christ; so that charity may be called the very livery of Christ."

Further on in the same sermon he explains Paul's putting love above faith. Paul is speaking only of the faith that moves mountains, not of the " lively justifying faith; for this right faith is not without love; for love cometh and floweth out of faith. Love is a child of faith; for no man can love except he believe; so that they have two several offices, they themselves being inseparable." [13]

Just as Latimer preaches the Christ and the doctrine of the New Testament, so his face is against that which is against it or beside it, the " will-works " as he calls them, such as are denounced or not commanded in the Bible; like pilgrimages and the cult or care of images, purgatory also, and all those things which are set by the counterfeiters of God's coin, like ceremonies and money-redemptions.[14] Likewise, of course, the slack and evil preaching of the prelates, and always the oppression of the poor by the rich and mighty. For Latimer by no means confines himself to ills within the Church or caused by its clergy. He had spoken up boldly before King Henry; [15] and in his sermons before Edward had much to say about the duties and character of a righteous King. It was before him that he spoke in a grand sermon upon covetousness and lust, all breeding sedition and rebellion; a sermon upon grasping landlords, and the hard lot of the ploughmen. Passages from its direct Anglo-Saxon diction are not readily to be matched:

" They in Christ are equal with you. Peers of the realm must needs be. The poorest ploughman is in Christ equal with the greatest prince that is. Let them, therefore, have sufficient to maintain them, and to find them their necessaries. A plough-land must have sheep; yea, they must have sheep to dung their ground for bearing corn; for if they have no sheep to help fat the ground, they shall have but bare corn and thin. They must have swine for their food, to make their veneries or bacon of: their bacon is their venison, for they shall now have *hangum tuum,* if they get

[13] Compare, in general, his Sermon on the Armour of God, *Sermons,* o. c. pp. 490 sqq.
[14] See *Sermons,* pp. 36, 52.
[15] See also a letter to Henry in Strype, *Ecc. Mem.* 3, 1, pp. 379 sqq.

any other venison; so that bacon is their necessary meat to feed on, which they may not lack.   They must have other cattle: as horses to draw their plough, and for carriage of things to markets; and kine for their milk and cheese, which they must live on and pay their rents.   These cattle must have pasture, which pasture if they lack, the rest must needs fail them: and pasture they cannot have, if the land be taken in, and enclosed from them.   So, as I have said, there is in both parts rebellion.   Therefore, for God's love, restore their sufficient unto them, and search no more what is the cause of rebellion.   But see and 'beware of covetousness'; for covetousness is the cause of rebellion." [16]

[16] *Sermons*, p. 249.   See also the excellent sixth sermon on the Lord's Prayer, ib. pp. 389 sqq.

CHAPTER XXV

PURITAN DOCTRINE

ANOTHER preacher, like Latimer ordained to martyr-dom, represents more specifically the beginning of Puritan repugnance to the garb which the English Church com-manded its priests to wear. This controversy as to vest-ments opens the great Puritan movement which im-presses itself upon the people, then is checked, and subse-quently gains for a while a disturbed ascendancy, making England austere beyond her temperament.

Through Edward's reign the vestiarian controversy ran high, reams of argument coming from the most con-siderable pens of the Reform. It lay not in the national churchly sense of decency, even under its most protestant impulses, quite to denude itself of ecclesiastical habili-ments. Yet Puritan souls, who still were kept within the established church, scrupled to wear them. The con-troversy focussed around the episcopal consecration of the excellent John Hooper. In Henry's time he had so-journed abroad in Germany and Switzerland, and had been intimate with Bullinger, Zwingli's influential suc-cessor at Zurich. Returning to England when Somerset was Lord Protector, Hooper became a noted London preacher, and was nominated by the King to the bishopric of Gloucester. Eight months of argument were required to quiet his scruples against wearing the episcopal robes and taking the oath of canonical obedience. Prelates and divines took part in the amicable controversy.

First Hooper requested Archbishop Cranmer to dis-pense with these matters. Cranmer refused; and there-upon was solicited to comply by the Earl of Warwick and the boy King himself. Still he felt that even such solicita-tions would not protect him in a clear violation of the law.

Ridley, bishop of London, was deputed to satisfy Hooper's conscience by argument. The discussion came to some heat between them. Hooper could not thus be brought to wear the vestments which had been worn by papal bishops. The King's council summoned him to present his arguments before it. Cranmer in the meanwhile consulted Bucer, then professor of divinity at Cambridge, and Peter Martyr who filled a like post at Oxford. His inquiry was whether the ministers of God may use garments prescribed by the magistrates without offending God? and whether he who refuseth sinneth?

These two unquestionable protestant luminaries signified their dislike of vestments, but counselled Hooper to accept them as ἀδιάφορον — indifferent. Still he could not see it so; and wrote learned counter arguments, urging in fine, " That whatsoever was not of faith was sin." Since he would not submit, but continued to preach against these unclean trappings, he was committed first to the archbishop's custody, and then to the Fleet. Finally he permitted himself to be persuaded to comply, and was consecrated bishop. He proved to be an admirable one, renovating and cleansing his diocese, preaching everywhere the word of God, and finally sealing his faith with martyrdom under Mary.[1] He is an early and eminent example of Puritanism within the Church, which he had entered with so many painful scruples.

In manner peculiarly English the vestiarian controversy presents the budding conscience, or the opening self-consciousness of Puritanism. The doctrinal tenets of the English Church, with its vigorously sprouting Puritanical wing, were sufficiently established by the close of Edward's reign. Besides articles of faith, a book of Church services was composed, while fitting vestments for the clergy were retained or adapted from those previously worn. The Church's aim to conduct its course " in one uniformity of rites and manners . . . as also to be of one decent behaviour in their outward apparel " is exemplified

[1] See for the whole account Strype, *Mem. of Cranmer*, 1, 302–315, also in Appendix, nos. 47 and 48. Also Strype, *Ecc. Memorials*, II, I pp. 350 sqq.; ib. II, II, pp. 34, 444, 455, 456 sqq.

a few years later in the " Advertisements " of Archbishop Parker,[2] himself a perfect type of Anglicanism.
They were published in 1566 with special reference to the
" vestiarian controversy " and the extension of Puritan
objections to other observances as well.

During the reign of Mary a considerable number of
divines as well as laymen had fled the realm, and betaken
themselves to the Low Countries, to Frankfort and other
German towns, also to Zurich and most portentously of
all to Geneva. These " exiles " of various strains of
churchmanship, engaged in hot disputes among themselves in the centres of their sojourn; yet one and all were
confirmed in their Protestantism, and became acquainted
with church services which had been purified from Romish
rites. Many of them moved among churches which dis-
avowed the rule of bishops and governed themselves
under presbyterian-democratic forms. They brought
back to England a strengthened repugnance to whatever savoured of popery; and, of course, found many
there who hated things papistical. Among these returning exiles, and apart from them as well, currents of influence from Zurich and Geneva continued.

Puritanism in its course and manner was still to be
sufficiently English. Its non-conformity, as the word im-
plies, countered practices rather than denied doctrines.
Yet, while having little to do with abstract ideas, its dissent was based on a principle, which had been that of the
Lollards or ' Lay party.' The principle was that of sole
and exclusive reliance upon Scripture, and a literal adherence to it as far as possible, (or even farther!) coupled
with refusal to recognize authority outside of it. It is
not certain just when and where the name of Puritan was
first applied to this scriptural non-conforming movement,
but it was sometime before the year 1568.[3]

It visibly began with scruples like those of Hooper
against wearing the vestments of a bishop. Some returning exile, about to be made bishop scrupled the same in
the first year of Elizabeth, and sought counsel from

[2] Gee and Hardy, o. c. pp. 467 sqq.
[3] See Camden, *Annales,* p. 132, cited in Prothero's *Statutes,* etc., p. 195.

Zurich, as had before been done; the advice came back to
bear with these matters and accept consecration because
of the great need of ministers.[4]   In the same year the
Queen found it necessary to check the " breaking or defacing of monuments of antiquity . . . set up in churches
. . . for memory, and not for superstition." [5]   Yet it
quickly became evident that there was much tender conscience in the matter of images, which put itself into a
weighty petition to the Queen, fortified and lengthened
with arguments from Scripture.[6]   Iconoclasm was akin
to the dislike of vestments, which, far from dying down,
broke forth year after year.   It was taken up by a constantly increasing number of clergy, who refused the prescribed habits as popish, as defilements upon the priesthood of Christ and because they stood in human invention
and were a tyranny.   Some three hundred fellows and
scholars in St. John's College Cambridge could not endure
the surplice.[7]   A number of books were written against
the wearing of habits, and Beza, from Geneva, wrote to
the respected Bullinger of Zurich, adjuring him to send a
protest to the Queen, who not willingly would listen to
anything from Geneva, whence had come Knox's ' Trumpet Blast against the monstrous regiment of women." [8]

We may profitably turn from the specific controversy
touching vestments to the broader and deeper aspects of
the Puritan contention.   As early as 1562, Convocation
which met to consider Articles of Faith, evinced an inclination to proceed to the further reform of the rites
and practices of the Church.   Some thirty-three members
of the lower house petitioned for congregational singing
of the Psalms; also that kneeling in the Communion might
be left discretionary; that copes and surplices be done
away; that saints days be abolished.   A few days later,
upon a vote being taken, the following propositions were
lost only by a vote of fifty-eight to fifty-nine: 1. That
Sundays and the principal feasts of Christ be kept holy

[4] Strype, *Annals,* etc., I, I, pp. 256 sqq.   z
[5] Ib. p. 279.
[6] Strype, *Annals,* I, I, p. 330.
[7] Strype, *Annals* I, 2, p. 125 and p. 153.
[8] Strype, *Annals,* etc., I, II, pp. 163–175.

days, and all other holy days be abrogated. 2. That the minister in common prayer turn his face to the people. 3. That making the cross on the child's head in baptism be omitted as tending to superstition. 4. That kneeling in Communion be left to the minister's discretion. 5. That it is sufficient for the minister to use a surplice. 6. That the use of organs cease.[9]

Clearly a good part of the lower clergy, and doubtless an equal proportion of the laity, were inclined toward the further reformation of the Church. But it does not follow that as strong a party would have subscribed to the advanced Puritan positions soon to be taken by Thomas Cartwright and his supporters at the university of Cambridge. Cartwright was a scholar and man of parts, who would have received preferment had he not objected to " the cope and other ornaments." He and his followers were now to pass on from such incidentals to an attack upon the order and government of the Church. They wished to abolish archbishops and arch-deacons, and to bring back the functions and emoluments of bishops and deacons to the Apostolic rule. They main-tained that the government of the Church was not com-mitted to the bishops and archdeacons, but to the minister and elders of each congregation (ministrum et presby-terium ejusdem ecclesiae) who are not to be made by the bishops, but chosen by the churches. In reforming the Church, everything should be brought back to the Apos-tolic pattern.[10]

This Cambridge movement came to a head in 1570, and resulted in a storm which deprived Cartwright of his fellowship in Trinity and his place as Lady Margaret reader in divinity. His chief opponent was Dr. Whitgift, afterwards Archbishop of Canterbury.

The Puritans now transferred their main efforts for reform from the Convocation of the Clergy to the Parlia-ment of the realm, where many were of their party. A bill was introduced in the Parliament of 1572 to dispense

[9] Strype, *Annals,* 1, 1, pp. 500–06.
[10] See for this matter and the Latin text, Strype, *Annals,* I, II, pp. 372–383.

with the use of the Prayer-Book by those godly ministers
who desired to adhere more closely to Apostolic pattern;
but whatever chance it had for adoption was cut off by a
message from the Queen forbidding the House to consider bills concerning religion unless previously approved
by the Clergy. Thereupon, shortly before Parliament
adjourned, appeared the famous Puritan manifesto, in
the form of a pamphlet entitled *An Admonition to the
Parliament*.[11] It was anonymous, but its chief authors
were known to be two Puritan clergymen, John Field (or
Feilde) and Thomas Wilcox, who were at once put in
Newgate. Measures to suppress the pamphlet led
merely to another somewhat enlarged edition.[12]

The first part of the *Admonition* adjures the members
of Parliament to address themselves to " the restitution
of true religion and reformation of God's Church," which
the same lies " not only in abandoning all popish remnants both in ceremonies and regiment, but also in bringing in and placing in God's Church those things only
which the Lord himself in his word commandeth: "— the
last phrase states the kernel of the Puritan position. It
is not enough to remove evil; good must be placed in its
stead. And because men are so

" marvellously blinded, it hath been thought good to proffer to
your godly considerations a true platform of a church reformed, to
the end that it being laid before your eyes, to behold the great un-
likeness betwixt it and this our English church, you may learn either
with perfect hatred to detest the one, and with singular love to embrace, and careful endeavor to plant, the other; or else to be without excuse before the majesty of our God, who . . . hath by us revealed unto you at this present, the sincerity and simplicity of his
Gospel."

We in England have not even the " outward face " of
" a church rightly reformed." For all good writers ac-

[11] See W. H. Frere and Douglas, *Puritan Manifestoes*, Introduction
(Church Historical Society, 1907). My extracts from the *Admonition* are
taken from the text admirably edited in this volume.

[12] The *Admonition* is in two parts, and along with it, in both editions,
were published letters from Beza, Calvin's successor, and another noted
foreign divine. The two parts, in their two editions, are not to be confused with the *Second Admonition*, which followed them in a few months
from the pen of Cartwright. This also is printed in *Puritan Manifestoes*,
referred to in the preceding note.

cord that " the outward marks whereby a true Christian church is known, are preaching of the word purely, ministering of the sacraments sincerely, and eccesiastical discipline which consisteth in admonition and correction of faults severely." Touching the first, the substance of the doctrine is sound, but the ministers are not " according to God's word proved, elected, called, or ordained." They are not as " in the old church " tried as to " their ability to instruct " and " their godly conversation "; but " tag and rag, learned and unlearned " are appointed by the bishops, " a hundred at a clap," and not elected by the congregation; nor is each one called to a single flock, but frisks about, seeking to join living to living. Instead of preaching, they read homilies, articles and injunctions, and " are bound . . . to a prescript order of service and Book of Common Prayer in which a great number of things contrary to God's word are contained." They have strange and lordly titles, and subsist upon all manner of abuses, which should be abolished.

As to the second point, the ministering of the sacraments, there is much that is faulty and many borrowings from the Papists. In the third matter, ecclesiastical discipline, instead of Ministers, Elders and Deacons, there is the popish lordship of one man over many churches; archbishops and lord bishops instead of an equality of ministers. Excommunication is utterly and corruptly misapplied. It is now for Parliament, not to patch and piece, or go backward; " but altogether remove whole Antichrist, both head, body and branch, and perfectly plant that purity of the word, that simplicity of the sacraments, and, severity of discipline, which Christ hath commanded, and commended to his Church."

The second part of the *Admonition* has for its heading: " A view of popish abuses yet remaining in the English Church, for the which Godly Ministers have refused to subscribe." Parliament is bidden to review the causes which withheld them from subscribing to the prescribed articles in the time of the last parliament, for which they were removed from their offices. They must subscribe and acknowledge that the Book of Common Prayer and all its several contents are not repugnant to the word of God; whereas "this book is an unperfect book, culled and picked out of the popish dunghill, the Mass book full of all abominations. For some and many of the contents therein be such as are against the word of God, as by his grace shall be proved to you." The proof of this statement, which the text adduces point by point, may be passed over. Then the Archbishop's court is attacked as "the filthy quammire and poisoned plashe of all the abominations that do infect the whole realm," and the commissaries court "is but a petty little stinking ditch, that floweth out of that former great puddle."

As for the Article touching Sacraments and apparel, the ministration of the first is faulty, as before shown, and the apparel, which is alleged to be "for order and decency commanded, yet we know and have proved that there is neither order nor comeliness nor obedience in using it. There is no order in it, but confusion: no comeliness, but deformity: no obedience, but disobedience to God and the Prince . . . copes, caps, surplices, tippets and such like baggage, the preaching signs of popish priesthood . . . garments of the Idol . . . garments of Balamites, of popish priests, enemies to God and all Christians." From the which, may it please her majesty and this high court of Parliament to hear and defend us. "If this cannot be obtained, we will by God's grace address ourselves to defend his truth by suffering, and willingly lay our heads to the block, and this shall be our peace, to have quiet consciences with our God, whom we will abide for, with all patience, until he work our full deliverance," a sentence which recalls the closing of Calvin's dedicatory epistle addressed to King Francis, prefixed to his *Institute*. Calvin's spirit breathes in the *Admonition,* which stands upon his principle of adherence to the word of God taken as command, and on his conviction that a Christian church must be modelled on God's word and the practice of the Apostles. Two years later Travers's and Cartwright's *Book of Discipline* will illustrate more explicitly the manner in which Calvin and the English Puritans magnified the import of exceedingly small matters, because they visualized them as set in these principles.

Dr. Whitgift composed an elaborate answer to the *Admonition,* while its authors in prison drew up a confession of their faith, stating their opinions as to the ordering of the Church and the conduct of its services.[13] They vindicated their position also in an appeal to the lord treasurer Burghley, whose attitude toward such reformers was more tolerant than Whitgift's. The future archbishop already stood for firm repression of all divergence from the norm set for the Church, while Burghley was inclined to leniency and a more sympathetic regard for the reformers' consciences. Apparently his personal leanings, and those of certain others of the Queen's counsellors, were toward a larger tolerance of the religious instincts of these stalwart and loyal subjects of the Queen, who could be relied on as against the disloyal machinations of Catholics within or without the realm. More especially Sir Francis Knollys and others of the Council were in favor of permitting " certain good exercises of prophesyings and expounding of Scriptures," so long as " no seditious, heretical, or schismatical doctrine, tending to the disturbance of the peace of the Church, can be proved to be taught or maintained in the same." [14]

These so called "prophesyings or exercises " were much used throughout the realm, and were permitted by certain of the bishops. " In many of our archdeaconries " says a contemporary writer,[15] " we have an exercise lately begun, which for the most part is called a prophecy or conference, and erected only for the examination or trial of the diligence of the clergy in their study of holy scriptures. Howbeit such is the thirsty desire of the people in these days to hear the word of God, that they also have as it were with zealous violence intruded them-

---

[13] Given in part by Neal, *History of the Puritans,* Bk. I, ch. V.
[14] Letter to the Bishop of Norfolk, dated May 6, 1574, given in Neal's *History of the Puritans,* Part I, ch. V.
[15] Harrison's *Description of England,* Bk. II, ch. 1, given in Prothero, o. c. p. 207.

selves among them (but as hearers only) to come by more knowledge. . . . The laity never speak, of course, except some vain and busy head will now and then intrude themselves. . . ." The pious author deems them to have been a " notable spur " to ministers, impelling them to study rather than spend their time at hunting, dicing, shooting of matches, tippling at the alehouses, and the like.

The appointment of these exercises at Northampton, approved by the bishop and the Mayor, and the justices of the peace, affords a typical description as of the year 1571:

"There is on every other Saturday, and now every Saturday, from nine to eleven of the clock in the morning, an exercise of the ministers both of town and country, about the interpretation of scriptures. The ministers speaking one after another, do handle some text; and the same openly among the people. That done, the ministers do withdraw themselves into a privy place, there to confer among themselves as well touching doctrine as good life, manners and other orders meet for them. There is also a weekly assembly every Thursday, after the lecture, by the mayor and his brethren, assisted with the preacher, minister, and other gentlemen, appointed to them by the bishop, for the correction of discord made in the town: as for notorious blasphemy, whoredom, drunkenness, railing against religion or preachers thereof; scolds, ribalds, or such like."

The same document provided that the ministers of the shire, once a quarter, should repair to the said town, and confer among themselves as to their lives and manners. Those found at fault were admonished, and on failure to amend, reported to the bishop. It also gives specific directions for " the order of the exercise of the ministers, with a confession of the faith ": the writing down of the names of those who shall speak, the manner of their speaking to the close interpretation of their text, the action of the moderators, and the consultation at the end upon doubtful points. A confession of faith declared the subscribers' adherence to the Bible as containing perfect and sufficient doctrine;— the same should lie open and known to all men. "And we condemn as a tyrannous yoke (wherewith poor souls have been oppressed) whatsoever men have set up of their own inventions, to make articles of our faith, or to bind men's conscience by their laws and institutes." The confession proceeds to enumerate matters and doctrines of the see of Rome, which were to be abjured. Its silent implication touches certain ways and ordinances of the Church of England, which could scarcely be found either in the Creed or Bible.[16]

Clearly such " exercises," by no means contemplated in the Articles or the Prayer Book, would be to the taste of the " godly " within the English Church, to wit, those who were inclined to cling to Scripture as the sole and exclusive norm and standard of religion and church government. They continued to be held, constantly or sporadically, in a number of dioceses in spite of opposition, and even a prohibitive letter from the Queen (1577) in which she states that, to her grief, in sundry parts of her realm, " no small number of persons . . . do daily devise . . . and put in execution, sundry new rites and forms in the Church, as well by their preaching, reading and ministering the sacraments, as by procuring unlawful assemblies of a great number of our people . . . to be hearers of their disputations and new and devised opinions upon matters of divinity," unmeet for the unlearned and conducing to schism and disturbance of the quiet of the Church.[17] This Queen who so loved uniformity and her own will, after the disappointing laxness and even Puritan inclination of Archbishop Grindall, was to find an efficient agent in Whitgift, appointed to the Primacy of England in 1583. We need not follow here their partially successful measures to enforce conformity; but will for the moment examine a little book which was to prove the most influential and unifying of all statements of this early non-conforming Puritanism. It was written in Latin by a learned and clear-headed disciple of Geneva, Walter Travers, and quickly translated into English and printed abroad in the year 1574 apparently by Thomas Cartwright, under the name: " A full and plain declaration of Ecclesiastical

[16] Document given in Strype, *Annals*, II, 1, pp. 133–140.
[17] Prothero, *Statutes*, etc., p. 205. See also Strype, *Annals*, II, 1, pp. 480 sqq.; II, 2, pp. 544 sqq.

Discipline out of the word of God, and of the declining of the Church of England from the same." Acceptance of this book became a badge of Puritanism. It helped to give to non-conformists the name of *Disciplinarians*.

At the beginning, emphasis is placed on the need of discipline for states, if they would not perish. The Church, " which is a certain society and company of such as profess the true service of God," cannot neglect it. In contrast with the " popish hierarchy and counterfeit manner of governing the Church," (which infects the Church of England) the author will present the pattern of the lawful policy and government of the Church as Christ and his Apostles left it, and " note our faults and errors [to wit, those of the Church of England] in every point."

" I call therefore Ecclesiastical Discipline the policy of the Church of Christ ordained and appointed to God for the good administration and government of the same." Thereupon, with citations from the Old Testament and the New, the contention is disproved that men may make Church ordinances as they see fit. All must be as commanded by God: Moses ordained only what God commanded him.

" Now whereas I affirm that Christ hath left us so perfect a rule and Discipline, I understand it of that discipline which is common and general to all the church, and perpetual for all times, and so necessary that without it this whole society and company and Christian Commonwealth cannot well be kept under their Prince and King Jesus Christ." Papists deny that Christ has left us such ordinances, and " contend that it is lawful for their High Priest to rule and order that Church of God as he listeth." But St. Paul proves in 1 Timothy 6, 13, that Almighty God and Jesus Christ are the authors of the discipline which Paul taught as " constant and unchangeable, which may neither be broken by man's power or authority, nor altered for any man's favor."

" So all the corruptions which are in our church this day spring from no other head than this, that we have followed popish dreams and fantasies as most stickyng (stinking?) sinks and chanells leaving the pure fountain of the word of God. For I see . . . that the master builders of our Church in repairing of it again were so wholly bent unto the doctrine that they never thought of Discipline and so retained it still almost wholly such as it was amongst the Papists, whereupon it cometh that all the government of our church is not taken out of God's word, but out of the Canon law and decrees of Popes. . . . Out of this Canon law came all that Romish Hierarchy, primates, Archbishops, Lord Bishops. . . . Let this be the first article of the new reformation that all things be exacted as near as may be unto the word of God. That our particular laws ground upon this foundation, and let so much be admitted for Ecclesiastical Discipline as may be confirmed by the voice and authority of God himself."

Thus the writer has reiterated his position that every ordinance of the Church must be drawn from God's word; and that no ordinance of man is admissible. This countered not only the Roman teaching, but that of the English Church as put by Whitgift: " that though the Holy Scriptures were a perfect rule of faith, they were not designed as a standard of church discipline or government; but that this was changeable, and might be accommodated to the civil government we live under."

The remainder of the Travers-Cartwright book of Discipline consists in the carrying out and application of these fundamental Calvinistic Puritan principles. It will declare, first and chiefly, what pertains to those having the Church in charge, then briefly what touches the rest of the saints.

" To the bearing of any ecclesiastical office " a call or vocation is requisite. " It is the appointment of God to the bearing of some office in his church in such sort and manner as he hath ordained for every officer to be appointed by." References to the Old Testament and to the New bulwark this statement, which is then applied to distinguish ministers lawfully called from such persons as unlawfully administer the sacraments, and then to " Archdeacons, chancellors, commissaries, and the rest of that sort, who without any ground of the word of God take upon them authority to judge of all such causes *as belong to the assembly of elders to judge of and to govern the church, and to correct and punish not only the people but even the ministers themselves."* This is a statement of

the presbyterian doctrine; following upon which the need
of a specific call is finally proved by the example of Christ
himself, who exercised no office till his thirtieth year, but
" tarried for that voice of his father whereby being declared the beloved Son of God in whom only his father
was well pleased, he might be sent out to go of his em-
bassage." So let no man thrust himself forward, but
await his call,— a definite call, not to preach in general,
but to a " certain place and church,"— the last important
point is hammered in with argument and citation. Next
the examination of candidates and their ordination by the
Elders are considered.

The several offices are treated, first, that of a bishop
who " is to minister of the church in heavenly things and
such as pertain unto God,"— even as Christ said his
Kingdom was not of this world. But " bishop," as will
appear, is a generic term embracing doctors and pastors
or ministers; it does not signify a separate higher order.
The author launches forth against the secular occupations
and authority of prelates. The bishop's function is to
teach and preach the Word of God; he is but a minister
of the church. Let his wages suffice for his maintenance,
and not for pomp. Much space again is given to the
" calling to a certain place " of ministers, and to their
qualifications and maintenance; and a distinction is drawn
between Doctors and Pastors: " Doctors . . . I call
bishops who are occupied in the simple teaching and expounding of the holy doctrine and true religion . . .
without the vehement speeches whereby the minds of men
are either raised up and comforted, or beaten down and
made sad." While a pastor is " a bishop who applieth
the Scriptures to the divers occasions and necessities of
the church, and ministereth the sacraments to those which
do believe." Besides doctors and pastors, there are
deacons, who are " officers of the church set over the bestowing and distributing of the church goods and
treasury." There are also Elders who are appointed
deacons " to take heed of the offenses that arise in the
church." These " help the pastor, in the administration
of the Lord's supper . . . and take heed that none come

unto the Lord's supper whose religion and honesty is not known."

The text passes easily to the use of this famous term, Elders, which is good English for " presbyters." By it the author intends pastors and doctors, and those who are named and ordained elders; " deacons are not of this company," unless they have also been made elders. The final authority over the church is wielded by all the body of elders, which constitutes the Consistory. " For the Consistory or Council of the church is the company and assembly of the Elders of the church, who by common counsel and authority do rule and govern the same." [18] " Therefore, as Lacedemon had an assembly of Elders, Athens a high court named Areopagus, Rome a Senate, and finally every Kingdom and commonwealth a Council whose authority is chief and sovereign in all affairs, and by whom the rest of the society are governed, so likewise the church hath an assembly of Elders, by whose authority ecclesiastical and church matters are governed and administered." The Consistory has the power to admonish, to suspend, to excommunicate. The last and extreme correction is thus defined:

" Excommunication therefore is a sentence given by the Assembly of the Elders, whereby the party that is convicted of some grievous crime and offense, and can by no means be brought to repentance, being first forbidden to come to the Lord's table without prescription of any other certain time than of his repentance, is driven out from the church, and cut off from the communion and fellowship of the faithful." This definition and the subsequent treatment of excommunication is, of course, Calvinist: the member is cut off from communion with the church till he repent; he is not damned to hell.

Our book of Discipline did not regard the government of the church as a democracy, but as a government of the carefully selected best, and so an Aristocracy. Having in view the threefold Aristotelian classification of gov-

[18] On page 160 it is said, " This Consistory therefore consisteth of these three orders, Pastors, Doctors and Elders which is called by S. Paul the Assembly of Elders."

ernment,[19] it makes the following explicit statement. " Therefore forasmuch as all things are ordered and governed by the authority of certain chosen men who are chief in the congregation in godliness and virtue, we may call the government of the church *Aristocracy*, that is that government and state wherein a few of the best do bear the rule: or rather *Theocracy*, that is the government of God, seeing that they have no authority to do anything but by the word and commandment of God." This same form of ecclesiastical government extends from the individual church to the Conference of a number of churches, and to Synods, which may be either provincial or national.

The treatise finds little to say of the remaining members of the church who do not conduct its government. They are included in the company " of all the Saints and faithful." " Under the name of Saints are contained all the rest of the church which do not exercise any public office or function therein, whose duty as in all other societies is only this, to suffer themselves willingly to be ruled and governed by those whom God hath set over them."

As for magistrates and princes, " although in respect of their civil authority the church be subject to them," they are not exempted from the Apostolic command charging every one " to be subject to those who in the Lord are set over them;" for the souls of magistrates are also committed to their charge. " For seeing they (the officers of the church) not only rule by the authority of Jesus Christ, but in a manner do represent his person, seeing they rule not as they themselves list according to their own will, but only according to his word and commandment, is it not meet that even Kings and the highest magistrates should be obedient unto them? " A number of instances are cited of the submission of civil rulers, including the famous incident of Theodosius and Ambrose. Yet it is for the civil rulers " to set in order and establish the state of the Church by their authority and to preserve and maintain it according to God's will, being once established. Not that they should rule the ecclesiastical mat-

---

[19] One may observe the influence of Aristotle through the treatise; both Travers and Cartwright were scholars.

ters by their authority, for this belongeth unto Christ alone and to him he hath committed this charge; but . . . they ought to provide and see that the service of God be established as he hath appointed, and administered by such as ought to administer the same, and afterward preserved in the same simplicity and sincerity undefiled."

For " Godly princes now a days," scripture affords the patterns of David, Solomon and Hezekiah and others, whose labor was notable " in appointing the order of religion according to the word of God and the voice of the prophets," and in restoring it when decayed. " By religion I understand not only the doctrine which we profess touching the manner of serving God and the obtaining of our salvation by his Son, but also the manner of governing the Church, of appointing the officers thereof, of correcting and taking away of offenses." This is the Calvinistic scheme of Church and State.

Concluding with an eloquent supplication to the Queen, the writer adds a slight recapitulation of his book, and a description of the seemly and distinctive spiritual apparel consisting of " godly and holy knowledge and profession of religion and an undefiled life and conversation " which shall clothe them that conduct the Church of God.[20]

The *Admonition* and the Book of *Discipline* set forth the tenets and ideals of early Puritanism, which were inspired by Calvin's system. Henceforth the Puritan struggle to maintain its non-conformity, and even to set up in the realm a system of presbyterian church government, centered in parliament, and tended to identify itself with the political struggle for parliamentary supremacy as against that of the Crown. The Puritans were a party in parliament and in the realm; and the movement seemed to make wide progress. But the time was not ripe, nor conditions sufficiently favorable. The authority of Elizabeth, and the efficiency of Whitgift, proved superior to

[20] Neal, *History of the Puritans,* Appendix, No. IV, gives " a directory of Church Government . . . found in the study of . . . Mr. Thomas Cartwright," and apparently entitled " The Sacred Discipline of the Church described in the Word of God." This document is an excellent commentary on the book we have just been drawing from, with which indeed it seems to have been often confused.

Puritan recalcitrancy and the assertion of a counter-parliamentary authority.

A few months after Whitgift became archbishop, he issued his insistent Articles, in October 1583.[21] He had consulted with his bishops, and the Queen tacitly approved. These Articles declared that the laws against Catholic recusants should be enforced. But far more explicitly they prohibited non-conformist " exercises," ordered the use of the prescribed ecclesiastical apparel, and restricted preaching, reading, and ministration of the sacraments to priests and regularly admitted deacons who had acknowledged the ecclesiastical supremacy of the Queen. These were required also to subscribe to the Book of Common Prayer, with the admission that it contained nothing contrary to the word of God, and to the Articles of religion, acknowledging them all to be according to God's word. Other matters were provided for and required. The Archbishop's Articles demanded little beyond the contents of unrepealed statutes; yet they were a peremptory declaration that matters questioned and detested would be insisted on. They served notice on the ministers and congregations of the " saints " that obedience to the ordinances of the Church of England would be required of them; they demolished the already widely operative organization of elders and deacons, consistories and assemblies.

The Archbishop procured the appointment of a new ecclesiastical commission to enforce his Articles and conduct processes to oust recalcitrant ministers. He had his way in spite of objections even from Burghley himself.[22] Protestations poured in; supplications to the Queen and council, petitions to parliament. The sentiment behind these protests partly directed itself against Roman Catholicism in the realm.[23] The Puritans were not inclined to admit that the Church of Rome was a

[21] Text in Gee and Hardy, o. c. pp. 481 sqq.

[22] See letter of Burghley to Whitgift, 1584, in Strype, *Whitgift,* III, p. 104.

[23] See for example, "A project for a remedy to prevent the present falling away in religion," said to have been offered to Burghley. Strype, *Annals,* III, 1, pp. 278 sqq.

true church at all; but a sheer mass of corruption. The most violent detestation of the papists and the deepest fear of some reinstatement of the Roman Church in England, were to be found among these men who scrupled to conform to Roman survivals in the English Church.

These tendencies and anxieties found eloquent expression in a " Supplication," from the pen of Thomas Sampson, addressed to the Queen and privy-council and to parliament in 1584.[24] Its chief burden was the dearth of suitable and learned preachers residing in the parishes and attending to their duties; and it prayed for the abolition of Roman practices surviving in the English Church, to the end that the danger of a relapse to popery might forever be averted from the realm. We may fitly close our citation of Puritan manifestoes by some sonorous extracts from this admirable state paper:

" That all and every of the said pastors be bound to be resident upon his own charge; to teach and to govern the people committed to him, according to the word of God. . . . That by the diligent travail of the pastors, the Lord blessing their labours, we, which are the people of God, and your subjects, may be brought to some good understanding of the truth of the religion of God; both to believe it in heart, to confess it with mouth, and to practice it in doing, in our lives reformed. . . .

" That also no popish idolatry be suffered . . . that we all thus being godly and diligently taught and exercised in the word of the Lord, may the better see, hate, and with sorrowful hearts lament our former ignorance and blindness, in which we are carried away in popery to adore that shameful idol of the popish altar, with that blasphemous Mass, and to admit the intolerable tyranny of the primacy of the bishop of Rome, with the whole abominations of popery, as we did of late. That we now, seeing our former fall herein, may both penitently confess our said former faults, and also publicly protest to stand hereafter against all popery: promising with all our hearts all dutiful obedience to the Lord our God, according to the truth of his most holy word. That by this means we, who are the people of this land, may be brought at length to have a stayed, grounded and settled conscience in the religion of God; and not be left wavering and inclinable to all such changes in religion as men shall make. There are at this time some to be found in this land, which do fully content themselves to be so

[24] See Strype, *Annals,* III, 1, pp. 320–329, giving the text of Sampson's preface; while the text of the petition itself is in Strype, *Annals,* III, 2 (Appendix), pp. 278–302. See also, Strype, *Whitgift,* III, pp. 118 sqq.

religious as the politique laws do prescribe; but they proceed no farther. Their loyalty to good laws is not to be discommended; but they must in religion proceed further, with desire to attain to that faith which is firm, sure, and stable, and constant in God and in Christ our Saviour. Otherwise these loyal and politique subjects are not unlike to change their faith and religion so oft as politique laws are changed.

" A fearful example of this change was given in this land when Queen Mary did succeed her brother King Edward. Now, if there be no more sure hold taken of the religion of God by us . . . than politique laws can procure, we may fear, that if another Mary should succeed our Queen Elizabeth,[25] the like change would follow. Therefore we humbly desire our rulers which are godly, to devise how by all godly means we all and every one of us may be bound to the true religion of God, now received and professed among us. So that as God himself is one, and not to be changed; and his religion is one, and not to be changed; even so we, by God's grace and good means, may be fast tied to God and his true religion; that we do never depart from it, nor change it for any other. . . ."

After protesting many abuses in the government of the English church, the supplication proceeds:

" Therefore may it please the Queen's highness, with the advice of her honorable council and authority of Parliament to take order for the removing of all that shall be found but abuse in the offices of the said archbishops and bishops of this Church of England and Ireland; and provide that hereafter bishops may be pastors in humbleness, diligence, and sincerity, to feed the flock of Christ: and not be *stately bishops,* bearing lordship among politic lords. . . . And to the end that the said bishops may hereafter do that office which shall be committed to them the more sincerely, we desire that all they, and every one of them, may be delivered from the burthen of all worldly pomp, honour and charge; and not be puft up any longer with the swelling titles and dignities of worldly honour and lordship: and that they also be set free from the administration of all civil causes and offices, that they may wisely apply themselves to the labor of the gospel and ecclesiastical function, in diligence and sincerity. . . ."

" That the Lord's day, even the sabbath day, which we do barbarously call Sunday, may hereafter be kept so holily, that it be not abused, nor mispent, neither in open feasting, nor in making or using any public shews, plays, or pastimes. Nor that there be any fairs or markets kept upon any sabbath day. . . . And that all games and pastimes of shooting, bowling, cocking, bearbaiting, dances, prizes of defense, wakes, May games, and all other such rude disports, be utterly forbidden to be used upon any sabbath

[25] Mary queen of Scots was still alive.

day: and that upon great punishment to be laid upon the offenders. So that the Lord's day may be kept holy, as it is commanded. . . ."

"Last of all, we English subjects most humbly beseech the most high and excellent majesty of the Lord our God, by whom all Kings do reign, and commonwealths do stand, to move the hearts of our noble queen Elizabeth, and her nobility, and of the high court of parliament, with due care to provide in time for the sure establishing of the Gospel among us and our posterity; and also for the continuance of civil peace in this land among the inhabitants thereof by setting the succession of the crown of England safely, surely, and in quiet; where it may rest after the death of our sovereign lady queen Elizabeth. And that all they may both foresee carefully, and prevent speedily, all such dangers as do now draw nigh to us; threatening to bereave us of all the benefits which we do enjoy, by the singular goodness of God, under the happy government of our dear sovereign queen Elizabeth; and do menace to bring upon us the plague of popish idolatry, foreign government and tyranny, with such other calamities, as we by our manifold sins do justly deserve.

"O! Lord God Almighty, we do humbly beseech thee in the name of thy beloved Son our Saviour Jesus, to save our queen Elizabeth, and be merciful to our Country, England. Amen." [26]

In the latter half of Elizabeth's reign there were men who went beyond Puritan non-conformity, and apparently sought to establish independent churches composed exclusively of godly people. Such a movement appears to start from the preaching of one Robert Browne, a truculent, but wavering, and in the end quite acquiescent personality. For he returned eventually to peace and quiet in the bosom of the Church, from which he had somewhat too vigorously kicked himself loose. But if he withdrew, he had disciples who went on, and even suffered death for their opinions in the late intolerant years of the Queen. These men would separate from the English Church because it included the wicked and profane; because its government was popish, its worship idolatrous, and its episcopacy against the word of God. The people of each parish ought to choose their minister or " bishop," which every elder may be. The elders should rule the churches, over whom the civil magistrates, the queen in-

[26] Strype, *Annals,* II, 1, pp. 398 sqq.; II, 2, pp. 214–226, 332–336, and 454 sqq. gives an account of other books and petitions against vestments and popish usages in the Church of England. See also ib. III, 1, pp. 175–179, 264–267.

cluded, have no spiritual or ecclesiastical, but only civil authority.[27] The Church of England is "no true church." Rather: "The Church planted or gathered is a company or number of Christians or believers, which, by a willing covenant made with their God, are under the government of God and Christ and keep his laws in one holy communion." (R. Browne).

These people were clearly *sectaries* or separatists; but the movement was discountenanced by the majority of the Puritans, and gathered no great head in Elizabeth's reign. And even the greater movement of Puritan non-conformity, if it did not actually decline in the last years of Elizabeth, at least created less disturbance in the Church: its recalcitrancy seemed for the time somewhat subdued. The firm rule of Whitgift depressed it; while his willingness to mitigate abuses left men fewer grounds of complaint. Parliament became less Puritan, and was less occupied with religion. Even the ridicule and male-dictions poured upon prelacy by the Marprelate Tracts [28] did not hold the receding tide, and were denounced by the staid Puritans, who liked not such clever scurrility. The severity of the act of 1593 against "the wicked and dangerous practices of seditious sectaries and disloyal persons" [29] was apparently well-timed to quell Puritan dissent and purge the realm of disobedience.

A few years before the passage of this statute, when Elizabeth's policy toward the Puritans had not displayed its final severity, Sir Francis Walsingham persuasively put the government's case as against them and the papists:

"I find that the Queen's proceedings both against papists and Puritans are grounded upon these two principles:

"The one, that consciences are not to be forced, but to be won, and reduced by force of truth, with the aid of time and use of all good means of instruction and persuasion.

"The other, that causes of conscience, when they exceed their

[27] See *National Dict. of Biography,* under Robert Browne, John Green-wood and Henry Barrow. Also extracts given in Prothero, *Statutes,* &c., pp. 223-4.

[28] Finally edited and reprinted by William Pierce, with sufficient intro-ductory matter, in two volumes.

[29] The statute is given in Gee and Hardy, o. c. pp. 492-498.

bounds, and grow to be matters of faction, lose their nature: and that sovereign princes ought distinctly to punish their practices and contempt, though coloured with the pretense of conscience and religion.

"According to these principles her majesty behaved towards the papists with great mildness, not liking to make a window into their hearts, except the abundance of them overflowed into overt acts of disobedience, in impugning her supremacy. . . .

"For the other party, which have been offensive to the state, though in another degree, and which call themselves Reformers, and we commonly call Puritans, this hath been the proceeding towards them: a great while, when they inveighed against such abuses in the Church as pluralities, non-residents, and the like, their zeal was not condemned, only their violence was sometimes censured. When they refused the use of some ceremonies and rites as superstitions, they were tolerated with much connivance and gentleness; yea, when they called in question the superiority of bishops, and pretended to a democracy in the Church, their propositions were considered, and by contrary writings debated and discussed; yet all this while it was perceived that their course was dangerous and very popular; as because papistry was odious, therefore it was ever in their mouths, that they sought to purge the Church from the relics of papistry, a thing acceptable to the people who love ever to run from one extreme to another.

"Because multitudes of rogues and poverty was an eyesore, and a dislike to every man, therefore they put into people's heads that, if discipline were planted, there would be no vagabonds, no beggars, a thing very plausible; . . . . besides they opened to the people a way to government by their consistories and presbyteries, a thing though in consequence no less prejudicial to the liberties of private men than to the sovereignty of princes, yet in first show very popular; nevertheless, this, except it were in some few that entered into extreme contempt, was borne with, because they pretended in dutiful manner to make propositions, and to leave it to the providence of God and the authority of the magistrate.

"But now of late years, when there issued from them [some] that affirmed the consent of the magistrate was not to be attended; when . . . they combined themselves by classes and subscriptions; when they descended into that vile and base means of defacing the church by ridiculous pasquils; when they began to make many subjects in doubt to take oaths, which is one of the fundamental parts of justice in this land and in all places; when they began to vaunt of their strength, and number of their partisans and followers, and to use comminations, that their cause would prevail through uproar and violence, then it appeared to be no more zeal, no more conscience, but mere faction and division: and, therefore, though the state were compelled to hold somewhat a harder hand to restrain them than before, yet was it with as great moderation as the peace of the Church could permit. Thus her majesty has always observed the two rules before mentioned, in dealing tenderly with consciences, and yet in discovering faction from conscience, and softness from singularity." [30]

This letter though unfair to the Puritans, shows the political wisdom of the government. The Puritan church system was unsuited to English society, and the principle of constraining all things to precepts forced from the word of God was impracticable. With all its strength and narrow sincerity, the Puritan temper and the rigid restraint it would set on life, could not reach even a temporary dominance until the time's abounding energies had had their fling. Moreover, a certain intellectual improvement now occurring in the Church was more in harmony with these energies of life, and tended to disparage Puritanism.

[30] Letter given in Neal's *Hist. of the Puritans,* bk. I, ch. VIII, taken from Burnet, *Hist. Ref.,* Vol. III, p. 419. It was written to M. Cretoy, the French minister.

CHAPTER XXVI

THE ANGLICAN *VIA MEDIA:* RICHARD HOOKER

THE revolutions of reform and change in England lowered the morale of the clergy and wasted the revenues of the schools and universities where the clergy should have been educated. These untoward conditions appearing in the time of Henry VIII, did not improve in the short reforming reign of the boy Edward. The Marian reaction or subversion had no sound restorative effect; and accounts agree as to the dearth of educated and decently behaving clergy in the time of Elizabeth. Seemliness overspread the Church under Whitgift's rule, while a certain Anglican intellectual revival was effected by Hooker's *Ecclesiastical Polity.*

Political and religious exigencies in the early years of Elizabeth had demanded a defense of the Church as against Roman Catholic recusants: the need was met by the excellent *Apology* of Bishop Jewel. Twenty-five years later a work of genius justified the doctrines, liturgy, and ceremonials of the Church as against the Puritan attack.

Bishop Jewel of Salisbury took counsel with other divines in the composition of his *Apology,* which was published in 1562 as the authoritative defense of the Church of England against the Romanists. It was soon translated into many tongues, an excellent and also authoritative English version coming from the pen of Lady Anne Bacon, wife of Sir Nicholas and mother of the great Francis. Everywhere it was accepted as the sufficient confession and defense of the Catholic and Christian faith of the English Church. So it remained. "Three great princes successively, viz. Queen Elizabeth, King James, and King Charles, and four archbishops were so satisfied with the truth and learning contained in it, that they enjoined it to be chained up and read in all parish churches throughout England and Wales." [1]

The Romanists cry out, declares the text,

" that we are all heretics and have forsaken the faith, and have with new persuasions and wicked learning utterly dissolved the concord of the Church; that we renew, and as it were, fetch again from hell the old and many-a-day condemned heresies; that we sow abroad new sects, and such broils as never erst were heard of; also that we are already divided into contrary parts and opinions. . . . That we have seditiously fallen from the Catholic Church and by a wicked schism and division have shaken the whole world. . . . That we set nought by the authority of the ancient fathers and councils of old time; that we have . . . disannulled the old ceremonies,"

— and that we are clean given over to all wickedness.

In reply to all such allegations, the *Apology* sought to establish the legitimacy of the Church of England as a true and ancient church, neither a heresy, an innovation, nor a schism.   Its office was to show

" that God's holy gospel, the ancient bishops, and the primitive church do make on our side, and that we have not without just cause left these men, and rather have returned to the apostles and old catholic fathers . . . not colourably or craftily, but in good faith before God . . . and if they themselves which fly our doctrine, and would be called catholics, shall manifestly see how all those titles of antiquity, whereof they boast so much, are quite shaken out of their hands,"

then they may bethink themselves indeed as to which side they might better join.

Jewel's *Apology* remains the classic statement of the Anglican as against the Roman position.   There is no need to follow its proofs of its main theses, nor its presentation of the sacraments, the ministry, scripture, and ceremonies; its counter attack upon the abuses and innovations of the Roman Church, or its consideration of councils and papal supremacy.   Nor need we notice the abundant replies by Roman Catholics, or Jewel's further

---

[1] Strype, *Annals,* II, 1, p. 147.   The *Apology* and Lady Bacon's translation are printed in Vol. III of Jewel's Works, Parker Society (1848). With Jewel's *Apology* compare his letter to one Scipio, as to the Council of Trent.— Strype, *Annals,* 1, II, pp. 60–68.

Defense of his *Apology*. Rather we turn at once to his protégé, the Judicious Hooker, the only man of the English Reform whose repute has fixed a title to his name, even as Aquinas was termed Doctor Angelicus (for his marvellous and holy intellect, rather than for his disposition, of which less is known) or Duns Scotus, Doctor Subtilissimus.[2]

Isaac Walton's lovely and *précieux* " Life " of this jewel of the English Church has fixed in our minds the impression of a sensitive intellectual nature, a being of precocious and extraordinary scholarship, an ecclesiastical philosopher with a beautiful reasoning and constructive mind: a man diffident, modest, with a " dovelike " disposition; a sweet and holy man, who most fittingly should meditate upon his deathbed on the nature and number of the angels, their blessed obedience and order, praying that it might be reflected among men. This impression is borne out by whatever else is known of Hooker and above all by the quality of his works. Their style is winning in spite of its inversions; " long and pithy," says the genial Fuller, " driving on a whole flock of clauses before he comes to the close of a sentence." Whether we search the ranks of the English Church of the sixteenth century, or look among objecting Puritans or Catholic recusants, Hooker seems the one unquestionable intellectual person whose delight is to reason on the things of God and man with sweetness and persuasion. For his all considering method, he may be likened to Aquinas, whom he had studied well. In England he had one intellectual predecessor, the Welshman Reginald Pecock, who had Hooker's reasoning mind, but lacked his judiciousness.[3]

Hooker was born in Exeter in 1554, of unemphatic parents, but under the auspices of a notable uncle, John Hooker, public official, antiquary, historian, and writer of good English. The worthy man recommended his nephew Richard to the patronage of Bishop Jewel, through whose assistance doubtless the studious lad found

[2] The term " Judicious Hooker " is in Cowper's epitaph on Hooker.
[3] Ante chap. XX.

himself at the age of fourteen a poor scholar in Corpus Christi College, Oxford, which had been the scholastic nurse of both John Hooker and the bishop. Under its rugged régime Richard studied, taught, graduated as Bachelor and then as Master, till in 1579 he became a fellow, and was appointed to lecture in Hebrew. His lectures in logic had already brought him reputation. His knowledge of Aristotle, even of Plato, of the serious classics generally, likewise of the Church Fathers and of Aquinas, will impress the reader of his *Polity*.

In 1581 Hooker was summoned to preach at St. Paul's, London, and three years later received a vicarage in Buckinghamshire. He gave that up to become Master of the Temple, a church already accustomed to Puritan views. Burghley wished to appoint Travers, the author of the *Discipline,* who was lecturing there in the afternoons, while Whitgift had another candidate. The Queen approved of neither, and so Hooker was given the place. At once arose an interesting dissonance between the new master's teachings, and those of the Puritan divine: as Fuller says, it was Canterbury in the morning and Geneva in the afternoons. This proved too much for Hooker's nerves, and the archbishop suspended his opponent, who thereupon in a Supplication to the Council complained of his removal without a hearing, and elaborately defended his position. Hooker replied, although already immersed in the plan of his great undertaking, which, as he wrote to Whitgift, " he intended as a justification of the laws of our ecclesiastical polity." The Temple was too distracting; London too noisy; he needed the quiet of the country to complete his work, the importance of which and the great talents of the author, Whitgift fully recognized. He placed Hooker in a quiet parsonage not far from Salisbury, from which some years later Hooker removed to a living given him by Elizabeth near Canterbury. He is said to have had an uncouth, ill tempered wife; but she managed his affairs, and he made her his executrix, calling her " well-beloved " in his will. The first four books of the *Polity* were printed in 1594, the fifth in 1595, and the three remaining, with or without the author's last revision, after his death which occurred in 1600.[4]

Two of Hooker's earlier sermons, the one on the Certainty of Faith, the other on Justification, shed light upon the temper of his mind. His delight in distinctions and analysis is evinced in the sermon on the Certainty of Faith, which would consider why faith seems weak even in those hearts wherein grace doth shine. Surely — who would dare gainsay it! —" that which we know either by sense, or by infallible demonstration, is not so certain as the principles, articles, and conclusions of Christian faith." Every churchman, Puritan, or Roman Catholic in the sixteenth century had to admit this, which it likewise was a necessity of Hooker's saintly soul to recognize. With exquisite intellectuality his distinguishing mind proceeds to adjust the difficulty to his satisfaction:

" Concerning which we must note that there is a Certainty of Evidence and a Certainty of Adherence. Certainty of Evidence we call that, when the mind doth assent unto this or that, not because it is true in itself, but because the truth is clear, because it is manifest unto us. Of things in themselves most certain, except they be also most evident, our persuasion is not so assured as it is of things more evident, although in themselves they be less certain. It is as sure, if not surer, that there be spirits, as that there be men; but we be more assured of these than of them, because these are more evident. . . . That which we see by the light of grace, though it be indeed more certain; yet is it not to us so evidently certain, as that which sense or the light of nature will not suffer a man to doubt of."

Note the clarity and correctness of language; the writer was one of the establishers of English meanings and distinctions. And here be it said, that these sermons and the *Polity* are the finished and final expression of Anglicanism, an expression never to be surpassed. Through fit discriminations, the sermon before us would comfort men who " in heaviness of spirit suppose they lack faith, because they find not the sugared joy and delight which indeed doth accompany faith, but so as a

[4] The completed but unpublished manuscript seems to have been destroyed after his death by his wife's relations, who apparently were Puritans. The connection between the three last books as subsequently printed and the supposed completed manuscript is obscure.

separable accident. . . ."   For which last there is good
reason:

"Too much joy even spiritually would make us wantons.   Happier a great deal is that man's case, whose soul by inward deso-
lation is humbled, than he whose heart is through abundance of
spiritual delight lifted up and exalted above measure.   Better it
is sometimes to go down into the pit with him, who, beholding
darkness, and bewailing the loss of inward joy and consolation,
crieth from the bottom of the lowest hell, 'My God, my God,
why hast thou forsaken me?' than continually to walk arm in
arm with angels, to sit as it were in Abraham's bosom, and to
have no thought, no cogitation, but 'I thank my God it is not
with me as it is with other men.'   No, God will have them that
shall walk in light to feel now and then what it is to sit in the
shadow of death.   A grieved spirit therefore is no argument of
a faithless mind."

Thus he concludes with a perfect sentence, which is the
logical conclusion of his argument.

A sermon or "learned discourse of Justification,
works, and how the foundation of faith is overthrown,"
points out with perspicuity the doctrinal agreements and
differences between the English Church and the Church
of Rome, and proceeds to argue at length against the
unsound tenets of the latter.   Admirably it presents the
Church of England's teaching:

"We ourselves do not teach Christ alone, excluding our own
faith, unto justification; Christ alone, excluding our own works,
unto sanctification; Christ alone, excluding the one or the other
as necessary unto salvation.   It is a childish cavil wherewith in
the matter of justification our adversaries do greatly please themselves, exclaiming, that we tread all Christian virtues under our
feet, and require nothing in Christians but faith; because we
teach that faith alone justifieth: whereas we by this speech never
meant to exclude either hope and charity from being always
joined as inseparable mates with faith in the man that is justified;
or works from being added as necessary duties, required at the
hands of every justified man: but to show that faith is the only
hand which putteth on Christ unto justification; and Christ the
only garment, which being so put on, covereth the shame of our
defiled natures, hideth the imperfections of our words, preserveth
us blameless in the sight of God, before whom otherwise the very
weakness of our faith were cause sufficient to make us culpable,
yea, to shut us out from the Kingdom of Heaven, where nothing
that is not absolute can enter."

After further argumentative explanation, Hooker comes to what may have been the chief point and reason for his discourse. He had been accused of admitting that the Roman Church was a true Church of Christ, within which many had been saved and possibly might still be saved. Doubtless he did not think that the heretical doctrine in the Roman Church might not utterly preclude the salvation of some of its members, a view repugnant to both Lutherans and Calvinist-Puritans. Her error, says Hooker, is " that she attributeth unto works a power of satisfying God for sin, and a virtue to merit both grace here and in heaven glory. That this overthroweth the foundation of faith, I grant willingly; that it is a direct denial thereof, I utterly deny." Hooker argues that Christ is the matter of the gospel, Christ as saviour; while works " are a thing subordinate." The Roman heresy regarding them is not like a denial of Christ or his saving power; it does indeed overthrow the foundation of faith, yet " being removed by a greater distance from the foundation . . . because of that weakness, which the philosopher noteth in men's capacities when he saith, that the common sort cannot see things which follow in reason, when they follow, as it were, afar off by many deductions; therefore the repugnancy between such heresy and the foundation is not so quickly nor so easily found. . . ."

We read between the lines of the pages following, that in such a point a man may pardonably err:

" How many just and virtuous men, how many saints, how many martyrs, how many of the ancient Fathers of the Church, have had their sundry perilous opinions; and among sundry of their opinions this, that they hoped to make God some part of amends for their sins, by the voluntary punishments which they laid upon themselves . . . shall we therefore make such deadly epitaphs, and set them upon their graves, ' They denied the foundation of faith directly, they are damned, there is no salvation for them.' . . . Except we put a difference between them that err, and them that obstinately persist in error, how is it possible that ever any man should hope to be saved? . . . Give me a man . . . yea, a cardinal or a pope, whom at the extreme point of his life affliction hath made to know himself; whose heart God hath touched with true sorrow for all his sins, and filled with love toward the gospel of Christ; whose eyes are opened to see the truth, and his mouth to renounce all heresy and error . . . this one opinion of merit excepted . . . and shall I think, because of this only error, that such a man toucheth not so much as the hem of Christ's garment? . . . Is it a dangerous thing to imagine, that such men may find mercy? . . . Let me die, if ever it be proved, that simply an error, doth exclude a pope or cardinal, in such a case, utterly from hope of life. Surely, I must confess unto you, if it be an error to think, that God may be merciful to save men even when they err, my greatest comfort is my error; were it not for the love I bear unto this error, I would neither wish to speak nor to live."

Wherefore Hooker is prepared to stand by a former statement of his, "that mother-sentence, whereof I little thought that so much trouble would have grown — 'I doubt not but God was merciful to save thousands of our fathers living in popish superstitions, inasmuch as they sinned ignorantly.'" Doubt as to their salvation had come hard to these Englishmen who had set up a purer church from which such corruptions had been expunged. To bring peace to these anxious doubters was one of the objects of Hooker's discourse,— in which so beautifully appears the sweet reasonableness of his mind. No one as yet had gone beyond this in recognizing that a man might err (that is, differ from you) in cardinal doctrine and not be damned.

Hooker's great treatise bears the title *Of the Laws of Ecclesiastical Polity,* in which title the first two little words "of the" (equivalent to the common Latin *de*) suggest that the work is not intended as an exhaustive presentation of that Polity and its Laws, but rather as a disquisition upon those aspects which were a cause of controversy. It is preceded by a lengthy and weighty address entitled "A preface to them that seek (as they term it [5]) the Reformation of the Laws and Orders Ecclesiastical of the Church of England." The object of this is to persuade those who would change the order of the Church not to hold the writer as an adversary of the

[5] Hooker always is precise; here he is careful to guard against any semblance of an admission.

truth which they have embraced, but as one who would embrace with them " the selfsame truth, if it be the truth." To this end he will first examine into the founder of their discipline, John Calvin, whom he thinks " incomparably the wisest man that ever the French Church did enjoy, since the hour it enjoyed him,"— a deferential but curious phrase.

Calvin's training and genius are characterized, and his founder's work at Geneva. Then through sympathetic sentences Hooker's hand finds it way to a source of grief : each particular church did what its leaders thought good, when some " small, common conference beforehand might have eased them of much after trouble." And while each church sought in its ordering to remove further from Rome, and discords sprang from the dissimilitudes among them, still greater heart-burnings might have been avoided, " if the orders which each church did think fit and convenient for itself, had not so peremptorily been established under that high commanding form, which tendered them unto the people as things everlastingly required by the law of that Lord of lords, against whose statutes there is no exception to be taken. For by this means it came to pass, that one church could not but accuse and condemn another of disobedience to the will of Christ, in those things where manifest difference was between them." Continuing the narrative of affairs at Geneva, and pointing out the troubles that arose from conceiving every accepted regulation of the church as necessarily an irrefragible command of God, Hooker pauses again to commend the great pains of Calvin in composing his Institutions [6] of the Christian religion, and " his no less industrious travails for exposition of holy Scripture according unto the same Institutions."

From the controversies among the continental Calvinists, Hooker seems to wander over to England, and remarks on the passing of " scrupulosity " from smaller contentions as to cap and surplice to the matter of those Admonitions to parliament directed " even against all

[6] Thus at this early time the title of Calvin's *Institute* or *Institutio* was pluralized in English.

the orders and laws, wherein this church is found uncon-
formable to the platform of Geneva." Their authors
were firmly convinced of the truth of their contentions:
we are fully persuaded otherwise; let us try " to find out
which part is in error."

The first means to employ must be human discretion,
which may perhaps lead men to look rather to the opinions
of those having knowledge of the matter. Calvin recognized that common men should not dispute on civil
polity; then why are they fit to judge as to the best
ecclesiastical regiment? This was the Tudor view, even
then not universally accepted, and long since popularly
discredited. Hooker considers how common men are
drawn to think " the Spirit to be the author of their persuasions concerning discipline," by whom also they are
sealed as God's children, and separated as the godly from
the world; then how the more learned are led to try for
what they consider universal rules laid down by the
Apostles; he next touches the Puritan demand for a
disputation, and adverts to the need of some authority.

The intent of the present work is then stated as none
other " than to make it appear unto you, that for the
ecclesiastical laws of this land, we are led by great reason
to observe them, and ye by no necessity bound to impugn
them . . . my whole endeavour is to resolve the conscience, and to show as near as I can what in this controversy the heart is to think, if it will follow the light
of sound and sincere judgment, without either cloud of
prejudice, or mist of passionate affection." He places
before them his arrangement of his topics. As it seems
desirable to clear the matter of doubts and ambiguities,
he will in his first book consider " what law is, how different kinds of law there are, and what force they are
of according unto each kind." The second book will be
devoted to " the very main pillar of your whole cause,
' That Scripture ought to be the only rule of all our
actions,' and consequently that the church-orders which
we observe being not commanded in Scripture, are offensive and displeasant unto God." The third book will

consider whether Scripture sets forth any particular and unalterable form of ecclesiastical polity. The fourth, the accusation that we have " corrupted the right form of church-polity with manifold popish rites and ceremonies," utterly unallowable. The fifth " examineth the causes by you alleged, wherefore the public duties of Christian religion, as our prayers, our Sacraments, and the rest should not be ordered in such sort as with us they are." The three remaining books will severally consider the propriety of the jurisdiction of lay elders, the jurisdiction and power of bishops over other pastors, and the ecclesiastical jurisdiction and authority of the prince. Then the " preface " concludes with a consideration of the " manifold strange and dangerous innovations " which would result from the changes advocated: of which the more staid non-conformists had already seen some fruit in the separatist movements of Independents and the violence of Anabaptists.

The first book of the *Polity* is the most philosophical. One feels that the author chose to lead his readers through the broad fields of philosophic discussion that their minds might be eased of polemic rancor, and perhaps a common interest in the dispassionate search for truth might be established as a bond of sympathy between himself and them. No other part of Hooker's work so clearly shows his joy in logical thinking and lucid presentation. In this book of humane disquisition he builds with the data of learning and the instrument of reason. One's curiosity grows to see how he will later fit his disquisition upon law and reason to his argument, to which this book is a persuasive prelude, a beguilement of the reader to look at things as Hooker does. We may find difficulties in his varied uses of the word " law," which in fact has so many meanings that though an author schedule and define them beforehand, he is likely to confuse his reader and himself.

Hooker opens with one of his disarming utterances:

" He that goeth about to persuade a multitude, that they are not so well governed as they ought to be, shall never want attentive and favourable hearers; because they know the manifold defects whereunto every kind of regiment is subject, but the secret lets [hindrances] and difficulties, which in public proceedings are innumerable and inevitable, they have not ordinarily the judgment to consider."

There follows more excellent matter to the like effect. The laws of our church have been called in question, and ourselves " accused as men that will not have Jesus Christ to rule over them. . . . Behold therefore we offer the laws whereby we live unto the general trial and judgment of the whole world." Let us begin with " the nature of law in general, and of that law which giveth life unto all the rest . . . the law whereby the Eternal himself doth work. Proceeding from hence to the law, first of Nature, then of Scripture, we shall have the easier access unto those things which come after to be debated."

The Creator and all parts of the creation act under law, fundamentally under the law of the Eternal, and more directly under that kind of law applicable to the nature and exigencies of each form of being. " That which doth assign unto each thing the kind, that which doth moderate the force and power, that which doth appoint the form and measure, of working, the same we term a Law." There is God's law for Himself: " The being of God is a kind of law to his working; for that perfection which God is, giveth perfection to that he doth." Hooker proceeds ordering his matter and filling out his pellucid statements with the substance of his extraordinary learning. His Greek quotations range from Homer through the philosophers, to Hermes Trismegistus and the Greek Fathers. Better than this, his reading has been transformed into himself, and has established his thought. It were hazardous to think to find in this Elizabethan Churchman strictly original conceptions; yet the result of his study and his thinking is his own, his own admirable creation, most admirable as it may seem to us, in this first book of his *Polity*,— which contains Hooker's conservative English expression of the volume of his learning and the product of his thought.

But one must not cite too lengthily from his quite delectable exposition of

"that law which, as it is laid up in the bosom of God, they call Eternal, [but which] receiveth according to the different kinds of things which are subject unto it different and sundry kinds of names. That part of it which ordereth natural agents we call usually Nature's law; that which angels do clearly behold and without swerving observe is a law celestial and heavenly; the law of Reason, that which bindeth creatures reasonable in this world, and with which by reason they may most plainly perceive themselves bound; that which bindeth them, and is not known but by special revelation from God, Divine law; Human law, that which out of the law either of reason or of God, men probably gathering to be expedient, they make it a law."

His discourse is heartily to be recommended, not omitting his lovely presentation of the law of angels, and his pertinent argument as to how man apprehends the law of God which rules him, and attains by will and the light of reason " unto the knowledge of things that are and are not sensible."

Section VIII sets forth " the sentence of reason," as " the natural measure " to determine our doings either in a mandatory or permissive manner:

"The law of Reason or human nature is that which men by discourse of natural Reason have rightly found out themselves to be all for ever bound unto in their actions. Laws of reason have these marks to be known by. Such as keep them resemble in their voluntary actions that very manner of working which Nature herself doth necessarily observe in the course of the whole world. The works of Nature are all behoveful, beautiful, without superfluity or defect; even so theirs, if they be framed according to that which the law of reason teacheth. Secondly, those laws are investigable by Reason, without the help of Revelation supernatural and divine. Finally . . . the Knowledge of them is general, the world hath always been acquainted with them."

They were not born to-day or yesterday, but " no man knoweth how long sithence "— Hooker quotes those most famous lines from Sophocles' *Antigone*. Through this part of the *Polity* one thinks of Bishop Pecock, who unfortunately for him had not Hooker's skill in preserving the necessary harmony between the law of reason and the written Bible.

The writer adverts to the benefits from following the "law which reason teacheth us," and the ruin which would ensue if the sun and moon departed from Nature's laws for them. He then proceeds to man's need of mutually helpful fellowship and communion in societies and states, which because of envy and violence, require regulation by human laws:

"To take away all such mutual grievances, injuries, and wrongs, there was no way but only by growing unto composition and agreement amongst themselves, by ordaining some kind of government public, and by yielding themselves subject thereunto; that unto whom they granted authority to rule and govern, by them the peace, tranquillity and happy estate of the rest might be procured."

This is the social compact, the effects of which are then discussed. The law-making power is in the people:

" and by the natural law, whereunto [God] hath made all subject, the lawful power of making laws to command whole politic societies of men belongeth so properly unto the same entire societies, that for any prince or potentate . . . to exercise the same of himself, and not either by express commission immediately and personally received from God, or else by authority derived at the first from their consent upon whose persons they impose laws, it is no better than mere tyranny."

Hooker passes on to discuss the variety and change of human laws, occasioned by the various and changing conditions of human societies; also the law of nations, which serves not merely the ends of traffic and confederacy, but the delights of farthest human intercourse, the natural desire " of society and fellowship with all mankind. . . . An effect of that very natural desire in us . . . appeareth by the wonderful delight men have, some to visit foreign countries, some to discover nations not heard of in former ages, we all to know the affairs and dealings of other people, yea to be in league of amity with them." Here is a true Elizabethan note, which has its almost conscious affinity with the first lines of the *Odyssey!*

Supernatural laws are revealed in Scripture for the

salvation and uttermost satisfaction of the highest desires of men, and their instruction in faith and hope and perfect charity. But also " Scripture is fraught even with laws of Nature," as to which " evidence of God's own testimony added to the natural assent of reason concerning the certainty of them, doth not a little comfort and confirm the same." Scripture and Nature supplement, and shed light upon each other: they " do serve in such full sort, that they both jointly and not severally either of them be so complete, that unto everlasting felicity we need not the knowledge of anything more,"— distinctly not the knowledge of the traditions which the Roman Church alleges to be also divine truth.

So he considers the various kinds of law, their nature and the grounds of their force.

" Lest therefore any man should marvel whereunto all these things tend, the drift and purpose of all is this, even to shew in what manner, as every good and perfect gift, so this very gift of good and perfect laws is derived from the Father of lights; to teach men a reason why just and reasonable laws are of so great force, of so great use in the world; and to inform their minds with some method of reducing the laws whereof there is present controversy unto their first original causes, that so it may be in every particular ordinance thereby the better discerned, whether the same be reasonable, just, and righteous, or no. Is there anything which can either be thoroughly understood or soundly judged of, till the very first causes and principles from which originally it springeth be made manifest? "

These sentences, especially the last one, are expressions of the writer's nature, and point his thesis. All the kinds of law which he has expounded sound in the nature and eternal law of God. His opponents " rightly maintain that God must be glorified in all things, and that the actions of men cannot tend unto his glory unless they be framed after his law, so it is their error to think that the only law which God hath appointed unto men in that behalf is the sacred Scripture." This is the very point of disagreement to which he has come, now fully equipped to show on his side that men glorify God as natural agents when they breath and sleep, and by yet another law glorify him in rational and moral acts, and still further by fitting observance of the human laws of society and nations. "Thus we see how even one and the selfsame thing is under divers considerations conveyed through many laws; and that to measure by any one kind of law the actions of men were to confound the admirable order, wherein God hath disposed all laws, each as in nature, so in degree, distinct from other."

Fresh from the conclusions of the first book, Hooker in the second directs his argument against those would-be reformers of the Church who hold that Scripture is the only rule in human affairs. Easily he shows that the position attacked is unwarranted either by Scripture or reason, or the consensus of human authority. He disproves the bearing of the Scriptural texts brought forward by the Puritans, and enlarges his own premises, pointing out again the many channels through which the divine wisdom flows to men, disclosing too his profound reverence for all forms of enlightenment:

"Whatsoever either men on earth or the angels of heaven do know, it is as a drop of that unemptiable fountain of wisdom; which wisdom hath diversely imparted her treasures unto the world. As her ways are of sundry kinds, so her manner of teaching is not merely one and the same. Some things she openeth by the sacred books of Scripture; some things by the glorious works of nature; with some things she inspireth them from above by spiritual influence; in some things she leadeth and traineth them only by worldly experience and practice. We may not so in any one special kind admire her, that we disgrace her in any other; but let all her ways be according unto their place and degree adored."

He would not with the Puritans "abate the estimation and credit of man" by insisting upon drawing "all things under the determination of bare and naked Scripture;" rather he points out the unavoidable need of human authority to accredit and explain the holy text; — though ten thousand general councils are not to be believed against "one demonstrative reason alleged, or one manifest testimony cited from the mouth of God himself to the contrary. . . . The testimonies of God are all sufficient unto that end for which they were given . . . the absolute perfection of Scripture is seen by relation unto that end whereto it tendeth." There are two opposite errors: the one of the schools of Rome which hold that Scripture alone, without tradition, does not contain all revealed truth necessary for salvation; the other of those who hold that Scripture not only contains all things necessary for salvation, " but all things simply, and in such sort that to do anything according to any other law were not only unnecessary but even opposite unto salvation, unlawful and sinful."

Proceeding along the general course of the argument, the third book addresses itself to the Puritan position that Scripture necessarily contains " a form of church polity, the laws whereof may in nowise be altered." Passing over his interesting and enlightening discussion, we may pause at some self-revealing passages touching the preciousness of all Knowledge and the just guidance of reason in matters of faith.

" There is in the world no kind of Knowledge, whereby any part of truth is seen, but we justly account it precious; yea, that principal truth, in comparison whereof all other knowledge is vile, may receive from it some kind of light; whether it be that Egyptian and Chaldean wisdom mathematical, wherewith Moses and Daniel were furnished; or that natural, moral, and civil wisdom, wherein Solomon excelled all men; or that rational and oratorial wisdom of the Grecians, which the Apostle St. Paul brought from Tarsus; or that Judaical, which he learned in Jerusalem sitting at the feet of Gamaliel: to detract from the dignity thereof were to injure even God himself, who being that light which none can approach unto, hath sent out these lights whereof we are capable, even as so many sparkles resembling the bright fountain from which they rise."

St. Paul teacheth " that nature hath need of grace, whereunto I hope we are not opposite, by holding that grace has use of nature." And he adds in another passage:

" Yea, whatsoever our hearts be to God and to his truth, believe we or be we as yet faithless, for our conversion or confirmation the force of natural reason is great. The force whereof unto those effects is nothing without grace. What then? To our purpose it is sufficient, that whosoever doth serve, honour, and obey God, whosoever believeth in Him, that man would no more do this than innocents and infants do, but for the light of natural reason that shineth in him, and maketh him apt to apprehend those things of God, which being by grace discovered, are effectual to persuade reasonable minds and none other, that honour, obedience, and credit belong of right to God."

Reason, moreover, is our aid to assure us rightly that the Spirit is really working in us. "Albeit the Spirit lead us into all truth and direct us in all goodness, yet because these workings of the Spirit in us are so privy and secret, we therefore stand on a plainer ground, when we gather by reason from the quality of things believed or done, that the Spirit of God hath directed us in both, than if we settle ourselves to believe or to do any certain particular thing, as being moved thereunto by the Spirit."

O sweet reason! how would the Judicious Hooker bring thee into things of grace! But he too must protest, and crave not so to be understood " as if any such thing by virtue thereof could be done without the aid and assistance of God's most blessed Spirit. The thing we have handled according to the question moved about it; which question is whether the light of reason be so pernicious, that in devising laws for the Church men ought not by it to search what may be fit and convenient." Again he turns to his conviction: " The light of natural understanding, wit, and reason, is from God."

The arguments of the fourth book are addressed to the Puritan assertion " that our form of Church polity is corrupted with popish orders, rites, and ceremonies, banished out of certain reformed churches, whose example therein we ought to have followed." At the close Hooker dwells upon the gradual and politic process of the English Reform; how that the Church of England in altering such of her previous ceremonies as hindered piety, considered " that the change of laws, especially concerning matters of religion, must be warily proceeded in." Human laws prove imperfect, even pernicious, and require abrogation. But " alteration though it be from worse to better hath in it inconveniences, and those weighty." The need must be clear, and the benefit substantial.

" Touching ceremonies harmless in themselves, and hurtful only in respect of number; was it amiss to decree, that those things which were least needful and newliest come should be the first that were taken away, as in the abrogating of a number of saints' days, and of other the like customs, it appeareth they did; till afterwards the Form of Common Prayer being perfected, Articles of sound Religion and Discipline agreed upon, Catechisms framed for the needful instruction of youth, churches purged of things that indeed were burdensome to the people or to the simple offensive and scandalous, all was brought at the length unto that wherein now we stand? Or was it amiss, that having this way eased the Church as they thought of superfluity, they went not on till they had plucked up even those things . . . which to abrogate without constraint or manifest harm thereby arising, had been to alter unnecessarily (in their judgments) the ancient received custom of the whole Church, the universal practice of the people of God, and those very decrees of our fathers, which were not only set down by agreement of general councils, but had accordingly been put in use and so continued in use till that very time present? "

For the Church of England violently to have cast forth things indifferent or even innocent because pertaining to the Church of Rome —

" this kind of proceeding might haply have pleased some few men, who having begun such a course themselves must needs be glad to see their example followed by us. But the Almighty which giveth wisdom and inspireth with right understanding whomsoever it pleaseth him, he foreseeing that which man's wit had never been able to reach unto, namely, what tragedies the attempt of so extreme alteration would raise in some parts of the Christian world, did for the endless good of his Church (as we cannot choose but interpret it) use the bridle of his provident restraining hand, to stay those eager affections in some, and to settle their resolution upon a course more calm and moderate."

The polity of the English Church had not before been set out so appealingly as in this passage,— indeed, as in this whole great work of Richard Hooker.

The fifth book is larger than all the first four and the ' Preface ' taken together. As comports with the extent and importance of the subject matter, Hooker makes his approach with dignified preambulatory step. The subject is presented in the body of the book, as follows:

"There is an inward reasonable, and there is a solemn outward serviceable worship belonging unto God. . . . Solemn and serviceable worship we name for distinction's sake, whatsoever belongeth to the Church or public society of God by way of external adoration." This is "ordered, partly, and as touching principal matters, by none but precepts divine only; partly, and as concerning things of inferior regard, by ordinances as well human as divine: about the substance of religion wherein God's only law must be kept there is here no controversy; the crime now intended against us is, that our laws have not ordered those inferior things as behoveth, and that our customs are either superstitious, or otherwise amiss, whether we respect the exercise of public duties in religion, or the functions of persons authorized thereunto."

The entire public worship of the Church is called in question and will be defended in this book.

The pleader requests the admission of four general propositions, or canons, which he thinks "no man of moderate judgment hath cause to think unjust or unreasonable."

First: That those external religious forms which appear or can be shown to promote godliness, "either as betokening the greatness of God, or as beseeming the dignity of religion, or as concurring with celestial impressions in the minds of men, may be reverently thought of," notwithstanding a few "curable inconveniences."

Secondly: "That in things the fitness whereof is not of itself apparent . . . the judgment of antiquity concurring . . . may induce" those to acquiesce who cannot allege a strong reason against it.

In regard to the third, he premises that "The Church hath authority to establish that for an order at one time, which at another time it may abolish, and in both it may do well. But that which in doctrine the Church does now deliver rightly as a truth, no man will say that it may hereafter recall, and as rightly avouch the contrary." He would have it granted, that where no law divine, nor any argument of reason, nor any public inconvenience, "make against that which our own laws ecclesiastical have (although but newly) instituted for the ordering of these affairs, the very authority of the Church itself . . . may give so much credit to her own laws," as to outweigh " any bare and naked conceit to the contrary."

Fourthly, seeing that necessity and great utility must sometimes sway, " we lastly require that it may not seem hard, if in cases of necessity, or for common utility's sake, certain profitable ordinances sometime be released."

Such were the premises or presumptions, persuasive and difficult to controvert, which Hooker asked his opponents to grant. To have assented would have made the Puritan position still more difficult. Hooker's work in fact led sweet reason captive to the Church, and left the Puritans to the bare poles of Scripture. Admirable is the pleading of this book in support of the whole Liturgy of the English Church, those exquisite prayers, lessons, and absolutions, those seemly, not too impressive, ceremonies all modulated in a ritual which is to the Roman as the perfect late Gothic church of St. Ouen is to the overwhelming Cathedral of Chartres. Likewise the book vindicates the Anglican sacramental attitude and corresponding practices. These controversies are no longer pressing, nor their substance as vital as it was in the sixteenth and seventeenth centuries. So we may pass over the last three questionably completed books treating of the alleged jurisdiction of lay-elders, of the jurisdiction and honored state of bishops, and of the King's ecclesiastical supremacy.

The *Polity* aptly concludes the period of Anglican schism and reform which created the Church of England. Throughout the course of separation, self-formulation and ceremonial establishment, the English Church evinces its English character and temper, and proves itself, and most clearly in the work of Hooker, a Catholic expression of English faculties, institutions, and social conditions. The Church is as clear an expression of England as the " English Constitution " or the Common Law. These were English products, effects having English social conditions, faculties and exigencies for their causes; yet in every phase of their evolution they were also *causes,* moulding the people from whom they sprang. Similarly the

Church was a result, an effect, and likewise a moulding cause, impressing its seemliness, its modulation, its ecclesiastical decencies upon the English race. But of course, just as all elements of the English Constitution have never been acceptable to all Englishmen, so the English Church was not tolerable to all. Roman Catholicism continued, Puritan non-conformity developed, not to mention more violent ebullitions of dissent.

The Puritan movement also was English. Doubtless it drew its immediately informing principles from Geneva. Possibly they proved an element, one cannot say of weakness, but of eventual impermanence; for Calvinism was not suited to the English mind and temper either as a system of belief or as a social and political method of control. The material abuses within the English Church, the unequal conditions of life in England, the hard lot of the laboring poor, were among the occasions or temporary moving causes of Puritanism, as they had been with Lollardy. One cannot observe the rise of Puritanism and follow its growth without perceiving that it was of old Lollard stock. Wyclif and the " Lay Party " were its forbears, and, in spite of gaps in the genealogy, the Lollard stock and temper re-emerge in Latimer and Hooper, and all who represented gospel tendencies within and without the English Church. In suggestive corroboration one may point to the intellectual affinity and occasional coincidence of position between Pecock and Hooker, the two most intellectual *opponents* of these protests against the established Church.[7]

Both author and translator of the *Book of Discipline* [8] regarded their church system as an aristocracy of the most godly. Tendencies in Puritanism toward political equality or freedom nevertheless lay in the asserted right of self-decision in religion, or more specifically in the right and duty in every man to read and understand Scripture for himself, and draw rules of life from it, by which he was commanded of God to guide his conduct. This also

[7] Though Wyclif lacked the doctrine of Justification by Faith, he was in some sense approaching it through his denial of the efficacy of pilgrimages and other observances of the Church, and of papal absolutions.

[8] Ante p. 145 sqq.

was akin to the tendencies of the Lollard " poor preachers " and their " lay party."

Calvin himself disapproved of riotous rebellion on the
part of subjects.   Yet he recognized the right of a people
organized under their appointed magistrates to take coercive measures against tyranny.   His followers and successors overruled his hesitations.   More than one powerful assertion of the principle came from the lips of John
Knox: for example in his argument with Maitland-Leth-
ington, who would take him to task for threatening the
idolatry of Queen Mary Stuart: " What harm should the
commonwealth receive, if the corrupt affections of ignorant rulers were moderated, and so bridled by the wisdom
and discretion of godly subjects that they should do wrong
nor violence to no man? . . . I speak of the people
assembled together in one body of one commonwealth,
to whom God has given sufficient force, not only to resist,
but also to suppress all kinds of open idolatry.   Such a
people, I affirm yet again, are bound to keep their land
clean and unpolluted." [9]

But the Puritan spirit was hard and narrow.   It detested, for example, the wit and zest and life in the
Marprelate Tracts, though they were directed against
its enemies.   It was unlovely and was not loved in
Elizabethan England, where there was no great sympathy with the Puritan horror of May games, dancing, and
" desecration of the Sabbath."   The broad currents of
English popular sentiment were in Shakespeare's plays,
which drew their themes from pride of nationality and
ardors of martial loyalty or equally martial feudalism,
and from all the lust and pride and energy of life which
was bursting forth in the England of the last half of the
sixteenth century.

[9] John Knox, *History of the Scotch Reformation,* Bk. IV.   Knox's *Confession of Doctrine,* and the Scotch (mainly Knox's) *Book of Discipline* (both
of 1560–61) were products of Scotch Calvinism.   The *Book of Discipline*
was especially potent in moulding the characters of those for whom it was
composed.   It was a militant constitution, calculated to keep the Kirk alert
and hostile to papistry.   It provides a system of mutual observation, almost
inquisition, admonition and disciplinary punishment; it presents a complete
organization of religion and education, and in spiritual jurisdiction steps
into the place of the Roman and English Churches.

Fully to realize why Puritanism might not then triumph, and why the Anglican Reformation could hold its broad middle way, sloughing off Romanism and rebuffing Puritanism with equal vigor, one must look beyond the religious movements to other phases of the spirit of Elizabethan England,— to its whole and vigorous love of life, the expansion of its daring, the vaunt and happiness of its poetry, and withal to its love of seemly form and fitting social conventions, which were conventions of the *via media*. The way of the Anglican Church was the only path religion could have trod. Elizabethan England could not re-enslave itself in popery: compare its literature with that of the Catholic reaction in Italy — Shakespeare with Tasso! Nor could it bind itself up in Puritanism. Either of these bands would have burst and much would have been spilled in the catastrophe.

The time of Elizabeth, and of Henry VIII as well, was not religious in the sense of other-worldly. It was entranced by the delights of living. With the Elizabethans, religion was an adjunct and a regulation of social life. As an institution of the State it ignored the recesses of the soul. The Church of England was adjusted both to the royal government and to the structure of English society. Its polity, ritual and doctrine agreed with the social and economic relations among the nobility, gentry and people. It interposed no barrier to commercial expansion or maritime enterprise, whatever the nature of the venture. It did not hamper the free human development of the open-minded, or deflect the intellectual progress of the thoughtful. It shed no blight upon the flowering of the lyric and dramatic genius of Elizabethan England.

CHAPTER XXVII

ELIZABETHANS

I

ELIZABETH, her statesmen, courtiers, ocean-adventurers, poets, seem to us complex, not readily decipherable. Their characters were not mediaeval, certainly not antique, and by no means a mere graft from the humane enlightenment and moral disillusionment of Italy. They were unlike the French: the brutalities differed on the two sides of the channel; nor did Elizabethans have the Gallic consistency and logic. Often their natures seem to lack unity. Sentiment and conduct do not agree, nor the acts of one day tally with the words of another. The actors are strangely affected by the personal exigency or opportunity and the turn of fortune. One suspects insincerity. Sometimes deceitfulness seems the unifying or explanatory element of their characters. Perhaps their remarkable faculty of expression opens a more interesting explanation.

The sixteenth century loosed the tongue of northern Europe; men had become voluble, with an extraordinary faculty of words. Royalty possessed the gift: Henry VIII, Elizabeth, Mary Stuart, Henri Quatre. So statesmen and Churchmen and reformers: Luther, Calvin, Knox, Hooker; so Montaigne and Rabelais. The very statutes of Henry VIII and Elizabeth are eloquent; they make out a case and are convincing. People of impulsive energy and vivid desire, when possessed of the gift, or by the gift, of facile emotional utterance, are apt to seem different beings at one time and another, as they may be affected by their impulses or carried along by their own eloquence. Expression enhances the emotional feeling, deepens the transforming effect; words make the man more passionate, more altogether what he feels at the moment and is expressing. And just as feeling is a phase

of personality, so is the expression. The two combine
in phases still more transforming. These very expressive
Elizabethans, so eager, so in love with their desires and
enamored of the vain-glory of life, seem to change under
adversity and the approach of a tragic end. As in the
flush of action they had shown themselves in the likeness
of the dominant desire, now final calamity resolves them
into an expression of appropriate sentiments and
thoughts: purified, they become sublime in the presence
of the executioner.

The natures of men have always been affected by altered fortunes. But the change was more vivid with the
Elizabethans. It was part of their dramatic faculty,
their Shakespearean power. Shakespeare's own characters, true Elizabethans, exemplify the same: his wicked
Dukes in *Tempest* and *As You Like It*. How marvellously sorry for himself does that useless footless King,
Richard II, become through the exquisite expression of
his sorrow for himself, which the poet gives him. And
Buckingham in *Henry VIII,* how beautifully does he die;
and at the end that harsh and grasping cardinal makes us
hate with him the " vain pomp and glory of this world,"
and with him wish that we had served our God with
somewhat more exclusive zeal.

There is even a curious parallel of phrase, showing
how the imagery used by the great dramatist might be
employed in speech or actual letters. Shakespeare's
Wolsey says to Crumwell:

> I have ventured,
> Like little wanton boys that swim on bladders,
> This many summers in a sea of glory,
> But far beyond my depth: my high blown pride
> At length broke under me, and now has left me
> Weary and old with service, to the mercy
> Of a rude stream, that must for ever hide me.

In 1530 when Crumwell was more busily employed in
ensuring his own fortunes than in stemming the tide which
overwhelmed his patron, a friend wrote him in congratulation and warning: " A merry semblance of weather often
thrusteth men into the dangerous seas, not thinking to be

so suddenly oppressed with tempest when unawares they are prevented and brought in great jeopardy. The winds are mutable, unsure, and will not be carried in men's hands to blow at a beck." [1] In such figures, thirty-four years before Shakespeare was born, men saw life's chances.

So perhaps the best key to the many-sided and often seemingly inconsistent personalities of the Elizabethans may be found in their abundant power of expression. It carried them along with it; made them for the time what they expressed; it brought reality to their apparent acting. Elizabeth herself was histrionic to the point of transformation: she seems verily to become, to change into the rôle she plays.

Elizabeth! There are some natures so many sided and unexpected and so dexterous as to slip through whatever net fate seems to spread for them. Character is fate! Elizabeth's endowment wove a fate for her full and glorious, vain-glorious as well to meet her vanities. Hers was a deft stepping amid whirlpools, her balance imperilled by ruffs and farthingales and furbelows — the whims and infatuations and enormous vanities of a woman pleased with pageantry and lusty shows, accepting the conventional adulation accorded English sovereigns, delighting in her popularity, and almost beyond sanity tickled by the preposterous sighings and wooings of adorers,— yet through her own vanities understanding men the better.

Another maid would have been wrecked in the perilous temptations which infested Elizabeth's unlovely girlhood. Her mother beheaded, she was reared not by wise, but by foolish women. Henry's last wife, Katharine Parr, for a while brought order to the entourage of the princess; but after Henry's death Katharine married that rapacious handsome rake, Admiral Sir Thomas Seymour, brother of Jane Seymour and of Somerset, and uncle of the boy-king. She could not keep that husband from romping with a hoyden girl, nor from questionable advances, which became unabashed proposals of marriage when he shortly became a widower. Elizabeth was not sixteen when she

[1] Merriman, *Life and Letters of Thomas Crumwell.*

had to repress her feelings for this taking swaggerer of
thirty-five, and disentangle herself from complicity in the
rebellious conduct which brought her would-be paramour
and husband to the block. Shrewdly she stepped over
the toils spread for her, and boldly cast back the imputa-
tions on her girlhood's honor. With a better governess
in charge of herself and her household, she betook herself
to study under her tutor Roger Ascham. Her mind had
always been inquisitive; she spoke French and Italian, and
from this time on, Latin, while she also learned some
Greek. The Greek and Latin classics were read with
Ascham, and Elizabeth began, or continued, a fruitful
study of history. She devoted herself to loving her royal
brother, and writing most proper letters to him, who evidently loved her in return.[2]

The princess of not quite twenty years who rode with
a brilliant and armed retinue to London to salute and aid
her sister Mary, was well equipped to meet the more
deadly perils which beset her in that jealous sister's reign.
Conformity to the re-established Catholicism, circumspect
abstention from all protestant and treasonable intrigue,
firmness of assertion and denial when accused and persecuted, helped to keep her neck from the axe, while the
loyalty of many an Englishman, and the re-considered
policy of Philip, in the end secured her life. Bitterly she
learned to know the Tower as a prison,— inquiring more
than once whether Lady Jane's scaffold had been removed.
It might have been left for her! Elizabeth did not want
to die; _her_ thoughts were not set on heaven, but pursued
the delights of living, of flattery, of seeing men kneeling
around her, of scheming, plotting, acting, deciding or refusing to decide, in a word, of being Queen.

Consummate actress — nay she rather was the rôle
she took! Dissimulator, nay she was her simulation! she
was everything she showed herself in that entrancing
entry into London after Mary's death; it was not acting
but being, through which she responded to every plaudit

[2] See Ellis, _Original Letters,_ 1st series, Vol. II, pp. 146, 160. Others are
in Miss Strickland's _Life,_ who seems elaborately to praise, and heartily to
detest, Elizabeth.

and good wish, and symbol of congratulation, and was
the pivot of her people's swirl of joy, kissing the Bible
handed to her, folding it to her breast, while she looked
into the people's eyes, and caught the crash of ordnance.
Elizabeth had life before her and would sip it — till she
saw the unavailing painted face of an old woman in the
bottom of the cup! [3]

She was fearless, having the best of nerves; she did not
worry, but tormented others.   She enjoyed the excite-
ments and perils of her reign.   She was in and of her
queenship and loyal to her realm.   She would hoodwink
her people, but never betray them.   Her welfare was
theirs, although she maintained herself and her court
after the manner of her day, and fed her favorites on
monopolies, since church and abbey lands had been distributed.   Late in her reign she realized that monopolies
might be a burden to the people.[4]   Clever as she was at
her accession, she learned from year to year, and
strengthened her policy out of her experience.   It was a
policy indeed, set with ruffs and frills, screened with preposterous coquetry, whimsical and elusive, and blind to
the keenest angriest eyes, disdaining no makeshift, using
every aid, merely deflected by obstacles, guided by opportunity.   Withal it was an English policy, that of the *via
media* at home, and abroad that of England holding the
balance between Catholic opposites, and sustaining the
Huguenots and Protestant Lowlanders.   Thanks to the

---

[3] Jusserand, *Literary Hist. of the English People,* gives in a note to Vol.
II, p. 328, the following extract from Hayward's *Annales,* descriptive of
the Queen: . . . "in coupling mildness with majesty as she did, and in
the stately stouping to the meanest sort.   All her faculties were in motion
. . . her spirit seemed to be everywhere. . . . Some she pitied, some she
thanked, at others she wittily and pleasantly jested, contemning no person,
neglecting no office; and distributing her smiles, looks and graces, so arti-
ficially, that thereupon the people redoubled the testimonies of their joys."
Ellis, *Letters,* 2nd Ser., Vol. III, pp. 191–196, contains interesting general
remarks by a contemporary upon the Queen's character, attainments, tastes,
and methods: referring to her "magnificence in apparel," her love of
jewels, her manner of delaying and at last freely granting offices, her
courage under danger of assassination, her hasty temper, quickly appeased,
her attainments in Latin, French, Italian and Greek, and then the manner
of her death. She translated for her recreation Sallust's *Jugurtha,*
Horace's *De Arte Poetica,* Plutarch's *De Curiositate.*

[4] See, Prothero, *Statutes,* &c., pp. 111–117.   James was obliged to abolish
monopolies in 1624, see ib. p. 276.

policy of Elizabeth and Burghley and to the energies of Englishmen, that England which upon Mary's death was likened to a bone thrown to two dogs, became the arbiter of other destinies besides her own.

To marry or not to marry, was a first personal and political question.   Elizabeth intended to be queen.   In the sixteenth century men thought that a woman-ruler needed a husband's tutelage: Mary had involved the realm in a Spanish tutelage.   Elizabeth intended to be queen herself, and no queen-wife to a husband ruling because he was her husband and she his wife.   Here was personal reason enough why Elizabeth would not marry; and as for reasons of state, political strengthenings or entanglements, time has shown that there was not one among all the actual or putative candidates whose marriage to the queen would not have been a bane to her reign and to her realm, and to England's future.   She replied with wise tergiversation to the anxieties expressed by her first parliament lest she should die childless:

" Concerning marriage, which ye so earnestly move me to, I have been long since persuaded, that I was sent into this world by God to think and do those things chiefly which may tend to his glory.   Hereupon have I chosen that kind of life which is most free from the troublesome cares of this world, that I might attend the service of God alone. . . . These things have I thought upon when I was a private person.   But now that the public care of governing the Kingdom is laid upon me, to draw upon me also the cares of marriage may seem a point of inconsiderate folly.   Yea, to satisfy you I have already joined myself in marriage to an husband, namely the Kingdom of England.   And behold, which I marvell ye have forgotten, the pledge of this my wedlock and marriage with my Kingdom."

She drew her coronation ring from her finger, and showed it to them.   Then, after a pause continued:

" Do not upbraid me with miserable lack of children; for every one of you, and as many as are Englishmen, are children and kinsmen to me. . . . I commend you that ye have not appointed me an husband, for that were most unworthy the majesty of an absolute princess, and unbeseeming your wisdom, which are subjects born.   Nevertheless if it please God that I enter into another course of life, I promise you that I will do nothing which may be prejudicial to the commonwealth, but will take such a husband, as near as may be, as will have as great a care of the Commonwealth as myself. But if I continue in this kind of life I have begun, I doubt not that God will so direct mine own and your counsels, that ye shall not need to doubt of a successour which may be more beneficial to the Commonwealth than he which may be born of me, considering that the issue of the best princes many times degenerateth. And to me it shall be a full satisfaction, both for the memorial of my name, and for my glory also, if when I shall let my last breath, it be engraven upon my marble tomb: Here lieth Elizabeth, which reigned a virgin and died a virgin." [5]

Often Elizabeth was ungracious with her Commons, rebuffing sharply every possible encroachment on the initiative and freedom of her royal prerogative. She could also open her mind and disclose her purposes to them as she rarely did to her own councillors. It was the truth she told this first parliament, that she wished never to marry; and it was the best truth she was capable of when she assured them she would do nothing injurious to the realm, and would in all her acts regard its welfare. That remained an aim inspired not merely by intellectual recognition of the identity of her own security with the safety and prosperity of her people, but proceeding from the one stable affection which she knew. She cared for her people, relied on their support as her chief strength, and rejoiced in their affection. If it was policy, it was also affection that led her frequently to declare: " That she could believe nothing of her people which parents would not believe of their children." [6]

For individuals among her servants and favorites she cared less steadily. With transient and often scanty gratitude she accepted services rendered with devotion. Sir Francis Walsingham, each year the poorer for his great services to Elizabeth and England, is said to have been buried at night that his poverty might not be seen.[7] Elizabeth accepted also the adulation of such as were expecting favours in return. She enjoyed it, though the

[5] As given in Camden's *Elizabeth,* under the year 1559. A somewhat different text is given in Nichols, *Progresses,* etc., I, pp. 63–65.

[6] Camden, *Elizabeth,* under the year 1579. And see her speech to the troops in Tilbury Camp on the approach of the Armada, given in Nichols, *Progresses of Elizabeth,* II, p. 536.

[7] Camden, o. c. under the year 1590.

all-flattered Queen was not likely to love the flatterers faithfully. At times they seemed to her like a pack of whispering servants.

Rough was her speech when angered; caustic her pen. Sir Robert Carey writes to his father, Lord Hunsdon, of the Queen's displeasure at his delay in going to his government of Berwick: " She grew into a great rage, beginning with ' God's wounds, that she would set you by the feet; and send another in your place, if you dallied with her thus, for she would not be thus dallied withal." [8]

Her anger was not lasting; but she had small pity. As early as 1571, when fifteen years more of captivity were still before Mary Stuart, who already plagued the Queen, Elizabeth writes to her:

" Madame, of late time I have received divers letters from you to the which you may well guess, by the accidents of time, why I have not made any answer; but specially because I saw no matter in them that required any such answer as could have contented you, and to have discontented you had been but an increase of your impatience which I thought time would have mitigated as it doth commonly where the cause thereof is not truly grounded . . . but now finding by your last letter of the 27th of the last [month] an increase of your impatience tending also to many uncomely passionate and vindicative speeches, I thought to change my former opinion and by patient and advised words to move you to stay, or else to qualify, your passions, and to consider that it is not the manner to obtain good things with evil speeches, nor benefits with injurious challenges, nor to get good to yourself with doing evil to another.

" And yet to avoid the fault which I note you have committed in filling a long letter with multitude of sharp and injurious words I . . . have chosen to commit to my cousin the Earl of Shrewsbury [Mary's very faithful keeper] the things which I have thought meet . . . to be imparted to you . . . wishing you the same grace of God that I wish to myself, and that he may direct you to desire and attain to that which is meet for his honor and your quietness. . . .   Your Cousin that wisheth
                                you a better mind." [9]

In fatal years to come, Elizabeth was to doubt long and sorely as to the execution of the ever-plotting Mary. [10]

[8] Ellis, *Letters,* 2nd Ser., III, p. 102, June, 1584.
[9] Ellis, *Original Letters,* 2nd Series, Vol. III, p. 1.
[10] See her " answer without an answer," to the Chancellor and the

She had vacillated very genuinely in another case, when
she wrote to Burghley staying the execution of the Duke
of Norfolk:

" My lord, me thinks that I am more beholding to the hinder
part of my head than well dare trust the forwards side of the same,
and therefore sent . . . the order to defer this execution. . . .
The causes that move me to this are not now expressed, lest an
irrevocable deed be in meanwhile committed. . . .

Your most loving Sovereign,
Elizabeth R." [11]

Adept as she was herself at prevarication and down-
right lying, she could despise lies in a character despicable
for its weakness, and could speak in excellent reproof, as
when she upbraided the young King James of Scotland
for breaking his word: " Among your many studies, my
dear Brother and Cousin, I would Isocrates' noble lesson
were not forgotten, that wills the Emperor his sovereign
to make his words of more account than other men their
oaths, as meetest ensigns to show the truest badge of a
prince's arms." And the letter proceeds to become
more specific in its recommendations.[12]

In spite of all that has been said of her queer familiari-
ties with favorites, her ready oaths and angry lapses from
decorum, Elizabeth possessed an inner dignity of mind
and temper suiting the outer stateliness of ceremonial
which surrounded and accompanied her. An instance of
her self-possessed dignity was her reply when nearly
sixty-five years old to the Ambassador of the Polish King,
who at his first audience harshly and unexpectedly blurted
out the demands of his master. Amazed, the Queen
answered him in Latin, the language which he had
used:

" Oh, how was I deceived! I looked for an ambassage, but you
have brought a complaint. I took you for a legate, but find you
a herald. Never in my life have I heard such words; I marvell indeed at such unusual boldness in public speech. Neither do I

Speaker presenting the reasons of parliament urging the execution of the
Queen of Scots, in Camden's *Elizabeth* under the year 1586.
[11] April, 1572, Ellis, *Letters,* 1st Series, II, p. 263.
[12] Ellis, *Letters,* 1st Series, II, 294 (August, 1583). A collection of
characteristic letters between Elizabeth and James of Scotland are published by the Camden Society (1849).

think that your King, were he present, would have used such
words. But if he has committed such matter to you (which I
doubt) I ascribe it to this: that your King is young, and a King
not by descent, but by election; newly chosen as he is, he does not
quite understand the manner of conducting a business of this nature
with other princes. . . . As for you, you seem to have read many
books, but not to have come upon the books of princes and to be
ignorant of uses among kings. Since you speak of the Law of
Nature and the Law of Nations, know this, that by the Law of
Nature and of Nations, when there is war between kings, it is per-
missible for one to intercept the other's war supplies brought from
any place, and to see that they be not turned to his injury; this,
I say, is the Law of Nature and of Nations. As you make much
of some new affinity with the house of Austria, remember that
there have been others of that House who would take the Polish
Kingdom from your King. As for the remaining questions, since
they are many and should be considered in order, accept what you
may hear from certain of my council assigned to this matter. In
the meanwhile, farewell and be quiet." [13]

One must realize Elizabeth as Queen. She might be
familiar with a favorite; but woe unto him if he presumed
in turn. There was said to be an affinity between her and
the baleful Leicester, from " the hidden consent of the
stars at the hour of their birth." She was infatuated
with him, in love with him; she tickled his neck as she
bestowed upon him in formal ceremony the insignia of the
Garter. Yet with what scorn and anger she wrote to him
years afterwards when he was swollen with vanity in the
Low Countries, and disobedient to her injunctions: " We
little thought that one whom we had raised out of the
dust, and prosecuted with such singular favour above all
others, would with so great contempt have broken our
commands in a matter of so great consequence and so
highly concerning us and our honour." And she commands him on his allegiance to do whatsoever her messen-
ger shall make known to him.[14] She had enriched him
with lands and monopolies; but when he died " in the
queen's debt, his goods were sold at publick outcry: for
the Queen, though in other things she were favourable
enough, yet seldom or never did she remit the debts owing

[13] Nichols, *Progresses,* etc., III, 416 sqq.
[14] Letter given in Camden's *Elizabeth* under the year 1586.

to her treasury." [15]   Her love for Leicester and her anger
were alike true expressions of Elizabeth.

As Queen, it was her garment's hem that was on the
level of her subjects' lips.   They addressed her kneeling.
She was their arbiter of life and death, the source of their
authority, well-spring of their honors and emoluments:
the delight, the cynosure of all eyes; to please her was
the subject's dearest privilege, his deepest happiness.   To
displease her meant banishment from court and privilege
and gladness; meant prison when she chose.   If she might
not kill without trial, she could pardon a convicted man.
In the summers she went on Progresses through her
realm,[16] when she was entertained by nobles, by universities and cities.[17]   The expense might almost ruin the host,
and men were in terror lest she *mislike* what they had prepared for her pleasure.   Women might well stay in the
background; they were usually objects of dislike and
jealousy.   Her favorites' secret marriages had best be
kept so; with reason enough she drove Leicester from her
when the emissary of the Duke of Anjou slyly divulged
his marriage; and on learning that Raleigh had married
one of her maids of honor, she imprisoned man and wife.
Elizabeth's coquetry with royal suitors was mainly diplomatic, and when it seemed most ridiculous, as with Alen-
çon, who was young enough to be her son, perhaps had
been drafted by Burghley in advance.   She always approached such matters *tam timido et suspenso pede!*[18]

With what pains Burghley arranged whatever he had
charge of is shown in some details of his management of
her reception by the University of Cambridge, whose
Chancellor he was.   It was in July 1578, and the college
heads made inquiry of him, as they signified their intention
of waiting on her majesty at Audely End, having in readi-

[15] Camden's *Elizabeth* under the year 1588.

[16] Nearly every summer Elizabeth made these progresses, which are mirrored and spread out at length upon the records, in Nichols, *Progresses of
Elizabeth,* in three large volumes.

[17] The anxious feelings of the Queen's expectant entertainers, as to the
expense and the uncertainty of her time of coming, and of the result of
their efforts to please, may be gathered from letters: see e. g. Ellis, *Original
Letters,* 1st Series, Vol. II, pp. 264–277.   Her Progresses were also a drain
on the exchequer.

[18] See Hume, *The Great Lord Burghley,* pp. 274, 277.

ness disputants upon two moral questions. If he approved, they would dispute *An clementia magis sit laudanda in principe, quam severitas,* and as a second topic *De fortuna et fato.* They intended to present the Queen with a book well bound.

"In answer, their high chancellor heartily thanked them; and that he liked well of their purpose of presenting themselves unto her majesty at Audely End. And that of the two questions, he liked better the first. And that the second might yield many reasons impertinent for Christian ears, if it were not circumspectly used. . . . That the present to her majesty he allowed of. But that they must have regard that the book have no savour of spike which commonly bookbinders did seek to add, to make their books savour well. But that her majesty could not abide such a strong scent. That they should do well to provide for the earl of Leicester, the lord chamberlain, and the earl of Oxford, some gloves, with a few verses in a paper joined to them, proper to every of their degrees; so that in number they exceeded not eight verses. That for himself he could spare them; so that others might have them. And that if Mr. Vice-chamberlain might have a pair with some verses, it should do well to conciliate his good-will, being a lover of learned men."

With equal care, Burghley prescribed other details of this modest academic reception.[19] The enormous expense, the elaborate spectacles, the endless masques and speeches, the bear baiting, the mock tourneys, the manifold adulation attending the entertainment of the Queen upon her Progresses may be gathered from the stately volumes which describe them. All kinds of fantastic flattery were lavished on her by gods and goddesses, nymphs, Ladies of the Lake, and Tritons, by " wilde men," giants and pilgrims. To please her taste, " Chastity " usually triumphed in the masques.[20]

Regarding the outer stateliness in which Elizabeth

[19] Strype, *Annals of the Ref.,* II, II, p. 203. When an academic disputation was too interminable, Elizabeth spoke out her weariness, as at her last reception at Oxford in 1592. Nichols, *Progresses,* etc., III, pp. 144–160. But she gave as good as she got, addressing the University in excellent Latin speeches expressive of her love of letters.

[20] Nichols, *Progresses of Elizabeth.* See especially the accounts of her entertainment by Leicester at Kenilworth, and by the town of Norwich, Vol. I, pp. 418–528; Vol. II, pp. 134–213; and the account of the charming fête at the seat of the Earl of Hertford in 1591, Vol. III, pp. 101–121. One notes improvement in the verses in the later Progresses.

moved, a foreign visitor describes an audience, the following year (1598) in the royal palace at Greenwich.

"We were admitted . . . into the Presence Chamber . . .
through which the Queen commonly passes in her way to Chapel:
at the door stood a Gentleman dressed in velvet, with a gold chain,
whose office was to introduce to the Queen any person of distinction that came to wait on her. It was Sunday, when there is
usually the greatest attendance of Nobility. In the same Hall
were the Archbishop of Canterbury, the Bishop of London, a great
number of Counsellors of State, Officers of the Crown, and Gentlemen, who waited the Queen's coming out; which she did from
her own apartment when it was time to go to prayers, attended in
the following manner: first went Gentlemen, Barons, Earls,
Knights of the Garter, all richly dressed and bareheaded; next
came the Chancellor, bearing the seals in a red silk purse, between
two: one of which carried the Royal scepter, the other the sword of
state, in a red scabbard, studded with golden fleurs de lis, the point
upwards; next came the Queen, in the sixty-fifth year of her age,
as we are told, very majestic; her face oblong, fair, but wrinkled;
her eyes small, yet black and pleasant; her nose a little hooked; her
lips narrow, and her teeth black (a defect the English seem subject
to, from their too great use of sugar); she had in her ears two
pearls with very rich drops; she wore false hair, and that red;
upon her head she had a small crown, reported to be made of some
of the gold of the celebrated Lunebourg Table. Her bosom was
uncovered, as all the English ladies have it till they marry; and
she had on a necklace of exceeding fine jewels; her hands were
small, her fingers long, and her stature neither tall nor low; her
air was stately, her manner of speaking mild and obliging. That
day she was dressed in white silk, bordered with pearls of the size
of beans, and over it a mantle of black silk, shot with silver threads;
her train was very long, the end of it borne by a Marchioness;
instead of a chain, she had an oblong collar of gold and jewels.
As she went along in all this state and magnificence, she spoke very
graciously, first to one, then to another, whether foreign ministers,
or those who attended for different reasons, in English, French,
and Italian; for, besides being well skilled in Greek, Latin, and
the languages I have mentioned, she is mistress of Spanish, Scotch,
and Dutch; whoever speaks to her, it is kneeling; now and then
she raises some with her hand. While we were there, W. Slawata,
a Bohemian Baron, had letters to present to her; and she, after
pulling off her glove, gave him her right hand to kiss, sparkling
with rings and jewels, a mark of particular favour; wherever she
turned her face, as she was going along, every body fell down on
their knees. The Ladies of the Court followed next to her, very
handsome and well-shaped, and for the most part dressed in white;
she was guarded on each side by the Gentlemen Pensioners, fifty in

number, with gilt battle-axes.   In the anti-chapel next the Hall, where we were, petitions were presented to her, and she received them most graciously, which occasioned the acclamation of " Long live Queen Elizabeth! "   She answered it with, " I thank you, my good people."   In the Chapel was excellent music; as soon as it and the service was over, which scarce exceeded half an hour, the Queen returned in the same state and order, and prepared to go to dinner.   But while she was still at prayers, we saw her table set out with the following solemnity: a Gentleman entered the room bearing a rod, and along with him another who had a table cloth, which after they had both kneeled three times with the utmost veneration, he spread upon the table, and after kneeling again, they both retired.   Then came two others, one with the rod again, the other with a salt-sellar, a plate, and bread; when they had kneeled as the others had done, and placed what was brought upon the table, they too retired with the same ceremonies performed by the first.   At last came an unmarried Lady (we were told she was a Countess) and along with her a married one, bearing a tasting-knife; the former was dressed in white silk, who, when she had prostrated herself three times in the most graceful manner, approached the table, and rubbed the plates with bread and salt, with as much awe as if the Queen had been present: when they had waited there a little while, the Yeomen of the Guard entered, bareheaded, cloathed in scarlet, with a golden rose upon their backs, bringing in at each turn a course of twenty-four dishes, served in plate, most of it gilt; these dishes were received by a gentleman in the same order they were brought, and placed upon the table, while the lady-taster gave to each of the guards a mouthful to eat, of the particular dish he had brought, for fear of any poison.   During the time that this guard, which consists of the tallest and stoutest men that can be found in all England, being carefully selected for this service, were bringing dinner, twelve trumpets and two kettle-drums made the hall ring for half an hour together.   At the end of this ceremonial, a number of unmarried ladies appeared, who, with particular solemnity, lifted the meat off the table, and conveyed it into the Queen's inner and more private chamber, where, after she had chosen for herself, the rest goes to the Ladies of the Court.   The Queen dines and sups alone, with very few attendants; and it is very seldom that any body, foreigner or native, is admitted at that time, and then only at the intercession of somebody in power." [21]

II

Personal expressions of piety with Christians tend to follow their fortunes and advantage, as well as their

[21] From Nichols, *Progresses,* &c., III, pp. 424-426 — taken from Henzner.

understanding of Christianity. So it was in the sixteenth, as well as in the twentieth, century. John Hawkins thanks God for a good haul of black slaves, and many another of those grand old buccaneers give thanks for the happy achievement of some bloody feat. Most famous of all Elizabethan sea-faring ejaculations is that of Sir Humphrey Gilbert, from the poop of his little foundering *Squirrel*,— " we are as near to heaven by sea as by land."

There were few open sceptics in those days. Statesmen referred to the established religion, used it and sometimes felt it, in their weighty business. Archbishop Whitgift made the enforcement of Anglican uniformity the purpose of his life and the standard of his righteousness. Walsingham by early education and conviction was a Puritan, and whatever scepticism penetrated his later thoughts, his Puritan instincts kept the sharp sword of his policy pointed against Spain. As for Elizabeth, her personal and royal nature was firm against papal authority; she had no fancy for Roman Catholicism, to which she had anxiously conformed with her life in peril under Mary. Had she not conformed, she would not have lived to rescue England. As queen she insisted upon obedience to her ecclesiastical authority, which she enforced as domestic and foreign exigencies permitted. Her philanderings with cross and candles were political. Her personal religiousness is one unknown element of the composite enigma of her character. William Cecil had also carefully conformed to Roman Catholicism under Mary; and so he lived to guide the policy of Elizabeth. He too was a politic in religion, prudent and inclined to moderation in that field as in all his statesmanship. One must nevertheless accord him many sincere religious thoughts.

In 1571 Elizabeth made Cecil Baron of Burghley, " as well for his long services [under Edward] . . . as also for the faithful and acceptable duty which he hath constantly performed from the very beginning of our reign and ceaseth not daily to perform . . . and also for his circumspection, valor, wisdom, dexterity, integrity of life, providence, care and faithfulness." [22]   True words for once.   The modern world owes much to him.   Elizabeth herself, an artist politician, perhaps was as intelligent as he; she was his equal in dissimulation.   But she had her fancies and infatuations.   Now and then she flung off from Burghley's unfailing wisdom.   It might become galling, so sure it was to circumvent her whims.   Without him, perhaps, this marvellous man-woman might have held her throne and kept England England; but seemingly Burghley's counsel kept the realm on even keel in perilous waters where many a tempest was eluded by these two shrewd navigators.

A moderator in matters of religion, a steadier of the realm in statecraft, William Cecil, born in 1520, was educated at St. John's, Cambridge, with John Cheke, Roger Ascham, Nicholas Bacon and other scholars, who incidentally were interested in Luther's writings.   Cecil was a hard student, just as he was to be a man of industry to the last week of his life.   Yet he disgusted his father, a substantial squire and thrifty courtier, by his early marriage to a sister of the lowly circumstanced Cheke. The young woman soon died, however, and a place was obtained at Court for Cecil in 1544.   Brother-in-law Cheke, a great scholar, was made Prince Edward's tutor, and friend Ascham the tutor of the Princess Elizabeth. In 1545 Cecil married one of those learned and intelligent daughters of Sir Anthony Cooke, another of whom married Sir Nicholas Bacon and became the mother of the famous Francis, and the translator of Bishop Jewel's *Apology*.

Protector Somerset made Cecil a confidential secretary, and later his approved qualities brought him a seat in the Council and the post of Secretary of State.   Prudently this Secretary accumulated goodly properties during the boy King's reign, and entered on a stately mode of life. He always cared for books, and heraldy and gardening. Maturity came soon upon him.   Never given to martial sports, his chief open air recreation came to be ambling upon a mule along his garden paths.   He was a martyr

22 Camden, *History of Elizabeth;* under the year 1571.

to gout, and with the increase of his fame, nostrums for its cure came from distinguished co-sufferers.[23]

When Mary was seated on the throne, Cecil proceeded to exculpate himself from his complicity in the plot to make a queen of Lady Jane Grey. In the careful note which he drew up there is at least one humorous paragraph: " When this conspiracy was first opened to me, I did fully set me to flee the realm, and was dissuaded by Mr. Cheke, who willed me for my satisfaction to read a dialogue of Plato, where Socrates, being in prison, was offered to escape and flee, and yet he would not. I read the dialogue, whose reasons indeed did stay me." [24] He had in truth had little share in that wild throw of the desperate Northumberland. Now he lived in partial retirement on his estates, managing his own properties, and those of others, very well. His prudence and business ability and willingness to bestow pains made his services in great request. At all periods of his career, even political enemies entrusted him with their affairs. Mary's government occasionally consulted him, and he was the adviser of the princess Elizabeth, who made him her Secretary of State immediately upon Mary's death.

With ample talent for mendacity, Burghley was an honest man. Nearly all the rest of Elizabeth's councillors took foreign bribes, if they were not bribed. " He can never be a good statesman who respecteth not the public more than his own private advantage." The veriest rogues have professed this maxim of Lord Burghley; but he practiced it at a time when Englishmen were corruptible. He was true to the Queen's and England's interests, as he understood them; and he understood them best of all. Yet he was careful of his own advantage and position, seeking his profit and advancement where he could prudently. He was not Quixotic, yielded no advantage to opponents, but circumvented and tripped them up by every wile. He was a cautious fox.

No novelist would attempt a plot as intricate as Eliza-

[23] See Ellis, *Letters,* etc., 1st Series, Vol. III, pp. 35 sqq. In England and Germany nearly all noted men suffered from gout. I have not observed such frequent talk of it among the French and Italians.

[24] Printed in Martin Hume's *The Great Lord Burghley,* pp. 40–43, a

beth's state polity.   Beneath its surface sinuousities, were
turns of queenly whim and temperament, eddies of intrigue and bribery and treason.   Religion, greed and
pride, distrust and lying, writhed and twisted within.
Yet the motives impelling the acts and words of Elizabeth
and her chief minister were beneficent, and we may be
thankful for the result.

Burghley's methods and Elizabeth's coquetting diplomacy were as English as the Church of England.   They
exemplified, and indeed were, the *via media*, even from
those first difficult months of the Queen's reign, when there
was need to re-establish the Church of England and break
the French hold on Scotland.   The first achievement has
been spoken of.   The second, representing the beginning
of Cecil's foreign policy, is too intricate for casual statement.   But the French soldiers evacuated Scotland.   We
cannot touch the diplomatic history of Elizabeth's reign,
even to tell, for instance, how Cecil discredited and drove
out one Spanish Ambassador after another, all of whom
acted as emissaries to the discontented Catholics of England.[25]   Yet these tales are better than fiction: so is the
whole story of this reign.

Possibly Elizabeth stood a little in awe of Burghley.
She treated him less rudely than any other of her councillors.   Yet dearly as he loved statecraft, and patient and
enduring as he was beyond other men, whom he also excelled as a counter-plotter, even he might show weariness
and a wish to retire.   Elizabeth would never let him go,
and on some occasion when apparently he had asked to
lay down his office, she wrote him the following often
quoted letter, addressing him by what seems to have been
her jocular name for this much tried councillor:

" Sir Spirit.   I doubt I do nickname [26] you.   For those of your
kind (they say) have no sense.[27]   But I have of late seen an *ecce
signum,* that if an ass kick you, you feel it so soon.   I will recant

book giving an excellent narrative of Burghley's career and intricate
statesmanship.

[25] See Hume's *The Great Lord Burghley,* pp. 126 sqq., and *passim* where
these affairs are clearly told.

[26] Misname, miscall.

[27] I. e. no sense of feeling.

you from being *Spirit,* if ever I perceive that you disdain not such a feeling. Serve God, fear the King, and be a good fellow to the rest. Let never care appear in you for such a rumour; but let them well know, that you rather desire the righting of such wrong, by making known their error, than you to be so silly a soul, as to foreslow [28] that you ought to do, or not freely deliver what you think meetest, and pass of no man so much, as not to regard her trust, who putteth it in you. God bless you and long may you last, *Omnino,* E. R."

Lord Treasurer Burghley endorsed upon this note, " Received the 8th of May 1583."

The Queen was fifty and he was sixty-three. If he was spirit because of sheer intelligence,— he lacked *esprit,* which the Queen shared with her younger royal contemporary, Henri Quatre.

After the sorely called for execution of the Queen of Scots in 1586, Elizabeth disclaimed responsibility, though she had signed the warrant.[29] In excellent rage, she poured her fury upon the ministers of her will and their own as well; among them Burghley. The Queen would not see him or accept his entreating letters. Whether or not he knew the storm would pass, or that it was but a stage tempest, the old councillor suffered the deepest depression. Reading the jottings of his meditations, one is in doubt whether the *Deus* that afflicts him is God or a *Dea-regina!* At all events they may be taken as a real expression of this never altogether vulpine personality:

Peccatum ignorantia commissum.
Anima si peccaverit per ignorantiam offeret arietem, et dimittetur ei, quia per ignorantiam.
      Quem deligit Deus, castigat.
   Non est sanitas in carne mea a facie irae tuae.
   Job. Ipse vulnerat, et medetur.

Notes of actual exculpating circumstances are thrown in. Then:

   Clementia. Leones prostratis parcunt.
   Nullum magis decet clementia, quam principem.
   Collant te servi tui, potius quam timeant.

[28] Give over.
[29] See her letter to Mary's son James of Scotland, Ellis, *Letters,* 1st Series, III, p. 22.

Ante senectutem curandum est, ut bene vivat.
Mors calamitatis terminus.

He sends letter after letter to the Queen: " finding my mind continually opprest with griefs for your displeasure, and mine old body and lame limbs by day and night vexed with pains . . . I will most plainly answer for thought and deed, as if God himself should call me to judgment, from whom nothing can be hid. My case alone is most miserable . . . your majesty doth condemn me more than others . . . through my lameness and infirmity not being able of myself to come into your presence . . . yet such is my earnest desire to appear before your gracious presence, as I am most willing to endure any pain, to be carried to some place, if to be laid on the floor near your majesty's feet, there to receive your gracious censure: hoping . . . that I shall find some drops of your mercy to quench the panting sorrows of my heart." [30]

When the mood was on her, the queen would console her old friend and councillor oppressed by gout and the weight of years, or perhaps banter him back into harness. To this double end would seem the purport of a playful and affectionate document indited by her while staying in 1591 at Burghley's seat of Theobalds:

" Elizabetha Anglorum id est, a vitore angelorum, regina formosissima et felicissima : to the disconsolate and retired spryte, the heremite of Tyboll, and to all other disaffected souls claiming by, from, or under the said heremite, sendeth greeting. Where in our court of chancery it is given us to understand, that you, sir Heremite, the abandonate of nature's fair works, and servant to heavens wonders, have . . . possessed yourself of fair Tybollt, with her sweet rosary the same time "— a passage of quite enigmatic banter follows: then the writing goes on: " We upon advised consideration have commanded you heremit to your old cave, too good for the forsaken, too bad for our worthily beloved councillor. And because we greatly tender your comfort, we have given power to our chancellor to make out such and so many writs as to him shall seem good, to abjure desolations and mourning (the consumer of sweetness) to the frozen seas and deserts, upon pain of 500 despights to their terror . . . if they attempt any part of your house again; enjoining you to the enjoyment of your own house, and

[30] Strype, *Annals of the Ref.*, III, 2, pp. 404–409. See also a fine letter ib. p. 410.

delight without memory of any mortal accident or wretched adversary. And for that you have been so good a servant to common tranquillity, we command solace to give the full and pacific possession of all and every part thereof: not departing until our favour (that ever hath inclined to your meek nature) have assured you peace in the possession thereof. Wherin we command all causes within the prerogative of our high favour to give you no interruption . . . *Teste meipsa apud Tybolls.*" [31]

Burghley's old age was prone to pious expression and the giving of wise counsels. On the death of his wife in 1588, with whom he had been so well mated for forty-three years, he took comfort in religious reflections and loving memories, and with his own sorrowing hand inscribed her deeds of charity.[32] Then he drew up a long Latin inscription suitable for a family monument, recording the life and death of his wife and a beloved daughter, the countess of Oxford, and the birth of his other children. His favorite son was Robert, an able coadjutor in affairs of state, and a continuer of his father's policy as councillor to Elizabeth and James. He was the first Earl of Salisbury of the present house. For him when young, Burghley wrote many instructions as wise as those of Polonius to Laertes; also loving letters.[33] Two years before his death Burghley wrote with reference to some clash of opinion, giving the principles of his conduct as minister of the Queen:

"My loving son, Sir Robert Cecil, Knt., I do hold, and will always, this course in such matters as I differ in opinion from her Majesty. As long as I may be allowed to give advice I will not change my opinion by affirming the contrary, for that were to offend God, to whom I am sworn first; but as a servant I will obey her Majesty's command and no wise contrary the same; presuming that she being God's chief minister here, it shall be God's will to have her commandments obeyed — after that I have performed my duty as a Councillor, and shall in my heart wish her commandments to have such good success as she intendeth." [34]

As he accepted his service to the Queen, so he accepted his religion, gravely. Once as Lord Burghley was

[31] Strype, *Annals of the Ref.,* IV, p. 108.
[32] The record printed in Strype's *Annals,* III, 2, pp. 125 sqq.
[33] Strype, *Annals,* IV, pp. 471–479.
[34] Hume, *The Great Lord Burghley,* p. 479, note.

coming in from prayers, Sir Francis Walsingham said " in merrie sorte " that " he wished himself so good a servant of God as Lord Burghley, but that he had not been at church for a week past; " Burghley replied gravely: " I hold it meet for us to ask God's grace to keep us sound of heart, who have so much in our power, and to direct us to the well doing of all the people, whom it is easy for us to injure and ruin; and herein, my good friends, the special blessing seemeth meet to be discretely asked and wisely worn." [35]

Burghley had no reason to cavil either at religion or fortune.   Still less had a certain overweening lord, who more justly might have girded at himself as the source of the unhappy issue of his state.   The Lord Treasurer, a few months before his death, was arguing with this Earl of Essex for peace with Spain in the Low Countries. When Essex insisted upon war, Burghley " drew forth a Psalm-book, and, saying nothing, pointed him to this verse, *Men of blood shall not live out half their days.*" [36]

As pointedly as the Ajax or the Oedipus of Sophocles, Essex proved the Greek adage: character is man's fate. His unbridled ambition and unbridled temper were as fate to this young man.   He possessed a certain magnificence of mind.   Failing to obtain the attorney-generalship for Francis Bacon, he presented him with one of his own manors — that Francis Bacon who knew well enough when to desert the ship which had so infatuate a pilot.

Essex was scarcely thirty-four when he laid his head upon the block, dying like an Earl.   He was unfit for the game of politics; he could not even control his temper with the old Queen who doted on this glorious young beauty.   She made him pay his debts to her, though he had to sell a manor; but made good his fortune without cost to herself by giving him the " farm of sweet wine," that same monopoly which had been Leicester's.   She was enraged at his secret marriage in 1590 with the daughter of Walsingham, who had just died.   Essex —

[35] From page 250 of Harrington's " Notes and Observations," given in Nichols' *Progresses of Elizabeth,* III, p. 419.
[36] Camden's *Elizabeth,* under the year 1598.

he was only twenty-three — bent before this storm, and, consenting that his wife should retire to her mother's house, was restored to favor. Yet he could not keep himself in hand when his imperious mistress showed her lack of confidence in his capacities. He gained the glory which he loved, and popular acclaim, by his valor in naval expeditions against Spain, when there were longer heads than his aboard the fleet. He was always quarrelling with those who thwarted him for their own advantage or England's. The Cecils were against him; Raleigh hated him. Fate would not long abstain from such a goodly victim. One sees it coming on him in a hot argument with the Queen, who would not send Sir George Carew to Ireland, so that Essex might be rid of him at court. He turned his back on her with a look of scorn. She gave him a box on the ear and bade him begone and be hanged. He swore aloud he would not put up with that affront, and laid his hand upon his sword. Some-one interposed, and he retired, but wrote an angry letter, saying he knew his duties as a subject and as an Earl and Marshall of England. He was no slave to submit to outrageous indignities from a passionate prince. "The queen's heart is hardened." His mind was be-sieged by the treasonable thought of driving his enemies from court by arms and forcing himself upon the Queen. Then followed discouragement and impulses of pious renunciation and retirement. Not long after, he brought himself to submit, and was received back into favor. "Yet hereupon his friends began shrewdly to fear his ruin, who had observed that Fortune is seldom reconciled to her foster children whom she hath once forsaken; and princes more seldom to those whom they have once offended." [37]

The next year, 1599, Fortune and the Earl's enemies assisted him to obtain for himself the fatal post of Lord Deputy of Ireland and General of the Army, with full authority to quell the Irish rebellion then exceptionally menacing. Furnished with an ample army, he set forth beset by hostile eyes. Almost at once he departed from

[37] Camden's *Elizabeth* under the year 1598.

the sounder lines of military policy which he had been enjoined to follow, and showed his incapacity either for
generalship or negotiation.   His deficiencies were made
glaring afterwards by the complete success, with slenderer
forces, by Lord Mountjoy.

The Queen was exasperated at Essex's failure, his
stubborn disobedience, and questionable negotiation with
the chief Irish rebel.   He was known to be violently discontented, and with good ground was suspected of a
purpose to return and overcome his enemies by arms.
The government had taken its precautions, when Essex
suddenly, without permission, accompanied by his friends
and gentlemen, crossed to England.   He had no well-
laid policy or plan of action.   Taken into custody he
showed repentance after a while, and was permitted to
go to his own house.   Next he was tried for his offenses
and sentenced to be suspended from all his offices and
to be kept in ward during the Queen's pleasure.   Again
he showed contrition and was relieved of restraint.   But
again he frustrated any chance of royal favor by impatiently following foolish counsels.   The result was a
pointless uprising of the Earl and his friends in London,
and the quick repression of this insurrection of a day;
then the trial, condemnation and execution of the Earl.
Fate accomplished itself upon him as cruelly as his enemies could wish.[38]

[38] Camden's *Elizabeth,* under the year 1601, gives a careful and very
interesting account of the trial of Essex, at which Camden was present.

CHAPTER XXVIII

RALEIGH, SIDNEY, SPENSER

THE Elizabethan time had many examples of that combination of temperament and aptitude which we call genius. The term will not be denied Sir Walter Raleigh, a complete and wonderful Elizabethan and a brilliant illustration of the variety of human phase attaching to the same " name and form." One would not call him good; nor was he religious: hatred, avarice, harbored in him; arrogance welled from his nature: a man of vivid desire, energy, imagination, vision, intellectual appetition; of jealousies and complainings, and of ready melancholy, with corresponding faculties of expression. His calamities proved a foil to his desires: they instructed him in sorrow and duress; to his worldly experience they added a more bitter realization of human hypocrisy, ingratitude, and treachery. His tragic lot evoked the further potentialities of his being.

No man of his time has attracted more biographers. Half-brother to Sir Humphrey Gilbert, he was born of fine Devonshire stock, possibly in 1552. The record of his Oxford life is scanty, and scanty the record of his youthful military service in France. The sea soon drew him. Besides other ventures, he made one voyage to the West Indies, another, and a tragic one, to the St. Lawrence, all before he went as an officer to harry Irish rebels in 1580. His brilliant service in Ireland was neutralized by his criticisms upon his superiors and his personal complaints. By the spring of 1582 he is found settled at Court and a prime favorite with the Queen. A gorgeous figure, bespangled with jewels, he also fastened attention by a display of knowledge, and his lively imaginative talk. He could make himself acceptable to other favorites, like Leicester; but proved a dangerous enemy to those who crossed him. His fortunes

advanced apace, the Queen bestowing on him sundry
estates and, what cost her less, a patent by which all
vintners in the kingdom should pay him annual license
fees.   This so-called " Farm of Wines " brought as much
as ten thousand pounds a year, reckoned in modern values.
A license granted him later to export woollen cloths may
have trebled his revenues.   He spent a good part of them
in fitting out expeditions to North America; for the
mantle of the drowned Sir Humphrey had settled upon
his opulent and energetic shoulders, and his mind dilated
with the vision of the West.

Raleigh's first expedition landed at Roanoke, and the
land was named Virginia; a second one attempted colonization.   At the same time, buccaneering ventures fed his
hostility to Spain and brought him timely gold; with which
he equipped other unsuccessful expeditions to Virginia.
In 1587 the youthful Essex, more magnificently overweening even that Sir Walter, became a serious rival for
Elizabeth's affection.   But Raleigh's sea-activities did not
lessen, while his repute for naval knowledge was enhanced
by the Armada year.   It was his clandestine marriage
with a maid of honor that in 1592 cast him out of the
Queen's favor — into the Tower.   The melancholy of
that temporary restraint drew from him an absurd letter,
written on hearing of the Queen's departure from
London:

" My heart was never broken till this day, that I hear
the Queen goes away so far off,— whom I have followed
so many years with so great love and desire, in so many
journeys, and am now left behind her, in a dark prison
all alone.   While she was yet near at hand . . . my
sorrows were the less . . . I that was wont to behold
her riding like Alexander, hunting like Diana, walking like
Venus, the gentle wind blowing her fair hair about her
pure cheeks, like a nymph; sometime sitting in the shade
like a goddess; sometime singing like an angel," . . .
and more besides, all written to the still friendly but
cold-blooded Robert Cecil,[1] at a time when Raleigh,

[1] Raleigh's Letters, ed. Edwards, p. 51 (Vol. II of Edwards' *Life of
Raleigh*).

recently married, was about forty and the goddess queen twenty years his senior. It was a long time before Elizabeth would see him.

No need to recount Raleigh's own voyage to Guiana, made in 1595, of which he has left a splendid story; nor to go over again the tale of his part in the attack upon Cadiz and the Spanish fleet, and the expedition against the Açores. His activities and expeditions went on till Elizabeth died. James hated him, and soon after the new reign began, Raleigh was somehow involved with others in a charge of treason. Sent to the Tower, he was harshly tried, convicted and sentenced to execution. Realizing his ruin, expecting death, in a mood which drove him to attempted suicide, Raleigh addressed a letter to his wife very different in tone from the one he had written to Cecil eleven years before: " You shall receive, dear wife, my last words in these my last lines. My love I send you, that you may keep it when I am dead: and my counsel, that you may remember it when I am no more. I would not, with my last Will, present you with sorrows, dear Besse. Let them go to the grave with me, and be buried in the dust. And, seeing it is not the will of God that ever I shall see you in this life, bear my destruction gently and with a heart like yourself." The letter continues speaking of herself, and their joint affairs, and closes with a prayer that God would show mercy to her and forgive her husband's false accusers.[2]

But he was not to die then. At the edge of the scaffold, the sentences of the alleged traitors were suspended, and Raleigh was left to an interminable imprisonment. Enough was rescued from the wreck of his fortune to enable him to occupy an apartment in the Tower with his wife, where he devoted himself to study and writing. The gall and wormwood of his life were tempered by his occupations. For a time he was permitted to use a garden, where he "converted a little hen-house into a still" and spent " all the day in his distillations." The ladies who passed by, and saw him from over the wall, begged his cordials and balsams. But his health was poor, and

[2] Edwards, o. c. II, p. 284.

he was ageing fast.   At the end of thirteen years, he was released and permitted — this man of nearly seventy — to equip and sail upon an expedition to Guiana, under the impossible terms of doing nothing to impair the King's good relations with his friends the Spaniards.   He sailed, infringed those terms, lost his son, and failed lamentably in his hopeless enterprise.   From somewhere, in his ship, he writes his wife —" I was loath to write, because I knew not how to comfort you; and, God knows, I never knew what sorrow meant till now." [3]   On his landing in England, after a brief trial, his execution came to him as a release, and gave him an opportunity to right himself with his contemporaries and posterity, speaking from the scaffold.

The brilliant activities of Raleigh's outer life, his over-splendid fortunes, errors of conduct, rancours, and his fifteen years of dolorous meditation in the Tower are mirrored in his writings.   One will remember, however, that verse and prose are apt to be more meditative and perhaps sentimental than action, and may render the man's life in other hues.   There was a vein of melancholy in Raleigh which appears in his verses, even while his fortunes were rising and most eagerly pursued.

Raleigh and Edmund Spenser had met before in Ireland; but it was not till the former's return there in 1589 that the intercourse between them became fruitful.   They were both souls of high romance; and although Spenser is using pastoral convention in his *Colin Clout's come home again,* it is clear that an impression had been made on him by the " strange shepherd " who " chanced to find me out " when seated piping " by the Mulla's shore."

> . . . himself he did ycleepe
> The shepherd of the Ocëan by name,
> And said he came far from the main sea deep . . .

Spenser turned into poetry the quite unpoetic complaints of this " strange shepherd."

> Of great unkindness and of usage hard
>   Of Cynthia, the Lady of the Sea,
> Who from her presence, faultless him debarred.

[3] Edwards, o. c. II, p. 359.

The same strange shepherd brought with him a long idyllic poem of his own, in which the *Ocean* told its love to Cynthia;[4] doubtless a charming poem, though one suspects it of lengthiness, without a beginning, a middle, or an end. Shepherd Spenser followed the duly pardoned Ocean Shepherd to Cynthia's court, and was presented to the goddess-queen. Soon the first three books of the *Faery Queen* appeared, prefaced with a noble sonnet by Raleigh, beginning,

> Methought I saw the grave where Laura lay —

The gift and fashion of verse was everywhere, and men of action had their lyric moods. Raleigh wrote love verses, as of course; but strains of cynicism or melancholy mark most of the poetry ascribed to him. The qualities discovered by the cynic in the world are those from which he is not free. Raleigh drew from his own nature when he wrote:

> Tell men of high condition,
>   That manage the estate,
> Their purpose is ambition,
>   Their practice only hate:
> And if they once reply,
> Then give them all the lie.

> Tell them that brave it most,
>   They beg for more by spending,
> Who, in their greatest cost,
>   Seek nothing but commending.

Cynicism is touched with melancholy in the next verse:

> Tell zeal it wants devotion;
> Tell love it is but lust;
> Tell time it is but motion;
> Tell flesh it is but dust:
> And wish them not reply,
>   For thou must give the lie.

Another poem is sad:

[4] The last book survives and is printed in J. Hannah's *Poems of Sir Walter Raleigh* (London, 1892), pp. 32–51.

> Like truthless dreams, so are my joys expired,
> And past return are all my dandled days,
> My love misled, and fancy quite retired;
> Of all which past, the sorrow only stays.
>
> My lost delights, now clean from sight of land,
> Have left me all alone in unknown ways
> . . . .
> Of all which past, the sorrow only stays.

The cynicism has vanished, while the sadness is touched by a gleam of faith, in the thoughtful verse written before his death:

> Even such is time, that takes in trust
> Our youth, our joys, our all we have,
> And pays us but with earth and dust;
> Who, in the dark and silent grave,
> When we have wandered all our ways,
> Shuts up the story of our days;
> But from this earth, this grave, this dust,
> My God shall raise me up, I trust.

In happier times he could view justly the fruitful ending of a heroic career. One fine verse in his poem on Sidney's death has the quality of noble epitaph:

> England doth hold thy limbs, that bred the same;
> Flanders thy valor, where it last was tried;
> The Camp thy sorrow, where thy body died;
> Thy friends thy want; the world thy virtue's fame.

Some years later, in 1596, when his own life was still unbroken, though it had been tried, he sent a letter of condolence to Sir Robert Cecil on the death of his wife, setting the lady's death in universal truth:

"There is no man sorry for death itself, but only for the time of death; everyone knowing that it is a bond never forfeited to God. If then we know the same to be certain and inevitable, we ought withal to take the time of his arrival in as good part as the knowledge; and not to lament at the instant of every seeming adversity, which, we are assured, have been on their way towards us from the beginning. . . ."

The letter warns against the harboring of griefs:

"I believe it that sorrows are dangerous companions, converting bad into evil, and evil into worse, and do no other service than

multiply harms. They are the treasures of weak hearts and of
the foolish. The mind that entertaineth them is as the earth and
dust whereon sorrows and adversities of the world do, as the beasts
of the field, tread, trample, and defile. . . ." [5]

Bacon was not the only man who could write like Bacon.

Some four years later another side of Raleigh's nature
sends a letter of malignant incisiveness to Secretary Cecil,
warning against clemency to Essex, lest it be ascribed to
" her Majesty's pusilanimity and not to your good nature.
. . . The less you make him, the less he shall be able to
harm you and yours. . . . For after-revenges, fear them
not; for your own father Lord Burleigh was esteemed to
be the contriver of Norfolk's ruin, yet his son followeth
your father's son and loveth him. Humors of men succeed not; [6] but grow by occasions and accidents of time
and power." He gives instances of heirs letting the
sorrows of their fathers sleep. " Look to the present,
and you do wisely. . . . Let the Queen hold Bothwell
[Essex] while she hath him. He will ever be the canker
of her estate and safety. Princes are lost by security, and
preserved by prevention. I have seen the last of her
good days, and all ours, after his liberty." [7]

Later, Raleigh saw the prisoner's lot from another
side: " For my own time, good my Lord, consider that it
cannot be called a life, but only misery drawn out and
spun into a long thread, without all hope of other end
than death shall provide for me, who without the help
of kings or friends, will deliver me out of prison." [8]

During his long imprisonment, partly for the instruction of James's heir, Prince Henry, Raleigh wrote a number of weighty treatises upon trade and commerce, upon
the laws and policy of England, and upon the navy and
service at sea. He also wrote the *History of the World,*
bringing the matter of his huge folio down to the Roman
conquest of Macedon. Perhaps he found more distraction dwelling in the labyrinth of ancient history than in
recounting the events of his own time; it was safer: " I

[5] Edwards, o. c. II, pp. 162–3.
[6] I. e. do not pass to their heirs.
[7] Edwards, o. c. p. 222.
[8] Edwards, o. c. II, p. 313, to Lord Cranborne.

know that it will be said by many, that I might have been more pleasing to the reader if I had written the story of mine own times, having been permitted to draw water as near the well-head as another.   To this I answer, that whosoever, in writing a modern history, shall follow truth too near the heels, it may happily strike out his teeth."   This passage comes toward the end of the long preface which most elaborately presents the wisdom that life and adversity had brought him,— now after eleven years of imprisonment, the time being the year of no grace for him, 1614.

He dared not omit some false and fulsome flattery of his stiff-necked royal foe — pardonable in a prisoner under suspended sentence.   Otherwise this interesting human document is a somewhat embittered and extremely censorious indictment of humanity, especially of the great.[9]   It has its lofty passages and poetic language: recognition of the writer's services to England now could yield him no other profit " than doth a fair sunshine day to a seaman after shipwreck."   It speaks of the triumph of history, which " hath carried our knowledge over the vast and devouring space of many thousands of years." Its opening notes might recall Orosius, or Augustine's *City of God*.   The first books of the work " have undertaken the discourse of the first kings and kingdoms," and since " the short life of a preface " cannot " travel after and overtake far-off antiquity to judge of it; I will for the present examine what profit hath been gathered by our own kings, and their neighbour princes; who having beheld both in divine and human letters, the success of infidelity, injustice, and cruelty, have (notwithstanding) planted after the same pattern."

Again, the sarcasm is dropped: " the judgments of God are for ever unchangeable; neither is he wearied by the long process of time, and wont to give his blessing in one age to that which he hath cursed in another."   Taking up the criminal record of England's kings, the indictment descends the series, noting no virtues, but only evil, till

---

[9] The Preface is sixty pages long in the Oxford (1829) edition of Raleigh's Works, Vol. II.

it declares of Henry VIII (Elizabeth being safely in her grave!) : "If all the pictures and patterns of a merciless prince were lost in the world, they might all again be painted to the life out of the story of this king."

Leaving the English kings, with a reference to the blameless record of King James, he lays bare a duplication of their crimes in the careers of the kings of France and Spain; — but "God is everywhere the same God;" and one and all have "pulled the vengeance of God upon themselves, their heirs, and their prudent ministers!"

"But what of all this? and to what end do we lay before the living the fall and fortunes of the dead: seeing that the world is the same that it hath been; and the children of the present time will still obey their parents!" — forgetting, like their parents, their experience, persuading themselves that God has guaranteed them in their hypocrisy and religious contentions; for the lives of these "comedians in religion" renounce the parts they play! They all chase after that which passes away, and neglect the things which are immortal.

"But let every man value his own wisdom as he pleaseth. Let the rich man think all fools, that cannot equal his abundance; the revenger esteem all negligent, that have not trodden down their opposites [enemies]; the politician, all gross [stupid] that cannot merchandise their faith; yet when we once come in sight of the port of death, to which all winds drive us . . . our own cogitations (those sad and severe cogitations, formerly beaten from us by our health and felicity) return again, and pay us to the uttermost for all the pleasing passages of our lives past." At the end a man "shall find nothing remaining but those sorrows which grow up after our fast springing youth; overtake it when it is at a stand; and overtop it utterly, when it begins to wither."

"Of all which past, the sorrow only stays."

Doubtless the Christian faith is the main solace; Aristotle satisfies us not; Hermes (Trismegistus), Lactantius, and Dionysius afford better aid, and Plato in Ficino's rendering, in the great matter of the world's creation and governance. Raleigh's illustrations show him to have been no more Copernican than Bacon. His philosophic matter is that of the thoughtful layman or amateur, to whom old arguments bring a new found conviction carrying a sense of proprietorship. In the very first paragraph of the main work he casts himself into the majesty of God's creation, and eloquently combines afresh the old thoughts of others.

He protests that he bears malice to no man, though all cannot be pleased.

> "I know that as the charitable will judge charitably, so against those *qui gloriantur in malitia* my present adversity hath disarmed (sic) me. I am on the ground already, and therefore have not far to fall. . . . All the hope I have lies in this, that I have already found more ungentle and uncourteous reaeders of my love towards them . . . than ever I shall do again. For had it been otherwise, I should hardly have had this leisure to have made myself a fool in print."

With these words he ends bitterly, as befits a man who had always been prone to complain of fortune's rufflings, and yet would dare her winds again. He was like his fellow Elizabethans, extremely vocal in adversity, but valiant and enterprising to the end of the venture which is life.

II

For the exceedingly expressive, dramatic, even histrionic, age when Raleigh wrote, the saying " Style is the man," is exceptionally true — meaning by " style " not the mere use and sequence of words, but the choice of matter to be uttered or omitted, the seizing upon facts which appeal to the writer, the ignoring of those which do not. Thus taken, style represents the man, his tastes and temperament, desires and aversions, and his faculties of observation and judgment. It may thus even represent his view of life. In this large sense, moreover, style, which still is form, becomes identical with substance — the substance of self-expression.

But " style " and modes of self-expression which are the very man, do not imply substantial originality, however formative they may be. For example, in the reformation of the Church under Henry VIII and Edward VI, the reforming thought had come mainly from abroad, and yet was readjusted and remade into what was palpably English, to wit, the English Reformation. Likewise the utterly marvellous literary self-expression of the Elizabethan time proceeded, especially in its lovely lyric phases, through the plastic use of appropriated matter. More splendidly than in religion, the work of foreign poets and story-tellers was transformed into English song, and with stupendous creativeness into English drama. So general and so overmastering was the impulse toward such new creation, with whatever materials came to hand, that the milder intellectual activities of humane and progressive scholarship were cast into the shade. The comparatively slight rôle of the Elizabethans in the progress of classical letters was to be of importance to the world because it was a means of bringing the classical material into the service of the English muse,— largely through translations from the French. Here classic form was of less consequence than classic matter. The poetic forms of Pindar and Anacreon, for example, did not affect English verse as they did the poetry of the French Pléiade, because no English poet directly mastered them as Ronsard did; and even had an English poet mastered them, he might have found them alien to his genius. The plays of Seneca instructed and perhaps hampered the Elizabethan drama before its exuberant strength flung Latin and Greek models to the winds. Only Fulke Greville in his *Alaham* and *Mustapha* tied himself to the classic scheme; and he was no playwright working for the stage, but a gentleman and servant of the State who passed his cultured leisure composing didactic poetry sometimes in dramatic form.

The more notable translators expressed themselves in their translations as amply as they rendered their original. Sir Thomas North put English gentlemen as well as Sir Thomas North into his grand version of Amyot's *Plutarch;* so Holland, although a classical scholar translating from the ancient text, put plenty of his English self and language into his rendering of Suetonius and Pliny; and Chapman, when he " spoke out loud and bold," transformed Homer in his way, though less brazenly than Pope did after him.[10]

Such then seems to be the double, closely related point of view from which this mighty field may be surveyed: that is to say through this potent and absorbing self-expression which is for the time the man, and also through the process of mastering and assimilating whatever was fed to it from the ancient world of Rome and Greece, and from contemporary Italy and France and Spain. We shall see the Elizabethans reacting upon, and expressing or re-expressing through themselves, the enlightenment of the time as it has come to them — the humanism and disillusionment of Italy, the French clarification, the German protest against whatever robbed the spirit of its due. In some way each Elizabethan expresses some phase of the contemporary world, and Shakespeare the impression of the universal whole. It is himself that he expresses through the universality of his illumination, or in any casual borrowing: — he, a sheer playwright, making plays for the theatre, following this business, inevitably expresses himself, and in and through himself the enlightenment and genius of the age. The transforming universality of his mind is not more evident than the unfailing beauty of his poetry. This also was himself; he could not help it,— as out of the gloom of *Measure for Measure,* and the outer degradation of the rejected Mariana, the lovely song breaks forth so unexpectedly:

> Take, O take, those lips away
> That so sweetly were foresworn.

It goes without saying that the field before us is so enormous that we can do no more than select a line of illustrations, tapping them, as it were, of some of their significance.

Sir Thomas Wyatt and the Earl of Surrey, in the reign of Henry VIII, made poems out of matter not their own, and fruitfully took verse-forms from Italy and

[10] Cf. C. Whibley's chapter on "Translators" in Vol. IV of the *Cambridge Hist. of Eng. Lit.*

France.   Wyatt died in 1542, at the age of thirty-nine;
and Surrey, when about thirty, was beheaded on a curious
charge of treason in 1547, just before the old king died.
Wyatt was the first English writer of sonnets, a fashion
which he gathered from his travels in Italy and from his
sojourns at Paris where Italian influence was strong.   A
number of his rather crude and labored sonnets were
translations from Petrarch, and in other verse he was
influenced by Marot.   Having written many love poems
of adapted theme and form, he still remains unforgotten
in those earnest lines to his poetic mistress, beginning

> Forget not yet the tried intent . . .

Surrey likewise wrote sonnets from the Italian; since
the sonnet had not yet come to its own in French.   As
he never crossed the Alps, it was chiefly in Paris that he
too fell under Italian as well as French influence.   He
learned the new Italian fashion of blank verse, inaugu-
rated apparently by the Florentine exile Alamanni, who
was publishing his poems at Lyons.   Certain of his countrymen, acknowledging his leadership, were using blank
verse in Virgilian translations.   Catching the idea,
Surrey translated into vigorous blank verse the second
and fourth books of the *Aeneid;* [11] thus inducting into the
language the mighty instrument of Marlowe and
Shakespeare.   His poems have more charm than Wyatt's,
though no single one attained the vogue of Wyatt's
Forget not yet.   The reader of Surrey will be sensible
of the pleasant temperament and fancy which belonged
to this nobleman who was a true poet, even in his translations and his treatment of conventional topics.

These two pre-Elizabethans seem as a false dawn of
the day-spring to come.   Insignificant are the poetic mur-
murings until the notes of Sidney and Spenser are heard
some thirty years later.   In the meanwhile across the
channel, Ronsard had come to his great fame: — the
Pléiade had made France the Parnassus of Europe, and

[11] See as to Alamanni's and other Italian and French influence in Surrey
and Wyatt,— Sidney Lee, *French Renaissance in England* (1910), pp. 109
sqq., and authorities cited.

incidentally had produced some thousands of French sonnets after Italian fashions, perpetuating the tradition of Petrarch. Sidney and Spenser drew upon these French sonnets, rather than directly from the Italian, when they re-lighted the torch quenched at Surrey's death.[12]

We make our first pause with the age's paragon Sir Philip Sidney, who, like Wyatt and Surrey, belonged in his life and death to the world of court and field. His influence upon literature was incomparably greater than theirs; and he comes before us as an ampler illustration of Elizabethan self-expression, through the assimilation of whatever it fed upon. The style was the man with him convincingly. His birth, his character, his deeds, his writings, and his death were noble. He was the perfect Elizabethan flower of chivalry. Having the passions of his youth and time, he was nevertheless staid and prudent, diligent and well instructed, eagerly acquisitive of a wide knowledge of affairs and possessed with a love of letters. From his childhood, he took himself very seriously, and society accepted him as a masterpiece. Fulke Greville, when an old man, forty years after Sidney's death, had " Friend to Sir Philip Sidney " carved upon his tomb. He says in his memorials of Sidney: " though I lived with him and knew him from a child, yet I never knew him other than a man: with such staiednesse of mind, lovely and familiar gravity, as carried grace and reverence above greater years. His talk ever of knowledge, and his play tending to enrich his mind."

Sidney's education at Shrewsbury School and then at Oxford, his travels on the Continent, his reception by princes, statesmen and scholars, his marriage to a daughter of Sir Francis Walsingham, his moderate influence at court, his dignified diplomatic missions, his watchful maintenance of Protestantism and advocacy of militant colonization, his setting out to fight Spain in

[12] The English sonnet-indebtedness to the French poets has been sufficiently treated and possibly over-emphasized in Sir Sidney Lee's *French Renaissance in England*: reference to which may be made for all details.

the Low Countries, the breaking of his thigh bone by a
shot, because he had laid aside his cuisses that he might
be no better protected than a friend who had not put on
his before battle, his giving the water brought him to a
dying soldier, supply the salient incidents of his life.[13]
His diligence and wisdom in affairs were remarkable.
He wrote a noteworthy treatise defending his father's
government of Ireland and an extraordinary letter to
the Queen to dissuade her from marrying Anjou; he
was constant in his hostility to Spain. Quite unique was
the impression which his manner, his knowledge, and his
stainless character made on all. The Earl of Essex,
who would have married him to his daughter, said when
dying: " If he go on in the course he hath begun he will
be as famous and worthy a gentleman as England ever
bred." Later the Prince of Orange declared that " if
he could judge, her Majesty had one of the ripest and
greatest councillors of state in Sir Philip Sidney, that
at that this day lived in Europe." Perhaps Fortune felt
herself unequal to carrying out the promise of this life,
and cut it off at thirty-two. Sidney's features were re-
produced by many artists. The early portrait made in
Italy by Veronese is unhappily lost; but few who once
have seen it will forget the miniature by Oliver, now at
Windsor, of Sir Philip seated beneath a tree, ornate,
precieux, romantic.

A nobleman of Sidney's vast repute (his estate was
small) would be a cynosure for poet's eyes. His own talents made him a moving centre of literary fashion and
creation. This canon of knightly virtue and noble seemliness was also the arbiter of poetic taste. As against
carping Puritans he advanced his knightly lance and
learned shield in *A Defence of Poesie;* also he wrote a
century of sonnets, which did much to bring the sonnet
into vogue; and his *Arcadia* became a wonder on both
sides of the channel.

With the poet Spenser and other friends, he formed
a society called the " Areopagus," that met for literary

[13] See H. R. Fox Bourne, *Sir Philip Sidney* (1891) ; and Sir Sidney Lee's
article in *Dict. of Nat. Biography.*

debate, the discussion, for instance, of the competing merits of metre and accent in English verse. No wonder Spenser dedicated to this " president of noblesse and chivalrie," his *Shepherd's Calendar,* and later humbly boasted of the patronage

> " of that most heroic spirit
> Who first my muse did lift out of the floor . . . . ."

No wonder also that Bruno, meeting this noble Protestant and unyielding enemy of popery, should dedicate to him his two most truculent and famous compositions.

We turn to Sidney's expressions of himself, first in his *Defence of Poesie.*[14] Seemingly it was occasioned by a Puritan attack dedicated to Sidney, by one Gosson, upon the playhouses and popular versemaking of the day. But Sydney's piece had predecessors and successors not merely in the task of poetry's defence, but in the field of critical consideration of what was faulty or commendable in verse. A broad controversy running through such essays related to the dependence of English poetry upon classic models, and specifically to the question of rhyme, and whether accent or quantity should be the moving principle of English rhythm. Diction and decorum also were discussed. Having but scanty traditions of its own, Elizabethan criticism drew upon the classics, often at second hand through Italian and French adaptations.[15] Yet the English writers seem to grope toward an expression of themselves in their appreciation of the qualities of English poetry. A notable manifestation of a writer's personality is Sidney's *Defence.* A good defence it is, large, ample, written with a noble enthusiasm scorning quibbles: it is learned too; sometimes acute and analytical. Out of his own mind, as well as from his reading, Sidney sets forth the almost divine dignity and worth of poets and their poems from Homer to the Psalms; his own sensitive nature discovers David's poetry and even method: — " For what else is the awaking his musical

---

[14] Written about 1583; published in two editions in 1595, one having the title " Apologie for Poetrie." Printed in G. Gregory Smith's *Elizabethan Critical Essays,* Vol. I, pp. 148 sqq. (Oxford, 1894).
[15] See generally G. Gregory Smith's introduction.

instruments; the often and free changing of persons; his notable *Prosopopeias,* when he maketh you, as it were, see God coming in his Majesty; his telling of the Beasts' joyfulness, and hills leaping, but a heavenly poesie, wherein almost he showeth himself a passionate lover of that unspeakable and everlasting beauty to be seen by the eyes of the mind, only cleared by faith." The union of a strain of Plato with this appreciation of the Psalmist's imagery shows Sidney giving out again that which he had made his own: — expressing his growing self with Plato's help. He argues upon the nature of the poet's art with arguments taken to himself from many ancient sources. " It is not rhyming and versing that maketh a poet . . . but it is that feigning notable images of virtues, vices, or what else, with that delightful teaching, which must be the right describing note to know a poet by." Thus he scorns to define the poetic art by its convenient, but not essential, means. He has well read his Aristotle's *Poetics,* rendering its famous *Mimesis,* and showing that neither philosopher nor historian can vie with the poet, who alone can give the general notion in the concrete instance, be that actual or fictitious,— a method followed by Christ himself in such parables as Dives and Lazarus and the Prodigal Son.[16]

Sidney's temper may be truer than his reasoning. The soul of him is in the confession of his " own barbarousness: I never heard the old song of Percy and Douglas that I found not my heart moved more than with a trumpet; and yet it is sung but by some blind Crouder, with no rougher voice than smooth style." Unhappily his mind and deference to current learned criticism continue thus: " which being so evil apparelled in the dust and cobwebs of that uncivil age, what would it work trimmed in the gorgeous eloquence of Pindar? " Critically he did not realize and could not justify the power of the ballad note. The closing pages of his noble composition ridicule rationally, and yet so futilely and un-

[16] Sidney finds the feigned Cyrus of Xenophon more instructive than the true Cyrus of Justinus, " and the feigned Aeneas in Virgil than the *right* Aeneas in Dares Phrygius "!

prophetically, the practices of the popular and irresistibly
romantic drama, which to be sure had shown little of
its coming power and magnificence when Sidney wrote,
or even when he died.

Sidney expresses or presents himself still more palpably in his sonnets and his *Arcadia*. He had caught the
sonneteering *furore* of France and Italy, while he absorbed ideas, or conceits from Petrarch as well as from
Ronsard and other Frenchmen. This absorption was
not incompatible with a genuine passion and sentiments
pressing to utterance. The current fashions of poetry,
with their store of ideas and phrases, afford the line of
least resistance to a poet's impulse to express himself,
his sentiments or passion. Besides, the notions and sentiments of love are much the same among all people of
similar tastes, or education; and identity of idea or phrase
may no more argue mutual influence than the worldwide
human custom of burying food and knick-knacks with the
dead.

Sidney was sometime in love with Penelope, daughter
of the first Earl of Essex and sister to his son whom
Elizabeth loved and beheaded. Although a marriage
with Sidney had been discussed, the young lady at nineteen
married Lord Rich and bore him many children. Two
years later Sidney married the daughter of Sir Francis
Walsingham, and no unhappiness came of it. But
Penelope is the English "Laura," the glorified Stella
of the long series of sonnets written mostly when both
Penelope and Sidney were married, and published after
Sidney's death under the title of *Astrophel and Stella*.
Assuredly Sidney expressed himself in them, whether or
not one will follow Thomas Nashe in his preface to their
first edition, of 1591, and find "the argument, Cruel
Chastity; the prologue, Hope; the epilogue, Despair."

Perhaps the first sonnet indicates the plan and nature
of the series:

Loving in truth, and fain in verse my love to show,
That She, dear She! might take some pleasure of my pain;
Pleasure might cause her read, reading might make her know,
Knowledge might pity win, and pity grace obtain;

I sought fit words to paint the blackest face of woe,
Studying inventions fine, her wits to entertain;
Oft turning others' leaves, to see if thence would flow
Some fresh and fruitful showers upon my sunburnt brain:
But words came halting forth, wanting Invention's stay.
Invention Nature's child, fled stepdame's Study's blows;
And others' feet still seemed but strangers' in my way.

.   .   .   .   .   .   ,   .

So he tells the purpose of the sonnets, and the wrong way in which he first went about to write them by " turning others' leaves,"— a process hindering composition. It is hard to make a poem out of others' ideas and images selected for the purpose. A better way had come to him:

Thus great with child to speak, and helpless in my throes;
Biting my trowand (truant) pen, beating myself for spite:
" Fool! " said my Muse, " look in thy heart, and write! " [17]

This, we may think he did, and stopped searching others' books. But when he looked into his heart and began to write according to its promptings, he found a heart, or mind, stored with love-thoughts and images derived from reading, which had become part of himself and his own musings. He could " look in his heart and write," and make use of all its thoughts and sentiments, whatever their provenance.

Thus others' conceits, appropriated, became expressions of genuine feelings; and others' thoughts were made part of a lover's argument, in Sidney's *Astrophel and Stella*. Sincerity of imagination is called for, rather than originality. Any poetic lover, gazing at the moon, might think in the conceits of Sidney's sonnet (XXXI) beginning:

With how sad steps, O Moon! than climb'st the skies!
How silently! and with how wan a face!
What! may it be that even in heavenly place
That busy archer his sharp arrows tries? —

and so forth.[18]   Sonnet LXIV seems to give a more unsuggested note:

[17] Compare Sonnet XV.
[18] Compare Shelley's " Art thou pale for loneliness . . ."

No more! my Dear! no more these counsels try!
O give my passions leave to run their race! . . .

The lady may have counselled something " Platonic ";
yet in sonnet LXIX, the lover is ecstatic over her granted
measure of conditional grace. If not in love with
Penelope Devereux, Sidney was in love with love; and
delighted in writing sonnets on this theme. They circulated in manuscript among his friends, assuring his
fame as lover-poet, which most of his circle aspired to
be. In a sonnet outside of this sonnet-series, Sidney expressed his mind's conclusion of a conflict, frequently
mentioned in the Stella sonnets, and by some thousands
of other men and women:

Leave me, O Love! which reachest but to dust!
And thou, my mind! aspire to higher things!

.   .   .   .

Then farewell, world! Thy uttermost I see!
Eternal Love, maintain Thy love in me!

This conclusion held while the mood of this sonnet
lasted; one cannot consider it the dominant of the
Arcadia, which Sidney wrote for his sister the countess
of Pembroke, when he was staying at her country seat,
disgusted with court politics, during the years 1580 and
1581.[19] It is a trying composition for us to-day; tedious,
endless, at least in the sense that it does not end, but
merely stops. It is written in " pure Sir Philip Sidney ";
that is to say Sir Philip's brand of that ornate and precieux manner of writing which was cultivated in Spain
and elsewhere before like fashions appeared in England.
John Lyly and his *Euphues* afford a contrasted illustration of the manner. Born the same year with Sidney,
and graduating at Oxford, feeling his aptitude for ladies'
society, this protégé of Lord Burghley came to London
to seek and find his social fortune. Sensing his true
audience, he wrote for the ladies, dedicating his work to
them, as Sidney says he wrote the *Arcadia* for his sister
— also a lady. *Euphues, the anatomy of wit* appeared
in 1578 or 1579, and its sequel, *Euphues and his England,*

19 See H. R. F. Bourne, *Sir Philip Sidney,* chap. XII.

in 1580, just when Sidney was occupying himself with the *Arcadia*. These compositions merit special treatment in the history of the English novel.[20] Doubtless, Lyly expressed his delicate and ladylike nature in his books. His style, quite as much as his topic, made him the fashion while he lived, and afterwards embalmed his memory. *Euphuism,* ornate, precieux, involute, antithetical, was stuffed with similes from the imagined qualities of gems and the fictitious ways of animals: — the last and loveliest use to which Pliny's *Natural History* and the Mediaeval Bestiaries were to be put! Of course it was absurd; yet Lyly's writing had its stylistic preciseness, its delicacy, balance, and modulation. These good qualities, separated from the chaff, appear to advantage in the pretty, almost charming plays which Lyly also wrote.[21]

Sidney vigorously disapproved of Euphuism in his *Defence of Poesie*. But in the *Arcadia,* while he omitted Lyly's natural history, he wrote as preciously. The style was expressive of his nature, as well as suited to his theme. Sidney was a part of his time's loftiest affectations and finest human qualities. He was the quintessence of its most scrupulous chivalry, of its nicest scholarship. Displace him from the sphere of politics and diplomacy, push him back just a little into Faery Land, and he might be an Arthur or a Red Cross Knight in Spenser's Poem, or a prince in his own *Arcadia*. Inevitably for this, his own prose poem, he would produce, out of himself and the time in which he wrote, a style imbued with the ornateness, graciousness, and highmindedness of Sir Philip Sidney. It also would reflect personal taste, which may strike us as his reflection of a contemporary fashion. Its chief artifices seem to lie in repetition of chosen words, worked into periodic antitheses, and in the poetic animism which ascribes motive and sentiment to trees and brooks and inert things.

[20] And have received it, charmingly, in Jusserand's *English Novel in the time of Shakespeare.* No one now can write of the *Arcadia* and not feel his debt to M. Jusserand.

[21] *Endymion, Alexander and Campaspe, Sapho and Phao,* etc. They also helped to form English prose.

The *Arcadia* is a sixteenth century romance of chivalry
cast in a pastoral setting: the princely knights and ladies
are the actors, while the shepherds of Arcadia, like its
vales and streams, make scenery and atmosphere, or incidentally assist the action.   The pastoral part (which
harks back through Sannazaro even to Theocritus) belonged to the same revival which is displayed in the rustic
Masques provided by English nobles for the entertainment of their Queen upon her Progresses.   Sidney had
composed a masque of this sort, and Spenser's *Shepherd's
Calendar* set the seal of lovely English verse upon the
fashion.   Spenser's poem was dedicated " to the noble
and virtuous gentleman " who was soon to write his
Arcadia.

As for this knightly and romantic story, its sources, its
forbears were everywhere, from Amadis de Galles to the
Arthurian knights; its inspiration sprang from the soul
of Philip Sidney and the renewed romance of the new
" temps aventureux."   The literary, romantic and chiv-
alric past is in this multitudinous tale: the perfect courage
of the knights, the point of honor, and the pink and white
lover traits which had delighted the ladies listening to
Chrétien de Troyes in the twelfth century.

Sidney's Romance was a covert declaration of himself.
First in the modest deprecating preface to his sister the
Countess:

" Here now have you . . . this idle work of mine; which I fear
(like the spider's web) will be thought fitter to be swept away . . .
It is done only for you, only to you; if you keep it to yourself, or
to such friends, who will weigh errors in the balance of good will,
I hope. . . . For severer eyes it is not, being but a trifle, and that
triflingly handled. . . . In sum, a young head, not so well stayed
as I would it were (and shall be God will) having many fancies
begotten in it, if it had not been in some way delivered, would
have grown a monster. . . . Read it then at your idle times, and
the follies your good judgment will find in it, blame not, but
laugh at."

Likewise he expresses himself throughout the book in
the characters and conduct of his heroes, for example

in the portrayal of Argalus, given by a court officer: " I
think no man for valor of mind and habilitie of body
to be preferred, if equalled to Argalus, and yet so valiant
as he never durst do anybody injury; in behaviour some
will say ever sad, surely sober, and somewhat given to
musing, but never uncourteous; his words ever led by
his thought, and followed by his deed; rather liberal
than magnificent. . . ." Here was no intended description of self (which Sidney seems to have given under
the humbler character of Philisides) ; but inevitable self-
expression. It is not always in the deeds and descriptions
or his heroes that an author declares himself; but quite
as truly in his manner of delineating, as it were, his opposites. Note this way of Sidney's self-expression in the
description of Parthenia, beloved of Argalus:

" fair indeed . . . and that which made her fairness much the
fairer, was, that it was but a fair ambassador of a most fair mind,
full of wit, and a wit which delighted more to judge itself, than
to show itself; her speech being as rare as precious; her silence
without sullenness; her modesty without affectation; her shame-
fastness without ignorance; in sum, one, that to praise well, one
must first set down with himself what it is to be excellent; for so
she is."

Sidney's devoted intimate, Fulke Greville, was palpably
didactic, in all his poems and dramas. Doubtless he
betrays himself when he says of Sidney's characters in
the *Arcadia,* " that in all these creatures of his making,
his intent and scope was to turn barren philosophy precepts into pregnant images of life; and in them, first on
the monarch's part, lively to represent the growth, state,
and declination of princes, change of government and
laws " and so forth. This was Fulke Greville's method,
rather than Sidney's. He may have said more truly,
that Sidney's " end was not writing, even while he wrote
. . . but both his wit and understanding bent upon his
heart, to make himself and others . . . good and great."
Sidney was a serious person; and may have had improvement in view even in his intellectual pastimes. Not
merely in the mediaeval centuries, but still in Sidney's

time, the writing and reading of works of the imagination carried an instructive purpose more frequently than now.[22]

III

We may come to a great poet through many avenues of sympathy. One way of approaching Spenser is by distinguishing between the actual and the real. The former is made up of the daily experience of mankind, in peace and war, in love and hate, in all manner of social relations and every mode of contact with the facts of mother earth. Imaginative literature makes use of this mass of data by selection, rearrangement, emphasis. It may enhance certain facts or human qualities, in the individual instance; intensifying human nature to the diabolic, or enlarging and raising it to the sublime; it may present it, so intensified or raised, in artfully constructed or plausibly imagined situations, which abound in humor or pathos, or attain the heights of tragedy. The facts may never have existed; but so long as the playwright or poet combines and rearranges his incidents along the lines of verifiable experience, and preserves possible proportions while raising his characters above the usual, he will not pass the bounds of truly imagined actuality. Herein Shakespeare is the supreme illustration.

The real includes the actual, but also transcends it. Without meaning to be metaphysical or mystical, one may say this much if one would understand either Plato or Spenser. The syllogism, the intellectual definition, the idea — things of the spirit all — were Plato's ultimate realities. The tangible data of daily experience which one may venture to call the Actual, were to him but as the apparent *tangibilia* by which he swung himself into the realm of spirit, where the idea, or the ideal, alone was real.

This crude analysis may answer for Spenser, who was

[22] The *Arcadia* became popular from the date or its publication (1590); both at home and abroad its vogue and influence were lasting. See Jusserand, *English Novel*, &c., pp. 260 sqq.

a poet, and incidentally a far-flung Platonist. The actualities of life chiefly meant for him his horrid surroundings
in Ireland or his disappointments at Court. In the world
of the actual, Spenser was a failure. We see him trying
for place — for a small place, then for a more comfort-
able place and *not* in Ireland. He may have been a pains-
taking administrator there; but it was his fortune to
rouse rancour at the man who in his minor way shared
greedily in the blind English policy, perhaps the only
policy with Ireland the impossible, then as now! Spenser got little comfort from his patrons, and little from
the positions held by him in Ireland. Willing to flatter
with the rest, he excelled all in the gorgeousness of his
poetic adulation of the Queen; that also brought him
little. He has left as his sole prose composition *A view
of the present state of Ireland,* which, except for its anti-
quarian diligence, is not above the level of the Administration in which he was a cog.

From all such squalid troubles and occupations, his
studious, musically sensitive, gloriously imaginative nature
would immure itself or fly away. Beyond his brief intercourse with such noble friends as Sidney and Raleigh,
nothing in his outer life ranked with his books and his
fecund fancy, so lively while he read or thought. Out
of his study and his thoughts, his imagination built
pastures of idyllic charm and worlds of knightly beauty,
and peopled them with beings of limpid excellence or
equally ideal wickedness. His people betokened human
qualities, were suitable type-ideas of holiness, temperance,
justice, courtesy, or cruelty and guile, or again types
of idyllic rustic joys and sorrows. Their natures and
actions were not merely imaginary, but were imbued with
symbolic significance and validity. Were not the virtues
real? and were not sins and vices facts? Real then were
their allegorical personifications, which not only lived so
vividly in the poet's vision, but also came to him
accredited with the stamp and sanction of tradition and
antiquity, of ancient thought and previous poetic creation.
His mind was reverential; his imagination was plastic
and constructive, building fantasies, nay realities, out of

the materials furnished by his devouring study and the reading of delightful books. Delight in imaginative creations, whether other men's or the poet's own, comes through their felt reality. They are shaped and formed by the imagination in accord with the predilections and best judgments of the poet, declaring and expressing himself in his omissions, choice, and emphasis.

So the world of Spenser's well-stored and wonder-making imagination, the world of the symbol, the allegory, and the type-idea, was a real world and a vivid one, moving in the life and strength of ethical principles and the underlying validities of human conduct, from which the actual Elizabethan world was swerving aberrantly and decadently. This is poetic Platonism,— all poets are Platonists — and rests on sound metaphysics, if any such there be. Imaginative contemplators have their intellectual rights as well as other people. The world made of their thoughts and of their universal consideration of causes and effects, is as real as the world of sense-experience. That poet in whom the visualizing and emotional imagination is dominant will build a world of living beings moving about and acting according to their own ideal laws of conduct good or ill, after the manner of men and women. Such a world will also be a reflection and expression of the poet's self.

Of such a world the poet Spenser was the builder, but by no means the demiurge. He did not create it, but marvellously put it together. He has taken to himself the matter of previous idealism, allegory, and romance. He brings a shaping knowledge of Platonism; prodigiously he possesses the antique pagan literature, using it as material for his world, fuel for his imagination; he is a catholic pagan in his temperament and in his tolerance of the heathen gods, and thereto a somewhat catholic protestant Christian, who has read the Bible reverently. A devotee of his own English Chaucer, he has gone far back of him into the writings of the mediaeval time. Of course, the *Romaunt de la Rose* is his, and he would seem to have appropriated the striking nature-allegories of Alanus de Insulis. He is indeed the final sacred vessel of mediaeval allegory: — is not the *Faerie Queen* a soul's conflict, *Psychomachia,* carrying back across the Middle Ages to the old Christian poet Prudentius? [23]   Likewise he is the poet of chivalry and of its holiest ideals; his is the spirit of romance, its matter too, with forests and enchantments, quests and valorous adventures. He has absorbed Tasso and Ariosto, possesses the latter's tricks and marvels, his witchery of combination; yet has somehow crowned Ariosto's spirit. The *Orlando Furioso* is sheer art; the *Faerie Queen* is art and religion too — the religion of chivalry, its final expression in a poem. Here Spenser is closer to Tasso than to Ariosto.

The matter of the *Faerie Queen* was too multiform to bring to narrative unity. Its disparate ingredients, that is to say, its insistent allegory, its matter of more veritable romance, its pagan and Christian piety, its mirage of living personages and political events, its reduplicated flattery of the Queen, who appears in several prototypes, are not happily fused. It gathers alike from pagan mythology and the Old Testament — the clashing rocks, the monster refreshed when hurled to mother earth, the Sirens, the Judgment of Solomon, what you will. The test lies not in the principle, but in the success of the procedure; [24] and usually Spenser is successful.[25]   The exquisite grace and beauty of the poem triumph, and throughout its entirety the plastic strength of the poet's temperament harmonizes recalcitrant elements, and charms the reader like a summer's day. It is a stupendous and beautiful example of a poet's veritable expression of himself through the transformation of whatever his learning had gathered.

A letter to Sir Walter Raleigh serves as preface to the first three books of the *Faerie Queen*. Even as Dante's letter to Can Grande set forth the intended mean-

[23] Cf. my *Classical Heritage,* etc., pp. 278 sqq.
[24] The unveiled apologetic for the execution of Mary Queen of Scots in the narrative of the trial and execution of Duessa is an unhappy instance. Book V, cantos IX and X.
[25] Though not in Artegal's copying of the Judgment of Solomon in the first canto of Book V.

ing, literal and allegorical, of the *Divina Commedia,* so Spenser's letter should explain the covert intentions of his poem. Spiritual antecedents of convincing power, extending back through the Church Fathers, even into paganism, argued that the veritable significance of historic fact and of the visible world lay in the symbolic meaning, which indeed represented the deeper reality. Dante's mastering realization of that which was carried by the allegorical or spiritual meaning, belonged to the mediaeval genius, of which he was the poetic summary and crowning illustration. Spenser had not this conviction in its singleness; for he was a man of the sixteenth century, touched with its enterprise and its discoveries, its consciousness of the counter-denials of the Catholic and Protestant faiths, its dominating humanism and further questings of the intellect. These multifarious influences produced a certain manifold of impulse in him, which barred the sheer assurance of the realness of the symbolical significance and content. Yet the old spiritual convictions enabled his powerful and well-stored imagination to construct a living world of allegorical romance out of the contents of his mind.

Dante's imagination created the *Divina Commedia* — most of it. He did not have the text of the Can Grande letter constantly in mind, nor did he tenaciously pursue the unhappy method of the *Convivio.* His imagination cast such shackles off, and made a poem. Likewise Spenser did not painfully abide by the edifying purpose stated in his letter to Raleigh, but gave his imagination play. Yet, even as Dante, Spenser was a teacher. In the *Faerie Queen* he is not averse to teaching by precept and admonition where the situation admits of it. But the poem teaches rather in the way of presentation — the presentation in action of the glorious and the ignoble, of that which should be imitated and shunned.

He says in the letter:

" Sir, knowing how doubtfully all Allegories may be construed, and this book of mine, which I have thought good . . . to discover unto you the general intention and meaning. . . . The general end therefore of all the book is to fashion a gentleman or noble person in virtuous and gentle discipline: which for that I conceived should be most plausible and pleasing, being coloured with an historical fiction."

The Book of the Courtier had tried for a like end in other fashion,— though Spenser does not say so. His own plan has both classic and modern sanction. Choosing " the history of King Arthur," he has

" followed all the antique poets historical; first Homer, who in the person of Agamemnon and Ulysses hath ensampled a good governour and a virtuous man . . . then Virgil, whose like intention was to do in the person of Aeneas; after him Ariosto comprised them both in his *Orlando;* and lately Tasso dissevered them again, and formed both parts in two persons, namely that part which they in philosophy called *Ethice,* or virtues of a private man, coloured in his *Rinaldo;* the other named *Politice* in his *Godfredo.*"

Having made these justifying statements, which strike us, so to speak, " as of the time," Spenser tells how he proposes to portray

" in Arthure, before he was King, the image of a brave knight perfected in the twelve private moral virtues, as Aristotle hath devised; that which is the purpose of these first twelve books; which if I find to be well accepted, I may be perhaps encouraged to frame the other part of Politic virtues in his person, after that he came to be King."

As a presentation of his theme through action, the six completed books of the *Faerie Queen* sufficiently fulfil the purpose outlined in his letter. Yet it would have taken the excellent pragmatical Fulke Greville, rather than the lovely poet Spenser, to have carried out this scheme specifically; in which case we should not now have the poem which bewitches our imaginations. In verses prefixed to the sixth book Spenser shows himself living and working in the poem, and discloses how real to him was that world of Faerie in which he lived and wrought.

The waies through which my weary steps I guide
In this delightful land of Faery,
Are so exceeding spaciöus and wide,
And sprinkled with such sweet variety
Of all that pleasant is to ear or eye,
That I, nigh ravisht with rare thoughts' delight,

My tedious travell doe forget thereby;
And, when I gin to feel decay of might,
It strength to me supplies and cheers my dulled spright,

Such secret comfort and such heavenly pleasures,
Ye, sacred Imps, that on Parnasso dwell,
And there the keeping have of Learning's treasures,
Which doe all worldly riches far excel,
Into the minds of mortal men doe well, [pour]
And goodly fury into them infuse.
Guide ye my footing, and conduct me well
In these strange waies where never foot did use,
Ne none can find but who was taught them by the Muse.

Reveal to me the sacred nursery
Of virtue, which with you doth there remain,
Where it in silver bower does hidden lie
From view of men and wicked world's disdain;
Since it at first was by the gods with pain
Planted in earth, being deriv'd at first
From heavenly seeds of bounty soverain,
And by them long with careful labor nurst,
Till it to ripeness grew, and forth to honour burst.

To Spenser, Parnassus was a mount of learning, and
for that reason too " the sacred nursery of virtue." The
Muses would impart such virtue to the poet whom they
chose to inspire, as with the grace of the gods, that it
should burst forth in honor. They had bidden this poet,
Spenser, early addicted to pastoral verse, to sing of arms
and princely knights:

There may thy Muse display her fluttering wing,
And stretch herself at large from east to west!

At their behest he devoted his life to writing the *Faerie
Queen.* It was the fullest expression of his poetic call,
and of that which to him was worthy and most real. It
should be beautiful, a beautiful creation: and in ever-
present, insistent, decorative and precious beauty, no
poem has since surpassed it. Herein the poet fixed his
enduring love and expressed himself most constantly.
His nature gives itself more unimpededly when his verse
is telling of the beauties of man and of nature, or is disclosing the soul's sensitiveness to beauty. Such fitting

ease of adequate expression is exemplified in hundreds of splendid passages or in perfect lines.

Scarcely less constantly his high-mindedness and adoration of the good and honorable — καλοκἀγαθία — press to expression; and his counter detestation of discourtesy and falsity, malice and vengeful spite,— " arguments of a vile donghill mind."

The *Faerie Queen* is an example of the veritable self-expression of a sixteenth century poet. It may be taken likewise as the expression of one phase of the tastes, fancies, and ideals of the Elizabethan time. None the less, it received and accepted its substance from the past. And one may profitably realize how this substance — the plan and contents, and the leading motives of the poem — had been transmitted to Spenser as completed forms of thought and feeling, that is to say, as language and forms of expression in which prior men and women had expressed themselves.

CHAPTER XXIX

THE DRAMATIC SELF-EXPRESSION OF THE ELIZABETHAN AGE

I

ALL things worked together to make the Drama a full and complete expression of the Elizabethan Age. Whatever entered that Age and contributed to make it what it was, or, at least, what its report has been, entered the Drama. To be sure, that had its natural exclusions. It was not religious, and had little to say of the soul's destinies beyond the grave. It recoiled from the Puritans who would have none of it, and tried to forbid it altogether. It passed over large portions of the people, and said little of their daily tasks. Neither those who dug and sowed, nor the city mob, appealed to it, though it used them when needed to fill out its action. Nor had it much to do with trade and commerce, and crafts or the professions, save that of arms. Yet it draws from them all as the story may require; and a merchant like Antonio may be a prime figure in a play. Doctors, priests, pedagogues fill out the action; though the clown and fool are better loved for their own sake, and as apter foils to the loftier characters.

Not written for dainty reading, but to be acted on the stage, the plays had to meet the tastes of a promiscuous audience, especially of the very live London public, whose passion was the theatre. The playwright's work was tried and tried again by popular insistence. He had need to put good matter in his play, and make it carry as a dramatic story, or lively pageant of human action. If, like most of Shakespeare's plays, it contained profound thought and reflections too fine for the common understanding, that troubled no one, since the action carried the audience across such stumbling places. This auditor-public was only somewhat less quick-minded than the Athenian demos, who heard, or *saw,* the plays of Aeschylus and Sophocles. Their moving and, usually, well-known legends would likewise help the stupider elements of an Athenian audience over any unfathomable comments of the chorus.

A London audience, composed of gentry as well as townsfolk, was a broader index of the age than a court society. Its demands were more apt to keep the plays broadly squared with life. It asked for, and condoned, whatever moved the time; and the plays presented such. National and patriotic " chronicle-plays " transcribed and glorified the nation's history. The enterprise, the chivalry, the heroism of the time were reflected in rugged, ancient incidents. Other plays, with subjects from the antique world, rendered the larger past, which was not England, yet had entered her throbbing veins. Still others drew tragic or romantic tales from Italy, the Orient, and Spain. Love, lust, ambition, the passions of mortal life, all were there, in English, Italian, or antique guise.

The plays embodied the current knowledge and information of the Age; and its yearning for still more knowledge. Marlowe puts a fine expression of this venturesome curiosity in Mortimer's last words in *Edward the Second*:

> Farewell sweet queen; weep not for Mortimer,
> That scorns the world, and, as a traveller,
> Goes to discover countries yet unknown.

And in *Tamburlaine* there is a soaring passage, which is not called for by the play or the character of the hero-speaker; but is just a flash of Marlowe's yearning:

> " Our souls whose faculties can comprehend the world,
>   And measure every wandering planet's course,
>   Still climbing after knowledge infinite,
>   Wills us to wear ourselves and never rest,
>   Until we reap the ripest fruit of all,
>   That perfect bliss and sole felicity,
>   The sweet fruition of an earthly crown."

The last four lines turn the theme to Tamburlaine's own ambition. Quite fantastic or sordid twists are given to these infinite yearnings in Marlowe's *Faustus*. That strange soul shows no detached desire for Knowledge of the glories of the Universe; he turns his magic to human and quite foolish ends, dramatic though they be. This is as befits the Elizabethan drama, which was not interested in physical science, or the advance of knowledge, save as these intellectual yearnings were very part of man. It is the dramatic moment which is given, the effect of the impulse or the vision on the soaring soul of man.

In this, as always, the drama is consistently and gloriously human, or even humanistic. The lesser playwrights as well as Shakespeare stand upon the human plain, their presentation of life extending to the full horizon of humanity. Where they cross the pale of death, it is but to portray the effect of the imminence or contemplation of death upon the human mind engaged with mortal aims or perceiving their nullity.

The Drama appears impersonal, an impersonal, rather than individual, self-expression of the Age. The production, the authorship, of the plays was often promiscuous. Until Ben Jonson, the playwrights, whatever they felt, display no vanity of authorship. Rather than ambitious poets, they were craftsmen working upon materials at hand. It cannot be said with certainty of a single Elizabethan play that the author is giving his own views, or intentionally expressing himself in it. So we are justified in treating the Drama as a general expression of the age, and may forego investigation of the authorship of plays and the qualities of individual playwrights,—which befits a critical history of the Elizabethan drama. My purpose is merely to suggest its most expressive notes, or, better, its symphonic harmony. Its antecedents, its preparation, its debt to recent foreign literatures and fashions, need be averted to only in the most general way, to salve our sense of human unity and influence. No cursory reader can fail to mark the dramatic progress in the last decades of the century, or fail to recognize the more striking differences between Marlowe and the much younger Webster, or between the fruits of their genius and the works of Jonson, Beaumont and Fletcher, and other gifted men, which belong rather to the Jacobean than the Elizabethan time. As for Shakespeare, the more one reads the other dramatists, the more lustrous becomes his singular preeminence; which consists less strikingly in distinctive qualities, than in the vast and all-inclusive power of genius and range of thought, and a loftier melodiousness in execution. He is worth all the rest; their sheer deification; — in him they have become a god. He lifts the expression of other playwrights, of the whole age indeed, to Pisgah heights, whence the entire range of human consideration and mortal incident is brought within the view and made part of the self-expression of this superman and the age of which he was incidentally the exponent.

The antecedents of the Elizabethan drama, as well as its own beginnings, may be regarded as themselves forms, or schemes, or categories, of expression, which passed on into the volume of the fuller time. Archaic schemes of dramatic representation were carried by the mediaeval mystery plays, and by the miracle or saints plays as well. All these gradually admitted human and comic elements, reflected from the manners of the time. Later followed another mode of the religious drama; the " morality," in which the characters were usually personified abstractions. The " morality " was a Psychomachia; the struggle between man's good and evil faculties made the drama. *Every-man,* originating in the fifteenth century, is a well-known " morality." All these " religious " representations fell under the disapproval of the Puritans, and their vogue was stolen by the secular Elizabethan drama, which proved a more living expression of the time.

This had its own crude popular antecedents in the recitals of minstrels and the representations of strolling performers, or men of the town or local guilds. For these in market-place or banquet-hall could perform an " interlude," a short simple play needing little preparation or machinery. It might be accompanied by " mummings " or " disguisings," which by the time of Henry

VIII made some approach to dramatic form, and were called "masques." All these had become a part of merry-making and good cheer.

In the sixteenth century, fashions of tragedy came from Italy or from the plays of Seneca. Under the latter influence, English tragedy set a native theme upon the stage in the play of *Gorboduc,* called otherwise *Ferrex and Porrex.* Here blank verse entered upon its career in English drama. The authors were Thomas Norton and Thomas Sackville, the latter a statesman who became Earl of Dorset. He expressed himself naturally in a play of good counsel, such as might emanate from one who wrote the wise "Induction" to the *Mirror for Magistrates.* In the play the chorus says that Gorboduc

"A mirror shall become to princes all."

The play was acted before the still young Elizabeth in 1562, and contained passages intended for her ear. The antique idea of fate, the fate of an accursed house, seems to direct this drama of the war between Gorboduc's two sons. Porrex, the younger son, dies by his mother's hand. The people rise and slay the murderous queen and old Gorboduc. Civil war ensues, with admonishings that it is a ruler's duty to present or name the heir of the crown, and for Parliament to confirm the act.

This tragedy was the self-expression of an Elizabethan statesman with dramatic gifts. He accepted the tragic modes of Seneca, his choruses, his messengers, and the classic scheme of five acts; also a sententious style. Tragedies were to follow with plots drawn from the Italian, and like their sources, were under Seneca's influence. Or, again, the tragic interest might swing back to English stories, the *Misfortunes of Arthur, The Famous Victories of Henry V, The True Chronicle History of King Leir and his three daughters.* In these the relatively living theme tends to break through the restraint of classic forms. But we have already reached the time of Shakespeare and his immediate known predecessors in tragedy.

As for the comic line of early growth, one Heywood

wrote vigorously in the reign of Henry VIII. His " in-
terludes " consisted of debates upon some theme, in which
the characters of the speakers begin to evince themselves
dramatically. Some pieces with veritable comic action
are doubtfully accredited to him. We have also *Calisto
and Melebea*, a clever adaptation from the Spanish; and
adaptations of the comedies of Plautus; and about the
middle of the century *Ralph Roister Doister* by Udall,
which had a plot. Adaptations from the Latin or the
Italian continue, till again we approach the time of
Shakespeare's youth.

John Lyly was born near the middle of the century and
outlived its close by a few years. This famous author
of *Euphues* brought a melodious and sophisticated prose
into the charming comedies which he formed from ancient
stories, to meet the taste of the ladies of the court and
of other people of refined wit. His mythical and traditional personages, delicate in their conduct, ingenious in
their language, unfold their gentle passions amid idyllic
scenes. They are quite proper for high comedy, through
which Lyly expressed his sense of charm. He had had a
humanistic education, and was a gently Italianate Englishman. The young Shakespeare read Lyly well, admits
his influence, and laughingly reflects it in *Love's Labour's
Lost*.

At the opening of Shakespeare's career, and toward
the tragic close of Marlowe's, certain college-bred and
clever men produced a number of plays marking a dramatic and, as it were, expressional advance. However
warped their lives and circumstances, they had some sense
of the poet's art. One of them, Thomas Nashe, whose
dramatic performance is rather indeterminate, thus expressed himself as to the poet and his worth:

" Destiny never defames herself but when she lets an excellent
poet die . . . Despised they are of the world, because they are not
of the world: their thoughts are exalted above all worldly ignorance and all earthly conceits. As sweet angelical queristers
[choristers] they are continually conversant in the heaven of arts;
heaven itself is but the highest kind of knowledge; he that knows
himself and all things else knows the means to be happy: happy,

thrice happy are they whom God hath doubled his spirit upon, and given a double soul unto to be poets." [1]

This almost Platonic passage in the mouth of a professed rogue, whose fictitious career was scarcely more disreputable than the author's, throws light upon the many-phased and voluble Elizabethan character, which so frequently seems to be just what it feels and expresses upon a given occasion. One recalls two lines from a poem of Robert Greene, a fellow novelist and playwright, whose life was as dissolute as its end was squalid, yet with its flashes of genius and fine feeling:

"Weep not, my wanton, smile upon my knee:
    When thou art old, life hath tears enough for thee!"

Greene seems to imagine this unforgettable refrain as falling from the lips of his own wife, whom with her babe the poet was just then forsaking!

Greene wrote some plays of fustian heroics, which had nevertheless a way of moving. Daintier work was done by another of the group, George Peele, whose pastoral play, *The Arraignment of Paris,* contained some charming verses. It was played in 1584 before the Queen, to whom as the beauteous nymph Eliza, the Golden Ball of Discord is in the end harmoniously awarded. Peele's fancy — the best part of him — played with the gods above, or delighted in flowery meeds, where

"Ye may ne see for peeping flowers the grass."

This man of rather slight dramatic power may have worked over the first and second parts of *Henry VI,* before Shakespeare took that chronicle play in hand.

The fashionings of Peele and Greene and Lyly did not leave the drama as it had been before. Of the same age with them was Thomas Kyd, a much stronger playwright. His *Spanish Tragedie,* probably written shortly before 1588, became deservedly one of the most popular of Elizabethan plays. Its author had read Seneca's Tragedies, and much French and Latin. But it was through

[1] Thos. Nashe, *The Misfortunate Traveller — the life of Jack Wilton,* ed. by E. Gosse (London, 1892).

his own dramatic talent that he made this telling tragedy (out of some source unknown), and put himself in it. Whether or not Kyd was the author of the *Hamlet* used by Shakespeare, the latter drew many a suggestion from the plays of Kyd, who was but six years his senior.

Doubtless Shakespeare owed more to Marlowe, who was born the same year (1564) with him. A spendthrift magnificence of speech expresses Marlowe and something of his time. Its tumult of desire is brought to mighty rhythmic utterance by the harmonic strength of a genius which had not lacked the leaven of classical training; for Marlowe took a bachelor's and a master's degree at Cambridge. He left the University in disfavor, naturally for London, and brought out *Tamburlaine*. Never was such a boisterous and lustful conqueror presented on the stage; he oppresses kings, wades in the blood of armies; unrelenting, remorseless, delighting in the wretchedness of his enemies,— upon whom his *honor* treads. Toward the end of the play, when Bajezeth's crazed queen has killed herself, and Bajezeth has dashed out his brains against his iron cage, Tamburlaine says of the spectacle:

> " All sights of power to grace my victory:
> And such are objects fit for Tamburlaine;
> Wherein, as in a mirror, may be seen
> His honor that consists in shedding blood
> When men presume to manage arms with him."

Tamburlaine's contempt is fathomless: he points to his adversaries before his last battle:

> " See a knot of Kings,
> Sitting as if they were a telling riddles."

His passion for his queen is equally extravagant; and he is magnanimous when men, at his first demand, submit. This famous, crudely constructed play had its own grandiose roaring, and moved with turgid force. Its dialogue calls aloud; the speakers wave their arms articulately: —

> " And ride in triumph through Persepolis! "

The desires of Marlowe's *Faustus* are kin to the ambitions of Tamburlaine. No sheer yearning to know impels him; but desire to get and have such things, and exercise such fantastic power, as magic and the devil's agency can bring. Yet this is part of the dramatic necessity. Elizabethan plays were plays of action; every motive had an active end, and must contribute to the action. There was no place for any sheer intellectual desire to know. Faustus uses his power rather childishly. He is loftily contemptuous, rather than rational: says of the Law:

> "This study fits a mercenary drudge
> Who aims at nothing but external trash."

He would "make spirits fetch me what I please," and "resolve me of all ambiguities." Still his desire for knowledge is desire for power:—

> "A sound magician is a mighty god
>
> .   .   .   .
>
> Philosophy is odious and obscure;
> Both law and physics are for petty wits;
> Divinity is basest of the three. . . .
> 'Tis magic, magic, that hath ravished me."

To satisfy his passions by its means, he surrenders his soul in return for twenty-four years of "all voluptuousness":—

> "The god thou serv'st is thine own appetite."

Mephistopheles is more spiritual. Faustus asks him how he had got out of hell: he answers:

> "Why this is hell, nor am I out of it."

In its construction, *Doctor Faustus* is a succession of scenes stitched together. But we have been looking only at its rough seamy side, indeed at the seamy side of the work of the poet and dramatist who had evinced his genius before a baneful knife prevented the unfolding of his powers.

> Come live with me, and be my love,
> And we will all the pleasures prove
> That hills and valleys, dales and field
> And rocks and craggy mountains yield.

He who wrote this little poem, and the warm sensuous *Hero and Leander,* might claim the name of poet,— even had his *Doctor Faustus* not contained four of the most splendid lines in English poetry:

> Is this the face that launched a thousand ships,
> And fired the topless towers of Ilium?
>
> .   .   .   .
>
> Oh! thou art fairer than the evening air,
> Clad in the beauty of a thousand stars!

No woman ever was as fair as this; but only womanhood in a poet's thought. The achievement of our poet was to advance the ten syllable line of English blank verse toward its Shakespearean perfection. But, besides the four incomparable lines just quoted, other lines and thoughts lift themselves toward Olympus in the plays of *Tamburlaine* and *Faustus.* Says the latter:

> "When I behold the heaven, then I repent."

In Marlowe's *Dido, Queen of Carthage,* which he drew from Virgil, come these lines of glorious extravagance:

> " O, that I had a charm to keep the winds
> Within the closure of a golden ball;
> Or that the Tyrrhene sea were in mine arms,
> That he might suffer shipwreck on my breast! "

It is in Marlowe's *Edward the Second,* written after *Tamburlaine* and *Faustus,* that his " mighty line " may be seen progressing toward its last excellence; while likewise in that play, which in so many aspects is the forerunner of Shakespeare's *Richard II,* the author's dramatic faculties attain the best expression it was given them to reach before Acheron sprung its gulf before him. Some of its finest passages have to do with death; one touching the death of Mortimer has been already cited. In another, a minor character exclaims:

> " Spencer, I see our souls are fleeting hence;
> We are deprived the sunshine of our life:
> Make for a new life, man; throw up thine eyes,
> And heart and hands to heaven's immortal throne;
> Pay nature's debt with cheerful countenance.

The play had opened with the recall from banishment of Gaveston, the royal favorite; who announces the extravagances with which he will at once beguile the King and waste the Kingdom. Edward's infatuation for this man, who " wears a lord's revenue on his back," is preposterous, yet no more so than that shown for " Steeny " Buckingham a generation after Marlowe's death, in the letters of James I. Edward, as his troubles close over him, is sorry for himself after the manner in which Shakespeare's Richard II. expresses himself more finely and more beautifully.

Marlowe's characters change with their circumstances, following not merely dramatic truth, but the truth of life, that men are not always the same. They recall the very actual Sir Walter Raleigh, his rapaciousness, his vanity that " wore a lord's revenue on his back," his bad temper and vengefulness; his none too steady sense of honor; and again, his melancholy temperament and poetic gifts, his intellectual vision, his almost sublimity, educed by a long imprisonment with its exit to the block.

II

Shakespeare's plays are impersonal in that they were written for the Elizabethan stage, and the author does not obviously give his own views and opinions in any one of them, not even in the *Tempest*. They are impersonal, moreover, in that the whole imaginative self-expression of the time finds its seraphic voice in them. Yet, on the other hand, they are supremely personal, as the transcendent works of genius perforce must be; in that they issue from their author, are the works of his mind, the embodiment of his genius; and no other man could have produced them. Necessarily they reflect the personality which has created them: even as philosophers have held the universe to be a reflection of its Creator. The plays of Shakespeare are as certainly an expression, a self-expression, of the master, and of no other man, as are his Sonnets, into which apparently he put those intimate sentiments which pertained to himself and his relationships to one or two other people. And the most transcendent and magnificent part of the revelation of William Shakespeare in the Sonnets by no means lies in their teasing indications of the writer's particular relations with another man or woman, or in their disclosure of an extraordinary attitude toward that other person; or in any such narrow torturing suggestion. No; the grand self-expression of the Sonnets rather consists in those same universal gifts through which the great playwright built out the human world which acts and speaks and thinks before us in his plays. In somewhat personally directed guise, the Sonnets exhibit the same qualities of temperament and character, and of thought and reflection, which in a somewhat different way are brought down from the empyrean, and directed to particular circumstances, by the characters of his plays. In both the plays and the sonnets, Shakespeare's thought, as a luminous rainbow, over-arches incident, passion or situation. He thinks the universal, and sets the concrete fact in its infinitude:

> " Not mine own fears, nor the prophetic soul
>   Of the wide world dreaming on things to come,
>   Can yet the lease of my true love control
>   Supposed as forfeit to a confined doom "—

The eternal heaven and the dreaming earth are wrought into the perpetuity of Shakespeare's very mortal love. As in the two sonnets, beginning:

> Like as the waves make to the pebbled shore

and

> Since brass nor stone nor earth nor boundless sea,

the waste of land and ocean and of human grace and beauty are contrasted with the closing somewhat conventional assertion of the immortality conferred on one whose name the Sonnets do not disclose. The Plays will afford many instances of universal thought brought to play upon the little circumstance.

Besides the sweep of over-thought in the Sonnets, comparable only to the sweep of over-thought throughout the Plays, the Sonnets otherwise disclose traits of Shake-

speare's nature in accord with the dramatic revelation of
the plays.   What other Elizabethan sonnets express so
sensitive a nature, or such tenderness? [2]   In the playwright, the sensitiveness of the sonnet writer is as an
Aeolian harp, responsive to every chord in the scale of
human joy and sorrow.   It feels the impact of every
passionate, ecstatic, or pathetic atom moving in the comic
tragedy of human life.   Through this playwright's sensitiveness his thought may apprehend each feature of life's
panorama.

In the Sonnets, the tenderness of Shakespeare turns
again and again to a forgiveness of his loved one's insensi-
bilities, and of his or her more positive faults or even
treasons.   Such forgiveness, which is tenderness meeting
the other's fault, rises from an enveloping, almost caress-
ing, knowledge of the other's nature.   This clear knowledge may also present itself in modes of scathing analysis.[3]

Such tenderness, forgiveness, and the great knowledge
in which these stand, become in the Plays a wonderful
understanding tolerance of everything in human nature
needing forgiveness or toleration.   If we may presume
to distinguish among Shakespeare's faculties, and separate
any one out of the living and dynamic unity of his nature,
— if we dare do this, perhaps it may be said that he
evinces no dramatic faculty or quality more important for
his art than this patient and so profoundly understanding
tolerance.   Linked with his other faculties, it enables him
to treat all human life with a discerning understanding.
It may be fundamental to his dramatic procedure, even
as a great understanding tolerance was fundamental to
Rabelais's handling of the human comedy.   Neither
Rabelais nor Shakespeare cast out any phase of life
through impatience.

The Plays bear varied witness to this tolerance.
Shakespeare's wit and his humor create by means of it.
Tolerance is the basis of the breadth of humor with which
he creates and handles Falstaff, as Rabelais creates Pan-
urge.   This is a master illustration of the demiurgic

---

[2] Among many, note sonnets LXXI–LXXIV, LXXXIX, XC, CXXXIX.
[3] As in sonnets CXLI, XCV, XXXV, LXIX.

quality of Shakespeare's tolerance.   Yet how constantly, and almost unexpectedly, it appears throughout his plays, reaching a sort of Olympian height in that forgiveness which has always understood, and now pardons, and will utterly ignore and forget the offense.

In *Midsummer Night's Dream,* Helena, the mean cat, runs and tells Demetrius of Hermia's and Lysander's flight.   Yet she shall be as happy in the end as anyone. What cares Shakespeare for so slight a foible in so slight a thing!   More serious and more questionable is it that neither the miserable Proteus in *Two Gentlemen of Verona,* nor the vicious Angelo in *Measure for Measure* meets with his deserts.   Both are pardoned, Proteus receiving for wife the lovely Julia, and Angelo, Mariana, who at least has sung one of the loveliest songs in all the plays.   In neither case had their vile attempts succeeded: and no more in Shakespeare's time than at present did the law punish *intent,* or even the *attempt,* as it did the perpetrated crime.   Conversely, as it were, Elizabeth, the Queen, said she was no searcher of consciences, but did insist upon outward *conformity* to the laws of the realm in the matter of religion.   At the close of *Measure for Measure,* the admirably reasoning Isabella obtains Angelo's pardon with like argument: "Thoughts are no subjects; intents but merely thoughts."

Even as Shakespeare himself, his royal personages will not merely pardon, but utterly ignore.   In *All's Well,* the King simply lets bygones be bygones in the case of the erring Bertram:

> "All is whole
> Not one word more of the consumed time."

But, of course, it is Prospero responding to Ariel's sense of mercy, whose largeness of mind most handsomely renounces vengeance on those who have so wickedly treated him:

> "Though with their high wrongs I am struck to the quick,
> Yet with my nobler reason, 'gainst my fury
> Do I take part.   The rarer action is
> In virtue, than in vengeance: they being penitent,

The sole drift of my purpose doth extend
Not a frown farther."

To forgive is the part of the " nobler reason," which
also understands. To ignore the unpleasant is the manner of a courteous mind. Says Prospero to Alonzo, who
is thinking backward with compunction:

> There, Sir, stop:
> Let us not burthen our remembrances
> With a heaviness that's gone.

Touching the self-expression of Shakespeare, conveyed
in his poems and plays, we are not attempting to extract
from them the so-called personal opinions and convictions
of the great dramatist, and still less are we seeking for
indications of his life and circumstances. With respect
to such incidentals, as we know, the Elizabethan drama is
impersonal and void of self-disclosure. This applies unqualifiedly to the plays of Shakespeare; and it is safest to
assume its application to the sonnets. But surely in the
plays as well as sonnets one may seek a self-expression, a
revelation indeed, of the faculties involved in their production; faculties which worked together, and together
made Shakespeare's effective genius. Moreover, in their
relatively stable sum, these faculties, together with more
passive tendencies, constitute a personality, which has a
personal equation, or aberration from the normal, a temperament and inclination. Such personal equation, temperament, inclination, affects the operation of the more
active or creative faculties; and cannot fail to reveal itself
in the subject's obvious preferences, in his conduct and
accomplishment, and (with a Shakespeare) in his
creations.

No one can gainsay the statement that the plays of
Shakespeare are an expression, even a self-expression, of
the genius, the unified efficiency of the faculties, which
produced them. One may pedal a little more softly when
looking to them for a disclosure, or expression, of temperament and inclination. Yet this is in them, if less openly
revealed than the more active dramatic and poetic faculties engaged in their composition. The sonnets and the

plays bear complementary testimony to Shakespeare's temperament, or disposition if one will, and predilections. Some of the sonnets show the poet's temperament stirred to active mood, gathered and directed in a channel, and so made visible. Yet characteristics thus revealed may also be detected through the plays, and sometimes in expressions which recall the sonnets. A sonnet-mood, an obvious revelation of the writer's self, may permeate, almost constitute, a character of a play: while, conversely, a preference or approval, perhaps abstractly stated in a sonnet, may be more personally directed in a play.

None can doubt that the writer of the Sonnets was one who not only understood, but felt, perhaps the most complete and extreme affection of one man for another ever revealed in literature. With its wonderful and manifold expression in the Sonnets, may be compared Antonio's love for Bassanio in the *Merchant of Venice*. Antonio is of a melancholy cast and one of the most perfect gentlemen it will ever be a reader's lot to meet. His purse, his person, his extremest means lie all unlocked to Bassanio's occasions in the first act of the play, and had been unlocked before. When Bassanio has won his Portia, and Antonio's ships have miscarried and his bond is forfeit, he writes this letter:

" Sweet Bassanio, my ships have all miscarried, my creditors grow cruel, my estate is very low, my bond to the Jew is forfeit; and since in paying it, it is impossible I should live, all debts are cleared between you and I, if I might but see you at my death. Notwithstanding, use your pleasure: if your love do not persuade you to come, let not my letter."

Afterwards, when apparently judgment has gone against him, and he expects to die, he says to his friend:

" I am a tainted wether of the flock,
    Meetest for death: the weakest kind of fruit
    Drops earliest to the ground, and so let me.
    You cannot better be employ'd, Bassanio,
    Than to live still, and write mine epitaph."

May we not think that in Antonio's words Shakespeare writes himself out as truly as in the passionate melancholy of the Sonnets?

Likewise in the affection of a different Antonio for Sebastian in *Twelfth Night*. He has rescued Sebastian from the waves, and fallen in love with the young man. Sebastian seems a little weary of his good services, and leaves him for Orsino's court, where Antonio has many enemies. The latter speaks:

> " The gentleness of all the gods go with thee!
> I have many enemies in Orsino's court,
> Else would I very shortly see thee there.
> But come what may, I do adore thee so
> That danger shall seem short, and I will go."

Conversely, compare the reflections of sonnet XCIV with the more personally directed statement in *Hamlet:*

> " They that have power to hurt, and will do none,
> That do not do the thing they most do show,
> Who, moving others, are themselves as stone,
> Unmoved, cold, and to temptation slow;
> They rightly do inherit heaven's graces,
> And husband nature's riches from expense;
> They are the lords and owners of their faces,
> Others but stewards of their excellence. . . ."

In *Hamlet* (Act III. sc. II) Horatio enters to Hamlet's call with:

> " Here, sweet lord, at your service."

Hamlet answers with the words

> " Horatio, thou art e'en as just a man
> As e'er my conversation coped withal."

Hor.   O! my dear lord —
Ham.   Nay, do not think I flatter;
   For what advancement may I hope from thee
   . . . Dost thou hear?
   Since my dear soul was mistress of her choice,
   And could of men distinguish, her election
   Hath seal'd thee for herself: for thou hast been
   As one, in suffering all, that suffers nothing;
   A man, that fortune's buffets and rewards
   Hast ta'en with equal thanks: and bless'd are those
   Whose blood and judgment are so well co-mingled,
   That they are not a pipe for fortune's finger
   To sound what stop she please. Give me that man

> That is not passion's slave, and I will wear him
> In my heart's core, ay, in my heart of heart,
> As I do thee."

The sonnet and Hamlet's words supplement each other, and together may be taken to express an approval of Shakespeare.

A more surface coincidence of thought and phrase between sonnet and play may be instanced. Sonnet LIII opens with almost mystic brooding words:

> " What is your substance, whereof you are made,
> That millions of strange shadows on you tend?
> Since everyone hath, everyone, one shade,
> And you, but one, can every shadow lend."

Then it descends:

> " Describe Adonis, and the counterfeit
> Is poorly imitated after you;
> On Helen's cheek all art of beauty set,
> And you in Grecian tires are painted new.
> Speak of the spring and foison of the year,
> The one doth shadow of your beauty show,
> The other as your bounty doth appear;
> And you in every blessed shape we know."

In the lighter vein runs the letter to Rosalind in *As You Like It:*

> The quintessence of every sprite
> Heaven would in little show.
> Wherefore heaven Nature charg'd
> That one body should be fill'd
> With all graces wide enlarg'd:
> Nature presently distill'd
> Helen's cheek, but not her heart,
> Cleopatra's majesty,
> Atalanta's better part,
> Sad Lucretia's modesty:
> Thus Rosalind of many parts
> By heavenly synod was devis'd,
> Of many faces, eyes, and hearts,
> To have the touches dearest priz'd.

One has here the same conventional conceit to which the brooding opening of the sonnet turns.

Our theme of Shakespeare's self-expression, or self-revelation, proceeds merely on the assumption that a man cannot put in the mouth of a " character " in a play a sentiment which he does not himself either feel or understand, any more than he can express the same directly in a sonnet. Yet but a moderate use of this apparently safe assumption will lead to some discovery of the quality of Shakespeare's mind and its poetic and dramatic faculties, as well as of his temperament and likings.

Something has been said already of Shakespeare's *over-thought,*— his constant mental habit of clothing the concrete fact or action with the import of the universal. Either he presents the fact in language of broad or even universal application; or else he adds reflections which set the fact within the light of principles controlling or illuminating human life. Thus the most famous of Hamlet's soliloquies — To be or not to be — (whatever other greatness belongs to it) indicates the reaction under stress of such a mind and temper as Hamlet's to the universal *pros* and *cons* of life and death.

Inasmuch as probably no other writer has presented such a range and variety of human fact and circumstance, one must assume that Shakespeare had an eye for every least detail of life. But obviously the facts in themselves did not satisfy him. He must think and express them in their universal relations, place them in their proper human category. To some dumb degree the like is true of every man; since to think a fact is necessarily to bring it under some general concept. The poorest human clod has a touch of this quality of Shakespeare, as a muddy drop partakes of the substance of the sea.

So much safely may be said as to an unfailing quality of Shakespeare's mind, disclosed in both plays and sonnets. Touching his poetic and dramatic faculties, the magic of his art, that may be left to any reader, and to the comment of the clever minds of many men of many tongues. One stands astounded before Shakespeare's all-comprehending, superhuman insight and understanding of man and woman, and the measureless magic with which he brings it to dramatic utterance.

Regarding the disclosure of his temperament in his plays, one realizes that their course and outcome offer a surer guide that the utterances of the characters. Yet possibly some of his ideas upon the proper method of the drama are suggested by Hamlet's advice to the players, which, as it proceeds, becomes as applicable to the writing of plays as to their acting: " Suit the action to the word, the word to the action, with this special observance that you o'erstep not the modesty of nature; for anything so overdone is from the purpose of playing, whose end it is . . . to hold as 'twer, the mirror up to nature; to show virtue her own feature, scorn her own image, and the very age and body of the time, his form and pressure."

The closing words declare the function of the Shakespearean drama, just as much as the proper manner of acting it.   They are also indicative of its human or " humanistic " attitude and accepted boundaries: which are exemplified by the entire content of the Plays.   Passages in them may doff the bonnet to the Christian faith; but only to meet the dramatic turn.   Shakespeare and his plays are most genially of this world, the plays having for their content the mortal life of man, its relationships, its passions, its sublimities and depths, its vanities and hopes of fame — but all on earth.   The conventional references to the superhuman, or the supernatural, are often pagan by affinity and seeming preference.   The *Tempest* has not a Christian touch; its machinery, its lovely visions as of Iris, Ceres, Juno, are as entrancingly pagan as Prospero's speech (Act V. sc. 1) beginning;

" Ye elves of hills, brooks, standing lakes, and groves."

It may be added that the masques and pageantry greeting Elizabeth's Progresses through her realm were likewise pagan.   In England, the age (outside of Church controversy) was not religious.   Rather it was a time when the energies, passions, ambitions, of eager men threatened to submerge the mystic anticipation of a life to to come.   No joyful anticipation of the bliss of heaven is expressed by Shakespeare.   In plays as well as sonnets, he has no love of death, but detests it, along with all " the wastes of time," and " time's thievish progress to eternity." Dismally death's injurious approaches sap the beauty and wit of woman, and man's strength and glory. Reconcilement to the fatal necessity, and a seemly end, are the most that can be expected. The motive and energy of *Measure for Measure* lie in the horror of being dead, which is by no means overcome by the incomparable reflections on the nothingness of life, with which the Duke fails to convince Claudio, who simply cannot bear to die. Shakespeare's plays move and breath, grieve and rejoice, and even consider and reflect, in the medium of the natural love of life and all its joys and glories. We recognize them as the most complete and splendid self-expression of the Elizabethan time,— " the Age of Shakespeare." Incidentally, along the ways of literary and intellectual influence, and of taste and fashion, this English age appears as the transformed magnificent effect of Italy and France and Spain: the Italy which, fed and illumined by the classic past, throve on the intrigue and comeliness of human life; the France which had appropriated and recast the enchantments of the land she had done so much to spoil and ruin; the proud and tragic Spain, conqueror, ruler, vampire among the nations.

Within these indicated boundaries, Shakespeare's plays touch the whole compass of life, and with genial, almost loving, consideration of every thread in the great woof. Their tolerance and compassion, akin to the loving tenderness of the Sonnets, has been spoken of. The same sensitive piteous nature had even appeared in " the first heir of my invention," the poem of *Venus and Adonis*, with its picture of the hunted hare:

> " By this, poor Wat, far off upon a hill,
> Stands on his hinder legs with listening ear,
> To hearken if his foes pursue him still:
> Anon their loud alarums he doth hear;
> And now his grief may be compared well
> To one sore sick, that hears the passing bell.
>
> Then shalt thou see the dew-bedabbled wretch
> Turn, and return, indenting with the way;

> Each envious briar his weary legs doth scratch,
> Each shadow makes him stop, each murmur stay:
> For misery is trodden on by many,
> And being low, never reliev'd by any."

That poem, besides, was an opening self-expression of Shakespeare's unashamed delight in the loveliness and passion of the flesh; a delight which in the Plays will, as it were, work itself out in a sex geniality as refined as is compatible with its life.

Here indeed we come upon a sweet and notable characteristic of Shakespeare's plays, which cannot be other than a veritable self-expression of his character: it is what is ordinarily understood by the term refinement, or delicacy. To appreciate this trait in him, one should read the plays of the other Elizabethan and Jacobean playwrights. Sex passion, with its accompanying intrigues and storms, set in an atmosphere of promiscuous appetition, is their common topic. Marlowe used other themes, and his rather incidental treatment of love combines idealism with extravagance. But for the most part, the plays of the other playwrights when handling their favorite topic, show sexual crudity and violence. The coarseness of their sex vituperation is extreme. These playwrights treated the relations between the sexes in a manner agreeable to their own natures and the supposed likings of their audiences. Likewise Shakespeare — and how differently!

The others have little share in the beauty of the expression, of the suggestions, of the reveries of love, so remarkable with Shakespeare. The words of Romeo and of Juliet relate themselves to all things fair and wonderful; the thoughts of Lorenzo and Jessica, in the last act of *The Merchant of Venice*, soar in realms of beauty. Coarse revilings are excluded from Anthony's realization of his overthrow through love, while Shakespeare's privity of insight reveals the mottled thoughts and twisting impulses of that bane to manhood, Cleopatra, whose invincible queenship holds the traits of Thais:

> Age cannot wither her, nor custom stale
> Her infinite variety!

The partly comic side, the semi-comedy of love, is still uniquely sweet and beautiful in Shakespeare, as in *Twelfth Night* or *As You Like It*. The time was free of tongue, and might be coarse in utterance; Shakespeare's heroines, judged by their time, do not fail in delicacy of speech.

It was given to this man through his sensitive delicacy, his sole and universal understanding of all men and women, his matchless human — feminine and masculine — imagination, to create an unapproachable and utterly wonderful array of super-womanly women; and to endow their several natures with every grace and faculty of wit and feeling, of devotion and atonement, known or hoped for on this earth. His evil women — in whom of course he is still Shakespeare — are few in number.

But the elevation and intrinsic refinement of Shakespeare's nature, which finds its self-expression in his plays, is not limited to his conceptions of women, and their relationships with men. It pervades his consideration of human nature and human relationships. It had already come to exquisite expression in the Sonnets. In the Plays it is not submerged by the stress of the action, unless in those, like *Cymbeline* or even *Much Ado About Nothing,* where Shakespeare dramatized some tale from the Italian which displeases us.

> Full fathom five thy father lies:
>   Of his bones are coral made;
> Those are pearls that were his eyes:
>   Nothing of him that doth fade,
> But doth suffer a sea-change
> Into something rich and strange.

Was ever an announcement of a death made with such charm and delicacy, such avoidance of the unbeautiful, and such full accord (the announcement being false) with the genius of life's high comedy.

Here one thinks of Shakespeare's wit. Of course the time loved sheer word-play, and Shakespeare has plenty of it. But, beyond this, his wit is intellectual, presenting for instance, a situation, which demands for its enjoyment by the auditor, the action of his mind. The plot against Malvolio in *Twelfth Night* may strike the reader as the funniest thing in literature: free from coarseness, it is intellectual, has daring and esprit. How both audience and playwright loved such a jest! Sir Toby in the play, amid his sobs of laughter, begs Maria, its deviser, to set her foot upon his neck — or on mine, chimes in Sir Andrew Aguecheek. Toby declares he could marry her (and so in fact he does) for this device —" And ask no other dowry with her, but such another jest."

If such were made at the Mermaid, there was verity in Beaumont's lines:

> " What things have we seen
> Done at the Mermaid! heard words that have been
> So nimble and so full of subtle flame,
> As if that everyone from whom they came
> Had meant to put his whole wit in a jest
> And had resolved to live a fool the rest
> Of his dull life."

Shakespeare's chief comic creation is Falstaff,— the creation of his wit and of his tolerance for human fault and foible. *Wit* be it said; and one should realize that the Elizabethan-Shakespearean usage of that word means mind or wisdom, the mental keenness which perceives the congruous and attainable, and devises fitting measures and apt words. It means this as well as the keenness which perceives the incongruous and impossible, and sees the humor, the pleasing innocuousness of the incompatibility, and puts it in pungent, quick contrasted, unexpectedly associated, words.

Falstaff has this wit, and also is the object or the butt of it. He is set and founded on the tolerance which comes from understanding; and he must breathe and move in such an atmosphere. Shakespeare's genius, which understands and tolerates, gives to this character an understanding and tolerance of itself. Falstaff understands himself and the Falstaffian macrocosmos, the world, seen in his eyes. He is tolerant of his cowardice, his moral weakness, and of every appetite and craving of his fat old body; also of the pretense which shields his vanity, and the lies which win him gear and drink. He moves and breathes and gets his living in a corresponding *milieu* of tolerance through understanding, as on the part of Prince Hal, who likewise has the wit to see the humor of Falstaff and enjoy Falstaff's wit. Finally, the audience, or reader, too, must have wit and understanding, and be beguiled to tolerance, in order to realize and enjoy the full humor of this character; which, as the creation of understanding and friendliness toward human fault and foible, was a part of the self-expression of Shakespeare.

Only prepossession will discover an intent to signify the close of the playwright's career in the words of Prospero abjuring " this rough magic "—

> I'll break my staff,
> Bury it certain fathoms in the earth,
> And, deeper than did ever plummet sound,
> I'll drown my book."

One might as well find some possible light touch of Shakespeare's mood in Ariel's fairy joy at freedom from all tasks.

Yet one cannot read *The Tempest,* without thinking of Shakespeare as expressing in his great magician some final moods of his own, some thoughts of farewell to the business of the world. There is in the play a strange, possibly an estranged, loftiness of view. Not only has Prospero tried the world, and found himself its victim in his outward fortunes; but since the time of his exile, or release, he has held it in the scales of his detached consideration, weighing it against his fancies, till it has become one with the stuff that dreams were made of in his mind. His dukedom of Milan is no more real to Prospero and perhaps less pleasing, than the visions of his Island, the

> Spirits, which by mine art
> I have from their confines call'd to enact
> My present fancies.

Life's actual sentiments, witcheries, infatuations, have become little things to him, even in those he loves:

> " Poor worm! thou art infected."

thinks he of Miranda so girlishly and beautifully in love with Ferdinand. And there is a touch of weariness at least in his reply to her happy wistful exclamation at the sight of the fine company:

> " O, brave new world,
> That has such people in't! "
>
> " *Tis new to thee.*"

We will not so identify Shakespeare with his magician as to have him say, as thinking of lovely Stratford:

> " And thence retire we to my Milan, where
> Every third thought shall be my grave."

And yet who will not find Shakespeare's self in the words following the vanishing of the vision-masque, which has astounded Ferdinand:

> " You do look, my son, in a mov'd sort,
> As if you were dismay'd; be cheerful, sir.
> Our revels now are ended.   These our actors,
> As I foretold you, were all spirits, and
> Are melted into air, into thin air:
> And, like the baseless fabric of this vision,
> The cloud-capp'd towers, the gorgeous palaces,
> The solemn temples, the great globe itself,
> Yea, all which it inherit, shall dissolve,
> And, like this insubstantial pageant faded,
> Leave not a rack behind.   We are such stuff
> As dreams are made on, and our little life
> Is rounded with a sleep."

Without any sure support from the play, one almost wonders whether Shakespeare does not mean that a man may find himself and at least the provisional truth of his nature, through realizing the insubstantial character of the phantasmagoria of the world.   Such a suggestion may be extorted from the words of Gonzalo, exclaiming on the issue of that wonderful voyage of theirs, through which one daughter of Naples found a husband,

> " And Ferdinand, her brother, found a wife
> Where he himself was lost; Prospero his dukedom,
> In a poor isle; *and all of us, ourselves,*
> *When no man was his own.*"

BOOK V
PHILOSOPHY AND SCIENCE

CHAPTER XXX

THE SCHOLASTIC ARISTOTLE, PLATONISM, AND NICHOLAS OF CUSA

I

THE Catholic philosophy of the Middle Ages through the whole course of its development evinces general characteristics which never were more strongly marked than at its culmination in the system of Aquinas. Still with the great Dominican, as before him, Scholasticism was acceptant, reverential, largely engaged in appropriation and re-expression; it was extremely formal through its endeavor to appropriate and re-express, and because the formal logic of Aristotle had been the chief moulding instrument. Furtherance of salvation was still the supreme sanction of knowledge; and the highest task of the philosopher was still to use his knowledge in the service of theology, and demonstrate philosophy's hand-maidenly accord with revealed Christian truth. The system of Aquinas exemplified this hardly won and soon to be lost coöperation between authority and reason, so necessary for a philosophical theology which had to digest the solid facts of revelation.

Intellectual conditions, past and present, contributed to the achievement of Aquinas, and conspired to render his Summa (along with Gothic cathedrals and the *Roman de la Rose!*) the typical constructions of the time. Much of humanity's best intelligence had long been consecrated to the Catholic or scholastic theology-philosophy. In spite of controversies and divergencies of attitude among its thoughtful, academic, and usually quite orthodox, promoters, the lines of progress had tended to draw together towards a common method and unity of system. This unity finally was established through the action of the

two closely connected intellectual forces which were promoting the advance of knowledge in the thirteenth century. One was the growth of Universities, facilitating
the exchange of thought, and making for its academic
ordering. The other was the introduction, first, of the
full logical *Organon* of Aristotle, and then of the body of
his substantial philosophy. As a result a genuine, and
the most comprehensive, classic system of philosophy re-
placed the current heterogeneous Augustinian Platonism.
It brought a revolutionary enlargement of Scholasticism,
and led to that final attainment of form and method,
through which these mighty Dominicans recast the Stagirite's philosophy in a Christian scheme.

The scheme of Aquinas seemed complete: seemed to
be such that nothing could be added or taken away. It
might be criticised, its premises might be impugned, its
method attacked, its conclusions shattered. But to aug-
ment or develop it as a whole was not possible. Moreover, from the close of the thirteenth century, the times
were unfavorable even for the continuance of the scholastic unity. There was an effective difference between the
Papacy at Rome and the Papacy broken by the French
king and domiciled at Avignon; there had come a corresponding change in the attitude of Europe. The universal unity of ecclesiastical Catholicism no longer reflected convincingly the power of God above. This depo-
tentiation of the principle of Church universality affected
Scholasticism, and was in turn affected by the modification
of scholastic principles.

Two men — one of the full blood, the other of the
half blood — of the scholastics were fatally to impugn
the joinder of dialectic and authority as supporters of
Theology. Duns Scotus proved, through tomes of metaphysics, that Theology was not a speculative science, but
a pragmatic means for salvation, and that it was based
(however rational its contents) upon revelation and not
on dialectic. Occam, more unreservedly than his master
Duns, argued against the testing of Theology by reason,
and restricted further the sphere of demonstrable truth:
the verities of Scripture are absolute, and neither require

nor admit the proofs of reason; Theology stands upon faith.

There was matter in Occam's teaching which could be turned to uses scandalously destructive of human certitude. Had he not shown how difficult was the proof of any correspondence between the propositions formed by the mind and the material realities of the world? Occamism was very popular; at Paris, for example. It was condemned time and again before as well as after the middle of the fourteenth century; but it was held by men of high repute for propriety of thought. Not against these were the papal censures directed, but against such an independent thinker as Nicholas of Autrecourt, who was affected by Occam's doctrines. Almost from his student years at Paris, his ideas began to disturb the authorities, and his opinions were finally condemned by the Avignon Papal Curia in 1349. Before then, this disturber of accepted thought had fled to Louis of Bavaria. Nicholas criticized the principle of causality, by holding positively that from the existence of one thing, the existence of another thing could not validly be deduced. He also denied the possibility of any certain knowledge of Substance, as something underlying the impressions made upon our senses. We have, therefore, no sure criterion of the truth of our perceptions, nor any certain knowledge as to the existence of material things. Likewise as to the soul; we experience its acts, but have no knowledge of its substance,— of any spiritual substance. He scouted the authority of Aristotle at every turn, and, apparently adopting the doctrines of the ancient atomists, would regard all natural processes merely as the coming together and dispersion of atoms.[1]

After the deaths of Duns and Occam, scholasticism became decadent, overloaded with logic, and inflated to perdition with words and sterile subtleties. There was no originality or progress left in it; and if men who were recognized scholastics, like Albertus of Saxonia or Meis-

[1] See Joseph Lappe, *Nicholaus von Autrecourt,* etc. (Baeumker's Beiträge, Munster, 1908); Rashdall, *Nicholas de Ultricuria, a mediaeval Hume.* (Proceedings of the Aristotelian Society, N. S., Vol. VII, 1906–7.)

ter Eckhart, were thinking and observing progressively, it was outside, rather than within, the circle of Catholic philosophy. There were still to be hundreds of professors teaching scholastic doctrines, who may be classed as Thomists, Scotists, Occamists. But they could not satisfy the insistence upon actuality which was dawning about them. Neither the understanding of life nor the sense of reality was with them: *Non ragioniam di lor* — let us not discourse of them. One merely need remember that even in the sixteenth century the universities still philosophized mainly from this same manifold volume of mediaeval thinking; while more independent thinkers drew from it their philosophic education, and found difficulty in divesting themselves of its categories and forms of expression.

Inspired by the revival of classical studies, and strengthened with the new knowledge of Greek, some men in the fifteenth and others in the sixteenth century sought to correct the mediaeval Aristotle with a better knowledge of his unadulterated doctrines, or were inclined to replace him with bits of the older Greek philosophies, or the teachings of Zeno, Pyrrho or Epicurus; while some would reinstate the blessed Plato and his Neo-platonic school. This independent or haphazard levying upon remote and noble sources was another factor in the philosophy of these centuries.

It would not have come into play but for the increase of knowledge and the development of taste and faculty which had taken place. If this human growth was shown in the Platonic revival and a more promiscuous levying upon the Ancients, it manifested itself more vitally and potently in the time's own philosophic contribution, its more original thinking. There had been a goodly lifting of men's eyes from parchment scrolls, and a fresh directing of them to natural phenomena; while the mind, with renewed freedom, was also reflecting upon humanity. A more independent view of the data and doctrines of philosophy, a more living conception of the forces of nature, and at last a reversal of the whole vision of the universe, became vital elements in the philosophy of the fifteenth and sixteenth centuries.

The scholastic Aristotelianism of the period was an academic waste, where men delivered expositions of the great schoolmen, or compiled commentaries upon Aquinas, altogether adding little to the world's understanding of life. In them dwelt the " instruction obtainable at the leading universities," in France, England, Germany, Italy. The reviving currents of Platonism had little effect upon this scholastic backwater; nor, until the seventeenth century, was it stirred by the new science and philosophy. Aristotelianism still was needed to steady men's minds, and as the source and stay of philosophic method. The most valuable Aristotelian labors were not those of the Dominican Cajetan (1468-1534) with his commentary upon the *Summa* of Aquinas, but rather those of the Protestant Melanchthon (1497-1560), seeking to simplify and utilize Aristotle's philosophy for the advancement of education in Germany, and as an aid to morals. This paragon of scholarship and eclectic thinking, with his genius for simplification, worked into his epoch-making text-books not only Aristotelian doctrines, but others which suited him from the store of antique thought. He deemed Aristotelian method of utmost importance, saying: " magnam doctrinarum confusionem secuturam esse, si Aristotles neglectus fuerit, qui unus ac solus est methodi artifex." [2] Certainly such a confusion did come upon the thought of the period, from the cult of various Greek philosophers, and an uncritical heaping together of their diverse opinions.

II

The revival of Platonism makes a picturesque and interesting story; one must not be beguiled into overestimating its importance. Plato had never ceased to be a name to conjure with. He was treated with reverence

[2] Cited by Ueberweg-Heinze, *Ges. der Philosophie,* p. 27 (10th ed.), B'd III, from Speech of 1536, in *Corp. Ref.,* XI, S. 282.

by Petrarch, who knew nothing of him except scrappily
at second hand.   Petrarch's way of speaking of him had
its effect upon generations who admired the famous
humanist.   Before meeting the philosopher himself, the
literati of the fifteenth century were prepared to sit at his
feet.   Nor, when they came to know him, were they dis-
appointed, either in him or in his reputed children, Plotinus and Porphyry, Jamblicus and Proclus.   The imagination of Plato was found divine, Plotinus presented a spiritual advance; the fantasies of Jamblicus were even more
attractive, and Proclus was a most congenial interpreter
of them all.

In philosophic, as in all productive, labor, beautiful
form is the finally achieved expression, and presents the
relief and joyfulness issuing from the philosophic process.
Plato's mind took great joy in the perfection of its
achieved form of expression, which was also destined forever to impart joy.   It goes without saying that the charm
of the Platonic Dialogues — even in translations! — had
to do with the vogue of Platonism in those fifteenth and
sixteenth Italian centuries, which cared for form
supremely.   But beyond this, Platonic modes of thought
and forms of expression became a moving contribution to
the enlargement and increasing suppleness of men's minds.

The story of the Platonic resurrection scarcely calls for
retelling.[3]   One should realize that Greeks from Constantinople and the Morea had never been infrequent
visitors to Italy, although the separation of the Greek and
Latin Churches had proved a barrier to genial intercourse
between the East and West.   Petrarch rather vainly
sought instruction in the Greek of Plato from Greek Ca-
labrians.   In the period following his death, the strait-
ened fortunes of the remnant of the Eastern Empire impelled more than one needy scholar to carry his preten-
sions to Italy; while the same straits induced the Greek
Church and government to reopen negotiations for religious union.   The Council of Florence in 1428 brought

---

[3] It is best told by Ch. Huit in *Le Platonisme pendant la Renaissance,*
published in *Annales de philosophie chrétienne,* N. S., Vols. 32–37 (1895–
1898).

many Greeks, and among them one Georgius Gemistus Pletho, a Platonist, and an inaugurator of the silly war on Aristotle.[4] With equal wordy rancor Gennadius and George de Trebizonde took up the Aristotelian cause, while the admirable Bessarion, himself a Greek and Pletho's pupil, showed the saner way of recognizing the greatness of both these princes of philosophy.

Pletho was, of course, an admirer of Porphyry and Proclus, as well as Plato. His fervor roused the interest of Cosimo de' Medici. This was in 1438, when Bruni was pleasantly translating the "letters" and some of the genuine dialogues of Plato;[5] others also were working in the Platonic grove; — which was to shelter Hermes Trismegistus, the Sibyls, Pseudo-Dionysius, and the Cabbala at last!

These Platonic, Neo-platonic, semi-mystical and Cabbalistic studies were not pursued altogether as scholarly investigations. Enlightening and guiding truth was expected from them. These people were not pedantically thrashing certain dry bones of the past, but looking for new life. While love of the beautiful stimulated the Platonic revival, its promoters were drawn on by the hope of mysteries to be disclosed, which in some way might strengthen and assure the lives of those upon whom the new mystic light was shed. Hear the young Marsilio Ficino, the best of Cosimo's Platonic protégés, and the chief light of the Platonic Academy of Florence: "The great Cosimo," says he in the preface to his translation of Plotinus, "at the time of the Council held at Florence, between the Greeks and Latins, often heard Gemistus [Pletho] as another Plato expound the mysteries of Plato." And Ficino's own term, "medicus animarum," suggests what even he was looking for in Plato.

Since Ficino's time (1433-1499), the world of scholarship has learned to distinguish between Plato and those who as early as the fourth century passed for his better self. Augustine's " Platonists " were what we call Neo-

---

[4] Selections from his voluminous Opera are printed in T. 160 of Migne, *Patrol. Graeca,* where (col 890-934) will be found his polemic *De Platonicae et Aristotelicae philosophiae differentia,*

[5] Ante, chapter II.

platonists, realizing some of the differences between the
two fourth centuries, the one before, the other after,
Christ.   For their ignorance of these differences, we must
not despise better men than ourselves, to wit, this same
Ficino and that princely prodigy, Pico della Mirandola.
The two were the sufficient luminaries of Florentine, that
is to say, Italian Platonism in the fifteenth century.

Cosimo, a penetrating judge of men, recognized the
merits of the little crooked youth, whom he heard reading
the first of his Platonic compositions at the age of
twenty-three.   Ficino had just finished his course of medicine at Bologna.   Cosimo bade him devote himself to the
cure of souls, and straightway made it easy for him to
follow this less lucrative profession.   So he gave himself
to the study and elucidation of Plato and those late followers of his, who were thought to have made his teachings more sublime, and to have brought them nearer to
the truth.

There are points to be noted in Ficino's temper and in
his attitude towards all those alleged followers of Plato,
as to whom he had to be his own enlightener.   He was a
sensitive soul, of ready sympathies; irascible, yet quickly
forgiving, and loyal to his friends; more prone to remember kindness than injury — a rare trait in that Italian
time.   He was attentive to his own and his friends'
digestion, and wore protecting amulets, changing them to
suit the day.   He also loved the seclusion of the villa
which Cosimo had given him, and was addicted to astrology.[6]   " Learned in his youth in the humaniores litterae,
he was fired with the love of Plato by Marcus Tullius,"
and then by other *latini Platonici,* for example Macrobius,
Apuleius, Boethius, and Augustine.

The young Ficino's ignorance of Greek was quickly
remedied through his own ardor and the instruction provided by his patron.   For his improvement he translated
(and then expounded) the " Hymns of Orpheus " and
those of the Neo-platonic scholastic commentator Proclus
(410 A. D.–485); also at Cosimo's request, *Mercurii*

---

[6] We have his *Vita,* written by Corsius in 1506, ed. by Bandini (Lucca,
1772).

Trismegisti librum de Origine Mundi. By the age of thirty-five, after five years' labor, he had translated into Latin the whole of Plato. Later, urged by Pico della Mirandola, he translated the works of Plotinus, which also took five years; then Synesius *on Dreams*, Psellus *on Demons*, Porphyry's *De Abstinentia*, and the famous " Jamblicus de mysteriis Aegyptorum," with more Neoplatonic writings; turning finally to " Dionysius the Areopagite."

One sees at once, that as the contemporary humanists might prefer the writings of the Latin silver age, so Ficino took naturally to the books of the last Greek philosophers, which had also been so congenial to the minds of the Church Fathers. No work of Plato interested him more than the probably apocryphal " Letters," in which he felt sure that he heard Plato speak in his own voice.

So we are prepared for the oft-cited letter written by Ficino to Bessarion, in which he speaks of that wisdom, that most precious gold, set by God in Plato's purest breast, but which his brilliant language somewhat obscured, and clothed in a terrestrial garb, so that the spiritual meaning was not clear to mediocre men. This gold was purified in the laboratory first of Plotinus, then of Porphyry, then of Jamblicus, and finally of Proclus; and now its shining fills indeed the world.

Thus Ficino became an all-absorbent Platonist, with at least the remnants of a Christian temper. Sometimes he drew close to Plato himself, as might be expected of one who had translated him so meritoriously. There is more of the real Plato in Ficino than in any of his older contemporaries or predecessors, even as his translations were better. But his interest in the classic philosopher resembled the interest of the Alexandrian Neo-platonists, and likewise the interest of such a one as Augustine, who was so close to the Neo-platonists both in time and spiritual need. Ficino was concerned with the soul's immortality, and his mind was fixed upon the question of man's *summum bonum*. Neo-platonism, with the affiliated " Mystery " literature, seemed to approach the Christian ethics, to point to a like " summum bonum," and fortify the path to immortality.   So Ficino was taken by it.   But the Platonic doctrines of love, which he found in the *Symposium* and the *Phaedrus,* appealed to him powerfully. They were more congenial to the fifteenth century, with its passion for all forms of beauty and its lay education in romantic lore, than they had been to Christians or pagans of the time of Augustine.

To have translated Plato and Plotinus was a prodigious feat.   But Ficino labored also as a philosopher.   Imparting the color of his time and personality to the concepts of these men he loved, he made an amalgam from them in his chief, quasi-original composition, entitled *Theologia Platonica*, or *De immortalitate animorum*.   The book was published, veritably *printed* (for the printing press had come!) in Florence in 1482.[7]   In his *pröoemium* addressed to Lorenzo de' Medici, Ficino praises Plato and reproves those who would impiously sever philosophy from religion.   He will set forth chiefly what Plato has on immortality: [8] — is there not Augustine's authority for finding Platonists to have been almost Christians? He hopes to give nothing save as *divina lex comprobet* [sanctions].   In the treatment of its subject the work is indefinitely scholastic.   It has much of Plato and Plotinus, and Hermes Trismegistus too; but it has also much of Thomas Aquinas.   For, though Ficino endeavored to reach back to Platonic sources, he did not cast aside his nearer mediaeval past, which indeed largely furnished his attitude and method, and the intellectual atmosphere which he breathed.

With the coming of Lorenzo to power in 1469, the band of eager Platonists, under his auspices and Ficino's guidance, were formed into the Florentine Academy in imitation of the immortal Academy at Athens.   They met at the Badia di Fiesole, furnished by Lorenzo.   Here the name of Plato was reverenced, and his sculptured

---

[7] I have used an excellent French edition of 1559,— a very complete piece of book-making: It sets forth the care with which the oldest codices have been compared, follows with a publisher's puff — Bibliopola ad Lectorem — which promises all that is known of all lofty themes drawn from all great philosophers and theologians; it has a table of chapter headings and a good index.

[8] In fact, the work is largely a presentation of the *Phaedo*.

image almost adored.   Here his writings were read aloud
and enthusiastically discussed; and then the company
would turn to the pages of Plotinus or Proclus.   Platonism became a lovely intellectual fashion among these
élite.   The Academy flourished through that esthetically
happy time, until Lorenzo's death in 1492.   A change of
mood and circumstance swept over Florence with Savo-
narola.   Ficino himself died in 1499, and there was no
one to take his place as leader, and perhaps no longer
call for such a leader or such a theme.   Five years before
him the marvel of the group, Pico della Mirandola, had
died at the age of thirty-one.

This prince, who for the sake of philosophy had renounced his princedom, was one of the wonders of the
quattrocento, and one of its noblest spirits.   As a child
and as a man, he was prodigious in his intellectual attainments and performances.   How many characteristics of
his time he represents!   Among others, that of being at
sea amid the newly flowing currents of Greek philosophy;
at sea, as well, with the larger knowledge (craved if not
yet won) of nature and the forces moving the universe.

Pico was closely knit in life and sympathy with the
Florentine group of Platonists.   Like his master Ficino,
he was encompassed by his scholastic Aristotelian inheritance, which furnished his habits of thinking.   Next, Platonism, in the very widest and loosest sense, may be
deemed the source, or rather base, from which sprang
his further proclivities, lucubrations, and noble consideration of life.   Looking even beyond Platonism, his mind
and temper sought appeasement from that fantastic, if
soul-satisfying, allegorical interpretation of the Old
Testament known as the Jewish Cabbala.[9]   With the
wise Rabbis and many Christian doctors, Pico believed
that its teachings had been secretly revealed by God to
Moses, at the time when He delivered to His prophet the
tablets of the law.   The Cabbala could helpfully be used,
he thought, in interpreting the Christian faith; in fact,

---

[9] Cf. Massetani, *La filosofia Cabbalistica de Pico d. M.* (Empoli. 1897);
also V. di Giovanni, *Pico d. M. nella storia del Rinascimento* (Mirandola,
1899).

(as we note) it's elastic symbolism could be compelled to
any meaning.   In it, moreover, could be discerned the
material and intellectual, or prototypal, worlds figured by
the Platonists.[10]   Holding with them, that a conception
is true when it corresponds to the Idea in the Creator's
mind, Pico held that our conceptions of the world must
accord with the original, immaterial, world existing in the
mind of God.

Pico's more direct thoughts of nature seemingly fall
within his conception of magic.   Let us not be repelled
by the word, or conclude at once that Pico's magic did
not contain wistful reflections touching nature's processes.
" Magia est pars practica scientiae naturalis," says he.[11]
But what he meant by *magia,* can be realized only by
one who can think in the terms of that Platonism which
was fluid enough to run in Cabbalistic moulds, and can
also place himself in the fifteenth century and share its
lack of a consistent view of nature and physical law.
Pico denounces the magic of his time, which relied on
demoniac agencies.   He wrote a book against Astrology,
in which he sought to free men from her deadly web.   It
is but reasonable to think that he meant something not
altogether foolish when he said that *magia* with him is
nothing else than " naturalis philosophiae absoluta con-
summatio ";[12] and again he calls it " nobilissima pars scientiae naturalis." [13]   It does no miracles itself, but gathers nature's powers which God scatters through the world,
and comes to nature's aid.   It investigates and works with
the affinities of things, and *marries* terrestrial objects with
the forces of the heavenly bodies.   There is no virtue
existing *seminaliter et separata* in heaven or earth which
the true *Magus* cannot *actuare et unire,*— educe, actualize
and join together.   Such is its value.   And so long as *we*
think that man can learn of God by reflecting upon His
works, we may understand how Pico came to make the following statement which gave umbrage to the Church:

[10] See Pico's *Praefatio ad Lectorum* to his *Heptaplus,* Also his *Apolo-*
gia, p. 175 of the Basel ed. of 1572.
[11] In his *Conclusiones.*
[12] *Apologia.*
[13] *Conclusiones.*

" Nulla est scientia quae nos magis certificet de divinitate Christi quam Magia et Cabala ": — no other science yields surer proof of the divinity of Christ than Magic and the Cabbala.

Something of Pico's mentality and the nature of his interests may be gathered from the drift of the nine hundred *Conclusiones* or propositions, which he linked together, to make of them perhaps a " golden chain " joining Platonism to Christianity. They were drawn from various sources, or were put forward as his own convictions. One notes the authors upon whom he mainly drew. Twelve propositions he takes from Porphyry, nine from Jamblicus, and from Proclus fifty-five. Then he draws from the supposed mathematics of Pythagoras thirteen, and six from the opinions of Chaldean theologians. Then from the Thrice-great Egyptian Mercury, ten, such as these: " Ubicunque vita, ibi anima; ubicunque anima, ibi mens ": —" omne motum corporeum, omne movens incorporeum." Forty-seven *Conclusiones Cabalisticae* follow, pertaining to the secret doctrine of the wise Hebrew Cabbalists, whose memory should be respected. The first one reads: " Sicut homo et sacerdos inferior sacrificat Deo animas animalium irrationalium, ita Michael sacerdos sacrificat animas animalium rationalium." He gives next a variety of *Conclusiones secundum opinionem propriam,* divided into physical, theological, Platonic, mathematical, Chaldaean, Orphic, Magic, Cabbalistical, " Paradoxas dogmatizantes," and " paradoxas conciliantes." His first statement is that Aristotle and Plato are really at one touching all matters natural and theological, although their language seems to conflict. Pico's interpretations were capable of reconciling anything; and so, besides making peace between these two great Greeks, he finds no difficulty in reconciling Aquinas and Duns Scotus. Here we quickly touch the scholastic substratum of his mind shown in his interest in analogies between the nature of an angel and the nature of the soul: " Sicut angelus necessario componitur ex essentia et esse, ita anima necessario componitur ex substantia et accidente."

Pico could be rational, according to our modern notions,

and consequently heretical, as when he opposed trans-substantiation, or maintained that Christ did not really descend into Hell, but only *quoad effectum*. Nor can he bring himself to admit the propriety of everlasting punishment for mortal sin. After this he passes to his *Conclusiones* as to Magic, already noticed, and then to the magical significance of the Orphic hymns, and then to the Cabbala.

He publicly supported these nine hundred *Conclusiones* in Rome in the year 1488. Then quickly, as he says in " twenty nights," he wrote his wide-ranging *Apologia,* defending those of his *Conclusiones* which had been dubbed heretical. It was a bristling composition, maintaining, for instance, that the Cross should not be worshipped, that in the Eucharist the substance of the bread remained, and that it does not lie " in the free power of man to believe that an article of faith is true." If he wrote his *Apologia* in " twenty nights," the process, brought against him for these published opinions, lasted intermittently through the remaining years of his short life.[14]

The magnificence of Pico's character, and his lofty consideration of man, appear in his letters, some of which were beautifully translated by Sir Thomas More, and in his oration upon *Human Dignity*.[15] In the first letter, to his nephew, he bids him never wish to please those to whom virtue is displeasing. Then with reference to the Christian faith, he gives his principles and practice: " It is madness not to believe the Gospel, whose truth the blood of the martyrs proclaims, the apostolic voices re-echo, miracles prove, reason confirms, the world attests, the elements utter, the demons confess; but it is far greater madness, when you do not doubt the Gospel's verity, to live as if you did not doubt its falsity."

To Lorenzo de' Medici he writes in courtly praise of his Italian poems, and to Politian in most friendly praise

---

[14] Cf. *Pic de la Mirandole en France,* by Dorez and Thuasne.

[15] *Joannis Pici Mirandulae Epistolarum liber,* ed. C. Cellarius (1682); *Pico della Mirandola, His Life, Three of his letters trans. by Sir T. More;* J. M. Rigg (D. Nutt, 1890), *De hominis dignitate,* published in Pico's *Opera.*

of him and dispraise of himself. As against a narrow classicism, he defends the writings of the great scholastics, showing how their language suited their substance. And in a letter to a man of religion he protests that his first and constant care is to unite piety with philosophy; and says that a sane, firm and robust intellect can be hoped for only from the integrity of life, from goodly conduct and from divine religion.[16]

The *Oration on Human Dignity* nobly expresses Pico's character and the result of his studies. It breathes a new sense of man's God-given freedom. Other creatures are coerced and limited by divine decree; but man's own decision is the arbiter of his nature. He is placed in the midst of the world, so that he may the better discern what it has to offer. God has made him neither heavenly nor earthly, neither mortal nor immortal, in order that he may mould himself to what he will, make himself a brute, or rise to the divine. This liberality from God is man's felicity; through which it is given him to have what he desires and to be that which he wills. Let a sacred ambition invade the mind, that we may strive with all our powers — as we may if we will. Let us despise the earth, and even the heavens, and beyond the courts of the world fly close to God. Thus Pico preaches the great principle — old Greek, human, or Christian — that it is for man to foster his higher nature and suppress the brute. He has taken the world's best to himself, and has brought his truth, the truth of his own nature, from afar: — from Plato, from Aristotle; from the Delphic Apollo's injunctions of temperance and self-knowledge; from the later mysteries — the " Chaldeans," the Cabbala, " Zoroaster," and from Christ.

Toward the close of his Oration, Pico denounces those who use philosophy as a means of gain, and proudly says: " For none other cause have I ever philosophized except in order that I might philosophize. Nor from my studies or my writings have I looked for any pay, or hoped or sought for any other fruit, than cultivation of the mind and the attainment of truth, which always and above all

---

[16] Epis. III, IV, XV, XXXIV.

things I desire." In conclusion he advocates wide reading; let one not swear by a single master, be he Thomas or Duns Scotus. Every school has some good of its own. And Pico comments on the merits of the great scholastics, and upon the Greeks; though the names of the latter which he mentions show him to have dwelt with the later and more questionable men, and to have turned more naturally to the commentator and paraphraser, than to the great originals. Yet in spite of much confusing of brass with gold, his scheme of education was a broad one, and his principles of life were of the loftiest.

Pico held a great deal of his time, and also, strangely mixed with it, a great deal of the past, his own genius furnishing the plastic principle, the personal result. He could handle the lucubrations of Scholasticism, and mingle them with Cabbalistic elements to a potent brew, streaked here and there with reason. With demonic energy he sought a short-cut to illumination, an endeavor proper to his time. His short-cut lay through the discovery of secret, hidden, mystery-enfolding writings, which could declare the mystery of life to adepts. He would have the *secret* books of Moses, of Esdras, of Zoroaster, of any dimly adumbrated ancient seer; and from them would draw so quickly the secret of life, suddenly, magically, getting something for nothing, in such mode as Plato and Aristotle knew to be impossible and foolish. The strong character-building and strenuous qualities in Pico knew this too; yet could not keep this Cabbalistic Platonist, this genius of the fifteenth century, from struggling for the short-cut which is folly's cul-de-sac.

Florence was the hearth of the revival of Platonism; and there it became the philosophic fashion. In its origin, it may be taken as part of the strong humanistic revival of letters, which for the fourteenth and fifteenth centuries, had its chief home in Florence. Many of those scholars who were fascinated by " Platonism," were devotees of letters rather than philosophy. So the Platonic revival influenced letters, and diffused itself as an element in art; as one may see in the sonnets of Michael Angelo and the frescoes of Raphael; nor had Leonardo before them been untouched by its suggestiveness.

The revival of any antique system of philosophy could not possibly have any such effect in the fifteenth century as the resurrection of Aristotle had in the thirteenth. Then the systematizing theology and philosophy, called Scholasticism, was reaching the climax of its energy, and was at the same time prepared to adopt the form of a great classic system. The philosophy of Aristotle could supply the desired form and method, and also fill the same with a store of universal knowledge and opinion such as the thirteenth century was very ready to receive. But fifteenth century thought was no longer disposed to bind a novel ancient system on itself; nor did Platonism offer a fresh store of tangible scientific knowledge. The fifteenth century did not expend on it the same unstinted diligence, with the same seriousness of purpose, that the thirteenth had consecrated to Aristotle. And the earlier foundation was not now to be shaken by its rival, which in a measure it had superseded in the late twelfth and thirteenth centuries.

An interest in Platonism passed on from Italy to Spain and France and England. In France, sundry scholars devoted themselves to the elucidation of the immortal Dialogues (poor Dolet did this to his deadly scathe, for the Aristotelianism of the Paris University could be vengeful). And Queen Marguerite of Navarre drew draughts of Platonism from the translations of Ficino.[17] In England, Sir Thomas More took delight in Pico's letters, and incorporated much Platonism in his *Utopia*. But everywhere conservative and anxious orthodoxy, especially at the universities, upheld Aristotle with a grip not to be loosed by anything which Platonism could offer. For indeed, philosophically, intellectually, scientifically, Platonism did not contain and could not offer, what the intellect of the coming time was to demand with a purposeful insistency becoming ever clearer. The call was for a new view of the universe, for new methods

[17] See ante, chapter XII.

of knowledge, new physical certainties and a larger volume of actually demonstrated fact.

III

In the thirteenth century (to look no further back) one observes scattered tastes for mathematics and for something like inductive physical science based on observation. Here labored the unappreciated contemporary of Aquinas, Roger Bacon, and Peter of Maharncuria of whom Bacon has so much to say.[18]   There were others who may have outstripped Bacon in mathematics; while in optics in which he worked with such delight, there was one Witelo, who was given to Neo-platonism and wrote a *Perspectiva,* and a younger man, Theodoricus Teutonicus de Vriberg, who seems to have flourished between 1285 and 1310.   He wrote *On Light, On Colors, On the Rainbow,* evolving as to the last a theory that was not forgotten.[19]   Somewhat later came Buridan, an important follower of Occam, and his friend and pupil, Albert of Saxonia, the two teaching at Paris in the middle of the fourteenth century.   With them there was a third, a certain Timon, the son of a Jew (himself apparently a Christian).   The voluminous writings of these three men upon physics or " natural philosophy " were in the form of *Quaestiones* upon the Aristotelian treatises, for example the *Octo libri physicorum,* the *Tres libri de Coelo et Mundo,* the *Quatuor libri Meteorum,* the *De Anima.* These works represented original consideration and experiment as well as study of the Stagirite, upon whose opinions touching the problems of physics they made some advance.   Beyond the labors of these men, such a fact as the coming of gunpowder into general military use evinces the application of intelligence to chemistry and mechanics.

In the first half of the fifteenth century, the expansion of the human spirit is represented by Nicholas of Cusa,

---

[18] See *The Mediaeval Mind,* chap. XLII.
[19] Baeumker, *Witelo, ein Philosoph und Naturforscher des XIII Jahrhundert* (Munster, 1908) ; E. Krebs, *Meister Dietrich, sein Leben,* etc. (Munster, 1906).

whose learning looked to the past, but whose genius shadowed forth the future.

He was born at Cues in the diocese of Tréves in 1401, whence his name Cusanus. A career of ecclesiastical diplomacy and affairs, as well as a life of devotion to philosophy, theology, and physics, lay ahead of this low-born lad. The foundations of his piety and learning were laid at Deventer, with the Brethren of the Common Life. Afterwards he went to Italy, and at Padua made his doctorate of laws in 1424. Within a few years, however, he had turned from law to the study of philosophy and the profession of the priesthood. The reformation of the Church drew his attention, while the still unsettled conflict between the Papacy and the Conciliar Party called forth his able *De concordantia catholica,* which made the superior authority of councils appear as the result of an historical inquiry. He presented the book to the Council of Basel, where he took active part until its intolerable measures drove him to change sides: he left Basel (1437) and joined Pope Eugene IV. The latter, disposed toward a council of his own, nominally with the object of uniting the Greek and Roman Churches, sent Nicolas to Constantinople to escort the Greek legates to Italy. On the homeward voyage there came to him, as he says,[20] the ultimate principle of his philosophy. We need not accompany Cusanus on his distinguished career as cardinal and bishop and papal diplomat until his death in 1464. Through all these years he applied himself as well to his philosophy and carried into many fields of thought that which he deemed had come to him upon the sea.

The principle which thus had flashed across his mind was the union of all contraries in the divine unity of God. The approach to it seems to have been through the state or method of *docta ignorantia,* whereby Nicholas stripped the ship of his philosophy down to those bare poles that might withstand all questioning, as after him Descartes did in formulating his *Méthode.* The idea and even the phrase *docta ignorantia* had a long history

[20] When closing his *De docta ignorantia,* III, 12.

from Augustine, and even from the Greeks.[21]   In the mind of Cusanus " learned " or " well-taught " ignorance never ceased to represent his consciousness of man's incapacity to know absolute truth.   From this it sharpened to a more specific and enlightening apprehension of the limits to our knowledge.   Through it next we realize that by reason of our inability to know the truth, every statement must remain an assumption or conjecture.[22] And while the truth may be approached through the balancing and discarding of these conjectures, we shall never know it so that we may not know it better.   The more profoundly we realize our inability to reach it the nearer becomes our approach.

Nicholas next proceeds to his principle of the unity of all contraries in God.   This ultimate conception may be set upon a universal antimony, which is fundamental to Cusanus's thought, that of the coincidence of opposites (oppositorum coincidentia), which the " prevailing Aristotelian sect deems heresy, though its recognition is the beginning of the ascent to Mystic Theology." [23]   " We, however, behold the opposites in the womb of the principle that unites them prior to their duality, that is before they were two things mutually opposed." [24]

Although this working principle of the coincidence or identity of opposites is alien from the Aristotelianism of Aquinas, Aquinas and other scholastics furnished the fund of thought from which Cusa naturally drew whenever he was not devising novelties.   So he reaches many conclusions of Aquinas, for instance, that God is the absolute actuality as well as the creative cause of all. But it was Cusa's novel thoughts and novel attitude that impressed those who followed him, and made his fruitful contribution to the intellectual changes of the fifteenth

[21] Its varying significance with Augustine, Pseudo-Dionysius, Bonaventura, as far as John Locke, is traced by J. Uebinger in *Archiv der Philosophie* for 1895, " Der Begriff docta ignorantia in seinem ges. Entwicklung." The phrase in Augustine is from the Ep. ad Probam, Ep. 130 (or 121), cap. 15, 28.   Est ergo in nobis quaedam, ut ita dicam, docta ignorantia, sed docta spiritu dei, qui adjuvat infirmitatem nostrum.

[22] Conjectura — this point seems brought out in Cusanus's *De Conjecturis*, written a year or so after his *De docta ignorantia*.

[23] *Apologia de docta ignorantia.*

[24] *Liber . . . de beryllo.*

and sixteenth centuries. His arguments, however, to prove the identity of the least and the greatest (maximum, minimum) in each order of existence, and finally the union of all *maxima* and *minima* in the absolute unity of God, may seem a juggling with scantily veiled fallacies.[25] But there can be no doubt of the earnestness of his endeavor to think God, and adjust his own existence to that absolute potency and actuality. We cannot really know God, because we must know by connecting the unknown with the known, and the infinite cannot thus be reached through the finite. Therefore since the Greatest, being *veritas infinita*, cannot be absolutely known by us, we reach it *incompraehensibiliter*, which is through the way of *docta ignorantia*. Mathematics also may help us along to our apprehension of the absolute union of opposites. An infinite line is at once triangle, circle, and sphere, and contains actually (*actu* — here we seem back with Thomas and Aristotle) everything that finite lines are *in potentia*. Likewise everything that lies *in potentia* in every least and simplest thing, exists actually in the greatest being: thus opposites disappear. The Greatest exceeds substance and accidents; but is more like substance (as Dionysius says) : i. e. it is *supersubstantialis* rather than *superaccidentalis*.

Surely this man had not cut loose from scholasticism; nor did he do so in applying his reasonings to the universe of concrete and finite things. Yet for himself he argues (at the opening of the second book of *Docta ignorantia*) that these must be known through the nature of their prototype and creator, and since that cannot be known (save incompraehensibiliter) we fall back on the method of *docta ignorantia*. Cusa's third chapter of Book II proceeds to show how the Greatest embraces or comprehends (complicet) and then evolves (explicet) all things in a way that we may somehow apprehend. The *Infinite Unity* is the *complicatio* of all things, holds them all within its unity; but God is also the *explicatio* or evolution of all things. Everything in him (as complicatio) is himself, and as *explicatio* he is in all things what they

[25] See e. g. the arguments of *De docta ignorantia*, I, 4.

are.[26]   Conversely finite things in their contracted or
concrete way have whatever the Greatest has in its greatest way.   Only the Absolute Greatest is infinite; the
Universe, the world of concrete things is not the Absolute
Greatest, which is God.   The Universe therefore is not
infinite; but neither is it finite, for it has no limit.

Since there is nothing absolute and self-existent save
God, the Universe is obviously from Him.   Through the
Universe as a whole the absolute Unity of God transfuses
itself into the plurality of created things.   Matter, which
is the potentiality of the Universe, could not exist without
the form in which it shall reach a non-absolute actuality.
Nor could that form exist but for the potentiality which
is matter.   That form is the soul of the world.   Matter
is predisposed toward it, is impregnated with desire for
actualization in it.   Reciprocally that form, which is the
World-soul, is drawn to its potentiality which is matter,
without which it could not be.   This desire for each other,
this living bond uniting them, is as the Holy Spirit uniting
Father and Son: and the Universe of concrete things is
the reflex, the *explicatio,* of the Tri-une God.

The microcosm, man, is constituted as the macrocosm.
The union between matter and the World-soul is repro-
duced in the union between the human body and the human
soul.   The life of man on earth hangs on the mutual
drawing together and realization of the two in this union.

Cusa was deeply interested in physical speculation,
even in observation and experiment; but his thoughts
upon natural phenomena always trailed his metaphysics.
There was metaphysics, if not mysticism, in his explanation of the movement of bodies.   It was affected by his
conception of the union of the World-soul with matter,
and the relationship of one and both to God.   Soul,
spirit, is the universal motor.   Involved in matter, it im-

[26] Lib. II, cap. 3 has the title — Quomodo maximum complicet et explicet omnia intellectibiliter.
    Maximum autem est, cui nihil potest opponi, ubi et minimum est maxi-
mum.   Unitas igitur infinita est omnium complicatio.   Hoc quidem dicitur
unitas, quae omnia unit. . . . scias Deum omnium rerum complicationem et
explicationem, et, ut est complicatio, omnia in ipso esse ipsum, et, ut est
explicatio, ipsum in omnibus esse id quod sunt.   Cf. Uebinger, *Die Gottes-
lehre des Nikolaus Cusanus* (Munster, 1888).

parts ceaseless motion, which thus becomes an attribute of the visible Universe. God is omnipresent in all that is. He moves it all. Matter, impregnate w:+h the World-soul, moves. Through the human soul, the human body moves. All things move; nothing is at rest. The earth is not the center of the Universe (*centrum Mundi*), neither can it ever lack manifold movement. Although Cusa did not discard the theory of the spheres, the earth is not for him the centre of the sphere of the fixed stars, but moves like the planets. Nor can either sun or moon or earth in its motion describe a true circle, *cum non moveantur super fixo*.[27] Cusa's thoughtful interest did not merely follow the grand lines of physical speculation; it was also turned upon an indefinite number of the problems of physics or mechanics.[28]

The quite sufficiently original mind of Cusa was also stored with learning. He had read and assimilated so very much and from such diverse sources. He had read, for instance, the famous Lully, and taken from him certain thoughts built round the phrase *quodlibet in quolibet,* everything in everything; he was filled with Neoplatonism, drawn from Plotinus, from the Hierarchies of Pseudo-Dionysius, and from a certain later Neoplatonic *Theologia Aristotelis;* he had also borrowed from many others much physical speculation.[29] In turn he influenced many and diverse men, among whom probably Leonardo da Vinci, and certainly the restless Bruno a century later. It suggests the continuity between mediaeval thought and that of the fifteenth and sixteenth centuries, to find Leonardo working with ideas which were close to those of Cusa's own fashioning and with others which Cusa had drawn from mediaeval men; or to find Leonardo making use of ideas which he might, or even may, have taken from such a fourteenth century Occamist and physicist as Albertus of Saxonia.[30] Appar-

[27] *De doc. ig.* II, 11. See Max Jacobi, *Das Universum,* etc., in *den Lehren des Nicolaus von Cusa.* (Berlin, 1904.)
[28] See generally Duhem's articles in *Bulletin Italien.*
[29] This is shown at length by Duhem, " Nicolas de Cues et Leonardo da Vinci," *Bulletin Italien,* VII (1907), pp. 87–134; ib. pp. 181–220.
[30] See Duhem, *Bulletin Italien,* VII (1907), pp. 314–329; ib. VIII, pp.

ently the thoughts of Cusa and Albertus affected Keppler and even the Copernican theory in general, for which Cusa's reasonings were suited to prepare men's minds.[31]

212 sqq.; 312 sqq., where Leonardo's direct indebtedness to Cusa is asserted positively.

[31] Duhem, *Bulletin Italien*, VIII, pp. 18–55.

CHAPTER XXXI

LEONARDO DA VINCI

THE philosophy of Cusa exemplifies how the mediaeval and antique past furnished much of the thought of even so constructive mind as his. The same will be true of the most original philosophies and physical investigations of the fifteenth and sixteenth centuries. But though that period drew masterfully upon its ancient sources, men had become restive under the authority of the past, and greater numbers than before were turning their thoughts directly to the world of nature. Criticism became more audacious, and novel shapings of opinion more in vogue. If the training of the past made possible these novelties, still the breath of life, which always is of the present, was in the latter. Many ideas drawn probably from the writings of previous men were made good use of in the eminently living and original works of the mind and hands of Leonardo da Vinci, who was twelve years old when Nicholas of Cusa died.

Leonardo's personality was complex beyond the verge of mystery. It seems possible to discern the master motives of his nature; but to name the chief among them were perilous; and perilous the attempt to find a unity of effort, of purpose, in his life. Perhaps no single motive unified those energies which pursued a confederacy of intellectual interests, or dispersed themselves through different provinces of investigation. Yet it was one Leonardo who became absorbed in science and in art. He, and not a part of him, was at the same time or successively, artist and engineer, investigator and writer, his faculties co-operating in the accomplishment of what might be a means or an end according to the purpose in his mind. Constantly, in his earlier life at least, he studied nature for the purpose of art, as when he dissected horses for the Sforza monument. Or he might use his draftsmanship to draw the human organs or the wings of birds for the ends of natural science, or of engineering.

Leonardo may have been a precocious boy in ways not noticed by his parents. His father did observe his gift for drawing, and placed him in the studio of Verocchio. Assuredly, then, from the first he was an artist,— painter, draftsman, carver,— fascinated by the appearances of men and things about him, impressed by their beauty, as it struck his eye. Opening his eyes to the world, he was caught by the surfaces, the fascinating appearances of things, and gave himself over to reproducing those visible forms. But, as every painter knows, the endeavor to reproduce the surfaces of things as the eye sees them, leads quickly to the study of their contours and substances, and the lights and shadows which, with substance and contour, contribute to the visible appearance, and must be considered by the artist who would reproduce that. This artist was led to investigate what seemed to him the natures of things, and the relationship of their appearances to their substance, with its color and form-giving envelope of light and darkness.

But even commonplace men have curiosity as to what things are, and how they come to be; and with Leonardo this curiosity amounted to insatiate genius. Just as he was born with a love of the beauty which filled his eyes, so was he from his youth inspired with an effective desire to know and understand the actualities surrounding him. Soon conviction may have come (befitting his benevolent and intellectual nature) that, in order to love, one must understand, and the more one understands, the more will be his love.

So it could not be otherwise than that Leonardo's curiosity should have passed beneath the visible surfaces of things, to their mechanism, the manner of their production and destruction. One motive, as his considerations upon painting testify, was to gain help in this art, that he might paint more truly, and do justice to the subtle beauty of the world. Nevertheless, it would be to ignore the rest of Leonardo's nature not to see that this motive was surrounded by the larger desire to know " la verità della cose," which is the " sommo notrimento delli intelletti fini." [1]

Leonardo never ceased to love the experiences of the eye. He meditated and reasoned upon things visible. The delight and wonder of seeing never ceased to lead and fashion the innermost meditations of his mind. That remained fixed on the things which it had received through vision. Constantly he lauds the sense of sight; and whenever his thoughts pass beyond the eye's experience, they seem to come to a strange land of deception and mirage, where there was, however, one form of truth — mathematics. Mathematics, reasoning from the sense data of number and proportion, is the one science that can securely pass beyond the experiences of the senses. Only by holding fast to mathematics can the mind safely penetrate the labyrinth of intangible and insubstantial thought.

The meditations of Leonardo would still have dwelt with the visible, with that which could be known through sense perception or its mathematical pointings, had not nature's overwhelming complexity driven him to a realization of the existence of infinite hidden reasons and causes beyond the data of experience: " La nature è piena d'infinite ragioni, che non furono mai in isperienza." Two thousand years before him, another keen observer declared that " Nature loves to conceal."

If those " infinite ragioni " were hidden from experience, he certainly would not accept any disclosure of them from authority — from the web of baseless syllogisms fabricated by the schoolmen. For himself, he would abide chiefly with physical investigations, aided, established, universalized through mathematics. In his physics, as in his study of anatomy and physiology, he

[1] *The Literary Works of Leonardo da Vinci,* 2 vols. (London, 1883), Vol. II, § 1168. My citations are taken mainly from this work, and from E. Solmi's admirable little *Frammenti letterari e filosofici* of Leonardo (Florence, Barbera, 1904). I would also refer to *Leonardo da Vinci, conferenze fiorentine,* by various scholars. (Milan, 1910.) Works on Leonardo are constantly appearing.

went far beyond the need of any painter's art,— which represented one phase of his practical energies. But these spent themselves also in the wide field of engineering, constructing canals as well as fortifications, and making the enginry of war. Through such undertakings, Leonardo applied portions of his science, as he applied other portions in his art of painting.

Through the decades of his life, the scientific interest, the sheer desire to find out and know, seems gradually to outweigh practice, both in engineering and in art. And doubtless the faculties of construction, as well as the efficient imagination and will to paint, were depressed by the activity of the scientific mind.

The various phases of Leonardo's practical, artistic, or more strictly intellectual, energies sustained and helped each other, partaking of each other's nature as well as aims. Yet they were also rivals, and, through their mutual interference, prevented, perhaps, the full achievement which the undistracted powers of Leonardo might have accomplished in some one field of effort.

A general knowledge of his life may be assumed. His painting has been spoken of already.[2]

Touching his achievements in architecture and engineering, one's eye is caught by what he is supposed to have written when in his thirties, to Lodovico Sforza. The Lord of Milan was beset by wars, and Leonardo offered to make him portable bridges, to carry with his troops, show him how to empty the water from the moats of besieged places, make him mortars for bombardment which will throw a tempest of small stones, or provide other ordnance, with a disclosure of new methods of mining and sapping; also armored chariots, and if the fight be at sea, machines for effective attack and defense. In time of peace, he can equal any man in architecture and the construction of public buildings and water ways; in sculpture and painting he can do whatever can be done.[3]

These promises may remind the mediaeval student of

[2] Ante, chapter V.
[3] See Richter, *Lit. Works*, &c., II, § 1340, for the presumptive draft of this letter.

what Roger Bacon once had vaunted as within the prowess of a certain Peter of Maharncuria.[4] All reports make Leonardo a wonderful expounder of projects. Yet his ingenuity might often make good his words; and his achievements as an engineer, especially in the construction of canals, seem to have equalled or exceeded those of any contemporary. He excelled all in mechanical and constructive devices, from flying machines to fortifications, as his sketches still show. No one of his contemporaries had so profoundly studied the power and currents of air and water; and probably no contemporary, unless it were his friend Bramante, knew more of the weights and strengths of materials and modes of building. He drew plans for many buildings and public improvements. But it was impossible that a man of his experimental temperament, with interests as diverse as his occupations, should have carried out his designs in the slower processes of actual building.

Leonardo was one held by the visible world of man and nature. To have passed beyond the range of objects seen by the eye, would have been as alien to his artistic temperament as it would have been alien to his closely related scientific mind to have passed beyond the sphere of the informing testimony of the senses. Through them had come delight and inspiration; through them came knowledge and practical as well as scientific certitude. Assuredly the canon of his scientific principles would be included within knowledge arising through sense perception. This observant artist and experimenting physicist held throughout to observation, investigation and experiment, all of which was embraced within his term *esperienza*. That is the *maestra vera* who will bow before no authority. And if men will reprove him, Leonardo, alleging that his proofs counter the authority " d'aliquanti omini di gran reverenza," he will reply that his proofs are born of sheer experience, the mistress of their masters. Very incredulous will be this mistress over the results of abstract reasoning when unsupported by the testimony of the senses, or the cognate principles of mathematics.

[4] See, *The Mediaeval Mind*, II, pp. 532–534.

" And if thou sayest, that sight impedes the steady and subtle thinking of the mind, with which it penetrates the divine sciences, and this hindrance once induced a philosopher to deprive himself of sight; — I reply that such eye, as lord of the senses, does its duty in giving a fall to those confused and lying, not sciences, but discourses, through which men are always disputing with noise and waving of hands. . . . And if that philosopher put out his eyes to lift the impediment from his discourses, such act was fellow to the brain and discourses, for it was sheer madness. . . .

" They say that that knowledge is mechanical which issues from *esperienza,* and that is scientific which is born and ends in the mind. . . . But, as it seems to me, those sciences are vain and full of errors, which are not born of *esperienza,* mother of all certitude, and which do not terminate in cognition (nota esperienza), that is, whose origin or middle or end does not come through one of the five senses.

" And if we have doubt of everything which comes through the senses, how much more should we doubt of things rebels to the senses, as the essence of God and the soul, and the like, about which one is always contending and disputing? And verily it always happens where reason fails, that clamor takes its place, which does not happen when things are certain. From which we say that where there is clamor there is not true knowledge (vera scienza), because truth has a single ending, and when that is made known, the contest is ended forever; and if the contest rises again, it means a lying and confused knowledge, and not certitude reborn.

" But the true sciences (vere scienze) are those which *la speri-enza* has caused to enter through the senses, silencing the tongue of the disputants, and not feeding its investigators upon dreams; but proceeds always upon true and known first principles step by step, and with true conclusions to the end; as is indicated in the elementary mathematical sciences, that is number and measure, called arithmetic and geometry, which treat with absolute truth of discontinuous and continuous quantity." [5]

For Leonardo, mathematics was the basis of all methodical investigation, experiment, and conclusion, that is of all science worthy of the name. " No human inquiry can be called true science, unless it proceeds through mathematical demonstrations."

" Proportions," says Leonardo in another place, " are found not only in numbers and measures, but also in sounds, weights, times and places, and in every force. . . . There is no certitude where some one of the mathematical sciences cannot be applied." With Leonardo all nature

[5] *Frammenti,* pp. 93–95.

is a field for the application of mathematics:— "The bird is a machine working through mathematical law." Nature's forces and operations are quantitative, and proper subjects of quantitative investigation and discovery. The economy of nature is quantitative, or one may say, mathematical. Its processes, even its *ragioni*, must be physical, quantitative, mathematical.

Man, the investigator, must realize that there is a profound rationality or consequence in Nature, which corresponds with the processes of human cognition, if not of human reason. "*La sperienza*, interpreter between plastic nature and the human race, teaches how that same nature works in mortals; constrained by necessity, it cannot work otherwise than its rudder, reason, requires it to work." But while Nature acts rationally, her investigator is obliged to proceed from *esperienza*, and afterwards demonstrate the rationality of the process which he has thus first verified in fact. Says Leonardo, " But I will make experiment (esperienza) before I proceed, because my intention is first to set forth the facts — l'esperienza — and then demonstrate by reason why such *esperienza* is constrained to work in such fashion. And this is the true rule to be followed by the investigators of natural phenomena (effetti naturali) ; while nature begins from *ragione*, and ends in *esperienza*, we must follow a contrary procedure, that is, begin from *esperienza*, and with that discover the *ragioni*." [6]

The necessity, which is Nature's mistress and instructress, is none other than her own *regola eterna*, or, in other words, Nature's law, *sua legge:* " Nature is constrained by the *ragione* of her law, which lives infused in her." Her essence, her inner being, may be beyond human investigation and knowledge; but the phenomena of nature may be followed, and we may know her effects — *effetti:* " The definition of the whatness — quiddità — of the elements is not in the power of man, but many of their effects are known." Nature's ways, or Nature's

[6] *Frammenti,* pp. 83, 85, 86, 88. In Leonardo's writings the *sperienza* or *esperienza* may (like *experientia* with Roger Bacon in the thirteenth century) waver in meaning between *experiment* and *experience*.

laws, are to be discovered in the courses of her phenomena, where each effect invariably answers to its cause. Leonardo may have seen the regularity of Nature's order in this correspondence, as well as in the absolute economy of Nature's operations: every one of her acts is done "per la via brevissima." [7]

This most unsystematic of human geniuses did not attempt to formulate a logical and complete statement of the principles which he followed in his scientific investigations. But evidently, both as stated in his maxims and as followed in his practice, his method was that of observation and experiment, and of drawing conclusions as far as possible along the ways of mathematical reasonings. Yet he who knows most loves most; and the questing necessities of Leonardo's mind, as well as his need to love the whole marvellous world, might project his thoughts beyond the data of his sensible investigations even when supplemented by mathematics. His admiration for the visible world, rather than any close reasoning, led him to recognize the rationality of Nature and her processes, along with her evident exhaustlessness. "Nature is full of *infinite regioni* which were never in esperienza." [8]

Leonardo's acquaintance with previous physical speculation and the extent to which he masterfully made his own the thoughts of others are puzzling questions. If the later mediaeval centuries were dominated by the authority of Aristotle, there were still inquirers whose minds were not completely fastened to the master's word. And there was some knowledge of the theory of the lever, the centre of gravity and the action of fluids, once demonstrated by that mighty mathematician Archimedes of Syracuse.

Two men were teaching in Paris in the fourteenth century whose physics showed some advance over Aristotle's: John Buridan, a distinguished follower of Occam, and his somewhat younger contemporary and probable pupil, Albert of Saxonia. [9] It does not appear that Leonardo

---

[7] *Frammenti*, pp. 97, 113, 121.   [9] Ante, chap. XXX, III.
[8] Solmi, *Frammenti*, p. 112.

used Buridan's work; but Albert drew on Buridan, and Leonardo seems to have studied Albert, drawing conclusions from his writings, or using them as spurs to his own views, which were not always nearer to the truth than those of the fourteenth century masters. Leonardo mentions an Albert, who likely was this Albert of Saxony; and more than once he refers by name to Archimedes and his writings. Though he does not name Nicholas of Cusa, probably he knew something of his writings. He was no scholar, as he admits, nor an incessant reader. But living at Milan for many years in intercourse with men interested in physical investigations, he must have gained some knowledge of these old physicists, if he did not read their writings.[10] This probability is confirmed by the apparent reflection of their opinions in his own manuscripts. It was not his habit to say much of other people, or mention any indebtedness to them. Relying on his own thinking and experiments, he certainly was not the man to accept the statements of others, but would use them as suggestions, and might soon forget their source. Even though Leonardo had no direct knowledge of these earlier men, they had still made mute preparations for his own achievements; for their work was an element of an antecedent time, which itself helped to make possible the later epoch and all that Leonardo's genius accomplished.

With these general considerations in mind we turn to Leonardo's interesting but difficult conception, force.

Impeto (impetus) and *forza* were cognate if not identical conception with Leonardo, and fundamental in his physics.

" Impetus is the impact of motion transferred from the *motor* to the *mobile* [the object thereby affected with motion]." Again: " Impetus is a *virtù* created by motion and transferred from the *motor* to its *mobile,* the latter receiving as much motion as the impetus has of life." " Every impact tends to be permanent. . . . Every action must be carried out (exercised, trained, *bisogna che s'eserciti*) through motion. . . . Motion is the cause of all life."

" What is *forza?* I say *forza* is a *virtù spirituale,* a *potenza*

[10] See G. Séailles, *Leonardo da Vinci,* pp. 370 sqq. (Second edition, Paris, 1905.)

invisibile, which through accidental external violence, is caused by motion, and set and infused in bodies thereby withdrawn from their natural state and given an active life of marvellous power."

Again: " I say that *forza* is a *potenza spirituale,* incorporeal, invisible, which with brief life is produced in bodies that through an accidental violence find themselves beyond their natural being and repose. I have said *spirituale,* because in this *forza* there is an active incorporeal life; and I say invisible, because the body where it is born does not increase in weight or form; of short life, because it always desires to vanquish its cause, and, that vanquished, it dies." [11]

Leonardo's *impeto* is in the main the *impetus* of Albert of Saxonia, to whose conceptions he seems to turn when thinking in terms of mechanics or sheer physics. When he looks beyond these, possibly suggestions from Nicholas of Cusa led him to endue his *forza* with life, making it as a very short-lived soul infused in a body.[12] He would thus maintain the connection of *impeto* and *forza* with life, indeed with spirit, intellect and volition. Recognizing that " no inanimate body moves of itself; but its motion is made (fatto) by something else (da altri,) he looked for the moving cause to something having intelligence and volition. Elsewhere he says:

" *Forza* is produced by the too-little or too-much *(carestia o dovizia);* it is the daughter of material motion and the grand-child of *moto spirituale,* and the mother and origin of weight. Weight is limited (finito) to the elements of water and earth, while *forza* is unlimited (infinita), since by it infinite worlds might be moved, if instruments could be made by which the force could be generated. *Forza* with material motion, and weight with thrust, are the four accessory (accidentali) powers with which all the works of mortals have their being and their death. *Forza* takes its origin from *moto spirituale,* which flowing through the limbs of sentient animals, swells their muscles; whereupon these swollen muscles shorten and draw back the tendons joined to them, and thus is caused the *forza* through the limbs of men." [13]

Albert had argued that the solid element of earth constituting the earth's greater part, tended to move toward

[11] *Frammenti,* pp. 124, 125, completed from Duhem, *Bulletin Italien,* VIII, p. 43.
[12] *Bull. It.,* VIII, pp. 29 sqq.
[13] *Frammenti,* p. 126; Richter, o. c. § 859.

a centre of gravity, and thus produce sphericity. Leonardo went further. Apparently quoting from Albert an opinion which the older man had stated for disapproval, he maintains that because of this tendency of the earth's solid part, the waters in time would cover it completely, and render it uninhabitable. Albert had also spoken of the action and effect of rain in this work of gravity; which Leonardo illustrates from his own experience as a hydraulic engineer. Finally Albert referred to the subsidence of coasts and the emergence of new land from the sea. Leonardo proceeds to substantiate this with his striking arguments drawn from the presence of fossil shells in sedimentary rocks far above the level of the sea, — arguments which made a beginning for the science of paleontology.[14]

If Albert had suspected that the earth might be as the moon and other celestial bodies, Leonardo advanced boldly to the view that the earth is not situated at the centre of the celestial world, nor at the centre of the circle of the sun, which is the central body and the source of light and warmth for all that world. The earth reflects light to the moon, as the moon to the earth; and, like the earth, the moon has days and nights. Thus Leonardo shuffled off the geocentric theory just at the time when Copernicus was commencing his studies.[15]

[14] *Bull. Ital.*, V, pp. 31, and 116 sqq., VIII, 316 sqq.; Richter, o. c. II, §§ 987–994; *Frammenti*, pp. 142–160. Duhem (*Bull. Ital.*, VIII, pp. 212–252, 312–346) shows how Leonardo influenced Cardan, and Cardan, Palissy; and therefore that, in tracing the influences upon Leonardo, we are considering the origins of modern geology. Duhem gives the following striking line through which notions on geology descended: — Aristotle; Theophrastus; Strabo; Straton of Lampsacus; *Liber de proprietetibus elementorum*, falsely attributed to Aristotle; Albertus Magnus; Vincent de Beauvais; Paul of Venice; Albert of Saxonia; Leonardo da Vinci. Leonardo discarded the sterilities of the Averroist commentators on Aristotle, put together the best theories of Albert and others, and also observed for himself. I have freely used these remarkable articles of P. Duhem in the *Bulletin Italien*, though hesitating to accept the positiveness of their conclusions. With further essays, they have been republished under the title of *Études sur Léonardo de Vinci; ceux qu'il a lus et ceux qui l'ont lu.* Three volumes (Paris, 1906, 1909, 1913). The work is virtually a history of physics.

[15] *Bull. Ital.*, V, p. 128 sqq.; *Frammenti*, p. 136 sqq.; Richter, o. c. II, §§ 858 sqq. Nicholas of Cusa had preceded Leonardo in stating that the Earth is not at the centre of a Universe, but a noble star, moving as other heavenly bodies move. Cf. also *Bull. Ital.*, VIII, p. 28 and pp. 116–147.

Passing over Leonardo's close observations of plants, we turn to his famous anatomical studies. He was convinced of the unity of the animal kingdom. To him man was the "prima bestia infralli animali," having duller sight and smell than many quadrupeds and birds. Conceiving a science of comparative anatomy, he examined the resemblances and differences between the muscles and bones of man, and of the frog or hare or horse or lion. He had carefully dissected animals — horses for the purposes of sculpture, but just as much to satisfy his scientific curiosity. And he had systematically dissected at least ten, and probably thirty, human bodies, removing the flesh carefully from about the veins.[16] He made careful notes, and exact and beautiful drawings, which he combined (this was a novelty) with his anatomical text. Also, he read the works of Galen and the serviceable Anatomy of the Italian Mundinus written early in the fourteenth century. Its author dissected bodies for himself, yet his book in the main followed Galen as given through translations from the Arabian commentators. Hereafter will be noted the chequered progress of the healing arts of medicine and surgery; but here it may be said that the science of Anatomy made little progress from the death of Mundinus in 1327 until Leonardo set his hand to it. There was dissection of animals before students, and more rarely the dissection of human bodies, which the Church objected to. This objection, coupled with the prejudice of learned doctors against working with their hands, led to the relegation of the dissections to the barbers or assistants, while the professor read aloud or lectured from Galen or Mundinus.[17] The anatomical drawings of the human body and its organs in the medical books were not made from dissections, but were conventional and served merely to assist the memory. They are not to be brought into the same category with those marvels of beauty and exactitude which Leonardo executed from the dissections before him, or from immediate

[16] Richter, o. c. II. §§ 796, 823, 824, 827, 829.
[17] See Charles Singer, "A Study in early Renaissance Anatomy" (*Studies in the History and Method of Science*, Oxford, 1917); M. Roth, *Andreas Vesalius*, pp. 1–55 (Berlin, 1892).

and vivid recollection of them.[18]   Indeed Leonardo's
profound study of the hearts of quadrupeds as well as
human beings, and his careful drawings of that organ
with its valves, makes one wonder that he did not seize
upon the principle of the circulation of the blood, especially as his investigations and dissections were always
animated by an interest in the vital function of each
organ.   Thus his anatomy joined hands with his physiology.   For him the body was more marvellous than any
machine of human invention.   Perfect were its functional
adaptations; and it was an organism, moved by a vivifying soul.[19]

Leonardo's generalizations might proceed through
analogies, as, for instance from the idea that man is a
microcosm, a smaller world, " mondo minore," as the
ancients said.   Man is composed of the four elements,
and has bones, as the earth has rocks, and a pool of
blood in which the lungs swell and contract, as the ocean
tide rises and falls; and as veins rise in that pool of blood,
and go branching through the human body, so the ocean
fills the body of the earth with infinite veins of water;
only the stable earth lacks sinews, which are made for
movement.[20]   As life or spirit makes the body a living
organism, so with the world, where nothing is born save
where there is life " sensitiva, vegetativa e rationale; " —
feathers growing upon birds, and changed each year, grass
in the fields, leaves on the trees.   " Hence it may be said
the earth has an anima vegetativa.[21]

Everyone is bewitched by analogies — inherited or of
his own discovery — which are so suggestive and so mis-
leading.   The inherited analogy between microcosmus
and macrocosmus bewitched Leonardo not a little, and
drew his eyes from what they might else have seen.   But

[18] These are chiefly contained in the manuscripts of the Royal Library at
Windsor, admirably published by Vangensten and others (Christiania,
1911 — the publication is not yet completed).   On Leonardo as an anato-
mist, see A. C. Klebs, in *The Boston Medical and Surgical Journal*, July,
1916; also F. Botazzi, "Leonardo biologico e anatomico," in *Leonardo,
Conferenze Fiorentine* (Milan, 1910).

[19] See Richter, o. c. II, § 837.

[20] Richter, o. c. II, § 929.

[21] Richter, II, § 1000.

he had a vision of Nature's constant destructions and re-
newals, the vast economy of the concatenation of living
organisms,— and what object was not living where all
things had, or might have, motion?

"Hast thou marked Nature's diligence?" he asks. "The body
of everything that takes nourishment, constantly dies and is constantly re-born; because nourishment can enter only into places
where the past nourishment has expired, and if it has expired it
has no more life; and if you do not supply nourishment equal to
the nourishment departed, life will fail in vigor; and if you take
away this nourishment, life is utterly destroyed.   But if you restore
as much as is consumed day by day, just so much of life is reborn
as is consumed; as the flame of a candle is fed by the nourishment
given by the liquor of the candle, which flame continually with
rapid succor restores from below what above is consumed in dying;
and from a brilliant light is converted into dark smoke; which
death is continuous as the smoke is continuous; and the continuance
of the smoke equals the continued nutriment; and at the same moment all the flame is dead and regenerated with the movement of
its nutriment." [22]

So he says elsewhere: "We make our life with the
death of others;"— how near he was to Heracleitus!
"In the dead thing life deprived of sense (vita dissen-
sata) remains, which reunited to the stomachs of the living, regains sensitive and intellectual life (vita sensitiva e
intellettiva)." [23]

Finally, he asks with enormous insight:

"Why did not Nature ordain that one animal should not live
from the death of another?   Inconstant and taking pleasure in
creating and making lives and forms without ceasing, since she
recognizes that they are an unfolding (accrescimento) of her terrestrial matter, Nature is more willing and swift in her creating
than time in its destruction; and so she has ordained that many
animals should be food for one another.   Not satisfied with this,
often she sends out certain poisonous and pestilential vapors over
the vast increasing multitudes of animals, and principally over men,
who increase greatly because other animals do not feed on them,
and, the causes removed, the effects would fail.   Therefore this
earth seeks to be deprived of its life, desiring continuous increase.
Through thy chosen and demonstrated argument, effects often resemble their reasons: animals exemplify the life of the world." [24]

[22] Richter, o. c. II, § 843.
[23] Richter, II, § 845.
[24] Richter, o. c. II, § 1219; *Frammenti,* pp. 169–170.

It would seem as if Leonardo was feeling his way toward a perception of the law of the conservation of matter, of energy, of life. "*Naturalmente* everything tends to maintain itself as it is — *in suo essere.*" But whatever by any cause is set in motion, tends to continue in motion according to the strength of the cause. These statements of physical law suggest a groping for such a universal principle. And one seems to sense the same in those considerations just noticed touching Nature's ways, which may have come to him from his studies in physiology and his ready adoption of the imaginative analogy between man and the world.

Leonardo's mind was drawn toward every natural science. In botany, anatomy and physiology, both human and comparative, his studies and experimental investigations were so broad and so penetrating that he may well be given the title of biologist. Whether to this the name of philosopher should be added, one may query.

In a sense, all thoughtful people are philosophers, desiring to refer their scattered knowledge to some principle of certitude, and place it in some unity of relationship to the knowing mind. Leonardo would refer his knowledge to experience, to the testimony of his senses, aided by mathematics. " Wisdom is the daughter of experience. . . . No human inquiry is worthy of the name of science unless it comes through mathematical proofs. And if you say that the sciences which begin and end in the mind possess truth, this is not to be conceded, but denied for many reasons. First because in such mental discourses there enters no *esperienza,* without which nothing by itself reaches certitude." [25]

Leonardo, as we have seen, said the like of this more than once. He would stand by mathematics applied to the experience of the senses, and would not go beyond. Possibly such a principle, however truncated it may be, might constitute a philosophy, if carried out systematically. But this is what Leonardo did not do. He passed his life seeing, examining, experimenting, noting his observations in language or with his marvellous pen-

[25] *Frammenti,* pp. 83–84.

cil; and he uttered pregnant maxims. So he filled manuscripts with notes to be a puzzle and surprise for men. He intended to devote his last years to an ordering of his notes and the composition of the systematic treatises, for which they held the necessary data. He never would have done this had he lived a hundred years. New observations, new suggestions, thronging on this restless mind, would still have thwarted its good intentions of systematizing its already garnered contents. If systematic coordination, assimilation, and presentation of one's knowledge and opinions are essential to a philosopher, Leonardo was not one.

Marvellously Leonardo represented the intellectual aptitudes of his time. Yet how uncertain and desultory seems the effect of his investigations and his manuscripts upon the generations who might best have profited by them! His manuscripts were tossed about and perhaps plundered, but excepting the portions touching painting, they were not published and seem not to have been systematically examined till our day. Yet one cannot believe that they remained quite unknown and void of influence. It is fairly certain that they were drawn upon by that interesting genius, Girolamo Cardano, whose father Fazio was a friend of Leonardo in Milan. Besides, one cannot think that so voluble a man as Leonardo would not have talked to his friends about his physical investigations, his dissections, his anatomical studies. There is the tradition of the " Academia Leonardo da Vinci," formed by him, or about him, in Milan. If it does not represent a concrete fact, it still testifies to his influence among his associates.

CHAPTER XXXII

ANATOMY, PHYSIOLOGY, AND DISEASE

LEONARDO interested himself efficiently in all physical science; and, along the pointings of his divers activities, one may follow the more special investigations of men who shared the same scientific spirit, pursued a like method, and would not acquiesce in the *dicta* of authority. It was not these *dicta* themselves, but rather their acceptance without testing their truth, that barred the way to free research. The men who were interested in the phenomena of the natural world, including the human body, differed among themselves in their mental processes and affinities; some of them indulged in the vagaries of loose speculation, or were affected by the superstitions or baseless sciences of the time, especially astrology; while some might follow more seriously and exclusively the method of direct observation and experiment, and the conclusions of rational or mathematical deduction. It is hazardous to draw lines of division among them; for the habits of the most effective intellects of the sixteenth century inclined toward many a slant that distorted their better thinking and retarded the progress of their more veritable knowledge. Those who most intelligently drew their conclusions from their own and others' observations are best entitled to be called men of science. Such did in fact enlarge their knowledge of the visible and tangible world, including the human organism. Their efforts did much toward placing, or replacing if one will, the physical sciences upon such bases as the Greek physicists as well as Leonardo would have approved and modern scientists might sanction.

In regard to these scientists and quasi-scientists of the sixteenth century, the matter of human interest lies in their intellectual attitude and the method of their studies and investigations. To what extent do they represent a change from the attitude toward fact and method of investigation followed in physical studies say by Albertus Magnus, or say, by Roger Bacon; or again by Albertus of Saxonia or Nicholas of Cusa? These four men differed among themselves in their ways of seeking truth; for in the main Albertus Magnus was a scholastic commenting on Aristotle, while Roger Bacon professed to set forth a new method and to discard much that struck him as perverse. Albertus of Saxonia was an observant physicist, although he still cast his writings in the form of commentaries on the works of Aristotle. Nicholas of Cusa, a later man, has the book-learning of his time, and knows the old authorities; but his face is half turned from them toward the new vistas, and he deeply ponders upon conceptions of the universe which shall tally with the needs and tendencies of his own thinking. He is quite as much of the coming time as of the Middle Ages; so indeed was Albert of Saxonia, and in another manner Roger Bacon. The minds of all of them, of course, were filled with thoughts and expressions from the past, and in the main their knowledge was its knowledge, which had come to them. But in their several manners they were also thinking for themselves and looking upon things about them and the revolutions of the stars above, which are beginning to shake their assurance of the primacy of their own Earth-globe. From them the way up, or the way serpentine, to the men of the sixteenth century, has many slopes and curvings, but no sudden break, nor even corners so sharp as to keep the old vehicles of thought from turning them.

The ways of human progress in knowledge are continuous beneath the apparently broken surface of the road. Thoughts may seem new and methods novel, but within them as their efficient moving core lies the self-transmission of the past, the moving content of knowledge and forms of thought and expression, as well as the impulse to perpetuate and add to it. This will remain true, although some of our sixteenth century men will show methods making a departure from those preceding them, while others show a more confused amalgam of the old thoughts and methods with their own by no means consistent thinking.

A few years after Leonardo's death the method of direct examination of the pertinent physical facts was established in the most direct and simple form in that very science of anatomy to which he had set himself so zealously. Andreas Vesalius was the author of this achievement. Judging by results and their continuity, it was he, rather than Leonardo, who founded the modern method and science of anatomy, and prepared the way for physiology. He was born at Brussels in 1514, just as the bells were ringing out the old year. For generations his forbears had been doctors. He went to school at Louvain, and entered the university. But his constant and passionate occupation was the dissection of animals. In his eighteenth year he made his way to Paris to hear Jacobus Sylvius (Jacques Du Bois) the most famous master of anatomy at that time. Sylvius was a hard conservative, who taught Galen, and used dissections to illustrate that great authority rather than as independent means of gaining knowledge. Vesalius could not endure that Sylvius should lecture from a book while barbers clumsily cut up a human body or far more frequently a dog's. What knowledge could be gained from having the roughly extracted viscera shown to him? This masterful auditor insisted upon conducting the dissection himself. " I had to put my own hand to the business." [1] Outside of the lecture-room, Vesalius dissected dogs, and haunted the cemeteries, where there were piles of human bones. He became so familiar with them that he could recognize any part of the human skeleton by touch, and name it with his eyes blindfolded.

After some three years of medical study in Paris, Vesalius returned to Louvain, and then went to Venice and soon to Padua, where at the end of the year 1537 he was made professor in the university. He was scarcely twenty-three.

[1] The quotation is from the preface of Vesalius' *Fabrica humani corporis*. See Sir M. Foster's Lectures on the *History of Physiology* (Cambridge, Eng., 1901). My facts as to Vesalius are gleaned from M. Roth, *Andreas Vesalius Bruxellensis* (Berlin, 1892).

Quickly casting aside " the ridiculous method of the schools," he demonstrated and dissected before his students, practicing also the vivisection of animals. But he used Galen in lecturing, at least until he became convinced that Galen had made his dissections and descriptions from apes, rather than from human bodies. After that, braving all opposition, he gradually freed himself and his demonstrations from the older author; and even used the bodies under dissection to show the many errors in Galen's descriptions when applied to the parts and organs of the human body. He was now demonstrating and lecturing from the facts alone, and from books no longer. He had five hundred students, and was already known beyond the university through his reputation and his *Anatomical Tables,* which circulated widely.

In order to establish the validity of his method before the learned world he set himself to the preparation of his great book, the *Humani Corporis Fabrica.* With it he composed a simpler *Epitome* for less advanced students. He set out for Basel to publish these works; and in 1543 the *Fabrica* was printed in seven hundred folio pages, with many illustrations. The text presented careful and minute descriptions of the parts and organs of the body, and then compared Galen's defective accounts of the same. Thus while setting forth a corrected and improved anatomy, it demonstrated Galen's errors by appealing not to authority but to the facts carefully presented. It was shown that Galen had made his descriptions from the dissection of apes and not of human bodies. Vesalius pointed to the Alexandrian physicians who centuries before Galen had really studied human bodies. By such arguments and biting sarcasm he sought to break the spell of Galen's infallibility. His polemic was directed as well against opponents, named and unnamed, who still relied upon authority in the face of facts. The attack was direct, the method incontestible; if only students could be prevailed upon to use their hands and eyes and reason.

This was the difficulty, since it meant a reversal of the long habit of seeing through others' eyes, and thinking in the forms of the traditional knowledge. Appeals to fact have proved futile quite as often as they have succeeded. But the time was ripe for the new method of investigation. Against storms of opposition, the book won such success that never more could professors at good universities read aloud from Galen, while barbers ignorantly cut up animals or even human bodies, and all present remained ignorant of the discrepancies between the facts before their eyes and the texts sounding in their ears. Vesalius's book was the foundation stone of a new anatomical science based upon dissection, and again dissection: — the dissection of human bodies and the vivisection of living animals.

The last was to be of enormous importance. For Vesalius's book did not stop with strictly anatomical descriptions, but considered, none too successfully, the functions of the organs: in a word, it proceeded naturally from anatomy to physiology. Its tone and contents were in themselves an argument against the many superstitions touching the care of health and the cure of disease. Its preface set forth the long decline of medicine and the contempt into which it had fallen: all due to the ignorance of the human body which had prevailed ever since physicians ceased to make dissections with their own hands.

Vesalius was not yet thirty, and his work as the founder of modern anatomy was done. Angered by the abuse which followed the publication of his *Fabrica,* he burnt the records of his further investigations, and became court physician to the Emperor Charles V. Intelligently and fruitfully he practiced medicine and surgery; but never again gave himself to systematic dissection. He brought out a second edition of his *Fabrica,* making some corrections and adding observations from his experience. He was not fifty when he died.

But others were ready to take up the study of " that true bible," as he called it, " the human body and the nature of man." Its study was to embrace the function as well as structure of the organs. Galen taught that the blood passed from the right to the left side of the heart through the septum between. This error, with the Galenic doctrine that there were two kinds of blood moving respectively in the veins and arteries, prevented any true conception of the circulation and its function in the human organism. And since the function of circulation is fundamental, these erroneous doctrines blocked the way to any valid science of physiology.

Vesalius hinted a doubt of Galen's view in the first edition of his *Fabrica,* and expressed it more plainly in the second. One Michael Servetus had studied at Paris under the same teachers that Vesalius listened to so impatiently. He was an investigator of the human body as well as of religion. In his book the *Restitutio Christianismi,* which was burnt with its author at Geneva in 1553, occurs a passage rejecting Galen's errors and describing crudely but correctly the passage of the blood from the right side of the heart through the lungs to the left side of the heart. Possibly Vesalius saw this statement before printing the second edition of his *Fabrica* in 1555. The position of Servetus is restated, with a claim to the discovery, by Realdus Columbus, a man of slightly questionable veracity, in a work published in 1559. A younger and better man, Caesalpinus, added something to the matter. More of a personage than either, and likewise a North Italian, was Fabricius ab Aquapendente. Yet through his long and useful career of teaching, Fabricius continued overawed by Galen, and his thoughts remained in error as to the action of the heart. He held the chair of Anatomy at Padua from 1565 till his death in 1619. And it was under him that William Harvey received his Degree in 1602.

Harvey was born in 1578 at Folkestone, and having graduated from Cambridge in 1597, proceeded to Padua. Returning to England, he became a member of the Royal College of Physicians in 1604 and Physician to St. Bartholomew's Hospital in 1609. From the year 1615, in Lectures on Anatomy at the College of Physicians, he began to advance his opinions concerning the movements of the heart and blood. These he set forth and proved them for all time in his closely reasoned *Exercitatio de*

Cordis Motu, published in 1628.   This small immortal
book demonstrated, more fully and correctly than had
been done before, the pulmonary circulation, that is to
say, the circulation of the blood through the lungs.   Then
it passed on to the great new field of the systemic circulation, and demonstrated the circulation of the blood
throughout the veins and arteries of the body.[2]   The
proof failed only to embrace the capillary circulation;
for without a microscope Harvey could not see these
minute vessels.   He had been enabled to reach and
demonstrate his great discovery through constant and un-
remitting study of the hearts and arteries of living
animals.

Throughout the original and free research of his long
life, which by no means stopped with the publication of
this book in 1628, Harvey continued a transmitter and
intermediary between the ancients and the moderns, for
whom he had founded a veritable science of physiology.
If he disproved Galen, he absorbed and continued in his
physiology many a principle from Aristotle, for instance,
his various animating or sensitive *souls,* though Harvey
would place them in the blood itself rather than in the
heart.   The authority of Aristotle was strong with him
to the end — " has always such weight with me," he writes
in his old age, " that I never think of differing from him
inconsiderately." [3]

From Vesalius and Harvey two human sciences had
received not merely a foundation, but as it were a sheet-
anchor principle, fixing them in method and fundamental
truth, so that thereafter they should never altogether
swing to and fro subject to the winds of fantasy and
speculation.   Both of these great men were themselves
affected, as were the best scientists of their time and yet
another generation, with many conceptions which later
knowledge has proved baseless, and even has placed
in the category of superstitions.   Yet these side issues
of the mind, children both of the past and of the six-

[2] See Lect. II of Foster's *Lectures on the History of Physiology* for a
fuller statement.
[3] See generally J. G. Curtis, *Harvey's Views on the use of the Circulation of the Blood* (N. Y., 1915).

teenth century, did not prevent Vesalius from anchoring anatomy to his basic principle, his method, of drawing the truths of his science from the direct study and dissection of the human body; nor did they prevent Harvey from attaining through dissection of the dead and the vivisection of living animals, his fundamental verity of the nature of the pulmonary and systemic circulation of the blood. Vesalius's method, and Harvey's consequent demonstration were of such fundamental and, as it were, standardizing nature as to secure the firm existence and sure progress of these two sciences. Thus they rendered to anatomy and physiology such a service as Descartes's *cogito ergo sum* rendered philosophy, in giving it a rational standard of certainty, for want of which the more speculative minds of the sixteenth century were swimming in oceans of uncharted speculation. But anatomy and physiology, adhering to these fundamental verities of fact and method received from Vesalius and Harvey, were destined gradually to free themselves from their alloy of baseless hypothesis or superstition, and repel the invasion of folly from without.

In their turn the sciences of Anatomy and Physiology were the only sure foundation for the healing arts of surgery and medicine. Yet the latter had been practised as far back as we have definite knowledge of mankind. Their vague and enveloping history makes no such concrete tale as that of the advance of anatomy and physiology, which may be credited to the liberation of these two sciences from the shackles of the books and to the untrammelled study of the bodies of animals and men. For them this freeing of the spirit came in the centuries with which we are occupied. The progress of surgery and medicine was neither so simple nor so obvious. A vast and veritable experience lay behind the surgery say of the year 1510 when Paré was born. A vast but less reliable experience, permeated with the vagaries of ignorance and superstition, lay behind the medicine of the somewhat earlier year of the birth of Paracelsus.

It may be that surgery is but a mode of treatment, and that surgery and medicine are or should be one. But the history of the two is not identical for the period before us, though the two were united by the best practitioners. Before the scientific foundation of anatomy by Vesalius, surgery had been learning more than medicine both from experience and from crude anatomical dissections. Its practice at Salerno in the early Middle Ages kept partially alive the better traditions of the ancients. But the University of Paris frowned upon men who worked mainly with their hands;[4] and the general tendency was to turn surgery over to a class of men who had no learning, but were gradually to gain much from experience. Surgery was less likely than medicine to become scholastic.[5]

Some surgery was taught at Paris in the thirteenth century when Lanfranchi, an able practitioner in both surgery and medicine, came to Paris from Milan. His better knowledge of the art, as set forth in his *Chirurgia Magna,* did much to help French surgery. After him came others, and then Guy de Chauliac, who used the work of his predecessors as well as the Anatomy of Mundinus, and produced in his *Chirurgie* the best textbook of the centuries before Paré.[6]

The most famous surgeon of the sixteenth century was an unlettered man.[7] Ambroise Paré knew neither Greek nor Latin, and was to write his treatises in French. Born in 1510, he was apprenticed to a barber-surgeon. By 1533 he had reached Paris, where he attended the lectures of Sylvius and, better still, obtained a post as house surgeon at the Hôtel Dieu. From that time till his death in 1590 he practised surgery, and very largely with the armies in the incessant wars. His own beautiful

---

[4] Chirurgie (Surgery) is from the Greek χειρουργία, meaning handicraft and then surgery.

[5] See Allbut, *Historical relations of Medicine and Surgery,* p. 22 and *passim* (London, 1904).

[6] The *Cyrurgia magistri Guidonis de Cauliaco* was produced in Latin in 1363, and soon put into French. It constantly cites Galen and Avicenna.

[7] Like his excellent contemporary Franco, a Provençal surgeon born in 1503, and apprenticed to an operating barber, just as Paré was. Some improvements in surgery seem due to Franco. A half century older was Benivieni of Florence (1448–1502), an excellent and progressive practitioner, who made autopsies. There were other Italian physicians who made dissections a little later.

story of his life and practice reflects his healthy bravery and cheerful ardor and the unfailing intelligence and judgment, and the skill of this great surgeon. As for experience, one doubts whether any other mortal ever treated as many wounded men. " I treated him and God cured him," was his favorite remark touching his famous cures. He realized profoundly the surgical value of the alleviation of suffering and the importance of inflicting the least possible amount of pain. He is best known for his rejection of boiling oil and cauteries in the treatment of wounds and amputations, and his use of the ligature upon the arteries under amputation. The ligature had long been used to stop the bleeding of wounds; but his novel use of it to control the hemorrhage in amputations made such major operations practicable. Besides the quite wonderful story of his journeyings and professional experience, he wrote an Anatomy, and a number of surgical treatises, among which perhaps the most famous was *La methode de traicter les playes faictes par hacquebutes et aultres bastons a feu* [fire-arms].[8] Paré believed many of the current superstitions relating to diseases and their cures; but this did not affect his surgery or his treatment of disease. He had been taught the methods of his time, and studied the *Fabrica* of Vesalius. But the school in which he never ceased to learn was the school of observation and experience.

Mediaeval medicine was more illuminated and, one may say infected, with learning than mediaeval surgery. There was less definite progress through observation and experience, and more constant resort to authoritative compilations, which were many and heterogeneous. The school of Salerno is a link between ancient and mediaeval medicine. It preserved much substance from Hippocrates and later Greeks and from Galen; it also kept up some systematic observation of disease and gave clinical instruction in its hospitals. But Arabian medicine, which was second-hand Greek, overspread Europe in the

---

[8] Vigo had written on arquebus wounds before Paré in 1514. Wounds from arquebus balls presented new surgical difficulties, and so pushed surgery forward.

twelfth and thirteenth centuries in Latin translations; and competed with the more direct Galenic tradition at the rising universities. The thirteenth and fourteenth centuries were prolific in compendia which combined debased material from muddied channels with notes of the actual observation of disease.

The fifteenth century, and the sixteenth finally, recovered the classical medical writings, and substituted these nobler sources for the distorting and obscuring commentaries of Arabians, Jews and mediaeval Latin compilers. The works of Hippocrates and Galen were translated directly into Latin and next were published in the Greek originals at the Aldine press about the year 1525. Before then the discovery in 1443 of the *De Medicina* of Celsus, an observant Roman of the first century, and the printing of the same in 1478, had given a knowledge of the practice of medicine in the Augustan time. Thus came about an advance in medicine, or a preparation for its advance, due to men who were scholars and humanists rather than practising physicians. If the practical result of the movement did not meet the hopes of the enthusiasts, some clarifying of the medical intelligence ensued, and doubtless some stimulus to direct observation must have come from the reading of Hippocrates, its greatest inculcator. At all events the clinical lectures of Montanus (1498-1552), given in the hospital at Padua, betokened a more effective medical training for practitioners.

There had been sensible practitioners in the preceding generation; yet at Florence the very heart of classical enlightenment, in the year 1494 when Lorenzo de' Medici lay on his deathbed, the last medicine given him was a draught of pulverized jewels. This treatment was sanctioned neither by Hippocrates nor Galen, but doubtless was drawn from current notions of the virtues of precious stones. Medicine is still a difficult art or science; and the principles of disease and healing were not so firmly established when Paracelsus was a child, and Fracastoro, that magic and astrology might not enter. A man younger than either of them, Girolamo Cardanus (1501-

1576), of whom there will be more to say, was an intelligent and successful physician, famed in Scotland, England, France and Italy; yet astrology had no more ardent devotee.

Paracelsus and Fracastoro are important persons in the history of the theory of disease. The former was a startling figure, and the latter the cultured author of an adventitiously famous poem. Any thoughtful physician cannot but tax his mind with questionings relating to the causes of the ills which it is his office to cure. Homer, and many a Greek after him, believed that the gods smote men and cattle with disease. Hippocrates looked to natural causes. He and his school, and the medical men of Alexandria, and Galen after them, all had their theories, which necessarily outran observation; for the causes of sickness are not easily to be searched out. The medical theories — unlike the excellent practices — of the old Greeks have been discarded; those of the periods following them are scientifically negligible. So all medical theories may become unless based on further knowledge than Paracelsus had. Had there ever been a more independent and incessant thinker? and practitioner too. He could not help thinking out for himself his theories of disease. They were broad and universal, having drawn wisdom as well as folly from many sources, and some knowledge from direct observation. They lacked the touchstone element,— some principle of rationality and truth capable of exposing the baselessness of whatever countered its cogency.

This strange and potent genius, whose name was Theophrastus Bombast von Hohenheim, is known to fame as Paracelsus. "Aureole" was another name bestowed by his admirers and caressed in Browning's drama. He was born at Einsiedeln, near the lake of Zurich, in 1493; and his father was a physician, who seems to have taught his son the rudiments of botany and alchemy and herbal medicine. He went to school at Villach, near the lead mines of Bleiberg. In after life he was intensely interested in metals and their mining and reduction. The youth entered the university at Basel, but soon left it to study with the Abbot Trithemius at Wurzburg, a man noted for his humanistic learning, and still more for his knowledge of alchemy, or chemistry, and other occult branches.

Alchemy or chemistry, medicine or magic? we may ask the question, which was it to be? Not so Paracelsus: "Alchemy is to make neither gold nor silver: its use is to make the supreme essences and to direct them against disease." [9] To Paracelsus all science, all existence, was impressed with mystery. The student of his career and writings may be puzzled to distinguish between his chemical or botanical investigations and his metaphysical or mystic or magical inductions or vagaries. Paracelsus recognized no such distinctions; all parts of his thinking and experimentation were equally valid to one for whom all visible and tangible things were but as envelopes of hidden virtues. He cherished the Cabala, like Pico della Mirandola. For both of them, magic was the wisdom which employs spiritual powers and hidden virtues to produce effects.

Yet this same Paracelsus balked as fiercely against devil lore and necromancy, and against astrology as well, as he did against the authority of Avicenna, whose works he burned in the market-place, as Luther had burned the papal bull. He despised baseless fabrications of the reason or unreason which countered the principles of life as he was seeking them, or which were hostile to his Christian faith in God. In the hidden virtues, the occult properties of things, this man, through his alchemy or chemistry, his botany, his physics, was following the principle of Life and its curative powers. That was his working philosophy of nature; and to its ends he employs both experience and speculation; he will even look to authorities, or to the rational principles set forth in them, and make his motto: *experimenta ac ratio auctorum*. For each disease he will seek in nature the counteracting or curative specific; for he relied upon the efficient correspon-

---

[9] Quoted from Anna M. Stoddart's *Life of Paracelsus* (London, 1911), p. 43 — to which rather enthusiastic book the present writer is much indebted for his Paracelsus lore. The unsigned article in the *Encyclopaedia Britannica* gives a good résumé of his life and works.

dence of the universal macrocosm with the human microcosm. Thus he even reaches the principle that like cures like; " similia similibus curantur "; a motto which, as one interprets it, will hold wisdom or folly.

All the while the mind of this remarkably efficient physician was set on fact, on the facts and causes of the diseases he was treating and their remedies. Observation and experiment! " The sick should be the doctor's books." He made some excellent innovations in the treatment of the sick by medicines and by surgery; his repute was vast and merited. He was hated too; for he was a medical revolutionist, one who not only despised all traditional quackery, but departed from usage by lecturing in German and not in Latin. The accepted calumnies of his brethren who hated him, have distorted the report of Paracelsus. In our own time quite personally devoted scholars have set themselves to re-write his life and establish his greatness. It is not necessary here either to follow his challenging career or attempt to set forth in detail his interesting opinions. His instruction to hosts of students was stimulating and enlightening. At Basel he lectured, for example, on the degrees and components of receipts, on diagnosis by the pulse, on diseases of the skin, on those from acidity, on the preparation of medicines, on wounds and ulcers. His energy and enthusiasm were irrepressible and often resistless. His insight into the processes of nature, and growth of trees, for example,[10] or the healing of wounds,[11] is astonishing. Ambroise Paré learned from his writings. A conviction of the healing power of nature, and of medicine founded upon nature, was with him as a religion. This conviction extended or sank to notions over which one might prefer to draw a veil; he could be over-hospitable toward that which exceeded proof! He believed in the *electrum magicum* of amulets, and held precious stones to be good remedies. Yet they had been tried and found wanting in the case of Lorenzo, whose death they did

[10] See the interesting extract given by Miss Stoddart at p. 205 sqq. of her *Paracelsus*.
[11] See ib. extract given on p. 213.

not impede when Paracelsus was a baby! Some of the good in him passed on to influence medicine and surgery; his foolishness was embalmed in the sect of Rosicrucians.

A very different man was Fracastoro of Verona, who was born before Paracelsus and outlived him some twelve years (1478-1553). He was a gentleman of ancient lineage, a poet, a man of wide learning, interested in all branches of knowledge or speculation. His medical education was obtained at Padua, where he may have been affected by Pomponazzi's lectures, which attempted to explain the world on a basis of natural law. Copernicus was a student there at the same time; and Fracastoro devoted some of his energies to globes and maps and astronomical problems. He became an eminent physician, and is said to have treated patients without pay. He wrote a Latin poem discussing an unpleasant disease which all peoples called after some other people's name. An urbane humanist, as well as penetrating diagnostician, Fracastoro accounted more politely for its origin by a pretty myth of ancient outrage done the altars of the gods: and the name of his unhappy hero was accepted as the name of the disease.

In 1546 he published his *De contagione et contagiosis morbis*. It led the way in the recognition and description of typhus fever, which then was ravaging Italy; it declared that phthisis, that is consumption or tuberculosis, is contagious; and it set forth the general principles of infection, or the transmission of disease from one sufferer to another. From the times of Hippocrates and of Galen, fevers had been ascribed to a corruption of the humors of the body, and no clear idea of their propagation had been given. Infection, vaguely recognized as a cause of disease, never vanished utterly from the medical view. Fracastoro, scholar and humanist, may have found his *seeds* of disease in Lucretius.[12] Yet he was the first to set forth a theory of infection definitely: " Contagion is an infection passing from one individual to another." The *seminaria contagionum* from the sick invade the bodies of the healthy. " There is a power in these seeds

[12] *De rerum natura*, VI, 1090 — passage cited by Singer.

that they may multiply and propagate their like." So they may be transmitted on and on. In some diseases the transmission takes place only through contact; in other diseases the *fomites,* or sparks of infection, may be transmitted by intermediate agents, garments for example; in still others the *fomites* may be carried from a distance by the air.

Paracelsus and Cardanus too had some idea of the seeds of disease. But Fracastoro stated clearly, with rational arguments, the explanation of the transmission of disease which has been demonstrated in our own generation. His works were widely read, and a hundred years after him Italian physicians, taking up his theory, demonstrated more adequately the nature of infection.[13]

As already remarked, the progress of one or another of the physical sciences in the sixteenth century seems to have hung upon the employment of some valid method of experimental observation which might lead to the grasp of a central fact or principle. This in turn served as a basis for further discoveries. Vesalius had used such a method; two generations after him Harvey grasped such a basic fact in his demonstration of the circulation of the blood. Without the foundation of Vesalius's anatomy, his contemporary Fracastoro presented a theory of infection which might have afforded a basic fact for medicine had the natural knowledge of the time and the means of biological investigation been adequate to demonstrate its validity. Vesalius had demonstrated the value of his method; Harvey also succeeded in demonstrating his great fact. But the nature and action of the *seminaria contagionum* were not demonstrated for three centuries. Until then Fracastoro's theory could not become the basis of new measures for the prevention and cure of disease.

Paracelsus, with his keen intuitions and experiments and his Will-o-the-wisp speculations, was a natural product of sixteenth century medicine, so conspicuously wanting

---

[13] The best account of Fracastoro is that of Charles and D. Singer: "The scientific position of Girolamo Fracastoro:" *Annals of Medical History,* Vol. I, pp. 1–34 (1917). See also A. C. Klebs in Johns Hopkins Bulletin, Vol. XXVI, No. 297 (1915), and a paper by Sir William Osler in the *Proceedings of the Charaka Club of New York.*

in valid conceptions of disease. Not in medicine alone
was there crying need to winnow the chaff from the common acceptances even of the learned and intelligent.
This might not come to pass until habits of testing facts
had become more prevalent, and general conceptions of
material probabilities and the regular action of natural
agencies had had time to enter men's blood. Girolamo
Cardan of Pavia and Milan (1501-1576) is another telling illustration of the opinions, sound and baseless, obtaining among the intelligent.

Of his difficult childhood and early struggles against
the hindrances of illegitimate birth and the merited antipathy of professional brethren, of his slowly won repute
as a physician, of his professional visits extending to the
ultima thule of Scotland, of his great fame as an author
and astrologer, and the calamities of his later years, he
has left the detailed and picturesque story in his *De vita
propria.*[14] His father, Fazio Cardan, a jurist and
mathematician, lived at Milan and was a familiar of
Leonardo da Vinci, and the son, Girolamo, Hieronimo,
or Jerome, from his youth was devoted to mathematics,
physical studies and gambling. Having studied at
Pavia, he graduated at Padua in medicine. He relied
on portents and dreams and his interpretation of their
forecastings, which assured him among other things, that
he was destined to strive for immortality. There was
no more careful and scientific astrologer in his time. He
won his first repute as a physician by cures effected in
Milan; where with boldness and acerbity he attacked the
current errors of practice in his first published work,
De malo recentiorum medicorum medendi usu. (Venice
1536). He had always written voluminously, even before he could get a printer.

Devoured with ardor and ambition, he published a
notable work on Arithmetic and another on Algebra,
which, with all allowance made for the writer's use of
others' formulae, was a substantial contribution to the

14 Henry Morley has followed this work and given its substance delight-
fully, along with further data, in his *Jerome Cardan* (2 Vols., London,
1854).

progress of that science. He worked and wrote prodigiously; no current topic of intellectual curiosity escaped
him — dreams, palmistry, ghosts, portents in earth and
heaven, and of course astrology. All these matters were
accepted by intelligent men, and verified by their observations, and by none more carefully and scientifically than
by Cardan. He also wrote tremendous commentaries on
Hippocrates and volumes of admirable moral aphorisms.
He was a man of versatility and manifold intellectual
aptitude. The two books which gave him widest and
most lasting fame were his *De Subtilitate Rerum,* worked
upon for years and published in 1551, and his supple-
mental *De Varietate Rerum,* published six years later.
They were encyclopaedic treatises upon the contents of
the universe, including the spiritual beings in it malignant
and benign — Demons, Angels and Intelligences. The
sciences were included, the arts, and the curiosities of
well-vouched for fact!

The *De Subtilitate* was written from a certain point
of view, and with an underlying (rather deeply buried!)
thought: it should set forth the principle of the
subtle nature and effects of things as apprehended, not
without difficulty, by the senses and the intellect. "Sub-
tilitas," says Cardan, is a " certain ratio, by which sensible
things are comprehended by the senses and intelligible
things by the mind *difficile,* with difficulty." [15] *With
difficulty;* so is it still and so will it be. With all imagin-
able increase of knowledge, the natures, origins, and
effects of things are not likely to become obvious.

Before leaving this natural philosopher we return to
the apparently innocent fact, that Cardan's father Fazio
was one of Leonardo's familiars in Milan. The son was
not a man gratuitously to acknowledge indebtedness to
any modern; in his book on Algebra he had used an
algebraic formula of one Tartaglia, though he had sworn
not to publish or divulge it; and of course, with no reference to its parentage. Likewise the *De Subtilitate* seems
mutely indebted to the writings of Leonardo upon paint-

[15] Quoted by Morley, o. c. II, p. 60.

ing and physics.[16]   Cardan probably had access to these writings, and would have been the last man to mention it; although he refers to the celebrated painter more than once.   He had passed his boyhood and youth literally in the service of his father Fazio, who died in 1524 when the son was twenty-three years old.   If Leonardo had, as he says himself, borrowed books from Fazio, why should not Fazio have borrowed something in return; and his son have used the material?

[16] This seems proved by Duhem, *Études sur Léonardo da Vinci*, I, pp. 223–245.

CHAPTER XXXIII

THE REVOLUTION IN ASTRONOMY AND PHYSICS

WE gathered in the last chapter that a number of opinions and beliefs which the enlightenment of our own time regards as superstitions made part of the scientific or quasi-scientific data of the sixteenth century, and might deflect or impede the progress of more valid knowledge or more consistent theorizing. Melanchthon in Germany was a clear thinker and a prodigy as a scholar, though of course not an investigator in physical science. He selected from what he found in books. But doubtless his firm belief in the influence of the stars on human fates would affect his presentation of the subject matter of his book on *Physics*. It is hard for us to discover a scientific mind or method in a man like Cardanus who was infatuated with dreams and portents, and an accomplished astrologer. Paracelsus rejected astrology, and yet involved his thinking in occultism, and accepted many things to us absurd. An independent but somewhat mystical genius like Paracelsus, and such a wonder of a Cabalistic Platonist as Pico della Mirandola, made use of conceptions which have since lost their validity; but they bent them to quasi-rational meanings.[1]

As is well known, the fifteenth and sixteenth centuries brought a marked revival of those beliefs and reasonings concerning the influence of the stars upon human affairs, with the casting of horoscopes, all making up the age-long pseudo-science of astrology. These beliefs permeated the opinions and judgments of mankind, and engaged the constant study of scholars, scientists and statesmen. Astrology was held the noblest of sciences, and its enlightenment and guidance sought in the most important affairs

---

[1] See ante p. 319 and p. 277 sqq. as to their handling of the conception of magic taken from the Cabbala.

of life. As an explanation of the world and human fortunes, it rivalled or peacefully paralleled religion and belief in the devil. Progress in physics and astronomy and firmer conceptions of physical law were gradually to dissolve this authoritative congeries of unsound conviction. In the meanwhile it made part of the mentality of a number of the great men of whom we have now to speak.[2]

The mass of knowledge and belief belonging to a period may not be consistent through and through. Yet it presents a view of the universe and man, and constitutes a whole, a sort of limping system, in which all the parts are somehow interlinked, and subsist through mutual toleration. He who attacks a single credence knows not how much of the entire conglomerate may be precipitated upon him. The minds of men who hold this sum of knowledge and opinion, or co-ordinated portions of it, are apt to have a common point of view. The mental processes of each mind make a way of thinking, indeed an intellectual organism wherein the disturbance of one element disturbs the whole and provokes its catholic hostility. This reaction, whether conscious or subconscious, makes for the rejection of every novel enlightenment.

For an example: Martin Luther could not have abandoned his conceived experience of personal combats with the devil without a re-adjustment of his mental and spiritual nature. Devils and sprites made part of the phenomena of the material world. George Agricola in 1556 published his *De re metallica,* an excellent and complete treatise upon everything connected with the mining and metallurgy of the time in Germany.[3] It treats of the origin of veins and ore deposits, and discredits the use of divining rods to discover veins of metal. But it recognizes devils, along with bad air and venomous ants, as among the pests encountered in mines. The demons are not all bad; there are peaceful Kobolds among them.

Such ideas are rarely dispelled by direct argument; their

[2] Cf. Troels-Lund, *Himmelsbild und Weltanschauung,* etc., 4th ed., pp. 194 sqq. (Leipsic, 1913).
[3] Agricola, *De re metallica,* translated with notes by Herbert C. Hoover, and L. H. Hoover (London, 1912).

roots are so entangled with all the rest of the man's convictions and mental habits. It is rather through a general change or advance in the sum total of the intellectualities of an individual or of an epoch that these beliefs are sloughed off as dead or inconsistent elements, which will no longer operate in harmony with the rest of the mental organism.

A remarkable illustration is afforded by the witch mania, which revived in the latter part of the fifteenth century and raged with unprecedented savageness for two hundred years in Germany and France and England. To-day an intelligent man can no more believe in witches than he could believe himself walking on his head, so complete a reversal would it entail of everything in his mind. But, in the centuries of the witch mania, to argue against the existence of witches and the ills they wrought would put the devil's advocate out of sympathy with his time, and might lead to his own condemnation as a witch. Thus the convictions, terrors, and passions of the community worked fearfully together. A certain Dr. John Weyer of Brabant in 1563 was brave enough to publish a book against the prevailing delusions. His arguments had little effect, although in some respects they also were very much of the time, and sought to give a benignant turn to much that the twentieth century would dub sheer delusion.[4]

Abler men than Weyer believed in witches. Ambroise Paré numbered sorcery among the causes of wounds, and agreed with Jean Bodin that the fact that God and men had made so many laws against sorcery proved its existence.[5] Indeed, if a man's mentality permitted him to believe in sorcery at all, its existence was abundantly established by those means which civilization had devised for the trial and proof of fact, to wit, the courts of law. Had there not been thousands of trials of witches or sorcerers followed by conviction? Such is one of the

[4] See for the whole matter and a sufficient account of the incredible prevalence and cruelty of the persecution of witches, E. T. Withington, "Dr. John Weyer and the Witch Mania," in Singer's *Studies in the History, etc., of Science* (Oxford, 1917).

[5] See R. Chauviré, *Jean Bodin* (Paris, 1914), pp. 125, 134.

arguments in the *Demonomanie des Sorciers* which Bodin, author of the famous *Republic,* wrote in reply to Weyer and his dangerous scepticism. The weight of testimony as well as the authority of Scripture was with Bodin. It is only a Montaigne whose very different mentality can prick the bubble of such testimony, at least to his own satisfaction.[6]

Not entirely unrelated to this acceptance of witchcraft and astrology by intelligent men is the more dignified fact that the most powerful intellects cannot always bring themselves to accept the best scientific conclusions of their own time. Francis Bacon would not accept the proof of the revolution of the earth around the sun. To be sure the proof may still have limped when Bacon rejected it. Yet the chief difficulty was that the mass of knowledge or belief, and conclusion, forming the intellectual nature and equipment of his mind acted as an inhibition against the acceptance of any fact that did not dovetail into his general understanding of the world. Another instance of Bacon's lack of adaptation (perhaps of his jealousy) was his belittling William Gilbert's remarkable *De Magnete,* which proved the earth itself to be a magnet and offered further arguments for the Copernican system.

Such a profound piece of harnessed argument and observation as this book of Gilbert's, published in 1600,[7] was indeed part of the advance not only of science, but of the human psychological adaptation, toward the acceptance of the new astronomy. This remarkable physician, a native of Colchester, England, carried in his mind many an old conception, holding for instance in the Aristotelian sense that the loadstone or magnetic quality of the earth was its proper form or completed nature (Book II, ch. IV). He was a great observer, using experiment and inductive reasoning, yet none the less inclined in large and somewhat intangible matters to fortify himself with authority. So he held that the earth had a soul (Bk. V,

[6] *Essays,* III, 11, on Cripples.
[7] Translated by P. F. Mottelay *On the Loadstone and magnetic bodies and on the great magnet of the earth* (New York, 1893).

ch. XII). In the absence of a more strictly physical theory of gravitation, the idea was not as foolish as it may seem.

The extension of navigation and the discovery of the New World were likewise preparing men's minds for the eventual acceptance of the new conceptions of the earth, which undoubtedly were made more vivid by the globes and maps of the Fleming, Gerhard Mercator (1512-1594). He had early shown gifts for mathematics and skill in making astronomical instruments. At Louvain he had learnt much from the Friesian Gemma, who taught medicine at the university and also mathematics (the two often went together in the sixteenth century) and had made a globe and a map of the world. Mercator finished a globe in 1541, finely executed with many corrections and improvements. In 1569 he produced his map of the world, his immortal "Mercator's Projection." In his earlier life he had thought to immortalize himself in a remarkable edition of the geographical works of Ptolemy; but his later years liberated him from deference to the old geographer and astronomer, and show his progressive reliance upon observation and the reports of navigators.

No novel piece of physical knowledge could fail to exert some effect upon the general mental attitude of those who could bring themselves to accept it. One may instance Palissy (1510?-1589), Huguenot and famous maker of glazes for pottery, and of "rustiques figulines." He was unlearned in Greek and Latin, but an apt worker with his hands and a constant penetrating observer of the processes of nature, and one may say an artist-lover of the same. He was an untaught geologist, who reasoned, often wrongly, on the facts as he understood them. The chief nugget of his contribution to knowledge of the earth was his statement as to fossil shells, to the effect that the species once lived where their fossil remains were found, to wit, in the rocks which formed dry mountain sides in Palissy's time or our own. "You must not think that these shells were made, as some say, by nature amusing herself with making some new thing. When I looked closely at the forms of the stones, I found that none of them could take the form of a shell or other animal, unless the original itself had built its form (si l'original mesme n'a basti sa forme)." Although Palissy did not proceed to the full conclusion that the ocean had at one time covered that very spot of earth, he dropped suggestions in that direction, and did much to establish the great rôle of the action of water in fashioning the face of nature and providing for the life of living things. The idea that fossil shells once housed marine creatures living in the mud and water where there was now dry land might carry to some minds the suggestion that opinions touching the earth might be revised.

Palissy was a worker and observer rather than a reader of many books. Yet when he enunciates such admirable maxims as " l'experience qui de tout temps est maitresse des arts," and " les sciences se manifestent a ceux qui les cherchent," [8] such is the coincidence of thought and phrase that one suspects him to have drawn something, through some channel from the writings of Leonardo da Vinci. The main channel for this borrowing, especially of ideas concerning the origin of fossils, was Cardan's book *De Subtilitate*, which had been translated into French; and Palissy refers to it by name when he chooses to refute its views, which appear not infrequently to have been indebted to the works of Leonardo.[9] In what other way snatches of Leonardo's thoughts may have been wafted to Palissy does not appear.

There had been some intellectual preparation for the stupendous change in the conception of the earth's place in the universe, which Copernicus ushered in well-masked in intricate mathematical demonstrations. Nicholas of Cusa had declared that the earth moved like the planets, and was not the centre of the universe. Albert of Saxonia before him had made disturbing suggestions. Likewise Leonardo asserted that the earth is not fixed at the centre of the celestial world, nor at the centre of the circle of the sun, which is the central body, and the source of light and warmth. The earth is a brilliant star.

[8] See E. Dupuy, *Bernard Palissy*, pp. 224–231 (2nd ed., Paris, 1902).
[9] Duhem, *Études sur Léonardo da Vinci*, I, pp. 245–253.

But these ideas were not as yet fortified with any proof.

One cannot consider the careers of those men whose labors manifestly established the new conception of the physical universe without feeling the force of their personalities and the power of their genius. Copernicus, Tycho Brahe, Galileo, Keppler, Huygens, Newton, are a galaxy which may well be termed sidereal. The new system made its way to acceptance slowly, against ridicule and more serious opposition. Yet the better intelligence of the sixteenth and seventeenth centuries was ready for its reception. Had these men not lived, the same change would have come, only more slowly and painfully for lack of the illumination of their genius. One is impressed by the coincidence of discoveries. The notable discoveries achieved by these great men are almost anticipated, adumbrated at least, or quickly followed, by their semblances in the work of less famous contemporaries. The progressive substantiation of the Copernican system resembles in some respects the manner in which the demonstration of the pulmonary and systemic circulation of the blood was finally accomplished.

Copernicus was twenty-one years younger than Leonardo. He was born at Thorn on the borders of Prussia and Poland in 1473. Destined for the Church, he showed a taste rather for astronomy and mathematics after he reached the University of Cracow, where he studied from his eighteenth to his twentieth year. He spent ten fruitful years in Italy, at Bologna, Padua, Ferrara, Rome, studying law and medicine, and also mathematics, astronomy and Greek. His uncle was a bishop, and Copernicus on his return home was installed as a Canon at Frauenburg, where he was to spend the greater part of his life. He took a not unimportant part in the affairs of the diocese, which, however, never seriously interrupted his devotion to astronomical calculations.[10]

Unsatisfied with the old explanation of the movements of the heavenly bodies, Copernicus turned to the con-

[10] All possible information touching Copernicus is contained in Prowe's *Nicolaus Coppernicus* (3 Vols., Berlin, 1883-4). Prowe's third volume is made up of portions of the Copernican writings. I would also express my indebtedness to A. Berry's *Short History of Astronomy* (N. Y., 1910).

trary supposition of the rotation of the Earth. This also had been suggested in antiquity and more than once in the century which gave him birth.[11] As this hypothesis seemed to him to afford a simpler and likelier explanation, he devoted himself to its mathematical demonstration. His calculations were based to some extent upon his own astronomical observations; but much more largely upon those furnished him by the ancients, although he realized their frequent inaccuracy. One must not think of him as a constant and marvellous astronomical observer; he had little skill in preparing instruments and did not even use the best the time afforded, which were made in Nuremberg. He was absorbed in the development and substantiation of his hypothesis. To this end he used his own and others' observations of the stars; and devoted himself to the mathematical calculations which served to reduce the data of the heavenly movements to general principles confirmatory of his hypothesis.[12] He retained some of the ancient mathematical devices and among them the epicycles and eccentrics of the Greek astronomers. For though he did all that one man could do, he had not succeeded in devising any better means of working out his system. To discard the old unreal encumbrances, and replace them with mathematical conceptions in accord with the observed movements of the planets was to be Keppler's task.

The circumstances of Copernicus's life were favorable to prolonged disinterested study. His temperament, perhaps his worldly prudence, and doubtless his absorption in his calculations withheld him from publishing his work. But his views were well-known by people interested in astronomy. About the year 1530, when the substance of his *De Revolutionibus* probably was complete, he composed a " little commentary," *Commentariolus,* for distribution in manuscript among his friends.[13] In

[11] Apparently Copernicus was unacquainted with the views of Nicholas of Cusa; for as Cusa was a distinguished cardinal, Copernicus would have cited his authority in the dedication of his own *De Revolutionibus* to the Pope.

[12] See Prowe, o. c. II, pp. 44–64.

[13] See Prowe, o. c. II, pp. 282 sqq. Prowe prints the Latin text in his third volume, pp. 184–202.

this, after a brief review of previous systems, he states his own heliocentric theory, beginning with its first principles thus:

" 1. There is no one centre for all the celestial orbits or spheres.[14]

2. The centre of the Earth is not the centre of the World.

3. All the planetary orbits (omnes orbes) circle around the sun at the centre of them all.

4. The distance between the sun and the earth compared with the altitude of the firmament is less than half a diameter of the earth compared with its distance from the sun.

5. The apparent movement in the firmament is due to the movement of the earth; accordingly the earth turns once a day on its unchanging poles, while the firmament and ultimate heaven remain unmoved.

6. Whatever movement we find in the sun is due to the earth and our orbit (nostri orbis) in which we are rolled around the sun; and thus the earth has several motions (pluribus motibus ferri).

7. The apparent irregularities in the movements of the planets are to be ascribed to the motion of the earth. The motion of the earth alone is sufficient to explain the apparent diversities of movement in the heaven."

After these general propositions the little tract proceeds to a more detailed statement of the movements of the earth, and other planets, and the moon.   It seems to have been made the basis of an exposition of the Copernican system before Pope Clement VII and his court in the garden of the Vatican.   The speaker was the papal secretary.   Three years later Cardinal Von Schönberg wrote a complimentary letter to Copernicus requesting

---

[14] The Latin of Copernicus is awkward and difficult. The text reads: Omnium orbium caelestium sive sphaerarum unum centrum non esse. With entire deference to Prowe's immense Copernican learning, I cannot see why he (Vol. II, 290) translates this: " Für alle Himmels-Körper und deren Bahnen giebt es nur einen mittelpunkt." Possibly Prowe, in his translations in Vol. II, pp. 288 sqq., did not use the final recension of the *Commentariolus* which he prints in Vol. III a year later. My own translation is faithful, but does not attempt to give every phrase in the Latin text.

further enlightenment touching his new astronomical system, which pleased the astronomer.[15]

Others felt their orthodoxy shocked.   Lutheran theologians discountenanced all revolutions save their own, Luther himself speaking of Copernicus with his usual emphasis: " The fool will overturn the whole art of astronomy.   But, as Holy Writ declares, Joshua commanded the sun to stand still and not the earth." [16] Melanchthon also disapproved.   But the matter would out.   Copernicus's enthusiastic follower Rheticus had thrown up his professorship in Wittenberg itself, in order to learn directly from the master, under whose direction in 1539 he composed his *Narratio prima,* his " first account," [17] of the great work which Copernicus had so far refrained from publishing.   But as the years of Copernicus were drawing to an end, the entreaties of his friends prevailed.   He composed the following preface addressed to Pope Paul III.[18]

Well he knows, begins the writer, that many people hearing of the publication of his work on *The Revolutions of the Celestial Bodies,* will cry out that such teaching is perverse.   He has long doubted whether it were not better to withhold his opinions from publication, and communicate them only by word of mouth to his friends, even as the Pythagoreans transmitted the mysteries of philosophy.   But his friends, and Cardinal Schönberg among them, had persuaded him no longer to hide that which he had kept back not merely nine years (as Horace suggests) but four times nine, saying that the book would be useful to mathematicians, and that as his doctrine had seemed absurd, so much the brighter would it shine when its darkness had been removed by demonstrations.

[15] Prowe, II, 273 sqq.

[16] Luther's Table Talk, cited by Prowe, II, 232: " The whole art," " die ganze kunst," of astronomy.   One recalls that astronomy was one of the seven liberal arts.

[17] This was at once printed, Prowe, II, p. 395.   Prowe gives the text in his third volume, pp. 295–366.   It is much longer than the *Commentariolus.*

[18] Prowe gives a full translation in II, 495 sqq., and the Latin text in III, 2 sqq.

" His Holiness will not wonder that I should give to light my slowly elaborated cogitations.   Rather will he expect to hear from me how I came to imagine the movement of the Earth against the received opinion of mathematicians and the common sense of mankind.   But indeed nothing moved me more to investigate the motions of the spheres than the variance of opinion among the mathematicians themselves.   I wearied of this incertitude among them concerning the scheme of movement of this world-machine established for us by the great Constructor, and I searched among the books of the philosophers until I found that some of them conceived the earth to move.   So I also took occasion to ponder on the earth's mobility; and though the idea seemed absurd, yet since others had felt at liberty to imagine what circles they chose to explain the phenomena of the heavens, I felt myself also permitted to try whether some firmer demonstrations might not be reached by assuming the movement of the earth.

" Now, on the assumption of the movements which I ascribe to the earth in the following work, I found after long observation that if the movements of the remaining planets be given to the earth, reckoning according to the revolution of each body, the courses of the stars and the phenomena of the heavens could be cleared of all confusion."

He speaks of the plan of the work, and expects that mathematicians who examine it carefully will agree with its conclusions.   No matter if some empty heads declare it not to accord wth Scripture.   Mathematics are written for mathematicians.   The work may also be of use to the Church in the correction of the calendar.

The *De Revolutionibus Orbium Caelestium* had been completed some years before its author wrote his Preface to the Pope in 1543.   The manuscript was forwarded to Rheticus for possible correction and for printing.   The place selected was Nuremberg, where there were good presses and much interest was taken in astronomy.   Rheticus saw the first portion through the press.   Then, as he was required elsewhere, he confided the task to Osiander, a noted Lutheran preacher and theologian, who occupied himself with mathematics.   This well-meaning man was afraid of his brother Lutherans, so sensitive as to their orthodoxy, and afraid as well of the so-called Aristotelians, who were fast bound to the old explanations of the heavenly movements.   So he wrote a preface to the work, showing that no exception need be taken to the author's hypothesis of the movement of the earth. It was the business of astronomers to observe the heavens, and form hypotheses to account for the observed movements of the heavenly orbs. To such attempts the present author had notably contributed. " It is not necessary that his hypotheses should be true or even probable, but merely and solely that they should present a scheme agreeing with the observations." The ancients had devised schemes of movement, to which no one ascribed verisimilitude. Astronomy cannot teach the real causes of these apparently irregular movements. Hence all that is demanded of an astronomical hypothesis is that it should account for the appearances; no pretense is made that the facts are really so. Thus the astronomer adopts the most congruous hypotheses, though a philosopher might prefer a deeper probability. " But neither of them knows anything for certain unless it has been divinely revealed to him. So let these new and ingenious hypotheses be placed with the old ones, which are not more probable." No one should expect from astronomy any positive and certain agreement with the facts.

This preface, printed with the book, was supposed to have been written by Copernicus. He lay on his deathbed, and had become unconscious before his book was brought to him on the last day of his life. He never read the preface, nor knew that his great work had been presented to the world as a mathematical hypothesis making no claim to actual truth.[19]

Copernicus assuredly was convinced that his theory of the movements of the earth and other planets substantially represented the actuality; as it did to an incomparably greater degree than the Ptolemaic theory, of which it was a reversal. Yet its imperfections were serious, and there were radical objections arising from the faulty conceptions prevailing in physics. The Copernican scheme had still to be conformed to the actual courses of the planets, and, for this, further observations were required and the genius to deduce general laws from them; while radical changes were needed in physics before

[19] See for the whole story, Prowe o. c. II, pp. 490–558.

the ceaseless rotation of the earth could be made credible. The further observations were to be furnished by Tycho Brahe, and the corrections in the mathematical theory as to the planetary courses were to come from the genius of Kepler; while his great contemporary Galileo was not only to discover in the moons of Jupiter a convincing illustration of the Copernican theory, but through his physical discoveries remove the difficulties in the way of accepting the rotation of the earth. It remained for Newton further to demonstrate the universal physical or mechanical law controlling the movements alike of the solar system and the countless orbs of the sidereal heaven.

Tycho Brahe (1546-1601) is the only one of these whose life falls entirely or even predominantly within our sixteenth century. He came of a noble Danish family and was educated at Copenhagen. Intended for an official career, his bent to astronomy and mathematics proved stronger. The appearance of a new star in 1572 finally drove from him all thoughts save those of astronomy and astrology. Undoubtedly the stars favored his career. King Frederic II of Denmark, convinced of the genius of his young noble, made over to him the island of Hveen between Copenhagen and Elsinore, and aided him to build a castle of astronomy, Uraniborg as it was named. Its foundations were laid in 1576 when Tycho was thirty years of age. And there, with numerous assistants, sumptuously and magnificently, but most effectively, he studied, calculated and observed the heavens for twenty-one years. His observations were more extensive, continuous and accurate than any made before. Firmly he had grasped the need of a continuous series of observations of the positions and movements of a heavenly body in order to determine its course with accuracy. So, for example, through many years he made daily observations of the sun. He was most ingenious in the invention and use of astronomical instruments.

The work of Tycho Brahe was admirably adapted to supplement that of Copernicus, as the sequel proved. But Tycho did not accept Copernicus' conclusions. He could not conceive the movement of the stable and heavy earth. Acknowledging the value of a number of the Copernican simplifications of the celestial movements, he nevertheless devised a system of his own in which the five planets circled around the sun, and all moved around the earth. Apart from this unsatisfactory generalization, his better working genius effected a number of useful astronomical discoveries.

Tycho Brahe was of his time in that his interest in astrological calculations paralleled his astronomical achievements. A devotee of scientific astrology, he deplored the ignorance of its practitioners. No one could cast horoscopes as skillfully as he. In his earlier years he believed that the stars exerted a direct physical influence upon human affairs; but later he dwelt upon their effect on the minds of men, and thus upon their acts and fortunes.[20] For him the universe and human destinies were interwoven with intangible influences, which still might be calculated.

In casting the horoscopes of King Frederic and his children, it is doubtful whether Tycho foretold the trouble to arise between himself and the King's eldest son, who as a mere child succeeded to his father's throne. Tycho's astronomy had been a drain upon the royal purse, and his rather violent and grasping temper offended many. As a result of disagreements with the young king and his council, Tycho left the kingdom, and eventually put himself under the willing but rather unstable patronage of the Emperor Rudolph II. Quarters were provided for him in Prague and a castle near that city. Thither came to him a greater and still more curious genius than himself, John Kepler, a young Würtemberger, born in 1571, who had already written a noteworthy book on the Mystery of the Universe. The temperaments of the two men scarcely harmonized; but they worked together from 1599 until Tycho's death in 1601. Kepler had worked for Tycho upon the difficult planet Mars, for the planetary tables which Tycho was preparing; and eventually he fell

[20] See J. L. E. Dreyer, *Tycho Brahe, a picture of scientific life and work in the sixteenth century* (Edinburgh, 1890), p. 51. Dreyer's book is a fountain of information. The third chapter shows how Tycho's work on the new star spurred his astrological zeal.

heir to the mass of Tycho's observations, with which he wrought after the power of his genius.

Apparently Copernicus cared little for astrology, nor do we hear of his casting horoscopes to which Tycho was addicted. With Kepler we return again to this entrancing and lucrative business, though with him we shall also pass beyond the theorems of Copernicus. Kepler was a marvellously fertile mathematician and astronomer; but his beliefs and temper were rooted in the sixteenth century, and were affected by divers still older traditions. All his life he cast horoscopes, tempering his prognostications with worldly wisdom and the prudence of equivocation. In his earlier career he ascribed the movements of each celestial body to a particular intelligence. Even then the surer side of his scientific nature looked for physical causes. He had been impressed with conceptions of *impetus* drawn from earlier physicists; but never could quite disillusion himself of analogies between *impetus* and the soul.[21] Rarely has such a predisposition towards imaginative speculation been combined with such scientific ardor and mathematical genius.

Kepler's services to astronomy were many. Chief among them were the " Three Laws " which went so far to correct and advance the Copernican system, and bring it into close accord with the celestial facts. They come to us as the residuum or resultant of numberless hypotheses which might be termed baseless or fantastic were it not for the intellectual honesty of their author, who laboriously tried out each one by the touchstone of observation, and found it wanting. It was because he would not rest satisfied with a discrepancy of 8′ between his geometric theory and Tycho's observations of the irregularities in the course of the planet Mars, that he pushed on till he reached the hypothesis that Mars (and each of the other planets) describes an ellipse in its course about the sun, which is at one focus of the ellipse. This is the first of Kepler's Laws, and has ever since been accepted as true.

He then set himself to formulate some law covering

[21] See Duhem, *Études sur Leonardo da Vinci*, II, pp. 201–211.

the planet's speed through different portions of its orbit.
Through observation he found the planet to move rapidly
when nearest the sun and more slowly when more distant.
And again, after trying out many unhappy suppositions,
he reached an hypothesis which he demonstrated to be
true, and so astronomers after him have found it: the
imaginary line connecting at any time the planet with the
sun will always describe or cover or " sweep out," as the
planet moves along its course, the same area in the same
period of time.

He had reached this second triumphant Law before
1609. His Third Law seems to have issued from the
compelling yearning of his mind to discover relations between the numerical quantities, temporal or spacial, observable in the solar system: the relation, for example, between the distance of a planet from the sun and the time
required for its revolution. At last his marvellous mathematical imagination struck out this hypothesis, which
proved to be correct: the squares of the periods of revolution of the several planets around the sun are in the
ratio of the cubes of their mean distances.

Kepler felt the need of some principle of gravitation
or mass attraction; and had studied Gilbert's treatise *On
the Magnet*. But his physics were too confused to admit of his logical or mathematical development of such
a theory. He died in 1629.

In the volume of Galileo's achievements in physics and
astronomy those features may be adverted to which most
notably contributed to the acceptance of the rotation of
the earth and the Copernican system.

He did not invent the telescope, but first among men
employed it in the limitless extension of astronomical
knowledge. With it he showed the irregular and moun-
tainous surface of the moon; with it he recognized the
spots on the sun, and demonstrated that they were on or
near its surface, and that by observing them the rotation
of the sun could be measured as well as proved. His most
convincing illustration of the Copernican system was his
telescopic discovery of the satellites of Jupiter, and his
demonstration of their periodic circulation around that

planet. Here was a smaller solar system shown in operation. Such discoveries and demonstrations opened men's minds to the Copernican theory.

Galileo's discoveries in physics were not less effective in overcoming objections. His wonderful career had opened in his eighteenth year when he turned his observation of the swinging lamp in the Pisan Cathedral into his veritable discovery of the law of the pendulum: to wit, that when a weight suspended on a string or chain is swung to and fro, its oscillations take place in a constant time period for any given arc, and in sensibly the same time for different arcs when these are small; but the time will increase with the lengthening of the string and diminish when it is shortened. Thus the oscillations of the pendulum afforded a measure of time, for the short period that they might continue. Seventy-five years later Christian Huygens, a native of the Hague, invented the pendulum clock, in which weights kept the pendulum in motion while the pendulum regulated the clock: an invention of exhaustless value in astronomy and other sciences.

Galileo (to return to his discoveries) also proved that every moving body tended to continue in motion forever in a straight line except as compelled to change. He determined the law of the uniformly accelerated motion of falling bodies. He showed that the same moving body might have more than one motion at the same time; and that, for instance, the path of a projectile combines a uniform transverse motion coupled with a uniformly accelerated motion of falling, making (apart from the resistance of the air) its path a parabola. He showed that all bodies on the earth or near it shared its motion, even clouds and air and mist, as well as a solid dropped from a height, which would therefore fall not quite vertically and reach the earth not west but east of the point it fell from. In all these respects he was approaching Newton, and there hovered in his mind something corresponding to the law of gravitation formulated by the great Englishman.

Galileo's scientific method, which he applied as well as often stated incidentally, was to prove its soundness through the times to come.   It combined experiment with calculation, effecting thus a passage from the particular instance to the general law: which should always be confirmed by a constant comparison of results.   For example, as he says in his *Two New Sciences*: " Let us take this at present as a *Postulatum*, the truth whereof we shall afterwards find established, when we see other conclusions, built upon this *Hypothesis*, to answer and most exactly agree with Experience." [22]

After Galileo it became difficult for an intelligent man not to abandon the old for the new system; yet Milton still held them in the balance!   He was predominantly a poet!   Galileo died in 1642, and the next year Isaac Newton was born.   Between the periods of their working lives, men younger than Galileo but older than Newton made important contributions to the knowledge of the celestial bodies and of the earth in its relations to them. The minds of scientific men became accustomed to the new conceptions, and were disposed to assume their truth.

Newton's greatest creative period extends from his graduation at Cambridge in 1665 to the publication of the *Principia* in 1687.   Though there was no longer call for arguments to prove the general truth of the Copernican theory, there was still need to rationalize it, and, so to speak, push back its why and wherefore to a further satisfying generalization sounding in some explanatory motive principle.

This was supplied by Newton.   Kepler had realized that the planetary motions could not be due to some central point, but must be ascribed to the influence of a central body, to wit, the sun.   Galileo showed that the motion of a body goes on in a straight line until stopped or deflected; and also demonstrated the law of accelerated motion in falling bodies.   Others pointed out the centrifugal tendency of any body actually revolving around a central point, a principle which when adjusted with Galileo's law of accelerated motion in falling bodies, re-

[22] *Two New Sciences*, p. 255 (Weston's translation).   Cited by Berry, *Hist. of Astronomy*, p. 178.

sults in the principle of acceleration directed toward a centre. After them came Newton.

Assuming Galileo's first law that a body in motion tends to move in a straight line, and making use of Kepler's Third Law as to the relation between the time of a planet's revolution and its distance from the sun, Newton set forth his law of the inverse square, in accord with which the motions of the planets might be explained on the supposition that the sun produces an acceleration toward itself proportional to the inverse square of the distance of the planet from the sun: i. e. at twice the distance the acceleration is one fourth as great, and at four times the distance one sixteenth as great.

Newton found both a proof and a further application of this law in the revolution of the moon about the earth. Next he devised or elaborated the conception of *Mass,* and identified the weight of a body with the force exerted on it by the earth. He reached the combined conclusion that the earth attracts any body with a force inversely proportional to the square of the distance from the centre of the earth and directly proportional to the mass of the body. Conversely this attraction or gravitation is reciprocal; and the finally generalized statement of the law will be: every material body attracts every other material body with a force proportional to the product of their masses and inversely proportional to the square of the distance between them.[23]

Such was Newton's final rationalization, or ascription to a general law, of the movements of the earth and all the heavenly bodies. As for the cause or reason of this law of gravitation he had no hypothesis. Thus far had the system of Copernicus been brought within a century and a half. It did indeed represent a change from the mental and spiritual attitude, and symbolic and scholastic conceptions, of a Hugo of St. Victor, an Aquinas or a Dante. In these the human spirit, religiously inclined, had beautifully worked. But the intellect, the sheer mind

---

[23] See Berry, *Hist. of Astronomy,* p. 228. Berry says that Newton formulated no such complete and general statement, but gave its parts in separate passages of the *Principia.*

of man, had never displayed itself as brilliantly as in that exposition of celestial physics which began, or rather, did not begin, with Copernicus, and was proved and perfected through the genius of Kepler, of Galileo and Newton, and the supporting labors of other mathematicians and astronomers. Within the compass of this theory or proven fact, the mind of pigmy man was calculating the courses of the stars in the unfathomable abysses of the universe.

CHAPTER XXXIV

THE NEW PHILOSOPHERS

I. TELESIO, CAMPANELLA, BRUNO

II. FRANCIS BACON

I

BESIDES anatomists and physiologists, physicists and astronomers, there were philosophers in the sixteenth century who vied with the scientists in their intellectual independence, and, as philosophers, surpassed them in the reach and looseness of their thought. The Aristotelians and Platonists have been spoken of. As followers of ancient systems they should not be classed with men whose thinking reflected the new thoughts of the time, scientific or otherwise. The latter were philosophers of nature, of the natural universe, terrestrial and celestial. Telesio (1509-1588), Bruno (1548-1600), Campanella (1568-1639), and Francis Bacon (1560-1626), greatest name of all, may be taken as their representatives. While their broad and independent and suggestive thinking held much of the past, it was impelled by the spirit of the time. With reservations as to Francis Bacon, their systems presented a certain magnificent confusion, and lacked a sure foundation in some irrefragable basic principle.

For they had broken with the authority of Aristotle, and had abjured the moulding power of logic and systematization which lay in the Aristotelian scholasticism. They were drawn in divers ways by thoughts from the antique,— of Plato, or " Pythagoras," of Democritus and Lucretius, not to mention the Cabala. Thus confusedly equipped, they were at sea with their own thinking upon the metaphysics of the universe. Rather than sheer eclecticism, their opinions present a certain synthetic originality. The wind-blown thinking of Telesio, of Bruno, of Campanella was to offer little guidance to future men. Its basic weakness lay in the lack of some fundamental principle of validity and certitude, such as Descartes was to discover in his *cognito ergo sum.*

It was not merely their metaphysics that were at sea. Their thoughts in general sprang from their imaginations pricked by the new physical theories and enlarging knowledge of the world. Their conclusions were not constructed painfully through inferences from the data of experience. Very different were the ways of these philosophers from the method of Vesalius, of Harvey, or of Galileo. Vesalius followed the teaching of his dissections; Harvey, likewise holding fast to his dissections of human bodies and his vivisections of animals, finally demonstrated his standardizing fact of the circulation of the blood; and what a Titan grasp had Galileo on the laws of motion, for example, which he had proved from his experiments. The sciences of physiology and of physics terrestrial and astronomical could never be shaken from these basic principles which served to test the validity of all new inductions. Our philosophers had no such tests of natural truth; and Bacon, interested in all the phenomena of nature, records in his encyclopaedia all sorts of untested notions and statements, many of them unsound and some of them absurd. We may find that he was not a serious man of science according to the standards of Harvey or Galileo or William Gilbert's *De Magnete,* which Bacon held to be rather small beer.

We proceed then to these philosophers of a new view of the world, which was untested by anything within their knowledge or their reasoning.

Telesio's polemic against Aristotle shows what originality lay in his philosophy, which Bacon, his admirer, said was better at pulling down. He attacked the Aristotelian conceptions of matter and form as two separables, arguing that they were strictly in and of each other. Form was but the result of any natural process. He would substitute the principle of force indwelling in all matter, impelling and vivifying it. His force was heat, conceived in interaction with its opposite, the principle of cold or death. Matter, impregnated with force, is not potentiality, but the veritable and sole reality. The end of Telesio's philosophy was the restoration of this sole reality to its true integrity, its re-integration, if one will; an integrity destroyed by the Aristotelian theory.[1] But, further, Telesio inveighed against Aristotle for his counter-principle of non-being; a mere word and no true or possible conception, he maintained. His own counter-principle of cold was no impossible non-ens, or privation, but a veritable counter principle, needed for Nature's world-process, where all generation and becoming imply the cessation of something else. The two are relative to each other, and attain an absolute reality only in their mutual strife, or reciprocal action as the force which fills all matter, realizes itself as matter's active part, and is one with that wherein it acts. This it is to explain Nature *juxta propria principia,* according to her own real principles; by means of observation, using the five senses, rather than abstract reason; and not by following Plato or Aristotle. Yet many a notion taken from the ancients, especially from what he knew of Parmenides or the system of the Stoa, filled out Telesio's philosophy. It was not a consistent system, and its details may be passed over. But one notes that Telesio made man quite veritably part of nature, of the whole material, force-impregnated, reality of the world. And for him the ethics of human life consisted in the self-realization of the man, his bringing himself to actuality and expression, just as the inner tendency of everything in nature is to realize and conserve itself.

Telesio, a native of Cosenza, near Naples, was a south Italian. So were Campanella and Bruno, the other chief exponents of a new philosophy of nature. Telesio was troubled by the monks; Campanella was imprisoned many years; Bruno was burned. Orthodox authoritative Christianity had long since made a bedfellow of Aristotle; but

---

[1] See G. Gentile, *Bernardino Telesio* (Bari, 1911), p. 68, to which little work these few pages are much indebted. Compare the strictures of Ramus upon Aristotle, ante, chapter XVI.

with self-conserving instinct it hated the new philosophy, which was hostile to its great Philosopher and was endowing Nature with a life within itself, making it real, absolute, infinite:— why not divine?

Inspired with ardor for natural truth and an admiration for Telesio, the young Calabrian Campanella came to see the aged master, only to find him lying on his bier. Campanella would be called to-day a "modernist." He loved truth, and he also loved the Church. Unhappily for him he entered the Dominican order, at a time when the new thoughts of nature and an infinite moving universe were gathering for their conflict with the Roman Catholic Aristotelian view of the world of earth and heaven. No one could be more eager for the Church's world-supremacy than Campanella; but his conviction that an equally direct revelation of God and man lay in nature, and that man's mission was to read the same, brought him under suspicion, and made him the prisoner of his Order, or of the Inquisition, for a large part of his life.[2] No cell could restrain the freedom of his spirit.

For him, faith on the one side, and, on the other, investigation, perception, consciousness, were the sources of religion and philosophic truth. Consciousness is a basic certainty, as Augustine had said, and as Descartes, near the close of Campanella's life, was to establish as the starting point of all knowledge. Man investigates nature through the consciousness of his experiences, which are to be compared with one another, and reasoned from. Through self-consciousness, also, one passes into a consciousness and unshakable conviction of God. This is the very pillar of our guidance,— the consciousness of the divine nature, the inner sense of the divine, the *tactus intrinsecus in magna suavitate,* which constantly brings us wanderers back to God; and more efficiently than either the syllogism or *authority,* through which we touch him only with another's hand.

From the infinite God proceed angels and immortal human souls, and space and transient things. All is alive, all sensitive to joy; and moved by sympathy and antipathy.

[2] He was also accused of conspiring against the Spanish Government.

The world is God's *living* image. Throughout the world, self-preservation is the law of every nature. Man's highest preservation is to overcome limitation and negation, and unite with God. Beyond this, Campanella, like Thomas More and Francis Bacon, all three following Plato, conceived a Republic of the Sun, where the welfare of men should be attained in justice and equality; where there should be common dwellings, common meals, common wives and common children; where mathematics and the natural sciences should be cultivated, and where all things should be rationally ordered for the good of the community. Anon this dream changed to a vision of a universal state under a perfect Pope, supported by the secular power of Spain! A Church philosopher might find himself drawn to such extreme transitions. A tragic dreamer was this Campanella, chained, yet free; unconquerable in his opposite desires of truth and Church supremacy.

There was no wish for Church supremacy in another South Italian, a Dominican also, to his bane, Giordano Bruno of Nola. With statues and acclaim the modern time has done its utmost to atone for the burning in the year 1600 of this man of genius and intellectual enthusiasm. His temper was as difficult as Abaelard's, and more heroic. In their different ways, both men were poets, which proves a certain molten eagerness in them. Moreover, while Abaelard's dialectic had little in common with Bruno's pantheistic philosophy of nature, each brought to sharp expression the master tendencies of his epoch. They were intellectual representatives of their time, though Abaelard had more effect than Bruno upon his own and later generations.

With a mind of power, Bruno possessed an architectonic imagination which drew vast conclusions. His imagination worked along lines of truth. Long afterwards slower and surer processes of the investigating reason were to reach many a position to which Bruno had boldly leaped.

Such an imagination, constructive, rational and fearless, would tally with the time's enlarging vistas, and see the significance of its new discoveries, and, above all, would grasp the meaning of that Copernican hypothesis which was to overthrow the fixed supremacy of the earth, and infinitely enlarge the horizons of its denizens. Bruno was the first who had the imagination and the courage to proclaim as an infinite fact that which had been timorously published as a mathematical hypothesis. Breaking with cautious limitations, he fitted the new thought not merely to the solar system, but to the universe freed for man's contemplation.

Indeed Bruno's entire philosophy, so far as it was entire, seems to issue from his conviction of the infinitude of the universe, within which moved the earth and sun and stars. That conviction fed the fervor of his thinking, permeated his conceptions of causation, of God and life, of force and mind and matter; filled out his view of human destiny, and gave his spirit joy. It also lifted him, if not into denial, at least into a sublime ignoring of the dogmas of the Church, and stung him to contemptuous attacks upon the methods and the nightmares of the persecuting hierarchies.

Of late years the tale of Bruno's restless life in Paris, in London and Oxford, in a very disagreeable Geneva, in a more genial Wittenberg, in Frankfurt, in a Venice so unwisely trusted, in the prison of the Inquisition at Rome, to the last scene in the Piazza Navona — has been told and told again.[3] Instead of repeating it, we may note his intellectual antecedents in those preparatory pre-Copernican doctrines of Nicholas of Cusa: the infinitude of God, and the union in Him of the contraries shown by the world; the relation of the world to God as the Unfolding (explicatio) of that of which He is the

[3] Sufficiently in J. Lewis McIntyre's *Giordano Bruno* (Macmillan, 1903) and Wm. Boulting, *Giordano Bruno,* etc. (no date). The documents relating to his trial, imprisonment and death are given by D. Berti. *Giordano Bruno da Nola* (1889). These two books give accounts of Bruno's philosophy. For further study one must turn to F. Tocco, *Le opere latine di G. B. esposte e confrontate con le italiane* (Florence, 1889). From this publication, one will gain more perhaps than from a desultory perusal of Bruno's voluminous works in Latin and Italian, of which there are a number of modern editions. The Italian and German literature on Bruno is large.

implicitude and union (implicatio); the rational conviction of man's inability to comprehend Him and the Universe, the thought that the earth moves, and is not the centre of the Universe, which can have no centre.

Greek philosophy as well as mediaeval Aristotelianism likewise afforded Bruno sympathetic data, or suggestively repelled him.   Living in city after city, he could understand the urban social quality of antique thought; and, as a child of the sixteenth century, he felt the swing of human interest toward the life which man lived so palpably on earth.   Such leaven promoted his appreciation of the old philosophies of the Eleatics and the Atomists, as well as the systems of Epicurus and the Stoa, and the works of Galen.   He was sufficiently dipped in the Neoplatonism, or fancied Neo-pythagoreanism, of his time. He was quite capable of weaving ideas drawn from all these systems into that infinitely heightened and extended Universe which his vision had created from the teaching of Copernicus.   What a field for the play of atoms! in numberless circles of worlds! none of them to endure as such; but everyone eternal in its mobile participation in the essentially changeless and unmoving All.   That All was permeated by the life-giving energy of the Ether, itself a measureless, substantial reality.   Even the environing sphere of the fixed stars was burst asunder: Bruno's universe, one, infinite, moveless, had no limit whatsoever.

And God?   The universe is His unfolding, *explicatio* as Cusa said; enfolds Him also, necessarily; for God is within it, not without.   And then, in thinking of the abiding unity of this infinitely unfolded deity, Bruno turns (among other ways of thinking it) to Cusa's *coincidentia oppositorum,* the union of contraries attained in infinite being.   So God, as the world-soul, permeates and energizes and vivifies the universe.   How could God's infinite energy have finite workings?   This universal energy, this divine substance, is absolutely one, and, with its unimpaired wholeness, fills all things wholly.   Everything is therefore animate, whether conscious or not, and moves to the fulfillment of its destiny.   Human souls may reach the blessedness of contemplating the divine spirit, with which they are imbued, and may re-unite with it upon the body's dissolution. Thus the Universe is divine; there is no other Heaven beyond it for immortal separated souls, whose true immortality is to unite with God all-present through the Universe.

Vital in Bruno's scheme was the principle of the imperishability of whatever is: material and spiritual substance were indestructible. The body might be dissolved into other forms, but, as part of the abiding material substance it would not perish. Likewise the spiritual principle is absolutely immortal. Beyond this, Bruno's expressions vary, quite naturally. He is found maintaining that individual souls endure forever; but his dominant thesis is that of the immortal substantiality of the universal spirit, of which individual souls are modes, and into which they most naturally return.

Proudly comforting and defending himself, when examined before the tribunal in Venice which was to deliver him to the Roman Inquisition, Bruno stated his philosophic creed:

" I hold to an infinite Universe, to wit, the effect of the infinite divine power, because it has seemed to me unworthy of the divine goodness and power, when able to create other and infinite worlds, to have created one finite world: so that I have declared that there are endless finite (particulari) worlds like this of the Earth, which with Pythagoras I take to be a star, like the moon, the other planets and the other stars. These are infinite, and all these bodies are worlds, and without number; they make up the infinite Universe in an infinite space. . . . Then, in this Universe I place one universal providence, though which everything lives, flourishes, moves, and stands in its perfection. And I understand this in two ways, first that in which the soul is present in the body, all in all (tutta in tutto) and all in any given part, and I call this natura, the shadow, the footprint, of the deity; next in the ineffable way in which God through essence, presence and power, is in all and above all, not as part, not as soul, but in a way that is inexplicable."

Thereupon Bruno states his conception of God in accordance with the opinions of accepted theologians and philosophers, yet admitting that he had held doubts (though he had not expressed them) of the Incarnation. As for the " divine spirit," he had not been able to conceive it as " a third person," but as the soul of the universe. " From this spirit, which is called the Life (Vita) of the Universe, there springs, according to my philosophy, the life and soul of everything having soul and life; and I deem it to be immortal, even as the substance of all bodies is immortal, there being no other death than separation and coming together." [4]

> " If the red slayer think he slays,
>   Or if the slain think he be slain,
>   They know not well the subtle ways
>   I keep and pass and turn again."

What folly is it for man to be troubled or afraid! This all embracing and pervasive unity and energy of life, laughs at apparent changes and destructions and comings into being; and we and all things are it. Nay, each one of us may feel himself that very All, which in each of us is wholly present. What sorrow can shake the happiness of that realization? Through such convictions, Bruno rises above the peace of Stoicism, in virtue of a profounder assurance. He lives "surrounded by the impregnable wall of true philosophic contemplation, where the peacefulness of life stands fortified and on high, where truth is open, where the Eternity of all substantial things is clear, where naught is to be feared but to be deprived of human perfection and justice."[5]

A man of such conviction might tell his judges that they gave their sentence against him in greater fear than he received it. In fear they surely were, before doctrines intellectually so revolutionary, practically so contentious and uncompromising. On this particular finite earth there was not room for Bruno and the Roman Catholic Church,— or perhaps for Bruno and Calvin and Luther!

---

[4] Text in Berti, o. c. pp. 400–402; see also McIntyre, pp. 76–78. This statement, one of the last recorded of Bruno, may not harmonize with earlier opinions, and was made by a prisoner accused of heresy. This fact may have influenced its form, if not its substance. Generally on the changes which Bruno's thinking passed through, see Tocco, o. c. pp. 331 sqq.

[5] From the *Spaccio,* quoted by McIntyre, o. c. p. 99.

Neither of the two latter cared for the swirling world of Copernicus; and the Roman Church was, and has since remained, between the devil and the deep sea, in its fear of such a doctrine as that *horrenda prorsusque absurdissima, mundos esse innumerabiles*.

Withal, Bruno is spoken of as a melancholy man. It was hard to laugh in the prisons of the Inquisition. Did he in some sort realize that his stanchness for the truth and his efforts to promote human enlightenment were to prove none too fruitful? Was he ever shaken in his own convictions, in his philosophy so imaginatively, so constructively, synthetic? He, at least, never perceived that his system was scarcely a system because not founded on some rock of well-proven certitude. If he stated many a view which men have since, on further grounds, held true, no one has exactly followed him, except perhaps in the waves of his pantheism,— not knowing whom they followed, yet swimming ever in those shoreless floods.

II

The vehement idealism, the intellectual enthusiasms, of this exceedingly expressive Bruno outsoared the certitudes of his natural knowledge. We are equally impressed by the abounding volubility of thought and language in his contemporary, that great Elizabethan, Francis Bacon. Indeed Bacon's catholic faculty of intellectual self-expression was a prime mover in the production of those voluminous writings which impressed his age and later generations. Through this compelling and transforming faculty the writer poured himself into his compositions, making them a grandiose mirror of himself. His works were animate. A tireless imagination, an inevitable aptness of phrase, a living power in the use of words gave forth his thought completely, even redundantly. Both his English writings and his Latin *opera* display the mighty abundance of a style that was the man. His pregnant mind imbued them with sententiousness; they moved with a stately magnificence and sweep.   The reader found them easy; was pleased with the excellence of their wisdom; they aroused his anticipation of complete intellectual satisfaction.   Their repetitions were no great drag, since few would read them all; and, in such a bewildering maze, men would ascribe their final failure to reach some certain goal rather to their own debility than to any lack of arrival on the part of the great philosopher.

The career of Bacon, from his early manhood until he became Lord Chancellor and fell from grace, has been too thoroughly discussed to require retelling.   With Burghley for an uncle and Salisbury for a cousin, Bacon's family connection virtually administered the affairs of England. Born in 1560 he lived through the reigns of Elizabeth and James, to die at the age of sixty-six in the second year of Charles.   According to the fulsome custom of the time, he praised these monarchs inordinately and absurdly; but gave them good advice when asked.

There has been much dispute as to the services of Bacon to science and philosophy, and men who have devoted their lives, or many years at least, to the study of his works have differed in the estimate of his accomplishment and the conception of his method.   Our own conclusions are not likely to prove convincing; and perhaps the least futile way to proceed will be to let the Lord Chancellor speak for himself.   Since it is inconvenient to put quartos into pages, we shall draw chiefly upon the impressive suggestions of plan and purpose, contained in his prefaces or *prööemia*.

Like other Elizabethans, Bacon was always asking for something from the hands of those who could bestow; but few men in begging letters set forth such glorious alternates to which in the case of refusal they would devote themselves.   When, as he said, he was waxing somewhat ancient, with one and thirty years already fallen in the hour-glass, he wrote to Burghley suggesting reasons for his advancement, making at the same time such professions of grateful admiration as one would use to an uncle who was Lord Treasurer and the most influential man in England.

. . . " I ever bare a mind (in some middle place that I could discharge) to serve her Majesty; not as a man born under Sol, that loveth honour; nor under Jupiter, that loveth business (for the contemplative planet carrieth me away wholly) ; but as a man born under an excellent sovereign, that deserveth the dedication of all men's abilities. . . . Again, the meanness of my estate doth somewhat move me. . . . Lastly, I confess that I have as vast contemplative ends, as I have moderate civil ends: for I have taken all Knowledge to be my province; and if I could purge it of two sorts of rovers, whereof the one with frivolous disputations, confutations, and verbosities, the other with blind experiments and auricular traditions and impostures, hath committed so many spoils, I hope I should bring in industrious observations, grounded conclusions, and profitable inventions and discoveries; the best state of that province.   This, whether it be curiosity, or vain glory, or nature, or (if one take it favorably) *philanthropia,* is so fixed in my mind that it cannot be removed. . . . And if your Lordship will not carry me on, I will not do as Anaxagoras did, who reduced himself with contemplation unto voluntary poverty; but . . . I will sell the inheritance that I have, and purchase some lease of quick revenue, or some office of gain that shall be executed by a deputy, and so give over all care of service, and become some sorry book-maker, or a true pioneer in that mine of truth, which (he said) lay so deep." [6]

In this letter Bacon already has in mind the kinds of empty headed disputers, followers of tradition, or inconclusive experimenters against which his weightier writings will never cease to declaim.   Many a youth has taken all Knowledge for his province, but only to find it more fruitful to retire and dig in some small corner.   But Bacon had his mediaeval forbears, his exemplars and justifiers.   He was nearer than we are to the thirteenth century when the prodigious compiling encyclopaedist Vincent of Beauvais had not only taken all knowledge for his province, but had, if not plowed, at all events garnered from the greater part of it.   The thirteenth century brought forth Francis Bacon's nearer prototype, another

[6] Spedding, *Letters and Life of Francis Bacon,* I, p. 108. Impatience for some profitable place does not interfere with such picturesque language as we find, for instance, in a letter to Foulke Greville a year or two later: " I have been like a piece of stuff bespoken in the shop, and if her Majesty will not take me, it may be the selling by parcels will be more gainful. For to be like a child following a bird, which when he is nearest flieth away and lighteth a little before, and then the child after it again, and so *in infinitum,* I am weary of it, as also of wearying my good friends. . . ."   Ib. p. 359.

Englishman, Roger Bacon, whose name and magician's fame lived in Elizabethan times, and indeed formed the subject of a play.[7]

Francis Bacon may never have read the writings of his namesake. Yet one still is struck, violently and repeatedly, with the intellectual and even temperamental affinities between the two. They both declaimed against the vicious methods of scholarship and science of their day; they both set forth at length, and most repetitiously, such a full inductive or experimental method as would rectify and enormously extend man's knowledge of his world; the intellectual aims of both were utilitarian and practical; and neither of them set any limit to his self-esteem. Besides these generalities, curious particular resemblances may be found between Roger Bacon's *offendicula* and *peccata studii,* which impeded all advance in knowledge, and Francis Bacon's *Idola* hereafter to be spoken of. These figures of denunciation were brought forward by each writer many times. Roger Bacon is constantly setting out the proprieties and prerogatives of his *scientia experimentalis,* even as Francis never leaves off expatiating on the unplumbed values lying in his inductive method. And there is curious analogy between the former's elaborately complicated example of the application of his method or science to the investigation of the rainbow, and the even more elaborate examples which the latter gives of his inductive method in the *Novum Organum.*[8]

One must not lay too much stress on these rather loose though fascinating parallels, which we will leave with this remark that the elder Bacon in his *scientia perspectiva* or Optics, seems to show himself a truer scientific investigator than the younger man ever proved himself to be.

Francis Bacon regarded himself with a seriousness justified by his intellectual powers. Undoubtedly he was

[7] R. Greene's *Friar Bacon and Friar Bungay* (1587). Legends or romances of Roger Bacon were printed too.

[8] See *The Mediaeval Mind,* Vol. II, chap. XLII, and *Novum Organum,* II, XI–XX on Heat, pp. 179–218 in Spedding's Translation, *Works,* Vol. VIII (cited from the American edition of 1863). Francis refers by name to Roger Bacon once, and in one or two other passages seems to have him in mind.

moved, as it were politically, with a desire to serve his
King and country and the English Church.[9] Like a true
Elizabethan he *was* this desire so long as he felt and was
expressing it. His still broader intellectual hope of
serving mankind through extending their dominion over
nature abode with him through life. In an introduction
written about 1603, intended as a preface to a work
on the *Interpretation of Nature,* he tells his personal
ideals:

" Believing that I was born for the service of mankind, and
regarding the care of the commonwealth as a kind of common
property which like the air and water belongs to everybody, I set
myself to consider in what way mankind might be best served,
and what service I was myself best fitted by nature to perform.

" Now among all the benefits that could be conferred upon mankind, I found none so great as the discovery of new arts, endow-
ments, and commodities for the bettering of man's life. . . . For
myself, I found that I was fitted for nothing so well as for the
study of Truth; as having a mind nimble and versatile enough to
catch the resemblance of things (which is the chief point), and at
the same time steady enough to fix and distinguish their subtle
differences; as being gifted by nature with desire to seek, patience
to doubt, fondness to meditate, slowness to assert, readiness to re-
consider, carefulness to dispose and set in order; and as being a
man that neither affects what is new nor admires what is old, and
that hates every kind of imposture. So I thought my nature had
a kind of familiarity and relationship with Truth."

His birth and education had drawn him into the business of State, and he hopes to do something for men's
souls in the matter of religion. But since his zeal had
been mistaken for ambition, he will address himself to
the perfection of a machine or *Organum* for the Interpretation of nature, though his years are not likely to
suffice for setting it to work. That must be done by
others.[10]

[9] See a splendidly written paper on the " Pacification and Edification of
the Church of England " addressed to James shortly after his accession.
Spedding, *Letters,* &c., Vol. III, pp. 103 sqq.

[10] Spedding's Translation, *Letters,* &c., Vol. III, pp. 84 sqq. Bacon
filled more important public offices after he wrote this preface than before. He was made Lord Keeper in 1617 and the next year Lord Chancellor. One has but to look through the seven volumes of Letters and
papers edited by Spedding to realize how busy he was with affairs. All
the while his passionate avocation was philosophy, in which he strikes one
as the greatest of amateurs.

Before proceeding further with those Introductions or other parts of Bacon's works which set forth the plan and scope of what he deemed his positive and supreme achievement, it were well to note his criticisms upon the state of learning and science in times past and his own day. These indicate the intellectual disagreements and aversions which led him to repudiate current and past methods, though to what extent he did in fact depart from them is another question. At all events his sweeping intellectual denunciations were put most tellingly and often truthfully. For mankind is human and limited and imperfect; and its ignorance and unsatisfactory progress in questionable knowledge lie open to many just criticisms. One need scarcely be an archangel to perceive that much human knowledge is foolishness.

Bacon's criticisms, or denunciations, are pithy as well as trenchant; some of them are acute, while others proceed from prejudice or ignorance. They abound in *The Advancement of Learning* (1605) written by Bacon in his own splendid English, and worked over into his more elaborate *De Augmentis Scientiarum.*

The first book, practically the same in *The Advancement* and in the *De Augmentis,* opens with an eloquent commendation and defense of learning, of which men cannot have too much:

"Let no man, upon a weak conceit of sobriety or ill-applied moderation, think or maintain that a man can search too far or be too well studied in the book of God's word, or in the book of God's works; divinity or philosophy; but rather let men endeavour an endless progress or proficiency in both; only let men beware that they apply both to charity, and not to swelling; to use, and not to ostentation; and again, that they do not unwisely mingle or confound these learnings together."

Bacon chides what he calls "three vanities in studies," or "three distempers" (he always loves to use many terms): "the first, fantastical learning; the second, contentious learning; and the last, delicate learning; vain imaginations, vain altercations, and vain affectations; and with the last I will begin."

He proceeds to criticise men whom we might call humanists for their over study and copying of the ancient eloquence, and says rather vaguely: " In sum, the whole inclination and bent of those times was rather towards copie than weight.   Here, therefore, is the first distemper of learning, that men study words and not matter."

He next criticises the contentious learning of the school-men, whose wits were shut up in Aristotle, and worked little upon matter, but rather spun laborious webs, and gave themselves to unprofitable subtilties.   And next, the third and foulest vice of " deceit or untruth," a vice which " brancheth itself into two sorts; delight in deceiving, and aptness to be deceived; imposture and credulity." Hereunder he groups the easy belief in the miracles of martyrs and hermits, the fabulous matter brought into works on Natural History; also astrology, magic, and alchemy.   He takes occasion to deplore the " overmuch credit " given to the ancient " authours in sciences."   One should neither bow down before antiquity nor gallop after novelty; and by no means fall into a distrust that anything remains to be found out.   It should be remembered that it is not the best and wisest of Antiquity that has survived; since " time seemeth to be of the nature of a river or stream, which carrieth down to us that which is light and blown up, and sinketh and drowneth that which is weighty and solid."

These criticisms except the last (which Bacon frequently repeats) reflect the more progessive spirit of the time when Bacon lived.   But he made them his own through his imagination, his irony, and his splendid Baconian style.   He finds further sources of error in " a kind of adoration of the mind and understanding of man: by means whereof men have withdrawn themselves too much from the contemplation of nature and the observations of experience, and have tumbled up and down in their own reason and conceits."   This was a new phrasing of what often had been felt; and one is reminded definitely of Roger Bacon when Francis proceeds to object to the mingling of philosophy with theology, and then to the building up of a philosophy on too few experiments and too narrow observation: " and Gilbertus, our countryman, hath made a philosophy out of the observations of a loadstone."

We turn from the first book of *The Advancement of Learning* to note Bacon's most famous sardonic strictures upon the mental habitudes of man: to wit the four kinds of " idols and false notions which are now in possession of the human understanding, and . . . beset men's minds that truth can hardly find entrance."[11]   There are first the Idols of the Tribe, which have " their foundation in human nature itself, and in the tribe or race of men," and pretend " that the sense of man is the measure of all things.   On the contrary, all perceptions as well of the sense as of the mind are according to the measure of the individual and not according to the measure of the universe.   And the human understanding is like a false mirror, which, receiving rays irregularly, distorts and discolours the nature of things by mingling its own nature with it."

Secondly, the *Idols of the Cave* appertinent to the individual man and his idiosyncrasies, and springing from his peculiar circumstances and education.   " For every one (besides the errors common to human nature in general) has a cave or den of his own, which refracts and discolours the light of nature."   Thirdly, the *Idols of the Market-place,* called so

" on account of the commerce and consort of men there.   For it is by discourse that men associate; and words are imposed according to the apprehension of the vulgar.   And therefore the ill and unfit choice of words wonderfully obstructs the understanding.   Nor do the definitions or explanations wherewith in some things learned men are wont to guard and defend themselves, by any means set the matter right.   But words plainly force and overrule the understanding, and throw all into confusion, and lead men away into numberless empty controversies and idle fancies."

" Lastly, there are Idols which have immigrated into men's minds from the various dogmas of philosophies, and also from the wrong laws of demonstration.   These I call *Idols of the Theatre;* because in my judgment all the received systems are but so many

[11] *Novum Organum,* I, XXXVIII sqq.   Bacon restated these *Idola* a number of times.

stage-plays, representing worlds of their own creation after an unreal and scenic fashion." [12]

And Bacon continues expounding these four kinds of Idols, pointing his strictures at current intellectual fallacies. The novelty lay in his picturesque expression of the troubles of the human mind, which men had dumbly realized before. Only at the last his conceit shows more originality when he likens to stage-plays the work of better men than he. He chooses to think that the pursuit of knowledge before he came was mistaken in its method and misdirected in its end. He had said in *The Advancement of Learning* that " the greatest error of all the rest is the mistaking or misplacing of the last and furthest end of Knowledge." Men have desired knowledge from curiosity or to entertain their minds, or add to their reputation or bring them gain: " as if there were sought in Knowledge a couch, whereupon to rest a searching and restless spirit; or a terrace, for a wandering and variable mind to walk up and down with a fair prospect; or a tower of state, for a proud mind to raise itself upon . . . and not a rich storehouse, for the glory of the Creator and the relief of man's estate."

The last is the true and worthy end of Knowledge; which as he says in his *Valerius Terminus*, " is a restitution and reinvesting (in great part) of man to the sovereignty and power . . . which he had in his first state of creation. And to speak plainly and clearly, it is a discovery of all operations and possibilities of operations from immortality (if it were possible) to the meanest mechanical practice." He had already asserted in the same treatise, " That all knowledge is to be limited by religion, and to be referred to use and action." Yet this was not his complete view; for he extols elsewhere, even in *The Advancement of Learning*, " the pleasure and delight of Knowledge [which] far surpasseth all other in nature." And it has its dignity and excellence in the raising of immortal monuments, like the verses of Homer.

[12] The above and other extracts from Bacon's Latin works are taken from the translations in the Spedding-Ellis, etc., edition of his Works.

Bacon's most grandiose indictment of the science of his time is contained in the preface to *The Great Instauration,* (or Renewal) of all Knowledge, and in the so-called *Pröoemium,* which begins: "Francis of Verulam reasoned thus with himself, and judged it to be for the interest of the present and future generations that they should be acquainted with his thoughts." It is in this *Pröoemium* and *Preface* and in the *Distributio* or plan of the work, which follows them, that he sets forth his great scheme and method. There is call for it indeed, if the case is as he says "whereas in what is now done in the matter of science there is only a whirling round about, and perpetual agitation, ending where it began,— vertigo quaedam et agitatio perpetua et circulus."[13]

That Bacon could have made this statement proves his lack of sympathy and understanding for the scientific movement of his time; for he spoke thus while William Harvey was establishing the circulation of the blood upon the surest foundations of observation and experiment, and Galileo was re-establishing physics upon certain laws. Bacon had taken all knowledge for his province, had vast thoughts of all the arts and sciences; — turning over the pages of his Works, time and again one is led to the conviction that he had no veritable conception of any single science whatsoever. And it is plain enough that had he been himself a sheer investigator, with commensurate perceptive powers, unhandicapped by an over-gift of language and sardonic lucubration, he would not have taken all knowledge for his province nor elaborated as his great achievement an unworkable scheme for its pursuit. No nimble scientific David would put on such Saul's armor — which this Saul did not wear himself. Bacon might commend or speak slightly of his contemporaries, and yet say nothing better than what Harvey said of him: "He writes philosophy like a Lord Chancellor."

In view then of the shortcomings of human knowledge and the self-made difficulties as well as inherent invalidities of human thought, Bacon perceived that there was

[13] This sentence from the *Pröoemium* is blown up further in the Preface.

but one course left for him, as he says in this *Pröoemium,*
— "to try the whole thing anew upon a better plan, and
to commence a total reconstruction of sciences, arts and
all human knowledge, raised upon the proper foundations." The enterprise seems large; but he deems that
"it will be found sound and sober;" for there is some
issue to it, and not a mere whirling in a circle, as he said
in the extract given above. He will make a beginning,
so "that in case of his death there might remain some
outline and project of that which he had conceived, and
some evidence likewise of his honest mind and inclination
towards the benefit of the human race."

The considerably longer Preface which follows is excellent reading and has more to say of the author's
mental attitude. Yet since it repeats much that has been
already noted, we may pass on to the *Distributio* or plan
of *The Great Instauration.*

The whole undertaking (which, of course, was never
completed) was to fall into six parts. The first of these
was to be a treatise on the divisions or classification of
the sciences, indeed of all human knowledge, and not
merely of what actually was known, but of what should
be known in order to fill up the waste regions in the intellectual globe. This had already formed the topic of the
second book of *The Advancement of Learning,* and is
still more elaborately treated in the second and succeeding
books of the *De Augmentis.* A real scientific investigator, like Vesalius or Harvey or Gilbert or Galileo, takes
little interest in this problem of universal classification;
but it was one which had weighed upon the students and
philosophers of the Middle Ages, who drew their
knowledge from the scattered storehouses of a greater
past. Like the long line of his mediaeval forbears,
Bacon, gathering his material from the works of other
men ancient and modern, lay under the same spell or necessity of attempted classification, to which he devotes so
many chapters.[14]

[14] Like some of those before him, Bacon drew from the works of Aristotle a strong impetus toward the classification of knowledge. Cf. *The
Mediaeval Mind,* II, chap. XXXVI.

The second part is entitled *The New Organon; or Direction concerning the Interpretation of Nature*. Bacon had discussed this matter in several of his shorter or unfinished works, and completed it in the *Novum Organum* itself, which although but a fragment of a projected treatise, remains as the most famous of his philosophical writings. The outlines of the Baconian method or Science may be drawn from the *Distributio* and supplemented from the *Organum* itself. The subsequent parts of Bacon's scheme, whether unattempted or partially achieved, will require but summary notice.

" To the second part," says Bacon, " belongs the doctrine concerning the better and more perfect use of human reason in the inquisition of things." . . . so that " the intellect may be . . . made capable of overcoming the difficulties and obscurities of nature. The art which I introduce with this view (which I call *Interpretation of Nature*) is a kind of logic,"— but very different from the ordinary logic. For, in the first place, " the end which this science of mine proposes is the invention not of arguments but of arts." Through the common logic an opponent is overcome by argument; through Bacon's, Nature is constrained by works.

Likewise the two kinds differ in the manner of their demonstrations. The common logic spends itself on the syllogism; I reject the syllogism, says Bacon, because it " consists of propositions; propositions are words; and words are the tokens and signs of notions. Now if the very notions of the mind . . . be improperly and rashly abstracted from facts . . . the whole edifice tumbles." He will throughout use induction as the form of demonstration which presses Nature most closely and is bound up in works. But he has revolutionized it, seeing that the old kind is puerile, proceeds by simple enumeration, and concludes at hazard.

" The sciences stand in need of a form of induction which shall analyze experience and take it to pieces, and by a due process of exclusion and rejection lead to an inevitable conclusion."
" I also sink the foundations of the sciences deeper and firmer; and I begin the inquiry nearer the source than men have done here-

tofore; submitting to examination those things which the common logic takes on trust. For first, the logicians borrow the principles of each science from the science itself; secondly they hold in reverence the first notions of the mind; and lastly, they receive as conclusive the immediate informations of the sense when well disposed. Now upon the first point, I hold that true logic ought to enter the several provinces of science armed with a higher authority than belongs to the principles of those sciences themselves, and ought to call those putative principles to account until they are fully established. Then with regard to the first notions of the intellect; there is not one of the impressions taken by the intellect when left to go its own way, but I hold it for suspected, and no way established, until it has submitted to a new trial. . . . And lastly, the information of the sense itself I sift and examine in many ways. For certain it is that the senses deceive; but at the same time they supply the means of discovering their own errors; only the errors are here, the means of discovery are to seek."

Brave words! grand plans for the discovery of truth. Yet the words are but words, and the plan shall be as one trying to pull himself up with his own bootstraps,— and having previously tied himself to the floor with sundry cords. Diligently, continues Bacon, has he sought on all sides for helps for the sense and for rectifications for its errors: (which shall all be as further *impedimenta!*); and he summarizes what he will have to say of the *Idola* in the body of the work.

Passing with him from the *Distributio* to the body of the work, we find more upon the deceptions of sense; for example: " By far the greatest hindrance and aberration of the human understanding proceeds from the dullness, incompetency and deceptions of the senses."[15] But Bacon's scheme will make all men alike sure discoverers of truth. " The course I propose for the discovery of the sciences is such as leaves but little to the acuteness and strength of wits, but places all wits and understandings nearly on a level." [16] Will it be a levelling up or a levelling down, one queries.

One reads on in the *Novum Organum,* looking for a clear and definite statement of the new scientific method of its author. One finds at least sufficient indication that

[15] *Novum Organum,* I, § 50.
[16] Ib. I, § 61.

Bacon, loving general discourse and reasoning, had not himself the temper of an investigator. He is impatient with a man like Gilbert for spending his labor upon the magnet "working out some one experiment." [17] He thinks that knowledge has "suffered from littleness of spirit and the smallness and lightness of the tasks which human industry has proposed to itself." Men flatter their failures with the pretense that nothing new and difficult can be discovered. "And even if a man apply himself fairly to facts, and endeavour to find out something new, yet he will confine his aim to the investigation and working out of some one discovery and no more; such as the nature of the magnet, the ebb and flow of the sea, the system of the heavens, and things of this kind, which seem to be in some measure secret, and have hitherto been handled without much success."[18]

These little minded men, who would confine themselves to some one discovery like the system of the heavens! "It is most unskilful," adds Bacon, "to investigate the nature of anything in the thing itself; seeing that the same nature which appears in some things to be latent and hidden is in others manifest and palpable."

Let no one feel too sanguine of surely finding Bacon's scientific method in this book which he wrote about it. The following is perhaps his clearest statement on the nature of futile and valid inductions:

"The induction which proceeds by simple enumeration is childish; its conclusions are precarious, and exposed to peril from a contradictory instance; and it generally decides on too small a number of facts, and on those only which are at hand. But the induction which is to be available for the discovery and demonstration of sciences and arts, must analyze nature by proper rejections and exclusions; and then, after a sufficient number of negatives, come to a conclusion on the affirmative instances; which has not yet been done or even attempted, save only by Plato, who does indeed employ this form of induction to a certain extent for the purpose of discussing definitions and ideas. But in order to furnish this induction or demonstration well and truly for its work, very many things are to be provided which no mortal has yet thought of. . . .

[17] Ib. I, § 70.
[18] *Novum Organum*, I, 88.

And this induction must be used not only to discover axioms, but also in the formation of notions. And it is in this induction that our chief hope lies." [19]

Here, as elsewhere, Bacon tends to ignore the part to be played by hypothesis in the ascertainment of truth. Yet the stimulating quality of these sentences is characteristic of the book before us; which is full of genius and the hope of greater knowledge, and warnings against paths of error. Some pages further on, Bacon says that man's noblest ambition is to " extend the power and dominion of the human race over the Universe." This empire of man " depends wholly on the arts and sciences. For we cannot command Nature except by obeying her." [20]

Fundamental to the knowledge through which we shall understand and command Nature is the discovery and investigation of *forms*. The term has always been a difficult one in philosophy, and Bacon's use of it lacks fixity and clearness. While in nature only individual bodies really exist, thinks Bacon, and therefore *forms* do not give existence,[21] yet it is hard not to ascribe some formative function to his conception of them. Says he: " the form of a nature is such, that given the form the nature infallibly follows," it is always present when the nature is present, and " if it be taken away the nature infallibly vanishes." Yet the form is the more abstract and general, seeing that " the true form is such that it deduces the given nature from some source of being which is inherent in more natures." [22] In another passage Bacon says: " When I speak of forms, I mean nothing else than those laws and determinations of absolute actuality, which govern and constitute any simple nature, as heat, light, weight in every matter and subject that is susceptible of them." [23]

We will not proceed further in the metaphysics of

[19] *Novum Organum*, I, 105.
[20] *Novum Organum*, I, 129.
[21] See *Novum Organum*, II, 2.
[22] *Novum Organum*, II, 4.
[23] *Novum Organum*, II, 17. See for a discussion of Bacon's *forms* T. Fowler's edition of the *Novum Organum*. Introduction.

Bacon's physics, so to speak, nor make further endeavor to reach a clearer idea of the Baconian method and the Baconian goal than the many other students who have differed concerning them.[24]   Practically it seems clear enough that his scheme includes the gathering of an infinite mass of data, all the facts of nature, if you will, upon which inductions should be based, giving man his full understanding of nature and command over her.   The scheme is outlined in the remaining four parts of the *Distributio,* to which for a moment we may return. Their titles are:

" 3. The Phenomena of the Universe; or a Natural Experimental History for the foundation of Philosophy. 4. The Ladder of the Intellect.   5. The Forerunners; or Anticipations of the New Philosophy.   6. The New Philosophy; or Active Science."

The full scheme of the *Instauratio Magna* embraced, as one may say, things worth knowing and all of them. But all received and current falsehoods should be excluded: such, says Bacon, " I proscribe and brand by name; that the sciences may be no more troubled with them."

Bacon did considerable work on *The Natural and Experimental History for the Foundation of Philosophy* which was to make the third part of the great *Instauratio.* For, as he says in the preface to this portion, men should " throw aside all thought of philosophy . . . until an approved and careful natural and experimental history be prepared and constructed."   Plato, Aristotle, Parmenides, Anaxagoras and others " invented systems of the universe, each according to his fancy, like so many arguments of plays."   And so have Telesius, Campanella, Bruno and others of the moderns.   " There is not and never will be an end or limit to this; one catches at one thing, another at another; each has his favorite fancy. . . . I know not whether we more distort the facts of nature or our own wits; but we clearly impress the stamp of our

---

[24] Bacon himself applies his method, or seeks to apply it, in the investigation of the *form of heat,* in the *Novum Organum,* II, 11 sqq., to which the reader is recommended.

own image on the creatures and works of God, instead of carefully examining and recognizing in them the stamp of the Creator himself."

So we forfeit a second time our dominion over the works of the creation,—" the power of subduing and managing them by true and solid arts." The true course is to discard these insolent fancies and humbly unroll the volume of Creation, and with " minds washed clean from opinions to study it in purity and integrity." His own *Organum* is not complete; but if any man wished to use it he would not have the means wherewith to address himself to philosophy; " My *Organum*, even if it were completed, would not without Natural History much advance the Instauration of the Sciences, whereas the Natural History without the *Organum* would advance it not a little. And therefore I have thought it better and wiser by all means and above all things to apply myself to this work." [25]

So Bacon composed a number of works, or compilations of statements, upon natural phenomena : the *Historia* of the Winds; the *Historia* of Life and Death,— a compilation of longevities and of remedies and incidents affecting health and length of life; the *Historia* of Dense and Rare; an Inquiry respecting the magnet; Thoughts on the nature of things; On the Ebb and Flow of the Sea, and others. These treatises, seriously intended, had little value, as Bacon's knowledge was not abreast of the best scientific investigation of his time. Much more puerile, to use one of his own favorite terms, is the " Silva Silvarum, or a Natural History," a foolish *omnium gatherum* drawn from all sorts of books, Pliny's *Natural History,* as well as works of Aristotle, Porta's *Natural Magic* and Cardan's *De Subtilitate* and *De Varietate*. He did it in his old age, and might not have published it himself; it was published after his death.

Bacon was a philosopher, desirous of laying the foundation of all knowledge, rather than seeking its substan-

[25] Bacon never uses one word where he can use two. One is struck by his constant habit of duplicating practically synonymous adjectives and adverbial phrases, as in the sentence just quoted.

tiation in details. He was a man uplifted upon the ranges of his thought, and borne forward upon the power and copiousness of his utterance. Often he was captivated by the imagery which crowded on his mind while thinking and writing. In physical science he was but an amateur. Had he not spoken with such assurance, he would less often have incurred reproach for the shortcomings of his knowledge, which have been much discussed.[26] The philosopher and amateur may be excused for not being at all points abreast of the best scientific knowledge of his time. Bacon ignored Harvey's teaching of the circulation of blood; but this was very new, and during Bacon's life had not won wide acceptance. His rejection of " the diurnal motion of the earth, which I am convinced is most false," [27] would have been excusable had he not kept to it after he knew of Galileo's discovery and exposition of the moons of Jupiter. He admired Galileo's feats with the telescope; but had no appreciation of the importance of his laws of motion. With some discrimination and intelligence he shared in the current notions of instructed men touching physical phenomena. He made no scientific discoveries himself.

But he was a great influence in his time and after, spurring men to independent thinking. He urged them to study nature and make experiments and hold fast to facts; and likewise to practicable purposes. With many others, he protested against subservience to authority; in language and imagery not to be forgotten he showed the Idola, the fetishes, the aberrances and pitfalls of human reason; he set forth a method of induction which, whether practicable or not, might tend to guard men against rashly drawn conclusions. And above all, with intellectual enthusiasm, he urged men on, proclaiming the sure and far-reaching powers of the mind for the attainment of serviceable truth.

[26] Excellently in Fowler's ed. of *Novum Organum,* Introduction, section 6 and passim; in Spedding's Summary of Ellis's Conclusions, in Spedding's Preface to the *De Interpretatione Naturae* (Bacon's Works, Vol. VI); and in the article on Bacon in the eleventh edition of the Encyclopaedia Britannica.

[27] *De Augmentis,* III, ch. 4. Copernicus and his doctrines are referred to by Bacon a number of times.

CHAPTER XXXV

FORMS OF SELF-EXPRESSION: THE SIXTEENTH CENTURY ACHIEVEMENT

WE have frequently spoken of expression as the completed form of the thought and emotion of which it is the utterance. And more than once we have remarked that the effect and influence, the efficient content, of the past passes on to succeeding periods in modes of expression. These constitute the enabling forms and substance through which the later time largely will express itself. But since the latter has thoughts and experience of its own, it will modify, and perhaps expand, the expressions which it has received, and may create forms of expression for itself.

The thought and feeling of the sixteenth century culminated in forms of expression, some of which have never been superseded or surpassed. If we would see them in their relationships to whatever made them possible, it were well to note the high points of the achievements of the past. These also manifested themselves as mighty forms of expression, in language as well as in stone and marble and the materials of civilization. Thus they transmitted themselves and their effect to the sixteenth century, and to the century in which we live.

Greece was a primal font of expression. The Greek achievement lived and moved and passed onward as a consummate presentation of valid human thought and human feeling, in beautiful and imperishable forms. They begin with Homer. They continue through lyric poets, Archilochus, Sappho, Pindar; through the great Athenian dramatists. Greek thinking reaches admirable form and expression with the philosophers: Heracleitus, Democritus, Socrates. It receives its perfect coronal in Plato. No less effectively Aristotle brought his logic

and his metaphysics to forms destined to remote and lasting dominance.   The Stoics and the Epicureans set their
adjustments with life in statements constantly recurring
to future men.   Besides these modes of speech, there had
come into being a beautiful and consummate expression
of Greek thought and feeling in religious and civic statuary
and architecture.

Under Greek influence, the Romans reached literary
and rhetorical expression imitatively or derivatively.
Out of their own genius, they found their calling in
methods of government, diplomacy and war.   In the
domain of private law, they expressed their very selves
imperishably.

Living in the Roman Empire, but spiritually apart, the
Jew essentially expressed himself in his religion.   Its
commands had been promulgated by law-givers in legal
and ceremonial detail.   Prophets and psalmists rendered
its universal significance and its abysms of emotion.

Out of Israel came Jesus and Paul: Jesus the Gospel,
the ineffable expression, of God's wisdom for man, and
of divine and human love; Paul, the impregnable formulation of the reconcilement, or spiritual supersession, of
the Law.   There followed the great endeavor (analogous to that of Paul) of the Graeco-Roman, ostensibly
converted, world to re-express Paul and the Gospel,
through terms of Greek philosophy and Roman law, in
creeds and supporting dogmas.   That also was a great
achievement in expression.

We pass over the period of transition to the Middle
Ages, and the continuous effort of the early mediaeval
centuries to learn and understand, and make their own,
their patristic and classical heritages.   These lessons
learned, this appropriation partially accomplished, the
time of articulate mediaeval expression opens with the
coming of the twelfth century.   In the twelfth and thirteenth centuries, the Middle Ages attain the forms of their
self-expression.   The language of the past, its expressional achievements, when they do not directly enter and
mould, or even constitute, the mediaeval forms, have at
least enabled them to be.   These final mediaeval achieve-

ments represent both an advance upon the immediate mediaeval past and a larger appropriation of the greater antique past which lay behind all the mediaeval centuries.

The basis of these mediaeval expressions was the Latin language. That had grown, and to some extent had been artfully constructed, to correspond with the needs of Latin civilization as broadened and enlightened by the infusion of Greek culture. It was a full-grown language, exact and logical and stately in its literature, looser and easier as spoken in the town and camp and province. It proved ample for the ethical philosophy of Rome, and exactly suited to jurisprudence, the ordered and even philosophical expression of legal principles and more special rules. It had been rendered elegant, even beautiful, in classical Roman poetry, history and oratory. Its structure had been loosened a little, somewhat declassicized, by the new Christian demands upon it for the expression of Christian thoughts. But still it held itself true Latin, rational and adequate, imposing and resonant, and so offered itself to half-barbaric, incipiently mediaeval, scholars. Sufficiently adaptable to new modes and sequences of thought, it proved a wonderful vehicle for scholastic theology and philosophy, while constraining them to logical exactitude in conception and expression. Its popularly spoken forms, its vernacular, were gradually to grow or change into the Romance tongues, Italian, Spanish, Provençal, and the marked varieties of old French.

The first expressions of scholastic thought were drawn from a Christian Augustine imbued with Neo-platonism; from the Latin version of the *Timaeus,* with its grand cosmic imaginings; and from the simpler logical treatises in Aristotle's *Organon.* The matter was worked over and re-set by the Scholastics, with a gradually clearer understanding of their problems of arrangement and restatement. Their special problem of " universals " was taken bodily from its expression in Porphyry's *Introduction* to the Aristotelian *Categories,* all in the Latin of Boëthius.[1] Through the latter half of the twelfth cen-

---

[1] See *The Mediaeval Mind,* Vol. II, chap. XXXVII (p. 369).

tury the more elaborate treatises of the *Organon* advanced the discipline, and complicated the modes, of logical expression in the schools. And still through these decades, and through the next century, Augustinian Platonism gave form and body to the devotional and constructive thought of such great Franciscans as Saint Bonaventura.

But the mightiest, and finally representative achievement of the Schools, was the work of Aquinas, set upon the labors of his master Albert. It consisted in the synthetic incorporation in the Christian scheme of the substantial philosophy of Aristotle. This was taken from those forms and statements in which it was expressed. Aquinas's recasting of it in his Christian scheme was the ultimate complete expression of scholastic Christianity. It was the summit of the mediaeval achievement in the catholic expression of its masterfully appropriated thought. Before Aquinas died, it was attacked, and afterwards frequently impugned. But it has not been superseded in Roman Catholicism to our day.

Another province in which the Latin culture afforded mental discipline to the Middle Ages, and even more directly transmitted a terminology, was the Civil Law. The whole story of the mastering of the contents of Justinian's *Digest* by the Bologna School of commentators is a story of the appropriation of advanced legal concepts adequately expressed, and of the acquisition of the intellectual strength to apply them.[2]

Thus far the mediaeval achievements in the Latin expression of philosophy, theology and law were largely a re-expression of old thoughts, systematically rearranged, but otherwise often preserving the transmitted form. Mediaeval thinking had not yet reached beyond the antique and patristic categories, and scarcely needed new forms of expression to convey novel intellectual contents. But mediaeval feeling, and especially the religious emotion emanating from the Christian faith, had developed in modes unexperienced and unknown in ancient Greece or Rome, and not attained by the first

[2] See *The Mediaeval Mind,* Vol. II, chap. XXXIV.

Christian centuries, when Christian thought was formulated by the Church Fathers. Through the early Middle Ages, Christian emotion gathers force; and before the vernacular languages were adequate to its expression, it found its voice, its many voices, in mediaeval Latin, prose and verse. By the twelfth century, mediaeval devotion has adapted Latin to its faculties and needs; can pour forth its devout passion — its holy detestations, its fears of the Judgment, and above all its love of Him who had drawn men from the jaws of hell. Devout voices no longer re-express what Hilary or Jerome or Augustine had said or thought. There has come a mediaeval soul, and it has found its tongue,— in Peter Damiani declaring his horror of the filthy world and his devotion to the hermit life, with greater power and beauty in St. Bernard thundering forth the terrors of the Judgment Day, or, with subdued passion, whispering his love of Jesus. His sermons on *Canticles* have attained a noble adequacy of language, an almost rhyming sonorousness, indicating their affinities with the Mediaeval Latin Hymn.

As the feeling, for instance, in the sermons of St. Bernard was largely of mediaeval growth, so not only the feeling of the mediaeval hymn, but the verse forms in which it was brought to such moving and beautiful expression, were mediaeval in their development. The *Dies Irae*, or the *Stabat Mater,* or the hymns of Adam of St. Victor, have no antecedent, either in feeling or verse form, among the Church Fathers or in the classical Latin or Greek literatures. These verses sprang from the mediaeval need to sing its faith; and, as utterances of religious emotion, have not been outdone.[3]

If we turn from all things written, and even from those uttered with intent and art, to acts and to words which fitted them, we find the life and sayings (for they are all one) of Francis of Assisi to have been a consummate devotional poem, and an expression of the love of God and man.

By reason of the vehicle, sometimes because of the matter, less originality might come to expression in the

[3] See *The Mediaeval Mind,* chap. XXXIII.

mediaeval Latin than in the vernacular: — the Romance tongues which had grown out of the old spoken Latin, and the Teutonic tongues which had their own northern origins, but were somewhat affected by Latin thoughts. Least affected by any Latin influence was the tongue in which the Sagas admirably expressed the unalloyed Norse character and the incidents of Norwegian and Icelandic life; in which also the Edda rendered the frozen heat of the old Norse soul.[4] The *Niebelungen Lied* is more generically Teutonic, and touched with ideas prevailing in Romance poetry.

The Arthurian legends, whether in prose or verse, were at once manifestations of the Romance tongues and, in another sense, the most fascinating and universal expression of the mediaeval spirit of romance and romantic lore. They made a home in Italy as well as France, and crossed the Rhine as blithely as the English Channel. In the fifteenth century, they renewed their life in the *Orlando Innamorato* of Boiardo and the perfectly delightful *Furioso* of Ariosto, and far away from Italy, in the rich English of Mallory's *Morte d'Arthur*.

Emotionally as well as intellectually, the final *Summa*, and a supreme expression, of the Middle Ages was the *Divina Commedia*. It was composed in the most stately and potent of the vernaculars. Beautified and vibrant with the quintessence of the gathering religious emotion of the centuries, it also brought to expression much that had hitherto had its exclusive home in Latin. For it re-set in *terza rima* the heart of Aquinas' *Summa Theologiae;* it held the natural knowledge of the time, hitherto kept in Latin; and it was intended to carry such fullness of spiritual allegory as Holy Scripture:— symbolism was inwoven in it. On the other hand, it rendered the very vernacular incidents and hates and loves of Dante's time, of Dante's self; it bore, as in a greater vessel, the matter of Trouvère and Troubadour, already told and sung in French and German and Italian. In fine it expressed what had grown up in the vernacular, and belonged to the spontaneous thinking and open speech of men, while

[4] *The Mediaeval Mind,* chap. VIII.

it also translated and re-expressed the loftier matters of theology and thought, which hitherto had been confined to Latin. Not merely from the fact that the *Commedia* was written in Italian, but from the nature of its translated Latin matter, it represents the turn of the noblest forms of expression from the Latin to the vernacular.

Something analogous may be said of the *Roman de la Rose,* which became more widely popular than Dante's poem. The first part, written by De Lorris, was an idyllic allegory, made of love fancies, close kin to those pervading the Arthurian stories. It was therefore an expression of matter which had arisen and taken form in the vernacular. But the second and longer part, by Jean de Meun, although continuing the love allegory of De Lorris, presented the whole range of Latin learning, and so was a vernacular translation and re-expression of the same.

Undoubtedly Petrarch, in his enormous concern over his *Africa,* and his affected depreciation of his beautiful *Canzoniere,* was not following his wisest instincts. But Boccaccio, after writing more Latin than became a fourteenth century story-teller, reached the final expression of his genius in the Italian *Decameron.* And he knew it.

At the time of Boccaccio's death, one might find somewhere in northern France or England, the worthy Gower, a man of Kent, writing with triple facility in Latin, Anglo-Norman-French and English.[5] His vast material is drawn from the mediaeval mirror of the antique; and Gower has not surely decided for any one vernacular as a literary vehicle of expression. But Chaucer is his English self; and, as the new genius of the passing show, fills his English poems, which are alive, with living vernacular incident. Like Boccaccio he had made his gradual literary passage from borrowed and translated mediaeval or antique matter, to the very living incidents and characters about him. He achieved a splendid English expression of it all. But Chaucer is not as great as Shakespeare, nor is the rough English of his contemporary,

---

[5] See his works, edited by G. C. Macaulay in four large volumes (Oxford, 1899–1902).

Wyclif, as good as Tyndale's. Between the fourteenth and the sixteenth centuries, the vernacular vehicle had grown ampler and more facile, and the thoughts expressed in it had freed themselves more completely from their mediaeval, and chiefly Latin, matrix.

In leaving the mediaeval time, we lift our eyes to its most glorious expression,— the Gothic Cathedrals. They were an organic mediaeval creation. Their earliest Christian predecessor, the Roman Christian basilica, spoke through its mosaic decoration; but the building itself was not, as a Gothic cathedral, articulate with the impulse of Christian aspiration and the ardor of Christian faith. The immediate forerunners of the great cathedrals were the Romanesque churches. Yet owing to the absence of mosaic and sculpture (our eyes are turned from Italy to the lands of France where Gothic came to its own) the early barrel-vaulted, or even the later cross-vaulted, Romanesque churches are rather dumb; and, while they are very solemn, as befits an age of painful learning, they lack emotional lift. But Chartres and Amiens and Rheims rear themselves as great organic voices of faith's passionate assurance and far aspiration. Their message is made distinct and explicit in sculpture and painted glass. Never had the passionate soul conceived or the devising mind constructed, in any time or place, more eloquent buildings.

These cathedrals are expressions beyond words, even as music may be; and yet so far as we may think of them as speaking, they seem to speak in the vernacular. For they had grown up and come to their own among the people of the Middle Ages, even among the very vernacular laity, the men and women of the market and the town. They were not the homes of monks, but civic structures; and though the services in them still were in Latin, the Cathedral spoke the vernacular of the unlettered folk who thronged it.

Its stained glass windows may be deemed more completely vernacular than its sculpture. The themes of both were drawn alike from the Biblical encyclopaedia; yet Gothic sculpture, in its consummate achievements (as that which still makes the shattered glory of Rheims) had learned from antique models, acquiring the old skill, borrowing something from the old patterns, yet transfiguring its carved figures with a solemn religious feeling, or investing them with a mediaeval and mortal vivacity. But the glass painting, untutored by the antique, was as utter a mediaeval creation, a mediaeval expression, as the mediaeval hymn. Both glass and stone have taken to themselves the love and fear and pity of mediaeval Christianity.

The Cathedral, the *Commedia*, the *Summa Theologiae*, such preeminent modes of mediaeval expression, such finished forms of the thought and feeling of the Middle Ages, were the culminations of prior stages of appropriation and attainment. They were complete and final. Along with them, were other mediaeval expressions, which were necessarily the forms taken by the thought and feeling entering them. More largely considered, however, they were not culminations, but rather beginnings or inceptions, destined to be either built upon or superseded. Their contents might be suited to the time and pleasing to the future, as the Arthurian legends for example. But, more often, judged by future standards, the thought is dull or otherwise lacks interest.

With some of them, their rough medium of expression was fatal to their enduring vogue. This was true generally of mediaeval vernaculars, the old French, English and German. But it was scarcely true of the Italian of Dante's *Commedia* and Petrarch's *Canzoniere*. These two poets either found an Italian which was adequate for the perfect expression of their matter, or through their genius fashioned what they found into a sufficient vehicle for their verse. One may find other favorable instances of the sufficiency of the vernacular medium: the *Roman de la Rose*, written in the best French of the thirteenth century, continued very popular for many generations; and so did the works of Boccaccio and Chaucer; but these come a century later.

Much water had indeed run under the bridges, between the thirteenth or fourteenth and the sixteenth century.

There had been progress in knowledge, a general increase in intellectual energy, and a great widening of
horizons, geographical, sidereal and mental. There had
come a considerable breaking up and loosening of men's
ideas. The passing of the universal reverence, or respect, or fear or apprehension, in which Europe had held
the papacy, had contributed to this. The Babylonian
Exile at Avignon, the Great Schism, the pressing of Councils into prominence, and withal a hardening of national
characters and antipathies, had prepared for the final
shattering of the Church.

For good or ill, it all made for the freeing of the human
spirit, and impelled as well as helped it to larger and
more independent modes of expression. No one could
now compose a *Summa Theologiae,* for there could be no
longer any accepted *Summa* of this all-embracing theme;
nor could the human scheme again be set in a " divine "
Commedia; and there remained no such unity of religious
thought and feeling as had built the Cathedrals. But
there was varied call and opportunity for all manner of
tangential statements of the multiform human Commedia,
and the aspiring knowledge and hopes of men; room also
for trenchant, though partial, restatements of man's relationship to God and to the militant churches on the
earth.

In the meanwhile, the vibrant and living and growing
vernacular tongues had come to man's estate; still young,
and pliant and elastic, but large-grown and fitted to express, either in prose or verse, whatever might spring
from human genius and come seeking a voice.

The vernacular tongues grew in richness and subtlety,
and advanced to conquer the fields of literary expression
and scientific exposition. The many-sided story has been
spoken of frequently in this book. We need recall it only
to illustrate the greatness of the sixteenth century lying
in the power, facility, and grandeur, with which it brought
its thought and feeling to expression in prose and poetry
and painting. As the thought and feeling did not then
and there begin, but were mainly derived and appropriated and clothed upon; so the modes of expression, rather

than invented, were appropriated and perfected, and finally transformed into a glorified self-expression of the age. Many, indeed, and mighty were the currents of intellectual and emotional influence, and glorious the antecedent forms, which often, in modes of finished expression, enabled the sixteenth century to express itself so beautifully.

Too deep significance is not to be attached to the vehicle, the medium, the vernacular languages themselves, of which we have been saying so much. Form and substance, the expression and its contents or message, are inseverable, and the expression is the finished shape in which the thought or feeling reaches actuality as well as utterance. This is true whether the thought and feeling be put in speech or writing, or expressed in sculpture and painting. Architecture is likewise the form and expression of a plastic conception or desire; so is the devotion of a scholar to his reading or of a scientist to his research; and so indeed is the conduct of any man in any sphere of life. But conception is not thus brought to such articulate expression as it is in language.

Moreover, inasmuch as the sixteenth century had reached so prodigious and exceptional a faculty of painting and language, there was little retarding drag between the thought and feeling and its utterance. Painter and poet, or even prose writer, rather than hindered, were carried along each by his voluble facility; each expressed himself more perfectly than was possible in cruder tongue-tied epochs, or when there was little skill with brush or chisel. Writers and painters give an unhampered expression of themselves, a self-expression, indeed, of rare force and clarity. In their case, style is the man with exceptional limpidity and truth.

From the point of view of the power and adequacy and beauty of its expression, the sixteenth century may be regarded as the crown of previous growth. We found the illustrations of this first in Italy in the scholarship of the humanists, which late in the fifteenth century came to such polished form in Politian. Then it was that Ariosto's *Furioso* clothed the spirit of Arthurian romance with finished art.   Ariosto's artistic detachment enabled him to render his themes in their pleasurable picturesqueness, and invest them with mirth.   Tasso, with a different temperament, writing beneath the chill of a sombre religious reaction, still reaches exquisite expression.   And already Machiavelli, in his *Prince,* had given such living form to political theory and precept, that his name became in all lands the symbol of the principles which his *Prince* exemplified.

These works were all in the Italian speech.   We followed also the course of Italian painting on to its splendid and classical expression of the Italian desire and genius for beautiful and consummate pictorial form.   In Italy, painting was a spontaneous mode of expression, a true vernacular, its works were never as translations from some ancient high-born language.   But Italian sculpture was more like a reflex, or continuation, of the antique style in bronze and marble.   Despite its vitality and power, it bore to painting almost the relationship of the Latin writings of the humanists to Italian poetry and prose.

Looking to the north, and to a different field, we behold Luther, the one significant and indeed tremendous personality of sixteenth century Germany.   Yet his utterances — and Luther was his utterances — were led up to and made possible by the forms and voices of the religious thought of men before him.   The constituent matter of his growth had not come to him separate from its expression, but enveloped and incorporate in that which was its living form.   Luther was himself a mighty voice, a rending expression of passionate thought.

One may say much the same of Calvin, a French incarnation, as Luther was a German.   Enabling influences and faculties entered into him, as they had come to Luther, in the form of expressed thought and feeling.   He, in turn, re-shaped and re-expressed whatever appealed to him, with a speaking intensity.   The power of the *Christian Institute* was in the power of its expression, in both the French and the Latin versions.

The English Reformation also, in its inception, in its growth, its culmination and its lasting effect, was a great

expression.   So it had begun in Wyclif, and so it had come
to fuller utterance in Tyndale and Latimer and the Puritans.   Its royal and political phase likewise found itself
a statutory voice, effective, sometimes eloquent, and coercive when not convincing.   This peremptory enunciation
of the Anglican *via media* came to exquisite and melodious
speech in the Book of Common Prayer.   It found another and rationally winning voice in Hooker.

We turn from religious reform to *belles lettres*.   Erasmus, the apostle of reason and education to all northern
Europe, confined himself to Latin, in accordance with his
scholar's nature.   He never used the vernacular, and his
writings lack its direct quality of life.   But the French
scholars and poets felt their nationality, and set themselves to the expansion and ennoblement of their native
tongue.   Building upon its power and vigor (one
thinks of Villon's verse), they drew enlargement of
thought and expression from both Greek and Latin, and
put classic qualities as well as words into their almost
modern French.   With a disciplined accuracy and new
confidence, they created nobler and ampler forms than
the French had known before.   To this achievement
Ronsard and his Pléiade, as well as the Étiennes, and more
than all John Calvin, contributed with different spirit and
different motives.   Whatever knowledge, forms of
thought and turns of feeling, they had drawn from Greek
or Latin or Italian, they appropriated with power, and
made over into forms of their own self-expression.   One
feels the process of transformation in Amyot's translation
of Plutarch.   More subtly Montaigne achieves a consummate personal self-expression through all that he has
taken to himself; and the self-expression of Rabelais is
so tumultuous and overwhelming, that we cannot tell what
is falling on us in the Rabelaisian avalanche.

Across the Channel, our Elizabethans were thinking
and speaking and singing in a language which was not
derived from Latin, like the French.   In their English
re-expression they will more utterly transform whatever
they have drawn from classic study, or from their French
and Italian contemporaries.   The process is observable in

Sidney's sonnets. Edmund Spenser, appropriating a prodigious compass of antecedent or foreign thought and
feeling, variously expressed, achieves a larger and more
beautiful self-expression, according to the richness of his
genius. Finally, in the sonnets and plays of Shakespeare,
incidental borrowings are transformed to the universal
human, while the poet and dramatist pours forth a
matchless human, or superhuman, expression of himself.

Leaning upon him, we need feel no fear in proclaiming
the glory of the sixteenth century, lying in the forms of expression which were then attained. Moreover, looking
to its effect upon succeeding times, one also realizes that
this effect still lay in the excellence and power of the expression. Though expression be inseverable from the
thought and feeling which actualize themselves in it, one
may here distinguish between form and contents. It was
not the new content of thought, or the emotional incre-
ment, that was to impress the sixteenth century upon the
future; but the influence lying in its expressional power
and charm and beauty.

Where else lay the effect of a Raphael or a Titian?
But so it is with the poetry and the prose — very clear
indeed as to the prose. The effect of Luther has endured through the manner of his utterances. His
thoughts still come to men in their ineradicable speech.
Calvin's *Christian Institute*, through the excellence of its
composition, continued to be the voice of radical Protestant conviction for generations.

Calvin's French version of his *Institute*, moreover,
pointed the development of its own medium of expression,
French prose; even as Luther's translation of the Bible
helped to form German. Our English Bible belongs
body and soul to the sixteenth century, although called
"The King James Version." Its dignity and noble
rhythm have permeated all English thinking and expression. And what enduring influence upon religious sentiment and conviction has been exerted by the harmonies of
language filling the Book of Common Prayer! It comes
from the reign of Edward VI, and Cranmer was its chief
artist. Its perfect expression has conserved the religious

thought of English-speaking peoples on both sides of the Atlantic, where the worshippers still think and feel in its phrases. So much has been done by the language of these great works to anchor religious thought and sentiment.

So in fields other than religious. The lines of Shakespeare beat forever in our minds. And the effect as well as fame of Bacon has lasted because of the splendid language in which he clothed both his wisdom and his vanity. In a politer land, the excellence of persuasive utterance in Montaigne's *Essays* set a point of view and suggested suave intellectual methods to Frenchmen.

An exception seems to be afforded by the works of physical investigation. The authors were devoted to the discovery of fact. Here all was brave inception, but as yet too crude to admit of finished statements. Great expressions were yet to come in the somewhat later formulations, in Kepler's laws or Galileo's, or Newton's still grander generalization.

INDEX

References are to volumes and pages, Roman numerals indicating the former, Arabic the latter. In a compound item, each volume reference carries until it is superseded by another.